Psychology and Criminal Justice

Psychology and Criminal Justice covers the ways that psychology intersects with the criminal justice system, from explaining criminal behavior to helping improve the three criminal justice pillars of policing, courts, and corrections.

The book is divided into two parts. The chapters in Part One describe how different areas of psychology can help us understand why people commit crimes. The Basics of biopsychology, developmental psychology, behavioral psychology, social psychology, personality psychology, and psychopathy are presented first in their respective chapters. These initial chapters conclude with a section called Explaining Criminal Behavior that applies The Basics to help explain criminal behavior. Part Two of the textbook begins with a chapter on three topics in psychology that are particularly relevant to the criminal justice system: mental illness, trauma, and substance use. In the remainder of Part Two, there are two chapters each for policing, courts, and corrections. Each of these chapters discusses the ways principles from psychology can help with criminal justice processes, including police investigations and officer mental health, psychological evaluations for court proceedings, juror selection and decision making, behavior change, and the effects of imprisonment.

After decades of overreliance on sociology-based theory and research, the field of criminal justice is looking to psychology for explanations and insight. This book is essential reading for upper-level undergraduate and graduate-level courses housed in both criminal justice and psychology departments.

Lesli Blair has been interested in both psychology and criminal justice her whole life. When she found her love for teaching while earning her doctoral degree, one of the first courses she taught was called The Psychology of Criminal Behavior. She honed this course over 10 years, never finding a textbook that fully met the needs of the course. Every existing textbook needed to be supplemented with other readings. Eventually, she realized that she needed to write this textbook. Hopefully, it will allow others to learn some of the many ways that psychology can help us understand crime and the criminal justice system.

Psychology and Criminal Justice

Lesli Blair

Routledge
Taylor & Francis Group
NEW YORK AND LONDON

Cover image: Getty Images/Cemile Bingol

First published 2025
by Routledge
605 Third Avenue, New York, NY 10158

and by Routledge
4 Park Square, Milton Park, Abingdon, Oxon, OX14 4RN

Routledge is an imprint of the Taylor & Francis Group, an informa business

ISBN: 978-1-032-16890-6 (hbk)
ISBN: 978-1-032-16813-5 (pbk)
ISBN: 978-1-003-25082-1 (ebk)

DOI: 10.4324/9781003250821

Typeset in Sabon LT Pro
by KnowledgeWorks Global Ltd.

Access the Support Material: www.routledge.com/9781032168135

Dad, 1946–2017

Boseph, 2009–2019

Julie, 1969–2020

I miss you all so much.

Contents

Boxes

Figures

Tables

Acknowledgments

This textbook has been years in the making, and it would not have been completed without the help and support of some important people. My colleague Deb Eckberg was immensely helpful as my main reviewer. She found my typos, suggested better wording, and offered valuable feedback on the content of each chapter. Additional reviews were provided by Susan McNeeley, my good friend from graduate school. Two of my close cousins, Edward and Stephanie, also gave laypersons' feedback to ensure the content was clearly written and point out areas that needed further explanation. And like everything in my life, I could not have accomplished writing my own textbook without the support of my mom.

1 Introduction

Introduction

This textbook is intended to be an introduction to the many intersections of psychology and criminal justice. Psychology has not been traditionally considered when exploring the causes of crime because criminology as a discipline developed from sociology. The study of criminal behavior often includes, and perhaps begins with, antisocial behavior. Indeed, the term antisocial behavior is used frequently throughout this textbook. This textbook predominantly discusses violent crime and aggressive behavior, including both instrumental and reactive varieties, as these are studied much more often than nonviolent crime and behavior. While the term forensic psychology is sometimes used to mean the application of psychology to any area of criminal justice, this textbook distinguishes between police psychology, forensic psychology, and correctional psychology. Due to the abundant use of scientific research throughout this textbook, this introductory chapter includes some notes on scientific research before finally providing an overview of how the textbook is organized.

A Brief History of Criminology

Criminology is the study of crime and criminal behavior. Since crime is a societal problem, it was first studied mostly within sociology. **Sociology** is the study of groups of people and societies as they develop and function as a whole unit. Many theories of criminal behavior have come out of sociology, and most criminology textbooks cover those theories. What is often not included in the study of crime and criminal behavior are the theories and principles of psychology. **Psychology** is the study of the mind and/or brain and its impact on behavior. Since psychology specifically investigates thinking and behavior, it has a lot to offer the study of crime and the criminal justice system. This textbook is designed to explore the ways in which psychology can help explain antisocial behavior and improve the criminal justice system.

Antisocial Behavior

When we hear the word "antisocial," we often think of someone who is not social. We might call someone who stays home instead of going to a party "antisocial." The word we actually should be using to describe this type of person is "asocial." The prefix "anti" means against something, whereas the prefix "a" means the absence of something. Therefore, a person who seems to lack a social life is "asocial." An "antisocial" person behaves in ways that are contrary to or against social norms. Throughout this textbook, you will see many references

DOI: 10.4324/9781003250821-1

to antisocial behavior. Remember that this does not mean behavior that is more reserved nor someone who is shy. **Antisocial behavior** is a behavior that violates social norms or expectations, including breaking rules that are not necessarily laws. Someone who vapes next to a sign that says "No Vaping" is behaving antisocially.

Antisocial behavior can be so pervasive in a person that they may be diagnosed with **antisocial personality disorder (APD)**. The *Diagnostic and Statistical Manual of Mental Disorders* published by the American Psychiatric Association is now in its fifth edition (DSM-5). The DSM-5 provides lists of diagnostic criteria and explanations of various psychological disorders. Personality disorders are in a special section of the DSM-5, as they are usually extremely stable over time. Indeed, they are considered a part of someone's personality. The personality disorders mostly associated with criminal and antisocial behavior will be covered in Chapter 6. APD will be discussed in Chapter 6, but will also be included in Chapter 7 due to its overlap and confusion with psychopathy. Psychopathy, sociopathy, and APD are often used interchangeably, but they are not necessarily the same.

Types of Crime Discussed

There are many different types of crime. Depending on the source, there are also different ways of categorizing the different kinds of crime. Very broadly speaking, there is violent crime and nonviolent crime. **Nonviolent crime** does not usually cause immediate, physical harm to another, as with theft or forgery. Whereas **violent crime** inflicts immediate, physical harm on another, such as sexual assault or murder. Throughout this textbook, we will mostly be discussing violent crime for two reasons. The first reason is that there is far more research on violent crime. As it is often considered more serious than nonviolent crime, this is perhaps not surprising. The second reason is that the field of psychology has studied aggression even though it has not always directly studied crime. As mentioned previously, the study of crime has traditionally and historically been the domain of sociology. Since aggression is usually a large part of violent offending, studies of aggression are included in this textbook.

Aggression Versus Violence

Aggression and violence often go together, but they are not entirely the same. **Aggression** is any behavior intended to inflict some kind of harm (e.g., physical, emotional) upon another against their will. Violence is inherently aggressive, but aggression is not always necessarily violent. Violence is a heightened level of aggression. **Violence** is an act, usually physical, that causes immense harm to another. There are also different types of aggression and violence that will be discussed in the coming chapters: instrumental and reactive.

Most scholars who study aggression and violence distinguish between instrumental aggression and reactive aggression. **Instrumental aggression** is aggression as a means to some other end and is often preplanned as a tactic to achieve some other goal. For example, one person may behave aggressively toward a store clerk as a distraction while their partner steals merchandise. Whereas, **reactive aggression** (also known as impulsive or hostile aggression) is aggression for the sake of aggression, often in retaliation or reaction to a real or perceived threat. This is likely the most common type of aggression. Typical bar fights are examples of reactive aggression. This distinction will come up throughout the textbook; specifically, we will revisit these ideas in Chapter 7, as psychopaths are perhaps more likely to employ instrumental aggression and violence.

What Is Forensic Psychology?

The term "forensic psychology" has proliferated in true crime circles as the genre has exploded with podcasts, books, fictionalized shows, docuseries, and more. The term has also found its way into academia with multiple graduate programs in forensic psychology. But what *is* forensic psychology? The word forensic loosely refers to anything to do with the law. This may be why "forensic psychology" seems to have come to mean any intersection of psychology and the law. However, as Neal (2018) recently pointed out, this definition needs clarification.

As you will see throughout this textbook, psychology and psychologists inform many parts of the criminal justice process. The more these two disciplines intersect, trying to encompass it all under one umbrella term is no longer feasible. Neal (2018) proposed that, much like the criminal justice process itself, the distinctions between these areas of psychology should be temporal, or based on when in the process they are used. For this reason, she suggested that forensic psychology should really be any application of psychology to the adjudicative process. Put simply, forensic psychology takes place in courts. Neal (2018) distinguished this from correctional psychology, which is the application of psychology to correctional settings (i.e., prisons, jails, probation, and parole).

This textbook adheres to these definitions and further adds police psychology to refer to the application of psychology to matters of crime detection and investigation. Indeed, in 1984, the American Psychological Association (APA) established the Police and Public Safety section of its Division 18 (Psychologists in Public Service). Interestingly, the APA has another subsection of Division 18 named the Criminal Justice section whose bylaws state that members are "principally involved in public service through their common responsibilities to carry out programs that are located in federal, state, county and private correctional settings" (American Psychological Association, n.d., para. 2). Clearly, this aligns with the term "correctional psychology" used in this textbook. The APA also has Division 41, the American Psychology-Law Society, which has historically been devoted predominately to the application of psychology in the courtroom. This is what Neal (2018) termed "forensic psychology." Therefore, the distinctions between psychology's application to the three pillars of the criminal justice system (i.e., policing, courts, and corrections) have always been there. Neal (2018) has just suggested clearer distinctions in the names of these disciplines.

Therefore, this textbook makes the following distinctions. **Police psychology** (or police and public safety psychology) refers to any intersection of psychology and the field of law enforcement. **Forensic psychology** specifically refers to any application of psychology to the courtroom and its processes. Finally, **correctional psychology** is the application of psychology to criminal justice correctional systems, including any punishment and/or rehabilitative efforts.

Some Notes About Scientific Research

Science is by its very nature an ever-evolving body of knowledge. Our collective knowledge evolves through scientific research. Yes, we should trust science, but we also must recognize its limitations. Scientific knowledge is essentially our best guess based on our current abilities to measure and isolate the variables involved. The main limitations that science encounters are with these abilities related to measurement and isolation. And in the social sciences, this can be especially difficult.

The ways in which researchers measure their variables are incredibly important to the outcome of a study. We will use the measurement of recidivism as an apt example. **Recidivism** is the term used for engaging in criminal behavior after a previous conviction. How do we determine whether someone has engaged in criminal behavior? There are many ways researchers use, each with its limitations. Perhaps one of the most common ways is whether or not someone has been arrested. However, there are a lot of people who are never arrested for their criminal behavior. Therefore, using arrest is not a perfect measure of criminal behavior, as some such behavior is likely to be missed. To capture crime for which there was no arrest, researchers will sometimes ask subjects to self-report their criminal behavior. This too is imperfect because there is no guarantee that respondents are being truthful. Often, then, criminal justice researchers will choose which measure of recidivism is best for their particular study, recognizing – and hopefully accounting for – its inherent limitations.

There are two words used when assessing the accuracy of a measure: reliability and validity. **Validity** refers to whether the measure is really capturing the concept we wish to examine. For example, if we are interested in determining whether someone has engaged in any criminal behavior at all, using arrest may not be a wholly valid measure (for the reasons described above). However, arrest is often used in criminal justice research as the best estimate for criminal behavior. **Reliability** means that the measure is consistent every time a measurement is taken/gathered. Using a very basic example, a ruler is a reliable measure of length because it will provide the same measurement every time you use it to measure the same thing. A measure of crime which may not be entirely reliable due to changing definitions over time is the **Uniform Crime Reports (UCR)**. In the early twentieth century, the federal government began collecting crime data from all jurisdictions that would voluntarily provide it. However, laws and definitions of crimes change, with new behaviors becoming illegal and others being decriminalized. Therefore, if you wanted to measure changes in crime rates in the United States over many decades, the UCR may not be a particularly reliable measure. Again, this is not to say it should not be used as a reasonable estimate of national crime rates. It is simply important to recognize the imperfections of the measures used in research.

You may have noticed that the examples used to describe invalid and unreliable measures are indeed used all the time in research. This is because, despite their flaws, they are the best estimates we have for certain variables. Unlike in many of the "hard sciences," social science research does not occur in a vacuum. Social science laboratories are embedded in the real world, with all of its many influences. When these other influences get in the way of what we are trying to measure, we call them confounding variables. **Confounding variables** are influences that affect the things we are trying to study, often unbeknownst to the researchers. When researchers are aware of possible confounding factors, they will usually include measures for them in the form of control variables. **Control variables** are measurements used by researchers to attempt to constrain their influence on what is being studied. Unfortunately, it is often not possible to include all possible control variables in a study. When studying the real world, the possible confounding variables are likely endless.

All of this information is not intended to cause you to lose faith in science. But it is important to understand the limitations of scientific research, particularly in the social sciences. This information will allow you to be a knowledgeable consumer of research with the understanding that it is imperfect and ever-evolving.

Systematic Reviews and Meta-Analyses

In part due to the limitations of any single scientific study, this textbook presents information from systematic reviews and meta-analyses when possible. These two types of scholarly publications are intended to synthesize the research knowledge that already exists.

A **systematic review** gathers all of the available empirical research on a specific topic and presents a comprehensive summary of what all of this research has to say on the topic. Any conclusions drawn from a systematic review are simply based on the preponderance of the evidence, to use a term from criminal justice meaning more likely than not. When there is enough existing research available on the topic of interest, a meta-analysis can be performed. A **meta-analysis** is a study of studies using specific research methods and statistics to reach an overall conclusion on a topic based on the results from many studies. The outcomes of a meta-analysis are referred to as effect sizes, and conclusions are based on the strength of these effect sizes and the overall statistical analyses using those effect sizes. Despite the improved nature of relying on evidence from many studies compiled together, systematic reviews and meta-analyses have their own limitations.

Both systematic reviews and meta-analyses strive to gather all existing research on a topic. This is often done by scouring databases of published empirical research. Problems can arise due to what is known as publication bias. **Publication bias** refers to the claim that scientific journals are less likely to publish empirical research that has "null" findings. This means that if a study does not find support for its hypotheses, it may not be published and therefore not able to be included in a systematic review or meta-analysis. Some refer to this as the "file drawer problem" because rather than being published, studies with results that publishers find less interesting languish in the researcher's file drawer. This can result in many more studies that support a claim being available for inclusion in these comprehensive reviews and analyses resulting in a bias toward an overall supportive conclusion. Luckily, most scholars who conduct meta-analyses and systematic reviews are aware of and account for this problem.

Organization of This Textbook

This textbook is divided into two parts. Part One contains several areas of psychology that may help us understand why people commit crimes. Part Two includes topics related to processes and practices of the criminal justice system that have been or may be improved by incorporating ideas from psychology.

As you may have noticed if you perused the table of contents, there is no chapter in this textbook dedicated to cognitive psychology. This may be surprising, as cognitive psychology is a discipline that is perhaps the most all-encompassing. Cognition is how we think and process information. Decartes' seventeenth-century assertion that "I think, therefore I am" illustrates the pervasive nature of thought and cognition. This is further evidenced by the fact that many other disciplines within psychology incorporate a cognitive aspect: cognitive-behavioral therapies, cognitive development, and cognitive neuroscience, to name a few. As such, cognitive psychology does not have its own chapter; instead, it is included throughout the textbook.

Part One

Each of the six chapters included in Part One covers a different discipline within the broad field of psychology. These chapters begin with a section titled The Basics, where principles from psychology that may help explain criminal behavior are described. These sections are intended to provide the knowledge foundation needed for the second half of each chapter. This second section of each chapter in Part One, Explaining Criminal Behavior, provides the reasoning and empirical research behind how the ideas from The Basics might help us understand why people commit crimes.

The next chapter, Chapter 2, describes the many ways our biology influences our psychology and therefore criminal behavior. Biopsychology contains a number of more specific fields of study, and Chapter 2 includes behavioral neuroscience, behavioral endocrinology, evolutionary psychology, and behavioral genetics. Chapter 3 then delves into developmental psychology as a process that transcends childhood. While cognitive and moral developments often occur in childhood, these concepts from developmental psychology can be utilized to create rehabilitation programs for both juvenile and adult offenders. Next, behavioral psychology is discussed in Chapter 4. This discipline is essentially the psychology of learning, so the chapter explores how offenders may learn criminal behavior and how best to teach prosocial behavior. The topic of Chapter 5 is social psychology, not to be confused with sociology. Social psychology is the study of interpersonal interactions and the psychology of behavior in groups. This discipline has researched antisocial interpersonal interactions for decades, so many ideas related to criminal behavior are presented. Chapter 6 covers personality psychology, including descriptions of common personality dimensions and specific personality traits that have been found to be more common among antisocial people. The last chapter in Part One, Chapter 7, describes two rare groups of people: psychopaths and serial murderers. The concept of psychopathy is fully explored, including why they may be prone to criminal behavior, before explaining that not all serial murderers are psychopaths and what research says about this uncommon type of killer.

Part Two

The second half of this textbook is devoted to the impact of psychology on each part of the criminal justice system: policing, courts, and corrections. Each of these pillars of the criminal justice system has two chapters. Due to the varied nature of these topics, the Part Two chapters do not share a common framework as the Part One chapters did (i.e., The Basics and Explaining Criminal Behavior). Therefore, the sections in the chapters in Part Two are much more diverse.

There are seven chapters in Part Two. Before turning to the pillars of the criminal justice system, Chapter 8 covers mental illness, trauma, and substance use. These three topics have obvious connections with psychology, yet our criminal justice system has historically treated these issues as if they were crimes. This first chapter of Part Two explains that mental illness, trauma, and substance use are often found within the same population and how we might better meet the needs of these citizens.

Chapters 9 and 10 focus on policing. The many ways psychology and psychologists can and do help police departments are discussed in Chapter 9. Topics include employment and fitness-for-duty evaluations, debriefing after a critical incident, informing hostage negotiations, criminal profiling, industrial/organizational psychology, and trauma-informed policing in Black communities. Chapter 10 describes the ways that principles from psychology may help improve specific police procedures, including suggestions for improving eyewitness interviews and identification of suspects, interrogation styles that limit the chances of false confessions, and the psychological reasons someone might confess to a crime they did not commit.

Subjects related to the courts are covered in Chapters 11 and 12. The ways psychology and psychologists assist in courtroom processes, including criminal competency, mental health courts, the insanity defense, and testifying in court, are the topics of Chapter 11. Expert witness standards are also reviewed, as psychologists are often asked to provide expert testimony on the stand at trials. Chapter 12 focuses on the psychology of the jury.

The chapter begins with a description of the jury selection process, and how and whether psychologists should assist in identifying suitable jurors. The bulk of Chapter 12 concentrates on the psychology of juror decision making, including why eyewitness and confession evidence are compelling despite the psychological flaws discussed in Chapter 10, as well as the deliberation styles of juries, jury instructions, and juror stress.

The last two chapters of the textbook, Chapters 13 and 14, are devoted to correctional systems. Chapter 13 centers on the psychology of behavior change and the great, evidence-based strides made in the field of corrections over the past several decades. The Risk-Need-Responsivity model guides the other topics in the chapter, including risk assessments, the stages of change, and correctional treatment programs effective at reducing recidivism. The concluding chapter, Chapter 14, covers psychology in secure correctional facilities, namely prisons and jails. Clinical psychology, counseling psychology, and industrial/organizational psychology are all utilized by psychologists working in prison. Chapter 14 also discusses the psychological effect on those who must spend time in a secure correctional facility, including both inmates and correctional staff.

Summary

This introductory chapter has provided an outline of what you can expect from the remainder of this textbook. You should now be able to distinguish between criminology, sociology, and psychology, as well as understand what is meant by the term antisocial. The distinctions between nonviolent and violent crime, aggression and violence, and instrumental and reactive violence were also presented. This textbook also distinguishes forensic psychology from both police psychology and correctional psychology. It will be important to keep in mind what you have learned about scientific research from this introductory chapter, as systematic reviews and meta-analyses will be presented throughout the remaining chapters.

References

American Psychological Association. (n.d.). *Bylaws of the Criminal Justice Section*. https://www.apadivisions.org/division-18/sections/justice/bylaws

Neal, T. M. S. (2018). Forensic psychology and correctional psychology: Distinct but related subfields of psychological science and practice. *American Psychologist*, *73*(5), 651–662. http://dx.doi.org/10.1037/amp0000227

Part One

Explaining Criminal Behavior

2 Biopsychology

Introduction

Biopsychology involves the study of the psychological effects of biological processes. This subdiscipline of psychology has grown immensely as we have learned more and more about human biology. There are several branches identified by the American Psychological Association that fit under the umbrella of biopsychology: behavioral neuroscience, behavioral endocrinology, evolutionary psychology, and behavioral genetics. This chapter will cover what each of these areas might contribute to our collective understanding of criminal behavior. But first, the basics. Given the extremely broad topic of "biopsychology," The Basics section will focus on those aspects/topics that are important for our subsequent discussion of how these concepts can help explain criminal behavior.

The Basics

Behavioral Neuroscience

The **nervous system** is responsible for information processing and communication throughout the body. The nervous system is separated into two parts: the central nervous system and the peripheral nervous system. The **central nervous system** consists of the brain and the spinal cord. The **peripheral nervous system** refers to the complex system of neurons responsible for relaying information between the other parts and systems of the body and the central nervous system. **Neurons** are cells built for communication throughout the brain and body; **neurotransmitters** are chemical messengers that originate in the nervous system. Neurotransmitters are transported by neurons to share information around the body and initiate other processes. Repeated use of the same sets of neurons strengthens **neural pathways** or networks, and just like a trail through a meadow, the more these neural pathways are used the more prominent they become. But the **plasticity** of the brain allows for changes to these neural pathways, as well. This section will cover the topics and processes of the nervous system relevant to our later discussion of criminal behavior.

The Brain

The brain is an incredibly complex organ. In fact, after centuries of study and decades of modern empirical research, we still do not fully understand how the brain works. Scientists make new discoveries every day. Given the complexity of the brain, this section will only cover the parts of the brain that research has linked with criminal behavior: the prefrontal cortex and the limbic system (specifically the amygdala).

DOI: 10.4324/9781003250821-3

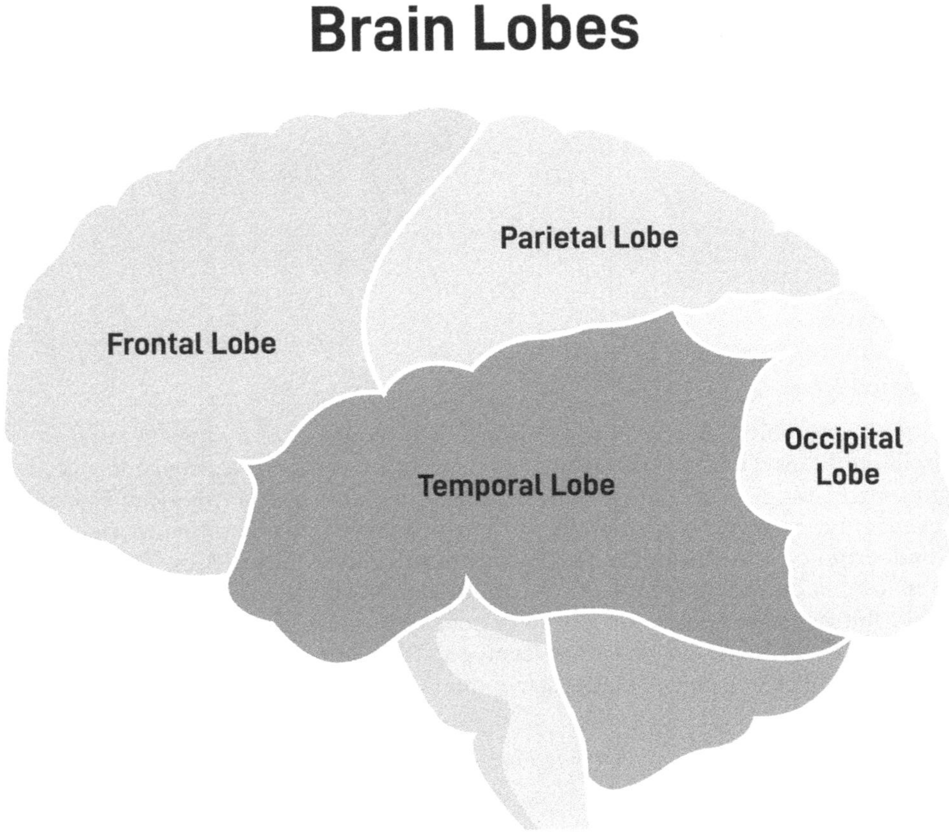

Figure 2.1 The lobes of the human brain.

Since our brains have two hemispheres (right and left), there are actually two of most structures in the brain. Based on their apparent functions, neuroscientists named four lobes of each hemisphere of the brain: frontal lobe, parietal lobe, temporal lobe, and occipital lobe (see Figure 2.1). As we have learned more and more about the brain, the lobes have been further divided into sections, also based on our collective understanding of the functions of those sections. The **prefrontal cortex** is the area of the frontal lobe directly behind your forehead. It is known for a collection of higher-level processes, which have been termed executive functions. **Executive functions** believed to be performed by the prefrontal cortex include decision making, self-control, planning, and regulating emotional responses from the limbic system. Essentially, the prefrontal cortex keeps the rest of the brain in check. It can be seen as the control center for the rest of the brain, particularly for emotions and planning.

It was once believed that the structures and processes in the **limbic system** were responsible for our experience of emotions and emotional memory, particularly the fear associated with the **fight-flight-freeze-or-fawn response**. This is a term for our biological responses to perceived external threats: fight the threat; flee from the threat; freeze, unable to respond immediately; or try to mitigate the threat by appeasing the source (fawn). For this reason, the limbic system can be thought of as our brain's alarm system. Neuroscientists now believe that the structures in the limbic system are responsible for much more than just emotions, including memory, pleasure, and reward response. Further, it has been discovered that many other areas of the brain seem to also be involved in our experience of emotions. So, we will focus on the part of the limbic system still believed to be the primary emotional center (and a brain structure frequently implicated in violent behavior): the amygdala. The **amygdala** is located in the medial temporal lobe, where much of the limbic system is located. "Medial" means toward the midline of the body, so our two amygdalae (one for each hemisphere of the brain) are located in essentially the center of our brains. The amygdala in particular, and the limbic system as a whole, are very closely connected with the prefrontal cortex that evaluates warnings from the limbic systems to decide the severity of the threat and how to respond.

Neurotransmitters

As previously mentioned, neurotransmitters are the chemical messengers of the nervous system. They are extremely fast-acting because they are transmitted by neurons (hence, "neuro" – "transmitters"). There are over 100 different chemical neurotransmitters! Neurons have specific receptors for specific neurotransmitters, and the number of these receptors impacts how easily the neurotransmitter is used in communication. The neurotransmitters most often identified as having a correlation with criminal behavior are dopamine and serotonin.

Dopamine causes us to experience pleasure. It therefore creates a rewarding feeling, increasing the likelihood that a behavior which led to a surge in dopamine will be repeated. For this reason, it is associated with learning and motivation (see Chapter 4). Since it is so closely related to the experience of pleasure, dopamine is associated with improved mood. **Serotonin** is more of a mood regulator, keeping us from staying too "high" or too "low" for too long. This is why low serotonin is often implicated in various forms of depression and anxiety.

Behavioral Endocrinology

Our body's endocrine system is responsible for creating and secreting chemical messengers called **hormones** into our bloodstream via numerous glands and organs, each responsible for creating and secreting various types of hormones. Hormones that have been most often implicated in criminal behavior are cortisol and testosterone. **Cortisol** is a hormone produced by our two adrenal glands, located atop each kidney. It is responsible for a wide range of things, but its primary role is in our response to stress. Consequently, it is known as a stress hormone. **Testosterone** is a sex hormone primarily produced in the gonad glands (i.e., testes in males and ovaries in females). Although both biological males and biological females have testosterone, it is found in much higher concentrations in males.

Evolutionary Psychology

As many know, Charles Darwin was the first to speculate that characteristics of species evolve over time based on what allowed the species to be successful in their environment. Darwin's *On the Origin of Species* (1859) put forward the idea of natural selection. **Natural selection** is the evolutionary process whereby members of a species with characteristics best suited for survival are able to pass on those characteristics to their offspring, whereas those members of a species whose characteristics are not well suited for their current environment will be unable to procreate, due to early death or simply lack of mates. You may have also heard the term "survival of the fittest" to describe the evolutionary process. In this saying, the word "fittest" simply means fit for the current environment, not necessarily strong or what we might consider "healthy." It is possible for there to be an environment that actually *favors* a trait we might ordinarily think of as "weak."

Darwin did not have a clear understanding of just how these environmentally-advantageous characteristics were passed onto offspring, though he had guesses. There was certainly an understanding at the time that offspring were similar to their parents, leading Darwin to tie his natural selection process to procreation. Around the same time as Darwin, Gregor Mendel was making his own discoveries about heredity. **Heredity** is the passing on of characteristics from one generation to the next. Mendel used pea plants to observe that the passing on of characteristics is not simply a matter of mixing the characteristics of the parents, as one would mix paint. This led him to speculate that there were dominant characteristics and recessive characteristics, with recessive characteristics only being passed down when *both* parents exhibited that characteristic and the dominant characteristic winning out in every other scenario.

Notice that the discussion of natural selection and heredity had no mention of genes. This is because those concepts pre-date our modern understanding of genetics. In fact, although he presented his findings in 1865, Gregor Mendel did not earn widespread recognition for his work until long after he had passed away in 1884. The twentieth century was the era of genetics.

Behavioral Genetics

Research in the first half of the twentieth century proved that there are essential building blocks in all biological materials that are responsible for the passing on of traits to offspring. These building blocks can be grouped into chromosomes, genes, and **deoxyribonucleic acid (DNA)**. DNA is the most basic building block in our bodies, a kind of assembly and operations manual. It is found coiled into 46 **chromosomes** in each cell of our bodies. We get 23 chromosomes from each parent; this is how we inherit our genes. **Genes** are sections of DNA responsible for the construction and maintenance of our bodies, as well as our individual traits and characteristics.

The biggest breakthrough in our collective understanding of inheritance came with the publication of Watson and Crick's discovery of the double-helix structure of DNA in 1953. A double-helix is essentially a twisted ladder; the twist simply allows the structure to be more compact. Each rung of the ladder is known as a base-pair. It is a pair because there are two sides to every rung of the ladder. These pairs consist of two of four nucleotides: adenine (A), cytosine (C), thymine (T), and guanine (G). For our purposes, the initial letter is sufficient. Because A is always paired with T and C always pairs with G, our bodies easily make copies of our DNA by "unzipping" the double-helix. Our bodies make two new strands of DNA using the now-separated base-pairs as a guide. However, errors are occasionally made in this duplication process. When these genetic mutations occur in the cells of an egg from a mother or a sperm from a father, the resulting abnormality *may* be environmentally advantageous. Recall the discussion of natural selection in the last section; these genetic mutations play a part in how evolution occurs over a great deal of time.

The second half of the twentieth century was devoted to molecular genetics, culminating in the completion of the Human Genome Project in 2003. **Molecular genetics** is the study of the sections of DNA that make up our genes and identifying what those genes do. Given that there are tens of thousands of base-pairs in our DNA, this is no small feat! The Human Genome Project was launched in 1990 to map the entirety of the structure and function of human genes. It took 13 years and many researchers at dozens of universities to complete the task. In the end, it was discovered that 99% of human genes do not vary from person to person. This is because the vast majority of our genes dictate what makes us human rather than another animal or plant. (Although we also share over 98% of our DNA with some other primates!) So, the entirety of variation in human traits is coded on just 1% of our DNA. It is these differences that are of interest to geneticists, including behavioral geneticists.

The twenty-first century has brought further complications to our understanding of how our genes influence our behavior. You are likely familiar with the term "nature versus nurture." It is a short-hand way to distinguish between genetic influences (i.e., nature) and environmental influences (i.e., nurture). Research on that 1% of our variable DNA has taught us that it is not as simple as one or the other. Many of our traits, especially our behavioral traits, are influenced by *both* nature *and* nurture. This has been called **gene-environment interaction.**

Gene-Environment Interactions

Two theories in psychology regarding how our genes interact with our environments to impact our behavior are diathesis-stress and differential susceptibility. The **diathesis-stress model** posits that our specific genes may make us more vulnerable to adverse environmental conditions. The word diathesis means a predisposition to something. According to this theory, those with and without the genetic predisposition will have similar behavioral outcomes when exposed to a positive environment. Differences in outcomes occur when "stress" is introduced via a negative environment. Those with the genetic predisposition are thought to have a much larger negative reaction to a negative environment than those without the genetic predisposition. Essentially, the environment can be thought of as an "on/off" switch in the diathesis-stress model. Stemming from the work of two different groups of researchers in the mid-2000s, the **differential susceptibility model** suggests that our genes affect how sensitive we are to our environments. Therefore, those with low sensitivity will not be affected much by environmental influences. However, those with high sensitivity will do better than even low-sensitivity individuals in a positive environment, but much worse in a negative environment.

Explaining Criminal Behavior

If the concept of nature *and* nurture isn't complicated enough, there are also interactions within the "nature" category alone. Our discussion here separates out the influence of regions of the brain, genetics, and biochemicals. However, in reality, these "nature" components also impact each other. Genetics can influence both the structure and function of the brain, as well as the biochemicals the nervous system uses to communicate. Genes can even be influenced by other genes, or gene-gene interaction scientifically known as **epistasis.** Biochemicals have interaction effects with each other as well. The environment, including the micro-environment of our own nervous system, can also impact how our genes are expressed. Scientists use the word **genotype** to refer to the physical sequence of genes, but they have a different word for how those genes are expressed within our bodies and to the world: **phenotype.** The term **phenotypic plasticity** is used to refer to the biological phenomenon of different phenotypes emerging from the same genotype. Phenotypic plasticity is exemplified in the fact that genetically identical twins (with an identical genotype) nonetheless look slightly different from one another – not to mention their differing personalities! In fact, scientists have long used twin and adoption studies to examine the varying impact of nature and nurture.

Twin and Adoption Studies

Before the mapping of the human genome, researchers relied on **heritability estimates** to determine whether our genetics play a role in our behavior. To isolate the effects of our genes, studies must control for (or hold constant) environmental variables. This is a tall order given the complexity of our environments! However, researchers began using twin studies and adoption studies to estimate heritability. The logic behind twin studies is that identical, or **monozygotic**, twins share the same DNA and, if raised together, similar environments. By comparing monozygotic twins to **dizygotic**, or fraternal, twins who share the same amount of DNA as regular siblings (approximately 50%), researchers can approximately control for environmental effects when both sets of twins are raised together.

Adoption studies take a different approach. When researchers compare adoptive children to their biological parents and their adoptive parents, they are theoretically isolating heritability. The adopted child's genetic makeup is similar to their biological parents, but their environment is different. This alleviates the concern that heritability has less to do with biology and more to do with the environment in which one is raised. Therefore, if adoption studies show that adopted children share similarities with their biological parents, it is more likely due to biology/genetics.

Combining these two research strategies was the ultimate in testing heritability, prior to molecular genetics. However, this required the identification of monozygotic twins reared apart from one another (i.e., in different environments). Since this is a relatively rare occurrence, some researchers in the mid-twentieth century stooped to unethical practices (see Box 2.1).

Even though the designs of these studies were imperfect, we were able to learn a lot from them! Perhaps most importantly, they gave rise to the understanding that *both* genes *and* environment matter (i.e., nature *and* nurture, rather than nature *or* nurture). Just prior to researchers shifting to molecular genetic studies, they were using twin and adoption studies to assess the differential impact of four different genetic and environmental factors: additive genes (symbolized in research as A), non-additive genes (symbolized in research with a D), shared environment (symbolized in research as C), and unshared environment (symbolized in research with an E). The distinction between additive genes and non-additive genes is beyond the scope of this discussion. Suffice to say, the inclusion of non-additive genes came after we began to understand the complex nature of how genotypes become phenotypes. An example of a shared environment is the home life of twins reared together, and an example of an unshared environment is the different friend groups of those twins. The symbols used for this research led these studies to be referred to as ACDE models (formerly ACE models), and you will often see results reported as the "best fit" model using these symbols. For example, if a research study found that non-additive genes did not contribute to outcomes, the study would report that the ACE model was the best fit.

Perhaps not surprisingly given our modern understanding of the complexity of the effect of genes and environment on behavior, a meta-analysis of twin and adoption studies assessing antisocial behavior conducted by Rhee and Waldman (2002) found that the best model fit was the complete ACDE model. This means that all four factors of our genes and our environment have some impact on antisocial behavior. They also point out that "parenting styles and behavior represent important environmental influences on antisocial behavior" (Rhee & Waldman, 2002, p. 521).

Elucidating the complex nature of the subject even further, Burt (2009) used meta-analysis to examine if there are differences in how our genes and environments impact aggressive

Box 2.1 Louise Wise Adoption Services – Child Development Center twin study

In the 1950s, Dr. Viola Bernard was the Chief Psychiatrist for Louise Wise Services (LWS), an adoption agency in New York City. She advised the agency to adopt identical twins into separate families, as she (misguidedly) believed this would be better for the children's self-identity and that families would be more likely to adopt a single child than take on two at once (Segal, 2022). She then told a colleague about this practice: Dr. Peter B. Neubauer, Director of the Child Development Center (CDC) at what is now called the Jewish Board of Family and Children's Services (or simply The Jewish Board) and a clinical psychiatry professor at New York University. LWS and CDC began collaborating to deliberately separate identical twins for scientific study.

However, the participants were not provided any information regarding the nature of the study. The biological parents and the adoptive parents were only informed that their child would be in an adoption study. Details were never divulged to the study participants – including that an identical sibling even existed! Despite records that Dr. Neubauer received a grant in 1965 from the National Institute of Health for "a longitudinal study of monozygotic twins reared apart" (Klitzman & Kelmenson, 2021, p. 657), no research results were ever published. All data and documents collected were endowed to Yale and Columbia Universities in the 1990s with the stipulation that they not be available to the public or other researchers for many decades (Klitzman & Kelmenson, 2021). Due to the secretive nature of the researchers and unpublished findings, it is unknown how many identical siblings were separated for this study. Those who have learned of their personal involvement in the study have struggled to gain access to these records as well (Klitzman & Kelmenson, 2021).

This case calls attention to the need for ethical guidelines in research on human subjects. Indeed, the Nuremberg Code, which describes basic rights for study participants such as the right to *not* participate, has been in place since 1949 after the discovery of abuse in the name of science at Nazi concentration camps. Further guidelines for ethical research using human subjects came after the revelation of the Tuskegee experiments, which did not inform subjects – mostly Black men – that they would be deliberately infected with syphilis. The resulting Belmont Report, mandated by the 1974 National Research Act, outlined three basic rights of human research subjects: respect for persons, beneficence, justice (National Commission for the Protection of Human Subjects of Biomedical and Behavioral Research, 1979). However, independent ethical oversight committees to ensure compliance with the Nuremberg Code and the Belmont Report, often called Institutional Review Boards (IRBs), did not become common practice in research on human subjects until the 1980s (Grady, 2015).

versus non-aggressive antisocial behavior (labeled by Burt as "rule-breaking behavior"). Limited by the research that existed at the time, Burt focused on these effects for children and adolescents. She concluded "that AGG [aggressive antisocial behavior] is primarily genetic in origin, whereas RB [rule-breaking behavior] is a function of both genetic and shared environmental influences" (Burt, 2009, p. 176).

Brain Structure and Function Studies

It has long been suspected that injuries to our brains cause changes in our behavior (see Box 2.2). Advances in medical technology have allowed researchers to examine both the structure and the function of the brain. Structural imaging technology provides static images of areas of the brain so researchers can determine if there are structural deficiencies, such as low/missing white matter (the bundles of neuron fibers found on the surface of the brain that communicate information), low/missing gray matter (the deeper parts of the brain that process information), lesions, or tumors. More recent functional imaging technology documents the areas of the brain that are stimulated during certain activities, thus examining how and how well the brain functions. An important caveat to this discussion of regions of the brain associated with criminal activity is that we are currently still learning a lot about how the brain functions, and there is a lot we do not yet know. Keep this in mind as we explore what we know so far.

Box 2.2 Phineas Gage, Charles Whitman, and Aaron Hernandez: Brain injury and disease impacting behavior over 150 years

Anecdotal cases of brain injury or disease leading to changes in behavior have been around for over 150 years. Anyone who has taken an introductory psychology course is likely familiar with the story of Phineas Gage. Gage was a railroad worker in the mid-nineteenth century when he was impaled through his head with a large iron rod. Miraculously, Gage survived but was never the same. With severe injury to his frontal lobe, there were many reports that Gage's personality and behavior were greatly changed and not for the better. Despite their popularity, some suggest that the stories of Gage's increased antisocial behavior after the accident may be overblown (MacMillan, 2000). Nonetheless, he inspired increased study of the effects of brain injuries on personality and behavior.

Over one hundred years later in 1966, Charles Whitman climbed a tower on the campus of the University of Texas at Austin armed with multiple firearms. After more than an hour and a half of indiscriminate shooting, 14 people were dead, 31 were left injured (one died of his injuries over three decades later), and Whitman was killed by police. He had felt something was wrong with his brain, requesting an autopsy in his suicide note. The doctor who performed the autopsy found a small tumor pressing against Whitman's amygdala. Scholars believe that while this tumor may have affected his mental state, it is likely not the only cause of Whitman's behavior that day.

Fast-forward another half-century to the murder conviction of former professional football player Aaron Hernandez in 2015. Hernandez was surrounded by violence his entire life, starting with an abusive father and continuing to his own involvement in violent behavior. After his murder conviction, he hanged himself in his prison cell. His brain was provided to Dr. Ann McKey, a neuropathologist at Boston University. Dr. McKey, an expert in chronic traumatic encephalopathy (CTE), said the damage to Hernandez's frontal lobe was the worst she had ever seen in a 27-year-old. He was posthumously diagnosed with Stage 3 (of 4) CTE caused by severe and repeated injuries to his head, which Dr. McKey noted is associated with "difficulty with impulse control, decision-making, aggression, often emotional volatility, and rage behavior" (Gonzalez, 2017, para. 6). The diagnosis has sparked widespread discussion of the safety of American football players – and those they encounter.

Executive Functions

The prefrontal cortex was mentioned earlier as an area of the brain long associated with executive functions. Due to this fact, "the prefrontal cortex has been most commonly recognized as the most crucial (although not the only) brain structure to be compromised in violent and antisocial populations" (Yang & Raine, 2009, p. 82). Upon further study, it is now believed that the prefrontal cortex can be further subdivided based on the function of different areas. As with most anatomical terminology, the specific areas of the prefrontal cortex are named for their location using directional language. According to a meta-analysis of brain imaging research on antisocial behavior (Yang & Raine, 2009), the brain areas most associated with such behavior are the right orbitofrontal cortex (right OFC; located just above the right eye socket), the left dorsolateral prefrontal cortex (left DLPFC; located in the back left of the prefrontal cortex) and the right anterior cingulate cortex (right ACC; recall that the brain has right and left hemispheres with the same structures on both sides). Although the anterior cingulate cortex (ACC) is technically a part of the limbic system, it is believed to also be responsible for executive functions.

There are several reasons that deficiencies in brain areas responsible for executive functions might lead to increased antisocial behavior. Cruz and her colleagues (2020) described how executive functions can be divided into three roles (an idea first proposed by Miyake et al., 2000): inhibition, shifting, and updating. The **inhibition** role of executive functions steps in to inhibit an initial, perhaps emotional, response to stimuli. The role of **shifting** is "defined as the ability to perform a new operation in the face of proactive interference" (Cruz et al., 2020, p. 2). Finally, the role of **updating** allows us to replace old information with newly acquired information. It is easy to see how one might get into trouble without the ability to inhibit a knee-jerk reaction, ignore outside attempts to provoke a negative response (i.e., "proactive interference") or replace old information with new information. Yang and Raine (2009) further suggest that **lateralization** (the differing functions of the right and left hemispheres) can be similarly explained:

> Overall, as suggested by lesion studies, it may be hypothesized that the reduction in the right prefrontal cortex, including the OFC and ACC, is associated with emotional deficits and poor decision-making in antisocial individuals, while the reduction in the left DLPFC is more linked to antisocial features of impulsivity and poor behavior control. (p. 86)

Amygdala

Research on the relationship of the amygdala to antisocial behavior has primarily focused on its role in the experience and processing of fear. Studies have shown that amygdala dysfunction is associated with decreased fear conditioning and difficulty recognizing fear in faces. **Fear conditioning** is a behavioral learning response (more on behavioral learning in Chapter 4) that inhibits behavior that has been associated with the experience of fear in the past. Those with amygdala dysfunction may not experience fear, or perhaps not as strongly as those with normal amygdala functioning. This is thought to lead to a sense of fearlessness that makes any natural or imposed punishments for criminal behavior less effective at deterring similar behavior in the future. Fearlessness toward threats to our own well-being may also lead to increased aggression, as the consequences of interpersonal aggression are lessened. Failure to recognize fear in the faces of others may also contribute to aggressive behavior since perpetrators will have difficulty understanding that their behavior is causing their victim to be afraid.

Interestingly, scholars believe that these two effects of amygdala dysfunction may be related to two distinct types of aggression introduced in Chapter 1. **Instrumental aggression** is used as a means to an end; it is often planned as a way to get something else that the person wants. Whereas **reactive aggression** is more impulsive, literally a reaction to a perceived threat. It would make sense, then, that reactive aggression is linked to the fearlessness of those with amygdala dysfunction, and instrumental aggression may be linked to the perpetrators' amygdala dysfunction causing an inability to recognize fear in others. Further, this distinction may be associated with the type of amygdala dysfunction, with *hypo*activity (i.e., decreased activity) of the amygdala potentially causing instrumental aggression and *hyper*activity (i.e., increased activity) being related to reactive aggression (Glenn & Raine, 2014). This hypothesis has been supported by a meta-analysis of gene-environment interactions involving a gene thought to impact the levels of serotonin affecting the amygdala (Tielbeek et al., 2016; see Molecular Genetics section in this chapter).

Chemical Messengers

Hormones

Two hormones that have been empirically linked with offending and aggressive behavior are testosterone and cortisol. Given that testosterone is most known as the male sex hormone and males are overrepresented in violent offending, it is not surprising that studies linking testosterone levels and aggressive behavior go back to the mid-nineteenth century. What is surprising is that more current research has been mixed. A recent meta-analysis of testosterone's direct effect on aggressive behavior concluded that "[a]n important 'take home message' from this meta-analysis is that relationships between testosterone and human aggression are relatively weak" (Geniole et al., 2020, p. 8).

Cortisol's important role in stress response has made it another good candidate for a direct relationship with offending behavior. After all, a major group of socio-criminological theories relate the experience of strains/stressors to offending behavior (i.e., Agnew, 1992; Merton, 1938; see Chapter 5). However, recent empirical evidence has shown that cortisol's direct role in antisocial behavior is also not well understood. New research has begun to look at the interplay of testosterone *and* cortisol on antisocial behavioral outcomes. A recent study examining this interaction concluded "that testosterone and cortisol may interact to influence criminal behavior with the positive association between testosterone and crime stronger when cortisol is low" (Armstrong et al., 2020, p. 7).

Neurotransmitters

It may seem that aggression is associated with negative emotions, such as anger and frustration. But research has shown that for those with low levels of dopamine, aggression can be associated with pleasure and therefore rewarding. Once thought to be related to impulsivity, newer research has shown that aggression can also be linked to sensation-seeking behavior, particularly for those with a gene associated with having fewer dopamine receptors (DRD2; Chester et al., 2016). Fewer dopamine receptors mean that more extreme levels of dopamine must be released to be "felt" by the few dopamine receptors available. Thus, those with this gene may be drawn to extreme dopamine-releasing activities, including aggression and violence. These findings support the **reward deficiency syndrome** put forward by Blum and his colleagues (1996) to help understand chronic substance use.

Similarly, lack of serotonin has been implicated in aggressive behavior since the 1970s. The **serotonin deficiency hypothesis**, coined by Duke and colleagues (2013), states that low levels of serotonin are correlated with increased aggression, particularly in men. Despite decades of published research supporting the hypothesis, a meta-analysis by Duke et al. (2013) found only minimal support: "we have found that serotonin explains just over 1% of the variance in aggression, anger and hostility" (p. 1159). A meta-analysis of the association of serotonin with amygdala responses to fear has produced similar results: the association is not as strong as once thought (Murphy et al., 2013; see next section on Molecular Genetics).

Duke and his colleagues (2013) provided four potential reasons for the divergent findings. Their first explanation is that the ways in which serotonin (the independent variable) and aggression (the dependent variable) are measured in studies lack reliability and validity. As mentioned in the introductory chapter, the ways in which researchers measure their variables are incredibly important to the outcome of the study. Are they measuring what they think they are measuring (i.e., validity)? And do the measures provide a consistent measurement every time (i.e., reliability)? Duke and colleagues (2013) question whether the measures used in the studies they meta-analyzed are accurately gauging both serotonin levels and aggressive behavior. The three other explanations they provide for their surprising meta-analysis findings are all related to why it may be difficult to measure the effects of serotonin. Serotonin is an incredibly complex and pervasive neurotransmitter with far more roles in the brain and behavior than neuroscientists initially realized (and likely even currently understand). This complicates correlational studies in three ways. (1) To some extent, serotonin may likely be correlated with many different functions, deficits, etc. (2) Serotonin may be responsible for some other function that is itself the cause of the relationship with aggression (i.e., there is a confounding variable of which we are not yet aware). (3) One of the specific functions of serotonin is related to aggression, and we have not yet been able to isolate that function. Additionally, Duke and colleagues (2013) point to the publication bias described in Chapter 1 to explain that perhaps studies *negating* the relationship between serotonin and aggression simply were not published. Clearly, much more research is needed on serotonin itself, as well as its potential relationship to aggression.

Molecular Genetics

The prevalence of the serotonin aggression hypothesis and the mapping of the human genome gave rise to research on variations (known as **alleles**) of the gene 5-HTTLPR, a serotonin transporter gene. This gene is responsible for "cleaning up" excess serotonin and returning it to be reused by neurons in a process called **reuptake**. When reuptake is limited, more serotonin remains available to continue its effects (whatever they may be). Some research has shown that the shorter allele of 5-HTTLPR may be linked to less reuptake and therefore more available serotonin. Much research has examined the effect of 5-HTTLPR alleles on amygdala response, particularly to aversive stimuli (Murphy et al., 2013, p. 512). While early research supported a connection between the shorter 5-HTTLPR allele and hypersensitivity to fear-inducing stimuli, a meta-analysis by Murphy and colleagues (2013) found that this association is statistically significant but small. The meta-analysis found that the 5-HTTLPR allele can only explain less than 5% of the variation in amygdala response to aversive stimuli.

In addition to the methodological issues outlined by Duke and colleagues (2013) described in the previous section, the inconsistent research findings on the effects of serotonin on behavior may also be attributable to gene-environment interactions. A meta-analysis was conducted to examine whether environmental adversity, "such as childhood maltreatment, lower family SES [socioeconomic status], and delinquent peer affiliation" (Tielbeek et al., 2016, p. 750) impacted the effects of 5-HTTLPR alleles. While Tielbeek and their team (2016) found a "robust overall interaction effect" (p. 757), they provided similar caveats as Duke et al. (2013). In particular, they noted that there should be extra concern about confounding variables when examining gene-environment interactions. After all, in these studies there are three measures vulnerable to measurement error: gene measurement, environment measurement, and outcome measurement, or the behavior we are supposing the gene(s) interacting with the environment are influencing. Nonetheless, Tielbeek and colleagues (2016) stated that the findings of their meta-analysis support a hypothesis put forward by Glenn (2011) that the longer allele of 5-HTTLPR causes *hypo*sensitivity to the environment (potentially leading to instrumental aggression), whereas the shorter 5-HTTLPR allele is linked to *hyper*sensitivity to the environment (potentially leading to reactive aggression).

The "Warrior Gene": A Lesson in Gene-Environment Interaction

Back in 2002, a landmark study was published by Caspi and his colleagues that identified a gene-environment interaction between the **monoamine oxidase A (MAOA) gene** and childhood maltreatment. The MAOA gene is responsible for regulating levels of both dopamine and serotonin. Alleles of the MAOA gene have been linked to aggression in animal and human studies, making it a candidate for study of potential gene-environment interactions. Since the gene is located on the X chromosome, of which males have two and females only one, there is also potential for it to help explain why males seem to be more likely to be aggressive than females. Caspi and his colleagues (2002) used data from a robust longitudinal study that measured relevant variables at 10 points in time over 23 years, including four different measures of antisocial behavior. Their study found "that the effect of childhood maltreatment on antisocial behavior was significantly weaker among males with high MAOA activity than among males with low MAOA activity" (Caspi et al., 2002, p. 853; see Figure 2.2). These findings have been replicated (i.e., additional studies of the same variables reached a similar conclusion), and a meta-analysis upheld the findings for males but not females (Byrd & Manuck, 2014). News of this discovery spread far and wide, earning MAOA the nickname "the warrior gene."

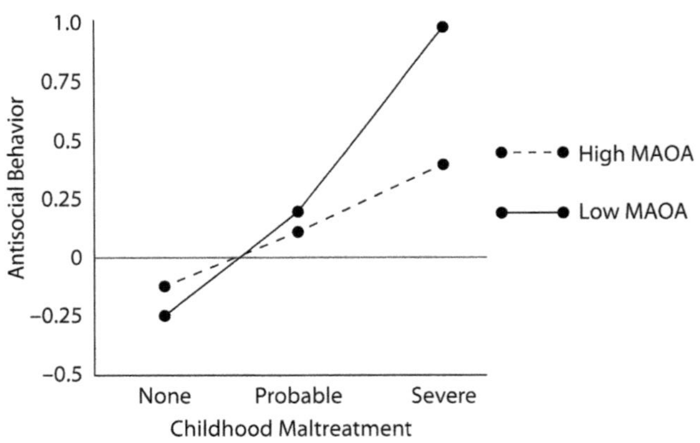

Figure 2.2 Diagram of the results of Capsi et al.'s influential study on gene-environment interaction.

Kolla and Bortolato (2020) published a comprehensive review of both human and animal studies on the interaction of MAOA alleles with maltreatment in early life and its effect on aggression and violence. While the overall findings support a connection between low MAOA, childhood maltreatment and aggressive behavior, their analysis also shows how much we have learned about the complexity of this particular gene-environment interaction in the last 20 years. Further, the authors suggested areas for future research regarding things we do not yet fully understand, such as the effects of the so-called "warrior gene" on females, interactions with other genes, and whether the effects of MAOA on dopamine levels can lead to a kind of addiction to violence. Importantly, Kolla and Bortolato (2020) point out that more studies on the effects of MAOA on aggression should examine the differential susceptibility model, rather than the diathesis-stress model, by looking specifically at the impact of *positive* childhood environments for those with the low-MAOA allele. Indeed, the visual model of the findings of Caspi and his colleagues (Figure 2.2) supports such a line of research. Given the complexity of the relationship and the ongoing nature of research in this area, it is alarming how much traction the "warrior gene" has gotten in popular culture and even our criminal justice system (see Box 2.3).

Box 2.3 The warrior gene as a criminal defense

We cannot fault criminal defense attorneys for grasping at any evidence that might exonerate or mitigate their clients' actions; in an adversarial criminal justice system, that is their job. The presiding judge has the ultimate say as to whether certain defense strategies and testimony are admissible (more on this in Chapter 11). Usually, this decision is made based on whether the evidence is generally accepted in the scientific community. So, it was only a matter of time until initial evidence of the so-called warrior gene made its way into the courtroom.

In *State [Tennessee] v. Waldroup*, the judge allowed the defense to introduce genetic evidence that the defendant possessed the "warrior gene" and had also experienced severe childhood abuse. And it worked. Bradley Waldroup was convicted of attempted second-degree murder, instead of attempted first-degree murder, in the machete attack on his estranged wife, Penny, and voluntary manslaughter, instead of capital murder, in the death of Penny's friend, Leslie Bradshaw. Both counts occurred in the same incident in 2006 when Penny arrived at Mr. Waldroup's home, with Ms. Bradshaw along for support, to drop off their shared children for a weekend custody visit. Mr. Waldroup was waiting for them with the machete and gun and at one point during the altercation told his children to say goodbye to their mother. Prosecutors had thought these things, among others, would be enough to prove premeditation and justify conviction on the higher-level charges they put forward. But the warrior gene defense convinced the jury that Waldroup's genes and childhood were at least partially responsible for his actions that day.

In 2021, the New Mexico Supreme Court ruled that the exclusion of warrior gene evidence in the murder trial of Anthony Yepez was perhaps unjustified (i.e., it should have been allowed by the judge) but ultimately did not impact Yepez's second-degree murder conviction. This case may still see further appeals, but it seems the warrior-gene defense may be here to stay.

Summary

Our brains and biology are extremely complicated, and scientists are expanding and refining our collective knowledge on the subject every day. The concept of nature versus nurture is outdated. We now know that our biology interacts with our environment in complex ways, essentially nature *and* nurture. Even more interaction effects are seen between different biological factors and between different environmental factors. Parsing out how all of these interactions impact our behavior, not to mention fully understanding the impact of our biology, will take time and a lot of further research. Luckily, rather than leading to calls for **eugenics**, the weeding out of undesirable genetic traits through barbaric interventions such as castration and extinction, as some have feared, embracing the effects of how our biology interacts with our environment can lead to more effective rehabilitative interventions. However, it is important to remember that this is an emerging and evolving area of study with many facets. Patience is called for in applying biopsychology to the field of criminal justice.

References

Agnew, R. (1992). Foundation for a general strain theory of crime and delinquency. *Criminology*, *30*, 47–87.

Armstrong, T. A., Boisvert, D. L., Wells, J., Lewis, R. H., Cooke, E. M., Woeckener, M., Kavish, N., Vietto, N., & Harper, J. M. (2020). Testosterone, cortisol, and criminal behavior in men and women. *Hormones and Behavior*, *146*, 105260.

Blum, K., Sheridan, P.J., Wood, R.C., Braverman, E.R., Chen, T.J.H., Cull, J.G., Comings, D.E. (1996). The D2 dopamine receptor gene as a determinant of reward deficiency syndrome. *Journal of the Royal Society of Medicine*, *89*(7), 396–400.

Burt, S. A. (2009). Are there meaningful etiological differences within antisocial behavior? Results of a meta-analysis. *Clinical Psychology Review*, *29*, 163–178.

Byrd, A. L., & Manuck, S. B. (2014). MAOA, childhood maltreatment, and antisocial behavior: Meta-analysis of a gene-environment interaction. *Biological Psychiatry*, *75*(1), 9–17.

Caspi, A., McClay, J., Moffitt, T. E., Mill, J., Martin, J., Craig, I. W., Taylor, A., & Poulton, R. (2002). Role of genotype in the cycle of violence in maltreated children. *Science*, *297*(5582), 851–854.

Chester, D. S., DeWall, C. N., Derefinko, K. J., Estus, S., Lynam, D. R., Peters, J. R., & Jiang, Y. (2016). Looking for reward in all the wrong places: Dopamine receptor gene polymorphisms indirectly affect aggression through sensation-seeking. *Social Neuroscience*, *11*(5), 487–494.

Cruz, A. R., de Castro-Rodrigues, A., & Barbosa, F. (2020). Executive dysfunction, violence and aggression. *Aggression and Violent Behavior*, *51*, 1–7.

Darwin, C. (1859). *On the origin of species by means of natural selection*. John Murray.

Duke, A. A., Bègue, L., Bell, R., & Eisenlohr-Moul, T. (2013). Revisiting the serotonin-aggression relation in humans: A meta-analysis. *Psychological Bulletin*, *139*(5), 1148–1172.

Geniole, S. N., Bird, B. M., McVittie, J. S., Purcell, R. B., Archer, J., & Carré, J. M. (2020). Is testosterone linked to human aggression? A meta-analytic examination of the relationship between baseline, dynamic, and manipulated testosterone on human aggression. *Hormones and Behavior*, *123*, 104644.

Glenn, A. L. (2011). The other allele: Exploring the long allele of the serotonin transporter gene as a potential risk factor for psychopathy: A review of the parallels in findings. *Neuroscience & Biobehavioral Reviews*, *35*(3), 612–620.

Glenn, A. L., & Raine, A. (2014). Neurocriminology: Implications for the punishment, prediction and prevention of criminal behaviour. *Nature Reviews Neuroscience*, *15*(1), 54–63.

Gonzalez, R. (2017, November 9). *Researcher says Aaron Hernandez's brain showed signs of severe CTE*. National Public Radio. https://www.npr.org/sections/thetwo-way/2017/11/09/563194252/researcher-says-aaron-hernandez-s-brain-showed-signs-of-severe-cte

Grady, C. (2015). Institutional review boards: Purpose and challenges. *Chest Journal*, *148*(5), 1148–1155.

Klitzman, R. L., & Kelmenson, A. M. (2021). Experiment on identical siblings separated at birth: Ethical implications for researchers, universities, and archives today. *Journal of Medical Ethics*, *47*(10), 657–661.

Kolla, N. J., & Bortolato, M. (2020). The role of monoamine oxidase A in the neurobiology of aggressive, antisocial, and violent behavior: A tale of mice and men. *Progress in Neurobiology*, *194*, 101875.

MacMillan, M. (2000). *An odd kind of fame: Stories of Phineas Gage*. The MIT Press.

Merton, R. K. (1938). Social structure and anomie. *American Sociological Review*, *3*, 672–682.

Miyake, A., Friedman, N. P., Emerson, M. J., Witzki, A. H., Howerter, A., & Wagner, T. D. (2000). The unity and diversity of executive functions and their contributions to complex "frontal lobe" tasks: A latent variable analysis. *Cognitive Psychology*, *41*, 49–100.

Murphy, S. E., Norbury, R., Godlewska, B. R., Cowen, P. J., Mannie, Z. M., Harmer, C. J., & Munafò, M. R. (2013). The effect of the serotonin transporter polymorphism (5-HTTLPR) on amygdala function: A meta-analysis. *Molecular Psychiatry*, *18*, 512–520.

National Commission for the Protection of Human Subjects of Biomedical and Behavioral Research. (1979). *The Belmont report: Ethical principles and guidelines for the protection of human subjects of research*. U.S. Department of Health and Human Services. https://www.hhs.gov/ohrp/regulations-and-policy/belmont-report/read-the-belmont-report/index.html

Rhee, S. H., & Waldman, I. D. (2002). Genetic and environmental influences on antisocial behavior: A meta-analysis of twin and adoption studies. *Psychological Bulletin*, *128*(3), 490–529.

Segal, N. L. (2022). Twins' continuing tales: New evidence reshapes thinking/appreciation and recognition: Honoring colleagues, honoring twins; remembering colleagues, remembering twins/in the media: Ukrainian twins in wartime; twins born in different years; identical twin surrogate; a quaternary family; abducted twins in Serbia. *Twin Research and Human Genetics*, *25*, 101–105. https://doi.org/10.1017/thg.2022.12

Tielbeek, J. J., Karlsson Linnér, R., Beers, K., Posthuma, D., Popma, A., & Polderman, T. J. C. (2016). Meta-analysis of the serotonin transporter promoter variant (5-HTTLPR) in relation to adverse environment and antisocial behavior. *American Journal of Medical Genetics Part B: Neuropsychiatric Genetics*, *171*(5), 748–760.

Yang, Y., & Raine, A. (2009). Prefrontal structural and functional brain imaging findings in antisocial, violent, and psychopathic individuals: A meta-analysis. *Psychiatry Research: Neuroimaging*, *174*, 81–88.

3 Developmental Psychology

Introduction

People sometimes think of **developmental psychology** as synonymous with child psychology. Indeed, much of our psychological development occurs in childhood and young adulthood. However, we continue to develop and change throughout our lives. Many of the theories we will discuss focus on the developmental stages in childhood, which may leave you feeling that hope is lost for those who had troubled childhoods. However, if we can identify developmental deficits, we may be able to counteract them, even in adulthood, through correctional treatment programs. This chapter will explore various developmental theories from psychology, how they can help explain criminal behavior, and how this knowledge can aid rehabilitation efforts in corrections.

The Basics

Piaget's Cognitive and Moral Development Theories

Jean Piaget was an early researcher in the cognitive and moral development of children. In the 1920s, Piaget began studying the way children of different ages seemed to think about and solve problems. He came to believe that children progress through stages in their cognitive development. He defined four stages from birth to age 12: sensorimotor stage, preoperational stage, concrete operational stage, and formal operational stage.

From birth until approximately age two, Piaget observed that children seem to be learning how to interact with the world using their senses and motor skills. He aptly named this stage the **sensorimotor stage**. During this early stage in cognitive development, children develop a sense of themselves as separate from the world around them, including an understanding that they have the ability to affect the world around them. The next stage, the **preoperational stage**, lasts from around age two until about age seven. The acquisition of language is indicative of this stage's focus on symbolic thinking, or understanding that one thing can be used to represent something else. However, children are still not able to understanding the different perspectives of others. This begins to change in the next stage, from around age seven until roughly eleven. In addition to understanding that their own thoughts and feelings may not be universal to everyone, the **concrete operational stage** is characterized by logic but only in a concrete (rather than abstract) way. Being able to think in an abstract and hypothetical way is the hallmark of Piaget's final stage of cognitive development: the **formal operational stage.** It is through abstract reasoning that those aged 12 and up (typically) can engage in thinking about things that are not "concrete," or directly and physically in front of them. This is why

DOI: 10.4324/9781003250821-4

reaching the formal operational stage of Piaget's cognitive development is required for any understanding of morals, which are based on abstract and hypothetical thinking about the world and one's role in it. It is important to note that although Piaget provided age ranges for his stages, the reality of cognitive development is likely more fluid with different individuals reaching different stages at different times. Indeed, it is possible that not everyone will even reach the formal operational stage of cognitive development, an important implication for moral development.

Recognizing the connection between cognitive development and moral development, Piaget also presented a two-stage theory of moral development in 1932. The first stage, from approximately ages five to ten, is **heteronomous morality** (heteronomous meaning from outside the individual, also known as moral realism). This stage is characterized by a strict following of rules handed down from authority figures, namely parents or guardians. What is "right" and "wrong" adheres closely to whether or not an action will be punished. This changes around age ten, and children move into what Piaget called **autonomous morality** (also known as moral relativism). This stage of moral development closely aligns with Piaget's final stage of cognitive development in that it requires the ability to think abstractly. This is because autonomous morality is not strictly dictated by rules. Children begin to think independently (or *autonomously*) and recognize that adherence to strict rules does not allow for consideration of the intention behind the act.

Kohlberg's Moral Development Theory

Following in the footsteps of Piaget, Lawrence Kohlberg (1976) created his own stages of morality which expanded upon the two stages outlined by Piaget. He grouped his six stages into three levels, each with two stages: preconventional morality, conventional morality, and postconventional morality (see Table 3.1).

Level one, **preconventional morality**, contains stage one and stage two of Kohlberg's moral development. Stage one focuses on **obedience and punishment**. This first stage is guided primarily by the behavioral psychology concepts of reward and punishment (see Chapter 4). The child does not understand the concepts of morality and ethics, but they understand that if something leads to punishment it must be bad. Conversely, if something leads to a reward, it must be good. However, since the rewards and punishments are initiated externally (usually from a parental figure), so too are the judgments of what is right and wrong. This changes in stage two of Kohlberg's moral development theory, which he called the **instrumental-relativist orientation.** In this stage, the child begins to learn that those in authority do not always share the same view regarding what is good or bad. In other words, what is right and

Table 3.1 Kohlberg's theory of moral development (Kohlberg & Hersh, 1977).

Level One: Preconventional reasoning
Stage 1: Punishment and obedience orientation
Stage 2: Instrumental-relativist orientation
Level Two: Conventional reasoning
Stage 3: Interpersonal concordance or "good boy/nice girl" orientation
Stage 4: Law and order orientation
Level Three: Postconventional reasoning
Stage 5: Social contract, legalistic orientation
Stage 6: Universal ethical principle orientation

what is wrong is relative (hence, instrumental-*relativist*) to the person making the judgment. The child begins to change their behavior depending on their audience, recognizing that they may be rewarded by certain people for certain behaviors. This is the "instrumental" piece of the stage, in that the child is using their behavior as a means to a reward.

The second level of Kohlberg's theory of moral development is known as **conventional morality**. The descriptions of the stages within level one named children because it is believed that most adults will reach at least stage three of the conventional morality level. (Whether or not this is true for adult offenders will be discussed later in this chapter.) The first stage of Kohlberg's second level of conventional morality (i.e., stage three) is an **interpersonal concordance** or "good boy/girl" orientation. At this stage, a person shifts from the hedonistic view of stage two to wanting to be perceived by others as "good," rather than simply doing what will get them rewarded in the short term. What seems to be judged by the majority of society as right and wrong begins to be internalized. This outward focus on uniform morality continues in stage four with an orientation toward **law and order**. An almost blind obedience to the laws of society is characteristic of this stage of Kohlberg's moral development theory. Those in authority are perceived to be the best judges of what is right and wrong, so the rules created by them should be followed without question.

It is believed that few people's moral development extends beyond level two's conventional morality. **Postconventional morality**, level three of Kohlberg's moral development theory, also consists of two stages. The first stage of this level, stage 5 overall, is focused on the **social contract** and individual rights. At this stage of moral development, the social contract, our collective agreement to sacrifice some autonomy and agree to abide by rules for the good of broader society, is paramount. The individual still values the legal system (as in stage four) but recognizes that people's perspectives on what is right and wrong are just that: perspectives and opinions. As such, all viewpoints should be considered when making societal rules and laws, and there is an emphasis on the changing nature of morality at this stage. Not surprisingly, the final stage of Kohlberg's theory of moral development is the most extreme. Stage six, the final stage of level three, is characterized by an adherence to **universal ethical principles**. While a person at this top stage views their moral guidelines as applying to everyone, these guidelines may not conform to the law. This is not to say, necessarily, that they believe they are above the law. Those at this high stage of moral development simply recognize that laws are created by people and, as such, are subject to flaws. They see it as an obligation to *dis*obey laws that do not abide by the universal ethical principles by which they expect everyone to live.

Although originally based on childhood development, Kohlberg's theory did not see people as fixed at any stage in moral development. In fact, we can move between stages in different situations, though usually only to the stages adjacent to the one in which we usually operate. Further, it is believed that our moral development stage can shift based on the stage of those with whom we spend the most time. **Cognitive disequilibrium** results when we socialize with people at a higher moral development stage. Essentially, our world view is challenged, forcing us to learn and grow in our moral development. This is good news for explaining criminal behavior and, more importantly, for encouraging desistance from antisocial behavior.

Psychosocial Development

Erik Erikson's theory of psychosocial development combines elements of developmental psychology, social psychology, and personality psychology. Erikson (1980) believed that our personalities develop from our interactions with others, especially significant others (e.g., parents, spouses), throughout our lives. He outlined eight stages that our psychosocial

Table 3.2 Erikson's psychosocial development with approximate ages.

Stage 1: Trust versus Mistrust	Birth through age 1
Stage 2: Autonomy versus Shame and Doubt	Age 1 through age 3
Stage 3: Initiative versus Guilt	Age 3 through age 6
Stage 4: Industry/Competence versus Inferiority	Age 6 through age 12
Stage 5: Identity versus Role Confusion	Age 12 through age 18
Stage 6: Intimacy versus Isolation	Age 18 through age 40
Stage 7: Generativity versus Stagnation	Age 40 through age 65
Stage 8: Ego Integrity versus Despair	Age 65 through death

development progresses through during certain approximate ages (see Table 3.2). Positive interactions with others during each stage will lead to "success" and allow progression to the next stage. Despite the stages being associated with particular age ranges, Erikson believed that one can advance through the stages at any age.

Stage 1 of Erikson's psychosocial development naturally takes place in infancy. This stage is labeled **trust versus mistrust**. Caregivers who respond promptly and consistently to the infant's needs will foster trust, while inconsistent and unreliable care will create mistrust. From around age one to age three, we are in stage 2 of Erikson's psychosocial development: **autonomy versus shame and doubt**. Toddlers who are allowed to explore their independence through doing things on their own – with help nearby – will develop a sense of autonomy, whereas an impatient caregiver who ridicules the toddler's efforts at autonomy will cause shame and doubt for the child regarding their ability to care for themselves.

As children begin to socialize more with other children, they enter stage 3 of Erikson's psychosocial development (approximately ages three to six). This third stage is labeled **initiative versus guilt**. The young child will begin to assert themselves during play with other children, and a delicate balance is required by caregivers to encourage this leadership without letting the assertiveness give way to aggression. However, children who are overly punished for their attempts to take control may develop guilt around their abilities. As the child enters school age, they begin stage 4 of Erikson's psychosocial development: **industry/competence versus inferiority**. Encouragement and accomplishments in school are very important at this stage and will lead the child to feel competent in their new role as a student. Discouragement or scorn around achievements will cause a sense of inferiority.

Adolescence is a time when we explore who we are and who we want to become. As such, stage 5 of Erikson's psychosocial development is labeled **identity versus role confusion** and lasts from around age 12 to about age 18. Being permitted to explore different ways of interacting with the world via their own choices will allow the teenager to develop a sense of identity. Restrictions to or directing emerging adult-like roles (e.g., work, political activism, volunteering) can lead to uncertainty about one's role in the broader world. As we enter the adult world, we also enter stage 6 of Erickson's psychosocial development: **intimacy versus isolation**. Lasting from approximately ages 18 through 40, this stage is characterized by our new intimate relationships outside our family of origin. Developing close, committed relationships with other adults at this time will lead to a sense of love and belonging.

Middle adulthood is characterized by career establishment and building a family. Stage 7 of Erikson's psychosocial development, **generativity versus stagnation**, lasts from around age 40 through to retirement age (i.e., approximately 65). Erikson coined the term "generativity" to refer to a sense of legacy and contributions to society that will outlast the individual. Without a feeling of purpose and contribution, someone in middle age may become stagnant and unproductive. Finally, late adulthood consists of reflecting back on one's life. Stage 8, the final stage of Erikson's psychosocial development, begins around age 65 and is referred to as **ego integrity versus despair**. This shift to a reflective perspective is due to our typical retirement from working, resulting in a decrease in our active contributions to the world. Given that most of us will likely have some regrets during the last stage of our lives, Erikson recognized that there will probably be some despair at this stage. However, he described ego integrity as "a sense of coherence and wholeness" (Erikson, 1982, p. 65). This can still be successfully accomplished even with a few regrets.

Attachment Theory

In the mid-twentieth century, John Bowlby (1958) theorized that interactions between a child and their caregiver cause the child to develop a consistent way of emotionally attaching themselves to others. He argued that attachment to a caregiver is an evolutionary necessity since infants must connect with and trust others for survival. Therefore, our interactions with our primary caregiver early in life dictate how much trust we put in others to provide care and support. Mary Ainsworth studied Bowlby's theory in what she called the "strange situation" experiment.

The **strange situation experiment** (Ainsworth et al., 1978) consisted of bringing a one-year-old infant and their primary caregiver into a room with toys. After a few minutes or so, a stranger enters the room and attempts to engage the infant in their caregiver's presence. Then the caregiver leaves the room, and researchers watch the infant's responses to being left alone with the stranger. Next, the caregiver returns to the room with their child and the stranger, while researchers note how the infant responds to their caregiver's return. The stranger then leaves the room. A few minutes later, the caregiver again exits the room, leaving the infant alone. Then the stranger returns. Finally, the caregiver returns and the stranger leaves. Observations are made regarding the child's reaction to each step of the strange situation. From these initial experiments, Ainsworth articulated three unique attachment styles, with a fourth added after additional research using the strange situation.

When the infants exhibited a **secure attachment style**, they were concerned when their caregiver left them alone, but not overly so. Further, securely attached infants welcomed their caregiver's return and quickly returned to play. Securely attached infants also freely engaged with the stranger when their caregiver was present.

However, there were two different insecure attachment styles articulated by Ainsworth: avoidant and resistant (sometimes referred to as anxious, especially in adults). Children who showed no distress when their caregivers left the room and were hesitant upon their return were labeled as having an **avoidant attachment style**. Indeed, some avoidant children literally avoided their caregivers by turning away from them when they returned to the room. In contrast, those infants categorized as having an **anxious attachment** (also referred to as resistant attachment) became incredibly upset even before their caregivers physically left the room and clung to their caregivers upon their return. Some of the resistant/anxious infants became so upset that the researchers ended the observation session.

Further research on Ainsworth's initial three attachment styles found that some infants exhibited unique behaviors that were not secure, avoidant, or anxious. Children placed in the new **disorganized attachment** category displayed inconsistent reactions to the strange situation; sometimes the infants would cling to their caregiver, while at other times the same infant would clearly avoid their caregiver.

How do these early attachment styles impact our adult relationships? It is theorized that our patterns of attachment to others continue into our adulthood. The reason is that whether we tend to securely attach to others or exhibit one of the insecure attachment styles is thought to be related to how much we trust that others can be relied upon for support in our times of need. Therefore, those with insecure patterns of attachment either rely too heavily on others for a sense of safety (anxious attachment) or do not trust others to have their back at all (avoidant attachment). Those with disorganized attachment patterns are perhaps unsure how to know whom to trust. It should also be noted that people may not always fit neatly into one attachment style; it is possible to display avoidant attachment behavior with certain individuals and secure attachment with others. However, it is believed that people have a tendency toward just one attachment style, which stems from their early experiences with their primary caregiver.

Explaining Criminal Behavior

How Can Moral Development Theories Help Us Understand Criminal Behavior?

The preconventional stages of Kohlberg's moral development theory are inherently self-serving. Stage 1 is characterized simply by the desire to avoid punishment; if it is perceived that punishment can be avoided, any behavior goes. In stage 2, this goes a bit further when the person realizes that different people may reinforce and punish different things. But the source of the moral judgment is external at both stages in the preconventional level. It is not until stage 3, the first in the conventional level, that we begin to internalize a moral compass. It is at this stage that we realize that our relationships are reciprocal. Our actions impact other people, and we want to be seen by others as "good." This interpersonal approach is still a bit hedonistic, but those at this stage at least care about how their behavior impacts others. It is for this reason, and empirical findings, that Gibbs (2003) advocated for a simplified focus on "immature" (stages 1 and 2) versus "mature" (stage 3 and above) moral development.

Meta-Analyses

A robust meta-analysis of 50 studies concluded that "moral judgment of juvenile delinquents is substantially lower compared to that of nondelinquents, with a large overall effect size of $d = .76$" (Stams et al., 2006, p. 708). In addition to verifying the clear connection between moral development and juvenile delinquency, Stams and his colleagues (2006) examined which other variables might impact this connection (known as moderator variables). Interestingly, they found that many variables did not impact their overall findings; type of delinquency, cultural background, socioeconomic status, gender, age, and intelligence did not change the association between moral development and delinquent behavior. However, they also found that institutionalization may be at least partly responsible for the inverse correlation between moral development and delinquency. Effect sizes were larger for studies that included youth who were incarcerated, rather than youth residing in the community. The concept of "institutionalization" will be discussed in full in Chapter 14. Suffice to say, juvenile detention centers house delinquents who have engaged in behaviors of varying severity, with petty criminals often living with violent offenders. Stams and his colleagues (2006) speculated that "[i]t could be that young people locked up in institutions for long periods cannot develop their moral judgment as much as they would in the outside world" (p. 713).

Another meta-analysis by the Stams team, this time led by Van Vugt, examined the connection between moral reasoning and recidivism while also testing the effect of methodological differences in the studies, such as how moral development and recidivism were measured (Van Vugt et al., 2011). There have traditionally been three different ways in which subjects' moral development stages are classified: recognition measures, production measures, and clinical judgment. **Recognition measures** are typically multiple-choice questions, allowing participants to merely differentiate between the various levels of morality. **Production measures**, on the other hand, often use vignettes, or stories, followed by open-ended questions requiring the respondent to *produce* or articulate their level of morality. Finally, **clinical judgment** is simply an evaluation by some professional, such as a psychologist. Van Vugt and her colleagues (2011) found that studies of recidivism which used production measures of moral development had stronger effect sizes than either recognition measures or clinical judgment. This might suggest that while recidivists may recognize higher levels of moral judgment, they may not be fully capable of producing – and therefore living at – those higher levels of moral judgment.

A similar finding regarding self-report measures of delinquency, namely that studies that used such measures, as opposed to more official reports, had larger effect sizes (Van Vugt et al., 2011), may point to the **social desirability bias**. This common methodological phenomenon typically manifests as over reporting desirable behaviors and under reporting undesirable behaviors. However, among offenders, especially juvenile offenders, the reverse may be seen as desirable. This has been called the **preservation of reputation hypothesis** (Emler & Reicher, 1995). The tendency to manage how others perceive us may also help explain why effect sizes were smaller when respondents were given multiple-choice options using a recognition measure of moral development rather than having to produce an explanation of moral standing on their own. Multiple choice response options may allow those at lower stages of moral development to nonetheless "fake" an understanding of a higher stage.

Despite interesting caveats regarding moderator variables, the overall findings of these meta-analyses are strong. There is a clear inverse relationship between moral development and criminal behavior. However, some research has found that delinquents who recidivate may actually have a higher level of moral development than those who do not recidivate (Petronio, 1980, as cited in Stams et al., 2006, p. 700). It has been suggested that perhaps cognitive distortions may explain this finding. **Cognitive distortions**, sometimes called "thinking errors," are patterns in thinking that help to neutralize any guilt or shame that might be felt for negative or antisocial behaviors. Albert Bandura (1986) called this moral disengagement, and Sykes and Matza (1957) called it techniques of neutralization.

Techniques of Neutralization and Moral Disengagement

Surprisingly, this was a time when criminology was ahead of psychology, as Sykes and Matza published their theory in 1957 and Bandura didn't publish his until 1986. The theories are similar to one another with only minor differences; see Table 3.3 for a visual comparison of the theories side by side.

Sykes and Matza (1957) identified five techniques of neutralization: denial of responsibility, denial of injury, denial of the victim, condemnation of the condemners, and appeal to higher loyalties. When using **denial of responsibility** to neutralize the guilt associated with antisocial behavior, the offender positions themselves as a helpless victim of circumstances. Perhaps their crime truly was an accident but someone employing denial of responsibility will claim that their actions were beyond their control even if they were purposeful. "I had no choice," may be something uttered during denial of responsibility. **Denial of injury** justifies

Table 3.3 Techniques of neutralization compared with moral disengagement.

What is being minimized	*Technique of neutralization*	*Moral disengagement strategy*
Immoral nature of the behavior	Condemnation of the condemners Appeal to higher loyalties	Moral justification Euphemistic labeling Advantageous comparisons
Responsibility for the behavior	Denial of responsibility	Displacement of responsibility Diffusion of responsibility
Consequences of the behavior	Denial of injury	Disregard or distortion of consequences
Worth of the victim	Denial of victim	Dehumanizing Attribution of blame

antisocial behavior by saying their actions have not truly caused irreparable harm. Sykes and Matza (1957) themselves point out the distinction made in legal theory that some actions are *mala in se*, or wrong in and of themselves, while other actions are *mala prohibita*, or wrong because the law says they are wrong. By their very nature, *mala prohibita* laws are philosophically debatable. However, delinquents using denial of injury might also claim that the victim "can afford the loss/damage" due to insurance or wealth. **Denial of the victim** flips the script on who is morally at fault. Even if someone acknowledges that what they did was wrong and caused harm, they may justify their behavior as morally correct because it serves as a retaliation against the victim. In the offender's mind, this makes them not a victim at all, but the initial perpetrator deserving of revenge. Similarly, **condemnation of the condemners** is a neutralization technique that pins the blame on someone else, this time the law and those who enforce it. One who is condemning their condemners will point out that everyone breaks the law, including police, lawyers, and judges. This neutralizes guilt by identifying the "condemners" as hypocrites whose opinions should not be trusted. Finally, when **appealing to higher loyalties**, the offender recognizes their behavior as wrong and/or contrary to the law. However, they claim loyalty to something they see as more important than the law and whose interests or ethics conflict with current legal standards. A common example of those who might appeal to higher loyalties is gang members whose loyalty is with their fellow gang members above all else.

Bandura (1986) situated his eight moral disengagements within four categories: minimizing the immoral nature of the behavior, minimizing personal responsibility for the behavior, minimizing the consequences of the behavior, and minimizing the worth of the victim or blaming the victim. You can see that Sykes and Matza's techniques of neutralization can fit into these categories as well (see Table 3.3). Bandura (1986) placed three types of moral disengagement under the category of minimizing the immoral nature of the behavior: moral justification, euphemistic labeling, and advantageous comparisons. **Moral justification** reframes the supposed moral transgression into a moral virtue by justifying a means to an end. Bandura (1999) used killing by a soldier in wartime as an example of the moral justification of taking a human life (p. 195). However, he argued that the ability of humans to make these moral justifications leaves open the possibility they are used for less-than-honorable acts as well. **Euphemistic labeling** is essentially calling a behavior something different so that it does not sound as bad or so that one's behavior seems justified. Once again, Bandura (1999) invokes the language of war as an example: civilians killed in military operations are often referred to as "collateral damage" (p. 195). This is a much more palatable way to digest one of the human costs of war. Finally, Bandura argues that the immoral nature of one's behavior can be "disengaged" by making **advantageous comparisons** to acts that seem even more immoral. "Well at least I didn't..." might be a common phrase when using this type of moral disengagement.

There are two techniques for moral disengagement under Bandura's category of minimizing personal responsibility for the behavior: displacement of responsibility and diffusion of responsibility. **Displacement of responsibility** can be summed up as "just following orders." If one can place the blame for their actions on someone else in a position of authority, they will be more likely to commit immoral acts. Bandura (1999) used the famous Milgram (1963) experiment as an example. Participants in the Milgram (1963) experiment inflicted more intense electrical shocks to a confederate of the study (no one was actually harmed) when told to do so by an authority figure in a white lab coat (see Chapter 5). **Diffusion of responsibility** is of course similar. When more people are involved in a criminal enterprise, each individual can feel justified in claiming less moral responsibility (more on this in Chapter 5 as well). It could be argued that this is one of the reasons that corporate crime, the violation of the law in the operation of a business, is difficult to prosecute.

Bandura placed only disregard or **distortion of consequences** under the category of minimizing the consequences of the behavior. This moral disengagement is extremely similar to Sykes and Matza's denial of injury. The perpetrator minimizes their guilt or shame by arguing to themselves and others that no real harm came to the supposed victim. Bandura (1999) contended that the further removed from the victim an action is, the easier it is to disregard the consequences of one's actions.

Finally, Bandura said there are two ways to minimize the worth of the victim: dehumanizing and **attribution of blame**. He argued that our basic humanity leads to psychological distress in the face of doing harm to a fellow human. Therefore, **dehumanizing** a victim is a way to morally disengage from the act(s) committed against them. But depending on the perpetrator's closeness to the victim (physically, emotionally, or otherwise), they may have difficulty in convincing themselves that their victim(s) is subhuman. Alternatively, Bandura suggested that one may disengage their own moral responsibility by attributing blame to the victim. Victim blaming may be so effective as to shift public opinion, and sometimes even the victims themselves come to believe that they are culpable for what happened to them. This is unfortunately evident in many cases of sexual assault.

Moral Reconation Therapy

Little and Robinson (1988) set out to create a correctional treatment program designed around Kohlberg's moral development theory. The result was **Moral Reconation Therapy** (MRT). Conation is a term referring to the cognitive process of making intentional decisions. The idea of *re*conation was coined by Little's mentors Wood and Sweet in 1974 (Moral Reconation Therapy, 2016). In fact, Wood and Sweet's Reconation Therapy for use with chronic substance users can be seen as a precursor to MRT (Little & Robinson, 1988). The theory behind MRT fuses elements from Erikson's psychosocial development with Kohlberg's moral development theory.

The aim of MRT is to move people to higher levels of personality development. This progression is based on the following stages of personality (Little & Robinson, 1988). Disloyalty is the lowest stage in MRT's personality development and is characterized by extreme antisocial behaviors bordering on psychopathy (see Chapter 7). Those in the next stage, opposition, have a *slightly* better moral compass that still functions on hedonistic ideals. The third stage, uncertainty, is exemplified by the same interpersonal mistrust as previous stages but with more willingness to engage in behaviors for the good of others. People in the fourth stage, injury, recognize that their behavior is the source of many problems for themselves and their loved ones but may not be ready to make positive changes. Those in nonexistence, the fifth stage, lack direction and commitment in their lives but are more likely to make decisions based on how they impact others. The danger stage, the sixth, is marked by a goals orientation and only occasional use of preconventional moral reasoning that may leave the person feeling as though they have had a setback. This goal orientation increases in stage seven, emergency, with the emergence of and commitment to goals focused on the greater good for all; setbacks will still occur, but a person in the emergency stage will quickly recognize and rectify them. The penultimate stage, stage eight, is called the "normal" stage and is characterized by a contented life with a good balance of communal and ethical considerations in moral decision making. Similar to Kohlberg's final stages of moral development, MRT's final stage, called grace, is unlikely to be achieved by many people. Those in grace view the world and their place in it holistically, and moral decisions are almost exclusively made based on universal ethical principles.

MRT clients are assisted in moving through to higher stages via structured group treatment. Group treatment is facilitated in 12–16 sessions over six to eight weeks. Two sessions are offered per week, each lasting approximately one to two hours. The content of the sessions is proprietary, requiring official training for facilitators. The sessions are guided by seven personality/behavioral elements:

1 Confrontation and assessment of self (beliefs, attitudes, behavior, and defense mechanisms).
2 Assessment of current relationships.
3 Reinforcement of positive behavior and habits designed to raise awareness and moral responsibility.
4 Facilitation of positive identity formation through exploration of the Inner Self and goals.
5 Enhancement of self-concept through ego-enhancing activities and exercises.
6 Decrease the hedonistic orientation of clients by the development of delay of gratification expectations.
7 The development of higher stages of moral reasoning (Little & Robinson, 1988, p. 144).

Since it follows a cognitive-behavioral approach, MRT meets the criteria for general responsivity. Part of Andrews and Bonta's Risk-Need-Responsivity model (i.e., the RNR model), general responsivity states that correctional treatment programs should adhere to psychological processes empirically shown to facilitate behavior change, namely cognitive-behavioral interventions (CBI; see Chapter 13 for a full discussion of the RNR model). In theory, this should mean that MRT is likely to reduce recidivism. Indeed, Ferguson and Wormith (2012) conducted a meta-analysis of 33 studies and found that "MRT had a small, but important, effect on recidivism" (p. 1091). The overall treatment effect showed that offenders who completed the MRT program recidivated at two-thirds the rate of offenders who did not receive MRT treatment.

How Can Attachment Theory Help Us Understand Criminal Behavior?

Since crime is inherently interpersonal, it makes sense to explore whether attachment styles might impact criminal behavior. It is also reasonable to hypothesize that those with insecure attachment styles (resistant/anxious or avoidant) are more likely to criminally offend than those with secure attachment styles. Indeed, research has found connections between attachment styles and violent offending and, unsurprisingly, intimate partner violence (IPV) in particular. It is important to note here that violent offending is much more rare than insecure attachment styles are estimated to be. It is believed that approximately 40% of the population has an insecure attachment style, while many scholars have argued throughout the years that fewer than 10% of offenders are responsible for most crimes (see Wolfgang et al., 1987). Therefore, it is unlikely that insecure attachment styles alone cause all offending behavior. However, research has shown that insecure attachment styles may play a role in violent offending, specifically IPV.

Attachment and Violent Offending

Ogilvie and her colleagues (2014) elucidate why we might consider insecure attachment styles to be linked with violent behavior. They argue that much research has shown that violence is a very common coping strategy in infants and toddlers, which indicates that violent behavior is likely *unlearned* rather than learned. They conclude that "where the home environment is dysfunctional and the child is unable to form secure attachment bonds, the process of unlearning violence becomes disrupted" (Ogilvie et al., 2014, p. 325).

The findings from the meta-analysis conducted by Ogilvie and her colleagues (2014) show that offenders are more likely to have an insecure attachment style than non-offenders. Interestingly, they found that offenders with a diagnosed mental illness were more likely to have an avoidant attachment style, whereas non-offenders with a mental illness tended to have an anxious attachment style. The meta-analysis found that violent offenders were more insecure in their attachment styles than non-violent offenders. Specifically, rapists were shown to have a more avoidant attachment style, but those who perpetrated sexual violence on children were more likely to have an anxious attachment style. However, it should be noted that this last finding was based on only one empirical study that analyzed the connections between attachment styles and sexual offending specifically (Stipe et al., 2006).

Attachment and Intimate Partner Violence

If it is reasonable to expect attachment styles to impact offending behavior in general, it makes even more sense to speculate that they may be connected to intimate partner violence (IPV) in particular. As such, there was a separate meta-analysis done by Velotti and her colleagues (2022) specifically with studies of attachment styles and IPV. The authors found it particularly important to distinguish between different types of IPV, specifically physical, psychological, and sexual. They argue that the studies that examine only "generic violence" (i.e., not separating out different types of IPV) could be missing important distinctions, leading to inconclusive or inaccurate results. Indeed, their meta-analysis found no significant relationship between avoidance attachment styles and generic IPV. Further, they found weak support for a connection between avoidance attachment styles and even specific types of IPV. Anxious attachment styles, however, were found to be greatly associated with generic, psychological, and sexual IPV and moderately correlated with physical IPV perpetration (Velotti et al., 2022). Contrary to what you might expect, the gender of the perpetrator did not impact any of the associations between attachment style and IPV.

Summary

This chapter explored how developmental psychology can help us understand criminal behavior. Various theories within developmental psychology explain how we develop our patterns of thinking and understanding of right and wrong. This chapter also presented empirical support for a connection between developmental deficits and antisocial behavior. Luckily, understanding developmental psychology processes can help guide correctional treatment programs even for adults, despite most of these processes typically taking place during childhood. This means that even if someone did not have a good upbringing, they can still make positive changes as an adult.

References

Ainsworth, M. D. S., Blehar, M. C., Waters, E., & Wall, S. (1978). *Patterns of attachment: A psychological study of the strange situation*. Erlbaum.

Bandura, A. (1986). *Social foundations of thought and action: A social cognitive theory*. Prentice Hall.

Bandura, A. (1999). Moral disengagement in the perpetration of inhumanities. *Personality and Social Psychology Review*, *3*(3), 193–209.

Bowlby, J. (1958). The nature of the child's tie to his mother. *International Journal of Psycho-Analysis*, *39*, 350–373.

Emler, N., & Reicher, S. (1995). *Adolescence and delinquency*. Blackwell.

Erikson, E. H. (1980). *Identity and the life cycle*. W. W. Norton & Company, Inc.

Erikson, E. H. (1982). *The life cycle completed*. W.W. Norton & Company, Inc.

Ferguson, L. M., & Wormith, J. S. (2012). A meta-analysis of moral reconation therapy. *International Journal of Offender Therapy and Comparative Criminology*, *57*.

Gibbs, J. C. (2003). *Moral development and reality: Beyond the theories of Kohlberg and Hoffman*. Sage Publications.

Kohlberg, L. (1976). Moral stages and moralization: The cognitive development approach. In T. Lickona (Ed.), *Moral development and behavior: Theory, research and social issues*. Holt, Rinehart & Winston.

Kohlberg, L., & Hersh, R. H. (1977). Moral development: A review of the theory. *Theory into Practice*, *16*(2), 53–59.

Little, G. L., & Robinson, K. D. (1988). Moral reconation therapy: A systematic step-by-step treatment system for treatment-resistant clients. *Psychological Reports*, *62*, 135–151.

Milgram, S. (1963). Behavioral study of obedience. *The Journal of Abnormal and Social Psychology*, *67*(4), 371–378. https://doi.org/10.1037/h0040525

Moral Reconation Therapy [@moralreconationtherapy9366]. (2016, September 30). *The term "reconation"* [Video]. YouTube. https://youtu.be/Hp6OiHKcfF4

Ogilvie, C. A., Newman, E., Todd, L., & Peck, D. (2014). Attachment & violent offending: A meta-analysis. *Aggression and Violent Behavior*, *19*, 322–339.

Petronio, R. J. (1980). The moral maturity of repeater delinquents. *Youth & Society*, *12*, 51–59.

Piaget, J. (1932). *The moral judgement of the child. Penguin education*. FreePress.

Stams, G. J., Brugman, D., Deković, M., van Rosmalen, L., van der Laan, P., & Gibbs, J. C. (2006). The moral judgement of juvenile delinquents: A meta-analysis. *Journal of Abnormal Child Psychology*, *34*, 697–713.

Stipe, T., Abracen, J., Stermac, L., & Wilson, R. (2006). Sexual offenders' state-of-mind regarding childhood attachment: A controlled investigation. *Sexual Abuse*, *18*, 289–302.

Sykes, G. M., & Matza, D. (1957). Techniques of neutralization: A theory of delinquency. *American Sociological Review*, *22*(6), 664–670.

Van Vugt, E., Gibbs, J., Stams, G. J., Bijleveld, C., Hendricks, J., & van der Laan, P. (2011). Moral development and recidivism: A meta-analysis. *International Journal of Offender Therapy and Comparative Criminology*, *55*(8), 1234–1250.

Velotti, P., Rogier, G., Beomonte Zobel, S., Chirumbolo, A., & Zavattini, G. C. (2022). The relation of anxiety and avoidance dimensions of attachment to intimate partner violence: A meta-analysis about perpetrators. *Trauma, Violence, & Abuse*, *23*(1), 196–212.

Wolfgang, M. E., Figlio, R. M., & Sellin, T. (1987). *Delinquency in a birth cohort*. University of Chicago Press.

4 Behavioral Psychology

Introduction

Behavioral psychology, also called behaviorism, was one of the earliest subdisciplines in the field of psychology. Perhaps unsurprisingly, it is the study of behavior but more specifically how we acquire behavior. In other words, it is the study of how we learn. We now know that learning does not only occur via a single process or even a series of processes. However, behavioral psychology was the first discipline to focus on observable phenomena to understand unconscious processes. This was in stark contrast to the prevailing psychological theory at the time: psychoanalysis. Sigmund Freud developed the practice of using talk therapy over many years to draw conclusions about the inner psyche. Behavioral psychology was developed out of direct observations of behavior, and early discoveries did not even come from psychologists.

Behavioral psychology began with Pavlov's dog, the now famous phenomenon of a dog salivating at the sound of a bell. Around the same time, another researcher discovered that rewarding experiences were likely to be repeated, whereas actions that resulted in negative consequences were unlikely to be repeated. Further research throughout the early twentieth century led to the refinement of this idea of learning via the consequences of behavior. The mid-to-late-twentieth century brought the ideas of observational learning, or acquiring behaviors by watching the behavior of others, to both psychology and criminology. The Basics sections of this chapter will explain these theories in depth. In the Explaining Criminal Behavior section, the evidence as to whether or not criminal behavior is learned via these principles will be presented from several different angles.

The Basics

Classical Conditioning

If you have heard of Pavlov's dog, you are likely already somewhat familiar with **classical conditioning**. Ivan Pavlov (1897/1902) was studying digestion in dogs in the late nineteenth century when he inadvertently discovered learning by association. He noticed that the dogs he was experimenting on would salivate simply at the sound of the bell that indicated meal time, before food was even present. Recognizing that there would be no inherent reason for a dog to salivate at the sound of a bell, Pavlov deduced that the dogs must be associating the bell with food. And because salvation is a reflexive response (i.e., not under the direct control of the dog), he further reasoned that this association was unconscious.

DOI: 10.4324/9781003250821-5

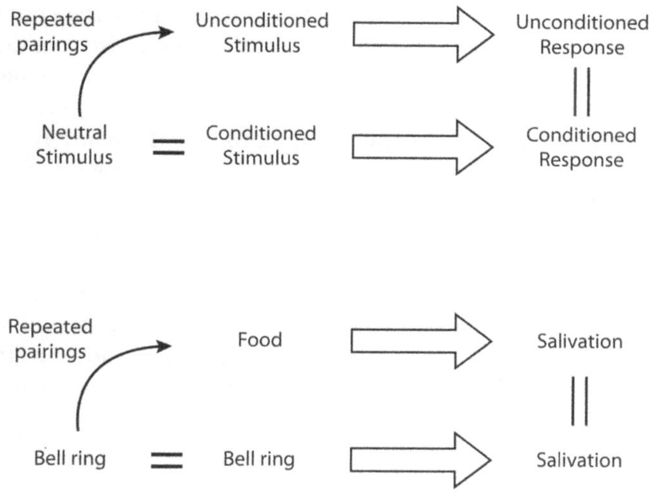

Figure 4.1 The process of classical conditioning.

Additional research into this phenomenon led to the identification of the components of classical conditioning. These components can be somewhat difficult to keep straight, so use Figure 4.1 to follow along visually. To begin, let's look at just the reflexive response that naturally happens. An **unconditioned stimulus** is presented, resulting in an **unconditioned response.** For Pavlov's dogs, the unconditioned stimulus was the food and the unconditioned response was salivation. A **neutral stimulus** is then paired with the unconditioned stimulus, meaning they are presented together at the same time. The bell was originally the neutral stimulus for Pavlov's dogs. With repeated pairings, the neutral stimulus becomes associated with the unconditioned stimulus, turning it into a **conditioned stimulus** that now elicits the same response as the unconditioned stimulus. This response to the conditioned stimulus is known as a **conditioned response.** Therefore, the bell that was once the neutral stimulus becomes the conditioned stimulus, and salvation is now both the unconditioned response and the conditioned response.

The conditioned stimulus on its own (i.e., without pairing with the unconditioned stimulus) will continue to elicit the conditioned response but not forever. This initial process of creating the conditioned stimulus and conditioned response is known as **acquisition.** However, if the unconditioned stimulus is presented numerous times without the conditioned stimulus (for Pavlov's dogs, this meant feedings not paired with a bell), the association between the two will eventually break down causing the conditioned stimulus to be a neutral stimulus once again. This phenomenon is known as **extinction.**

Pavlov's discovery coincided with a push for the discipline of psychology to be seen as its own field of science. John Watson led this charge and officially founded behavioral psychology in 1913. Watson and his colleague Rosalie Rayner also demonstrated a number of properties of classical conditioning, as well as proof that it works with humans, in a now highly controversial study. Watson and Rayner (1920) studied the classical conditioning of fear using an infant known as Little Albert. Little Albert was presented with the neutral stimulus of a white rat, of which he was not initially afraid. However, a hammer was used to cause a loud noise (unconditioned stimulus) causing Little Albert to become fearful and cry (unconditioned response). After repeated pairings of the loud noise with the white rat, Little

Albert became classically conditioned to fear the white rat (now the conditioned stimulus) and would cry when it was presented even without the loud noise (conditioned response). Watson and Rayner (1920) also wanted to study the idea of **stimulus generalization**, or the broadening of a conditioned response to stimuli that are similar to the conditioned stimulus. They demonstrated that after classical conditioning to fear the white rat, Little Albert also showed the conditioned fear response when presented with other white furry things, including a fur coat and a Santa's beard.

Another study around the same time was able to demonstrate the opposite phenomenon: stimulus discrimination. In 1921, Shenger-Krestovnika was able to teach dogs to distinguish between a circle and an oval by only pairing food with the presentation of a circle and not an oval. After repeatedly receiving food when presented with a circle and *not* receiving food when presented with an oval, the dogs would only salivate when shown a circle and not when shown an oval (Gray, 1987). This is **stimulus discrimination**, or the ability to tell the difference between similar but different stimuli.

Operant Conditioning

In classical conditioning, we learn by association. In **operant conditioning**, we learn from the consequences (both pleasant and unpleasant) that come from our behavior. Just like in classical conditioning, this learning can happen naturally, as all behaviors have natural positive and negative consequences. Many associate operant conditioning with BF Skinner, whose work is indeed important. But the basic idea underlying operant conditioning, namely that consequences shape future actions, was originally put forward by Edward Thorndike.

The Law of Effect

Like Pavlov, Thorndike was studying animals at the turn of the twentieth century. Instead of dogs, Thorndike (1905) studied how long it took cats to find their way out of a puzzle box to get to a piece of fish on the outside. He noticed that after they stumbled across the lever that let them out of the puzzle box, the amount of time it took them to escape got shorter and shorter with each trial. Clearly, they had learned! Thorndike theorized that behavior that is followed by a pleasant consequence (accessing the fish) will be repeated in the future, and if a behavior is followed by an unpleasant consequence, it will be less likely to be repeated in the future. Thorndike called this the **law of effect**, and it became a critical foundation for Skinner's later work developing the principles of operant conditioning.

BF Skinner

Taking Thorndike's lead, Skinner developed the Skinner box in the mid-1930s. The Skinner box simply contains a lever that will either administer food or stop an electrical shock, depending on the experiment. Hungry rats were first placed in the Skinner box with a lever that would administer food when pressed. Inevitably, the rat would accidentally press the lever. When lever pressing was rewarded with food, the rats quickly learned to press the lever to receive the food. In a different experiment with the Skinner box, the rats were given an uncomfortable electric shock that would stop when they pressed the lever. Again, after accidentally stumbling into the lever and stopping the electric shock, the rats eventually went immediately to the lever to stop receiving the shock. With these experiments and others, Skinner (1938) developed the reinforcement and punishment principles of operant conditioning.

Reinforcements and Punishments

The basic principles of operant conditioning are positive reinforcement, negative reinforcement, positive punishment, and negative punishment. **Reinforcements** are used to increase behavior, whereas **punishments** are used to decrease behavior. Whether they are positive or negative depends on whether something is being added or something is being taken away. **Positive reinforcement** adds a pleasant experience or item to encourage a desired behavior (e.g., the food in the Skinner box). Whereas, **negative reinforcement** takes away an unpleasant experience or item to encourage desired behavior (e.g., the shock in the Skinner box). Since punishments are intended to decrease behavior, a **positive punishment** adds an unpleasant experience or item to discourage an undesired behavior and a **negative punishment** takes away a pleasant experience to discourage an undesired behavior. See Figure 4.2 for a visual depiction of these concepts.

These seemingly simple ideas can be incredibly confusing! To keep them straight, first decide whether a behavior is being encouraged or discouraged. If the behavior is being encouraged, a reinforcement is being used. If the behavior is being discouraged, a punishment is being used. Keep that in mind as you decide whether something is being added or

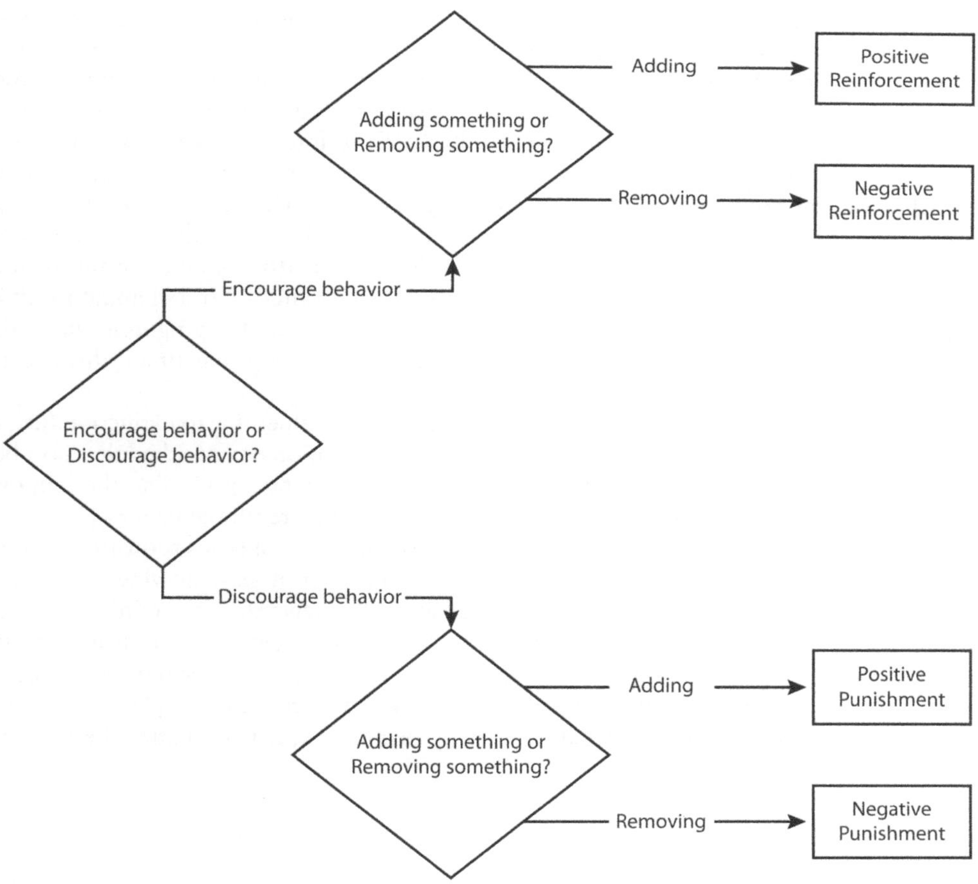

Figure 4.2 Positive and negative reinforcement and punishment.

something is being taken away from the person whose behavior is being impacted. If something is being added or given, it is positive. If something is being subtracted or taken away, it is negative.

Skinner (1951, as cited in Peterson, 2004) also developed the behavior modification concept called shaping. **Shaping** is a method of teaching more complex tasks by reinforcing successive approximations of the end-goal behavior. Anyone who has successfully trained a dog is likely somewhat familiar with this concept. To train a dog to roll over, for example, you must start by teaching the dog to lay down. Once the dog learns to lay down on command, you can then move on to teaching the dog to lay on its side. The next step may be to reward the dog for beginning to roll over onto its back. The final step, of course, is to reward the dog for fully rolling over on command. Shaping in operant conditioning can be broken down into as many steps as is necessary for the individual. For example, if the dog is reluctant to lay on its side, the trainer could begin to teach the dog to lay on its side by first reinforcing even a slight lean to one side. Once the dog learns to lean, reinforcement is not again provided until the dog goes a step further, perhaps by mostly laying on its side. It is easy to see why Skinner called this process shaping, and he even likened it to a sculptor shaping clay (Skinner, 1951, as cited in Peterson, 2004, p. 325).

Further research on these principles of operant conditioning led to the discovery of different **reinforcement schedules**. Reinforcement schedules describe different timing and delivery of the reinforcement. When a reinforcement is provided every time the desired behavior is performed, this is known as **continuous reinforcement**. When a reinforcement is provided only after the desired behavior has been repeated a specific number of times, this is known as **fixed ratio reinforcement**. Similarly, **fixed interval reinforcement** calls for the reinforcement to be delivered only after a certain amount of time, as long as the desired behavior was completed at least once during that time. The timing of reinforcement can also vary, rather than being fixed. This makes it somewhat unpredictable as to if and when a reinforcement will be provided. In **variable ratio reinforcement**, a reinforcement is provided after the desired behavior has been repeated a random and changing number of times. When a reinforcement is provided after a random and changing *amount* of time (and the desired behavior has been completed at least once during that time), this is called **variable interval reinforcement**.

Just as with classical conditioning, operant conditioning is vulnerable to extinction (i.e., the discontinuation of the desired behavior). However, certain reinforcement schedules have been shown to slow the rate of the extinction process. Because it entails providing the reinforcement every time the desired behavior is exhibited, continuous reinforcement is particularly susceptible to extinction. Once the reinforcement stops, the behavior stops soon after. Variable reinforcement schedules do particularly well at preventing – or at least slowing – extinction. This is because the subject does not know when they will receive the next reinforcement, as it varies each time. Therefore, it takes longer to recognize when reinforcement is not continuing. The desired behavior will continue longer, in the hopes that another reinforcement will be provided *at some point*. Without naturally occurring reinforcement to replace the artificial reinforcement, the desired behavior will eventually become extinct no matter the reinforcement schedule used.

Social Learning Theory

You may have noticed that both classical and operant conditioning involve hands-on learning, meaning that the person doing the learning is having a direct experience (i.e., experiencing two stimuli at the same time or experiencing reinforcement or punishment). We know now that learning does not only and always occur this way. Noam Chomsky (1959), often called the father of modern linguistics, rightly pointed out that humans do not only acquire language through operant conditioning as Skinner believed. Without getting into the complexities of biolinguistics, one of Chomsky's main points was that the learning of language often happens through observation and imitation of others.

Observational learning was studied extensively by Albert Bandura. Perhaps the most famous of his studies is referred to as the Bobo doll experiment (Bandura et al., 1961). This study is particularly relevant for this chapter as it examined the role of observational learning in aggressive behavior. Bandura and his colleagues designed an experiment where children witnessed adults playing with an inflatable toy (i.e., the Bobo doll). Some children saw the adults playing aggressively with the doll, while other children saw the adults play with other available toys. Later, those children who witnessed the aggressive play with the Bobo doll were more likely to repeat this aggressive play with the doll. Whereas, the children who did not witness adults playing aggressively showed almost no aggressive play. Bandura concluded that the children were learning by observation and imitation of behavioral **models.**

In a further refinement of his social learning theory, Bandura (1986) incorporated individual agency via cognition (i.e., thinking). Bandura outlined four stages of his **social cognitive theory**: attention, retention, reproduction, and motivation. The first phase, **attention,** requires the observer to pay attention to the model of the behavior. If the behavior is not observed, it cannot be imitated. The next stage, **retention,** recognizes that the observer must remember the behavior that they observed in order to imitate it. The third stage is **reproduction,** and this is the act of imitating the previously observed behavior. The final stage of Bandura's social cognitive theory is **motivation,** meaning that the observer must have sufficient motivation to continue to repeat this behavior. This is believed to occur through reinforcement of the new behavior, either experienced directly by the observer or indirectly via the observer seeing the model be reinforced for the behavior and therefore expecting their own reinforcement. This is known as **vicarious reinforcement.**

Additionally, Bandura believed that characteristics of the model impact whether or not an observer will even pay attention to their behavior (i.e., the first stage of social cognitive theory). He asserted that an observer will be more likely to pay attention to the model's behavior if they believe the model is similar to themselves. He also stated that models perceived to be of high status are more likely to have their behaviors replicated by others.

A similar theory was developed independently in sociology and criminology. Edwin Sutherland (1939) posited that who we associate with matters in whether we engage in criminal behavior. He also believed that we learned from these associates but did not describe how this learning happens. Robert Burgess and Ronald Akers then added the learning process from Bandura's work to Sutherland's ideas.

Differential Association Theory

Sutherland developed his theory of **differential association** in 1939 with nine principles regarding how he believed criminal behavior is acquired (see Table 4.1 for all nine principles). Note that this was prior to the full development of the learning theories from behavioral psychology described above. Therefore, Sutherland simply stated that criminal behavior is learned in the same way that other behaviors are learned, but he did not describe this learning process. Rather, the crux of his differential association theory is the sixth of his nine

Table 4.1 The principles of differential association.

1	Criminal behavior is learned.
2	Criminal behavior is learned in interaction with other persons in a process of communication.
3	The principal part of the learning of criminal behavior occurs within intimate personal groups.
4	When criminal behavior is learned, the learning includes (a) techniques of committing the crime, which are sometimes very complicated, sometimes very simple; and (b) the specific direction of motives, drives, rationalizations, and attitudes.
5	The specific direction of motives and drives is learned from definitions of the legal codes as favorable or unfavorable.
6	A person becomes delinquent because of an excess of definitions favorable to violation of law over definitions unfavorable to violations of law.
7	Differential associations may vary in frequency, duration, priority, and intensity.
8	The process of learning criminal behavior by association with criminal and anticriminal patterns involves all of the mechanisms that are involved in any other learning.
9	While criminal behavior is an expression of general needs and values, it is not explained by those general needs and values, since noncriminal behavior is an expression of the same needs and values.

Source: Sutherland (1939).

principles: "A person becomes delinquent because of an excess of definitions favorable to violation of law over definitions unfavorable to violation of law" (Sutherland, 1939). This is the "differential" part of Sutherland's theory. This is simply a fancy word for the difference between the number of positive and the number of negative influences. Sutherland is saying with his sixth principle that lawbreaking results when someone holds more positive beliefs about (i.e., "definitions favorable to") violating the law than negative beliefs about (i.e., "definitions unfavorable to") violating the law. Various other principles from Sutherland describe where we acquire these "**definitions.**" We learn them "in a process of communication" (principle two) "within intimate personal groups" (principle three). In other words, we learn our attitudes and beliefs about violating the law through interactions with our *associates*. Taken all together, the basic premise of Sutherland's theory of differential association is that delinquent behavior is learned when the balance of (i.e., differential) those around us (i.e., associations) hold a positive (i.e., favorable) view of violating the law.

Social Learning Theory (Criminology Edition)

Several decades later, Burgess and Akers (1966) refined Sutherland's theory to include the newly developed ideas from behavioral psychology, particularly Skinner's operant conditioning and Bandura's social cognitive theory. Their principles of **differential association-reinforcement** theory, as modified from Sutherland's original principles, are listed in Table 4.2. This revision of the theory addressed what was lacking in the original: an explanation of the learning process. However, it was not until Akers and his colleagues (1979) fully tested the theory that the four components of his **social learning theory** were established. They are differential association, differential reinforcement, definitions, and imitation. Differential association is conceptualized just as Sutherland did; it is the balance of the attitudes of those around you. The concept of definitions is also unchanged from Sutherland's theory in that they are simply the beliefs and attitudes one holds. Akers' social learning theory, however, notes that the balance of the definitions of those around us eventually becomes our own internalized definitions.

Differential reinforcement and imitation are concepts more clearly borrowed from behavioral psychology. Imitation is the same concept as Bandura's reproduction. We copy (i.e., imitate) the behaviors of those around us (i.e., models). Akers agreed with Bandura that

Table 4.2 The principles of differential association-reinforcement.

1	Criminal behavior is learned according to the principles of operant conditioning.
2	Criminal behavior is learned both in nonsocial situations that are reinforcing or discriminative and through that social interaction in which the behavior of other persons is reinforcing or discriminative for criminal behavior.
3	The principal part of the learning of criminal behavior occurs in those groups which comprise the individual's major source of reinforcement.
4	The learning of criminal behavior, including specific techniques, attitudes, and avoidance procedures, is a function of the effective and available reinforcers, and the existing reinforcement contingencies.
5	The specific class of behaviors which are learned and their frequency of occurrence are a function of the reinforcers which are effective and available, and the rules or norms by which these reinforcers are applied.
6	Criminal behavior is a function of norms which are discriminative for criminal behavior, the learning of which takes place when such behavior is more highly reinforced than noncriminal behavior.
7	The strength of criminal behavior is a direct function of the amount, frequency, and probability of its reinforcement.

Source: Burgess and Akers (1966).

we are more likely to imitate the behaviors of those we admire or with whom we identify. He also posited that behavior is more likely to be imitated if the observer sees the model reinforced or the observer otherwise anticipates reinforcement for the behavior. The concept of **differential reinforcement** combines operant conditioning with Sutherland's point that the attitudes of those around us differ. Akers recognized that learning happens most easily from reinforcement of behavior (rather than punishment). He also recognized that if the attitudes of those around us differ (i.e., differential association), then the behaviors for which we are reinforced will also differ depending on who is observing the behavior. Therefore, if we have more criminal associates than non-criminal associates, we will be more likely to be reinforced for criminal behavior.

Explaining Criminal Behavior

As will become apparent in this section, measuring the components of behavioral psychology can be difficult in humans. Much of the early evidence supporting these theories came from experiments on animals, as these studies have much fewer ethical restrictions. Indeed, one of the most difficult aspects of studying potential causes of criminal behavior is that it is unethical to deliberately induce such behavior in human subjects. This leaves sociologists and criminologists to only be able to study criminal behavior after it has already happened, which requires attempting to retroactively control for myriad other variables that may also influence criminal behavior (i.e., all other theories of criminal behavior). However, even in psychology, a field that has more often attempted to use controlled experiments to study phenomena, there is concern with Bandura's studies of human aggression.

Given the mixed empirical findings from direct studies of the social learning of criminal behavior, this section will also present indirect evidence that principles from behavioral psychology may impact antisocial behavior. Research on the influence of violent media, the effectiveness of deterring criminal behavior through punishment, and correctional treatment programs that are the most successful at reducing reoffending all contain elements from behavioral psychology.

Evidence from Criminology

Pratt and his colleagues conducted the first meta-analysis of Akers' social learning theory in 2010. Since these researchers wanted to synthesize the empirical evidence for Akers' theory, they specifically excluded studies of Bandura's social cognitive theory. They explicitly focused on Akers' four components of differential association, definitions, differential reinforcement, and modeling/imitation as predictors of criminal or deviant behavior. They noted that more studies focused on differential association and definitions than on differential reinforcement and modeling/imitation. While this indicates a need for further research in these areas, Pratt and his colleagues (2010) believed they still had more than enough information on these variables to draw a clear conclusion. That conclusion was that differential associations and definitions have a stronger relationship with delinquent and offending behavior than differential reinforcement and modeling/imitation. This is consistent with The Big Four risk factors for antisocial behavior (i.e., antisocial attitudes, antisocial peers, a history of antisocial behavior, and antisocial personality; see Chapter 13). However, it provides little support for the aspects of Akers' social learning theory taken more directly from behavioral psychology, namely the effects of reinforcement for antisocial behaviors and the impact of witnessing others engaging in such behavior. Still, Pratt and his colleagues (2010) encouraged further study of these two components of social learning theory.

Evidence from Psychology

Throughout his career, Albert Bandura and his colleagues conducted many experiments similar to his seminal Bobo doll experiment, modifying variables such as live versus filmed models and punishment of the models versus no punishment of the models. While these studies seemed to support the observational learning of aggression, the concept is not without its critics. The most prominent critique is that these experiments are not measuring aggression at all, but merely short-lived imitation of behavior as if it were instruction for how to play with the doll (e.g., Tedeschi & Quigley, 1996). This idea is supported by the other common critique of Bandura's studies; the supposed aggression exhibited following observed aggression does not seem to last beyond the experiment itself (e.g., Geen & Thomas, 1986).

These critiques and empirical findings point to the fact that aggression is not a simple concept, and the explanation of how aggressive behavior is acquired is likely not simple either. Baron and Richardson (1994) defined aggression as "behavior produced to cause physical harm or humiliation to another person who wishes to avoid it" (Ferguson, 2023, p. 1). Ferguson (2023) argues that intent to harm is a crucial component of aggression that is difficult to measure and unethical to induce for the sake of an experiment. Also inherent in aggressive behavior is its interpersonal nature, suggesting the inclusion of ideas from social psychology (see Chapter 5).

Media Violence and Aggression

The concepts of observational learning and vicarious reinforcement beg the question: do people learn to behave aggressively by consuming aggressive media? You have likely heard this argument. Some people believe that watching violence on television or in movies, or more recently, playing violent video games can lead to increased violent or aggressive behavior. This assertion has been empirically tested, but it is unfortunately still a source of controversy.

Recent research has focused on violent video games as they are presumed to be a more immersive medium. There are also a number of concerns about the effects on children who may play them, as children and teens are often their primary audience. Multiple meta-analyses have been conducted on the topic, including one commissioned by the American Psychological Association (APA, 2015). Unfortunately, they have reached different conclusions. The meta-analysis from the APA and a separate one by Anderson and his colleagues (2010) concluded that violent video games *do* lead to increased aggression. However, a reevaluation of the APA meta-analysis by Ferguson and his colleagues (2020) supported the findings from his previous meta-analysis (Ferguson, 2015) that violent video games have a negligible effect on aggression.

So, who is correct? Although this is still an ongoing area of research, recent studies have suggested a couple of possible reasons for the inconsistent results. After reanalyzing the data from three separate published meta-analyses, Mathur and VanderWeele (2019) concluded that there is "considerable common ground between these three meta-analyses" (p. 706). Namely, one camp is correct that there is a non-zero effect on aggression resulting from exposure to violent video games. However, the other camp is also correct in pointing out that this effect is quite small and possibly not worthy of concern. Additionally, Devilly and his colleagues (2023) conducted several studies in an attempt to identify possible mediating effects on the relationship between video games and aggression. One of their conclusions was related to the methodology used in many experiments on the relationship. Specifically, the limited amount of time study participants are typically allowed to play a video game under experimental conditions possibly causes frustration for the participants (see the discussion of the frustration-aggression hypothesis in Chapter 5). Devilly and his colleagues (2023) also observed that the personality characteristics of trait anger (i.e., generally being an angry person) and emotional suggestibility (i.e., emotions are easily influenced) mediated the effect of violent video games on state anger (i.e., being angry in the moment) and behavioral aggression (see Chapter 6 for more on personality characteristics related to aggression). However, they cautioned that "this does not discount the possibility that years of media consumption have previously influenced these dispositions" (Devilly et al., 2023, p. 111).

The Social Learning of Deterrence

The criminal justice notion of **deterrence** is theoretically based on behavioral psychology: the idea that punishment will reduce undesired (i.e., criminal) behavior. **Specific deterrence** aligns with direct operant conditioning, stating that a criminal who has been punished for a crime will be less likely to commit that crime in the future. **General deterrence** is more like Bandura's vicarious or observational learning, asserting that others who see someone punished for a crime will be less likely to commit that crime themselves. Despite its basis in modern psychology, the theory of deterrence dates back thousands of years to early criminal justice philosophers (Beccaria, 1764; Bentham, 1789; Hobbes, 1651). These early scholars recognized that for punishment to effectively deter future behavior, it needs to be swift, certain, and sufficiently (but not overly) severe. However, criminal justice systems have difficulty meeting these three criteria for effective deterrence.

Given the focus of modern Western governments on **due process** (i.e., the requirement of specific and thorough processes to be followed prior to depriving a citizen of life or liberty), **swift punishment** is difficult to achieve. The clandestine nature of criminal behavior does not allow for absolute **certainty of punishment** either; many crimes go undetected or unreported. It seems that the **severity of the punishment** is the only thing the criminal justice system can control. Unfortunately for deterrence theory, the severity of punishment is the least effective of these three criteria in affecting behavior change (Apel & Diller, 2017).

Stafford and Warr (1993) identified another big problem for deterrence theory. The lack of certainty of punishment created a different learning opportunity in **punishment avoidance**. They argued that when individuals repeatedly commit a crime and avoid punishment it may actually increase the likelihood of future criminal behavior. Similarly, people can witness others avoiding punishment for their crimes, creating a problem for general deterrence as well. The more often an offender experiences or witnesses punishment *avoidance*, the less certain punishment becomes. Stafford and Warr (1993) included the concepts of both direct and indirect punishment avoidance in their **reconceptualization of deterrence theory**.

From a behavioral psychology perspective, the larger problem with deterrence theory is that it focuses on the punishment of undesirable behavior rather than the reinforcement of desirable behavior. Research has shown that behavior change happens easier when reinforcement is used more often than punishment (Apel & Diller, 2017). This makes some intuitive sense. Punishments may effectively teach people what *not* to do, but that should be paired with an emphasis on what should be done instead by reinforcing desirable behaviors.

Nonetheless, there is some empirical evidence that vicarious punishment may curb behavior in others, which shows support for general deterrence. Malouff and his colleagues (2009) conducted a meta-analysis of studies of vicarious punishment in the psychology literature. Their overall findings showed support that people will be less likely to engage in a behavior for which they saw a model punished. The authors noted that all of the studies included in their meta-analysis measured the outcome variable (i.e., observer behavior) soon after they saw the model punished for the behavior, so the long-term effects of vicarious punishment remain unknown. Further, this meta-analysis provided evidence that there are likely intervening variables within the relationship between vicarious punishment and behavior. However, the authors were able to test a number of variables that may affect this relationship. Malouff and his colleagues (2009, p. 283) concluded:

> Vicarious punishment occurred with live and filmed models, severe and nonsevere consequences for the model, positive punishment for the model or combined positive and negative punishment, primary and secondary punishment or just secondary punishment for the model, adult participants and child participants, and female and male participants. Vicarious punishment occurred with various types of behavior, such as sharing, working hard, cheating, acting aggressively, and choosing items. Hence, one may conclude that the effect of vicarious punishment is robust across these variables.

Correctional Rehabilitation

As will be discussed in more detail in Chapter 13, the most effective treatments for reducing recidivism among convicted offenders are based on cognitive-behavioral principles. However, **contingency management systems**, as Skinner called them, have been in use by corrections agencies for a long time. You may be familiar with the concept of "good time" in relation to prison sentences. This is the common practice of reducing an inmate's sentence for good behavior while in prison. In behavioral psychology terms, this is negative reinforcement for good behavior. Another common system in corrections is token economies. **Token economies** use a symbolic "points" system, originally in the form of "tokens," which are awarded for positive behavior. These points or tokens can then be exchanged for various things seen as valuable (e.g., commissary items, increased privileges, etc.). This allows the recipient to choose a reward that is of most value to them. More recently, correctional programs are built in tiered "phases" of treatment, whereby advancement through the phases of the program is paired with increased privileges at each successive phase.

These contingency management systems have been effective at encouraging positive behavior while the system is in place. However, once the person is out of the system (i.e., released from prison or community supervision) and the reinforcement stops, the positive behaviors eventually go extinct. Of course, this is exactly what Skinner would predict. For behavior change to last beyond state supervision, the extrinsic motivation to change provided by the contingency management systems must be transitioned to intrinsic motivation via recognition of more natural reward systems for positive behavior, such as maintaining prosocial relationships. This is where thinking (i.e., cognition) becomes important in cognitive-behavioral treatments.

Summary

Behavioral psychology has a long history, and some of that history comes from outside the field of psychology. Early discoveries were made by non-psychologists, and ideas seemingly unrelated to how behavior is learned actually contain principles from behavioral psychology. While current empirical evidence suggests that aggressive and violent behavior may not simply be learned through imitation and observational learning, there may still be hope for using cognitive-behavioral principles for behavior change in correctional settings. More research is needed in all of these areas, perhaps due to the difficulty in accurately measuring these concepts. As with all research, behavioral psychologists must be open to the possibility that social learning is only one piece of the puzzle in understanding criminal behavior.

References

Akers, R. L., Krohn, M. D., Lanza-Kaduce, L., & Radosevich, M. (1979). Social learning and deviant behavior: A specific test of a general theory. *American Sociological Review*, *44*(4), 636–655.

American Psychological Association. (2015). *APA Task Force on Violent Media: Technical report on the review of the violent video game literature.* https://www.apa.org/pi/families/review-video-games.pdf

Anderson, C. A., Shibuya, A., Ihori, N., Swing, E. L., Bushman, B. J., Sakamoto, A., Rothstein, H. R., & Saleem, M. (2010). Violent video game effects on aggression, empathy, and prosocial behavior in Eastern and Western countries: A meta-analytic review. *Psychological Bulletin*, *136*(2), 151–173.

Apel, A. B., & Diller, J. W. (2017). Prison as punishment: A behavior-analytic evaluation of incarceration. *The Behavior Analyst*, *40*(1), 243–256.

Bandura, A. (1986). *Social foundations of thought and action: A social cognitive theory.* Prentice-Hall.

Bandura, A., Ross, D., & Ross, S. A. (1961). Transmission of aggression through imitation of aggressive models. *The Journal of Abnormal and Social Psychology*, *63*(3), 575–582.

Baron, R., & Richardson, D. (1994). *Human aggression.* Plenum Press.

Beccaria, C. (1764). *An essay on crimes and punishments.* W.C. Little & Co.

Bentham, J. (1789). *An introduction to the principles of morals and legislation.* T. Payne and Son.

Burgess, R. L., & Akers, R. L. (1966). A differential association-reinforcement theory of criminal behavior. *Social Problems*, *14*, 128–147.

Chomsky, N. (1959). A review of B. F. Skinner's verbal behavior. *Language*, *35*(1), 26–58.

Devilly, G. J., O'Donohue, R. P., & Brown, K. (2023). Personality and frustration predict aggression and anger following violent media. *Psychology, Crime, & Law*, *29*(1), 83–119.

Ferguson, C. J. (2015). Do angry birds make for angry children? A meta-analysis of video game influences on children's and adolescents' aggression, mental health, prosocial behavior, and academic performance. *Perspectives on Psychological Science*, *10*, 646–666.

Ferguson, C. J. (2023). An evolutionary model for aggression in youth: Rethinking aggression in terms of the catalyst model. *New Ideas in Psychology*, *70*, 101029.

Ferguson, C. J., Copenhave, A., & Markey, P. (2020). Reexamining the findings of the American Psychological Association's 2015 Task Force on Violent Media: A meta-analysis. *Perspectives on Psychological Science*, *15*(6), 1423–1443.
Geen, R. G., & Thomas, S. L. (1986). The immediate effects of media violence on behavior. *Journal of Social Issues*, *42*(3), 7–27.
Gray, J. A. (1987). *The psychology of fear and stress* (2nd ed.). Cambridge University Press.
Hobbes, T. (1651). *Leviathan: Or the matter, form and power of a commonwealth, ecclesiastical and civil*. Scolar Press.
Malouff, J., Thorsteinsson, E., Schutte, N., & Rooke, S. E. (2009). Effects of vicarious punishment: A meta-analysis. *The Journal of General Psychology*, *136*(3), 271–285.
Mathur, M. B., & VanderWeele, T. J. (2019). Finding common ground in meta-analysis "wars" on violent video games. *Perspectives on Psychological Science*, *14*(4), 705–708.
Pavlov, I. P. (1897/1902). *The work of the digestive glands*. Griffin.
Peterson, G. B. (2004). A day of great illumination: B. F. Skinner's discovery of shaping. *Journal of the Experimental Analysis of Behavior*, *82*, 317–328.
Pratt, T. C., Cullen, F. T., Sellers, C. S., Winfree, L. T. Jr., Madensen, T. D., Daigle, L. E., Fearn, N. E., & Gau, J. M. (2010). The empirical status of social learning theory: A meta-analysis. *Justice Quarterly*, *27*(6), 765–802.
Skinner, B. F. (1938). *The behavior of organisms: An experimental analysis*. Appleton-Century.
Skinner, B. F. (1951). *How to teach animals*. Freeman.
Stafford, M. C., & Warr, M. (1993). A reconceptualization of general and specific deterrence. *Journal on Research in Crime and Delinquency*, *30*(2), 123–135.
Sutherland, E. H. (1939). *Principles of criminology*. J. B. Lippincott.
Tedeschi, J. T., & Quigley, B. M. (1996). Limitations of laboratory paradigms for studying aggression. *Aggression and Violent Behavior*, *1*(2), 163–177.
Thorndike, E. L. (1905). *The elements of psychology*. A. G. Seiler.
Watson, J. B. (1913). Psychology as the behaviorist views it. *Psychological Review*, *20*, 158–177.
Watson, J. B., & Rayner, R. (1920). Conditioned emotional reactions. *Journal of Experimental Psychology*, *3*(1), 1–14.

5 Social Psychology

Introduction

Social psychology is the study of how we, as individuals, interact with and are impacted by society and other people. It is easily confused with sociology, which is the study of societies and groups of people as a whole. Since social psychology has always been interested in interpersonal interactions, it is not surprising that the field developed its own theories specific to aggressive and antisocial behavior. Further, as cognitive psychology has found its way into many psychology disciplines, social psychology has increasingly become the study of social cognition. **Social cognition** is the ways we, as individuals, think about and respond to our social interactions. The Basics section of this chapter will cover the social psychological concepts of schemas, scripts, deindividuation, diffusion of responsibility, the bystander effect, conformity, and obedience to authority, as well as early and popular theories of aggression from social psychologists. In addition to empirical research on these concepts and their relation to crime, the Explaining Criminal Behavior section of this chapter will discuss two more recent theories that have attempted to combine ideas from the earlier theories to create a more comprehensive theory of aggressive behavior.

The Basics

Schemas

Before we delve into the social psychological theories of aggression, it is important to explain that humans often employ mental shortcuts to understand our environment. We are constantly bombarded by social and sensory information. To aid us in processing this information, we develop mental shortcuts that psychologists call **schemas**. The various types of schemas will be discussed more thoroughly in Chapter 12 in relation to juror decision making. For the purposes of this chapter, it is important to note a few things about schemas. We each develop our own schemas based on our experiences and exposures. Schemas are formed when repeated experiences involving the same social and sensory information occur together, much like classical conditioning (see Chapter 4). They therefore contain powerful associations between things that are possibly unconnected in reality. Stereotypes are common examples of schemas. Additionally, a type of schema about events is known as a **script**. A script will specifically inform how we think a particular event will play out based on our past experiences. Cues from our current environment will trigger certain schemas to be activated in a process called **priming**. Once a schema is primed and activated, we use associations we have previously made about things we are currently experiencing to make

DOI: 10.4324/9781003250821-6

nearly instantaneous inferences about our current situation. Schemas, therefore, can greatly impact our interpretations of and responses to certain social situations. This means they likely play a role in social-psychological explanations of criminal behavior, and indeed the concept of schemas is included in many of the theories described next.

Early Social Psychological Theories of Aggression

Frustration-Aggression Hypothesis

In 1939, Dollard and his colleagues published *Frustration and Aggression*. The central tenet of their **frustration-aggression hypothesis** is that feelings of frustration lead to increased chances of aggressive behavior. It should be noted that some scholars (e.g., Berkowitz, 1990) believed the original frustration-aggression hypothesis stated that all frustration will lead to aggression and that all aggression can be traced back to a frustration. This was a source of criticism of the theory, which led to some of the reformed theories we will discuss later in this chapter (see cognitive neoassociation theory).

Dollard and his colleagues (1939) believed that the relationship between frustration and aggression could explain a wide range of aggressive behaviors, even when the target of the aggression is not the source of the frustration. This was due to their adherence to Freud's psychoanalytic theory, which was popular (if not all-encompassing) in psychology at the time. Defense mechanisms, in psychoanalytic theory, are ways in which people handle negative emotions such as frustration. The particular defense mechanism applicable to the frustration-aggression hypothesis is displacement. **Displacement**, as a defense mechanism, means taking out negative emotions on someone or something other than the cause of the negative emotion, usually when that cause is unavailable or seemingly inappropriate to attack. A classic example is a man who is frustrated with his work and, instead of taking it out on his boss, he beats his wife when he gets home.

The relationship between frustration and aggression is fairly intuitive. Even those of us who are incredibly non-violent have likely experienced the urge to act out aggressively (e.g., punch a pillow or scream and yell) when we are frustrated. The concept makes so much sense that the idea developed independently within sociology. In 1938, Merton published his now famous **strain theory**. Merton's original theory focused primarily on the frustration of goal blockage in the attempted attainment of the American Dream. However, his theory was later expanded by Agnew's **general strain theory** (1992), which noted that there are many sources of stress and frustration that may lead to aggression and antisocial behavior. You can learn more about strain theory, and other sociological theories of criminal behavior, in any basic criminology course or textbook.

Excitation Transfer Theory

Zillman first published his excitation transfer theory of aggression in 1971. At a basic level, **excitation transfer theory** states that because emotional and physiological arousal does not immediately dissipate, such excitation can be transferred to subsequent encounters unrelated to the original source of the arousal. Through further research, Zillman and his colleagues (1972) determined that even physiological arousal via exercise impacts subsequent aggressive behavior. In addition to physiological and emotional arousal, our thoughts play a role in excitation transfer theory. Remaining in an environment free of distractions may allow someone to more easily ruminate on the original source of their anger or frustration, and this rumination has been shown to delay the natural decrease of excitation. However, the reverse has also been found to be true. Studies have shown that being told information that mitigates someone's rude behavior *prior* to a negative encounter with that person results in much less retaliatory behavior than being given such information *after* experiencing the person's rude behavior (Zillman, 1988). The implication for excitation transfer theory is that our thoughts impact our level of emotional and physiological arousal, but the same emotional and physiological arousal can also impact the ability of our thoughts to mitigate our behavior. Some scholars have even used excitation transfer theory to explain police officers' willingness to use excessive force (Barton et al., 2000).

Hostile Attribution Bias

The term hostile attribution bias was first used by Nasby and his colleagues (1979) in their study of aggression among adolescent boys. **Hostile attribution bias**, also known as hostile intent attribution, is the tendency to perceive ambiguous social cues as having a hostile intent. It has been argued that this bias is learned through repeated exposure to hostile events, such as child abuse. When someone is continually confronted by situations and people that mean them harm, they will develop an assumption that hostility is a common interpersonal occurrence. Therefore, when they find themselves in a more ambiguous situation, they will be more likely to assume hostile intent.

Cognitive Neoassociation Theory

After decades of research on the frustration-aggression hypothesis, Berkowitz began presenting some revisions to the theory that eventually became his cognitive neoassociation theory. The first idea put forward by Berkowitz (1990) was that frustration alone does not always lead to aggression, particularly if it does not elicit a negative emotion. The concept of frustration had previously been defined as a thwarting of the achievement of an anticipated goal. Research has shown that this did not always lead to aggression, causing Berkowitz (1990) to theorize that frustration must cause an unpleasant response in order to lead to aggressive behavior. This seems to be a reasonable modification to the operational definition of the concept of frustration. After all, if someone is blocked from attaining a goal that they did not particularly care much about, it is less likely to lead to a sense of frustration as we commonly understand that feeling. It makes sense to note that the concept of frustration must be accompanied by a negative affective response to really be considered frustration.

Berkowitz's **cognitive neoassociation theory**, therefore, states that negative affective is the true underlying cause when frustration leads to aggression. The theory further adds that aspects of the situation that trigger schemas associated with negative affect and/or aggression will increase the odds of aggression in the present situation. As with the concept of priming, these schemas need not be directly related to the situation at hand. When there are cues present in a situation that have been cognitively linked with negative affect or aggression in the past, these schemas will be activated, leading to an increased chance of aggression. This idea was first developed by Berkowitz and his colleague LePage (1967) in the discovery of what is now known as the weapons effect (see Box 5.1).

Box 5.1 The weapons effect

In the late 1960s, Berkowitz and LePage (1967) set out to test whether the mere presence of a weapon would increase levels of aggression. Their experiment had subjects evaluate each other on a task by giving a varying number of electric shocks based on how well their partner did. One of each partnered pair, however, was a confederate who was actually in on the experiment. The tests had a number of variables, including how many shocks the confederate first gave the subject (either one, intended to not provoke anger or seven, intended to provoke anger). More importantly, the tests varied as to whether a shotgun and revolver were on the table, sports equipment was on the table, or nothing was on the table. The dependent variable was the number of shocks the subject chose to give the confederate upon evaluation of their performance of the task. Their findings clearly showed that the presence of weapons increased the number of shocks the subject gave the confederate, especially in a retaliatory fashion when the subject was upset at first receiving seven shocks from the confederate. Berkowitz and LePage (1967), recognizing one experiment cannot confirm a finding, called for further research on the association between weapons and aggression.

Many such studies have been conducted in the decades since this pioneering experiment. Benjamin and his colleagues (2018) did a meta-analysis to assess the effect of the presence of weapons on aggressive behavior, aggressive thoughts, and hostile attribution bias. They found a weapons effect for all three. Indeed, they concluded that "[t]he weapons effect is quite robust" (Benjamin et al., 2018, p. 359), including for weapons other than guns such as knives, swords, hand grenades, and even toy weapons.

Social Information Processing Theory

Social information processing (SIP) theory likens the brain to a computer, with inputs that inform outputs. Like a computer, this social information processing is presumed to be automatic and rapid. Unlike a typical computer (artificial intelligence notwithstanding), perception and prior learning play a large role in social information processing. The theory was first applied to behaviors in children by Dodge in 1986, and he and his colleague Crick conceptualized the full social information processing theory of aggression in children in 1994 (Crick & Dodge, 1994). Huesmann separately developed the model with aggression in adults (1988, 1998). Huesmann (1998) described the minimal differences in the models: "One, developed by Huesmann and colleagues, initially focused particularly on scripts, beliefs, and observational learning, whereas the other, developed by Dodge and colleagues, focused particularly on perceptions and attributions" (p. 87; original citations removed). Given the similarities in the overall process, we will use Crick and Dodge's (1994) circular model to explain the theory (see Figure 5.1).

When faced with a social situation that requires a behavioral response, **social information processing theory** states that there are six steps that happen as we choose our behavioral response in a social situation: "(1) encoding of external and internal cues, (2) interpretation and mental representation of those cues, (3) clarification or selection of a goal, (4) response access or construction, (5) response decision, and (6) behavioral enactment" (Crick & Dodge, 1994, p. 76). As can be seen in Figure 5.1, each of these steps is informed by our internal, personal database of memories, rules, schemas, and other social knowledge. One of the reasons different people behave differently in the same or similar situations is due to the differences in this

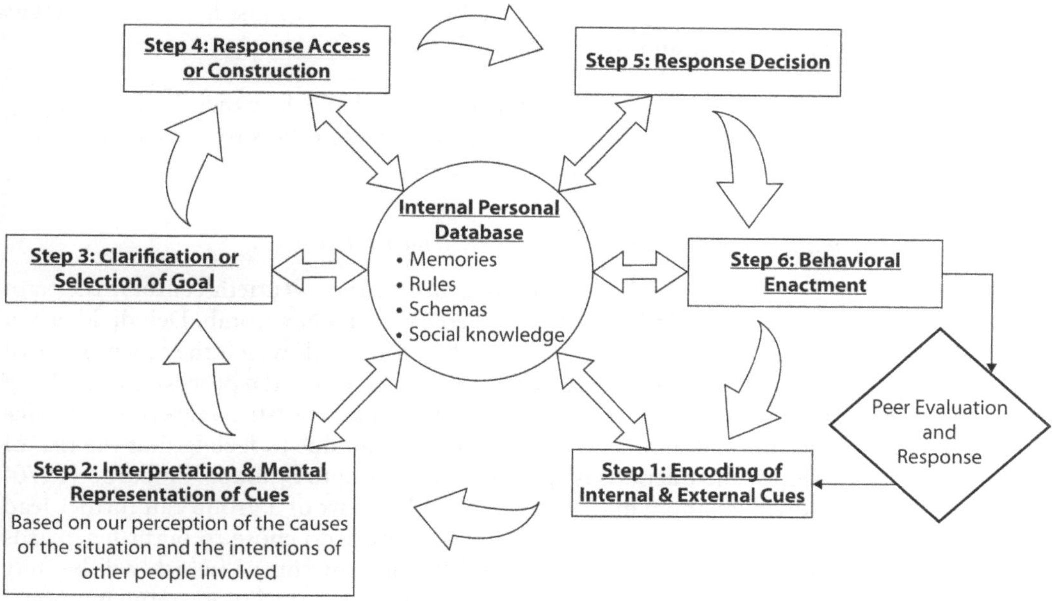

Figure 5.1 Social information processing theory (Crick & Dodge, 1994).

accumulated information within each of us. Additionally, the way we interpret social cues (i.e., step 2) is a matter of our perception of the causes of the situation and the intentions of other people involved. Indeed, a lot of empirical research has included hostile attribution bias and schemas as important influencers in SIP theory (Tuente et al., 2019; Verhoef et al., 2019). Crick and Dodge (1994) made the model circular to illustrate that every social incident serves as new data for similar encounters in the future.

The original theories by both Crick and Dodge (1994) and Huesmann (1998) focused on cognitive errors made in our social information processing that cause maladaptive responses such as aggression. Lemerise and Arsenio (2000) recognized that our emotions likely also influence each step of social information processing. For example, our emotional arousal, including excitation transfer and cognitive neoassociations, likely impacts our ability to clarify what we want out of the situation (i.e., our goals in step 3). In addition to emotions felt in the immediate situation, deficits in our ability to regulate our emotions as well as personality traits that may make us prone to certain emotions are thought to influence our social information processing (Lemerise & Arsenio, 2000).

Psychology of Behavior in Groups

As mentioned in the introduction to this chapter, sociology is the study of groups or societies as a whole, and social psychology is the study of individuals in their interactions with groups or societies. This line gets even more blurry when studying the individual psychology of the behavior of people in groups. However, there are several concepts from social psychology that have been used to explain such behavior: deindividuation, diffusion of responsibility, the bystander effect, conformity, and obedience to authority. The first work identified with social psychology was Le Bon's *The Crowd* published in French in 1895 and translated to English the following year (Le Bon, 1896). The ideas just listed were evident even then. According to Paulus and Kenworthy (2022),

> [a] major theme of Le Bon is that the members of a crowd may lose their individuality and may be easily swayed by their leader and the actions of others to behave in ways contrary to their personal beliefs and values (p. 204).

Deindividuation, Diffusion of Responsibility, and the Bystander Effect

Despite first being explored by Le Bon before the turn of the twentieth century, the term deindividuation was coined in 1952 by Festinger, Pepitone, and Newcomb. **Deindividuation** is the loss of a feeling of oneself as separate from the group with which they identify or of which they are currently a part. Further research helped determine the processes underlying how this phenomenon can lead to increased, and even uncharacteristic, aggression and violence. The individual's normal inhibitions may become weak due to feeling that the risk of negative consequences for their actions is spread among the entire group. Zimbardo (1970) theorized that the individual anonymity experienced when part of a group can further lead to this **diffusion of responsibility**. Indeed, this is why Zimbardo chose to outfit his guards with mirrored sunglasses in his infamous Stanford Prison Experiment (which will be fully described in Chapter 14). He expected this to cause the guards to feel more anonymous and therefore more likely to act as a cohesive group rather than as individuals (Zimbardo, n.d.).

A concept related to deindividuation and diffusion of responsibility has become known as the bystander effect. Latané and Darley (1968, 1970) were prompted to begin their line of research on this phenomenon after the much-publicized murder of Kitty Genovese in mid-1960s New York City (see Box 5.2). It had been reported that neighbors were apathetic

Box 5.2 The murder of Kitty Genovese

Kitty Genovese was a 20-something-year-old living at Kew Gardens in Queens, New York, in 1964 when the unthinkable happened. Returning home late one night, she was attacked multiple times by a stranger, sexually assaulted and stabbed. She died from her injuries. A *New York Times* article two weeks later famously reported that 38 of Genovese's neighbors failed to come to her aid or even call the police (Gansberg, 1964). The appalling behavior of these would-be Good Samaritans inspired the pioneering work of Latané and Darley (1968, 1970) on the bystander effect.

Despite the original narrative put forward by the *New York Times*, later analysis – and anniversary articles published by the *Times* itself – indicated that neighbors did in fact intervene to help Ms. Genovese (Manning et al., 2007). At least one neighbor indeed called the police and held Kitty until they arrived. In the documentary *The Witness* (Solomon, 2015), a woman recalls phoning the police and being told they had already received calls, and retrieved police records indicated at least one call about the incident. However, simply calling the police was not as easy as it is today; citizens had to call their local police department directly. That changed in the late 1960s, partly in response to this high-profile case. In addition to leading to the psychological study of the bystander effect, Kitty Genovese's murder and its aftermath played a part in the establishment of our national 911 emergency response system as well (Cook, 2014).

to the screams for help that must have been heard in the middle of the night. Darley and Latané (1968) suggested that this was due to the diffusion of responsibility felt by those living in such a populated urban area who likely believed someone else would call the police. The problem of the **bystander effect** occurs when everyone believes someone else will get involved and therefore no one gets involved.

To help explain the bystander effect, Latané and Darley (1970) described the steps required in deciding to help in a situation. First, one must notice the situation. Second, one needs to believe the other person needs help. Third, one must feel personally responsible for helping. Fourth, one needs to feel they have the ability to help. And fifth, one must make the decision to take action to help. This cognitive process of course happens very quickly, especially when the situation is perceived as an emergency. However, Latané and Darley (1970) also described the aspects of group situations that may interfere with this process, leading to the bystander effect. First, as mentioned, is diffusion of responsibility. Second is the fear of others judging that we are misunderstanding the situation (i.e., there is not a need for help), causing us to look at how others are reacting to the situation. This can lead to the third contributor to the bystander effect as identified by Latané and Darley (1970): pluralistic ignorance. **Pluralistic ignorance** is the tendency to believe others see things in the opposite way that you do, which causes us to go along with the crowd – a phenomenon known as conformity.

Conformity and Obedience to Authority

Classic studies by Solomon Asch (1951, 1956) in the 1950s demonstrated the power of **conformity** or the tendency for humans to follow others when they are part of a group, even if they think the group consensus is wrong. Asch proved just how influential this social-psychological effect is in a simple experiment. Asch (1956) presented a group of people with a series of lines of different lengths, one serving as the benchmark by which the other three were compared. Among the group of people viewing the lines, only one was the subject of the experiment while the others were **confederates**, meaning they were in on the experiment and indeed an integral part of it. A dozen different groupings of lines were presented, one set at a time. Each time, there was only one line that was clearly the same length as the benchmark line. Everyone was asked to audibly indicate which line they believed it to be, with the subject of the experiment always going last. For the first few sets of lines, the confederates and the experimental subject all chose the "correct" line. This was to ensure the subject believed the other "subjects" were of sound mind. After establishing this trust in the group, all of the confederates deliberately chose the same wrong line in the next set when asked to audibly indicate the matching line. They continued to unanimously choose the incorrect line on most of the remaining sets, occasionally choosing the correct line to not raise too much suspicion in the subject.

Astonishingly, subjects went along with the group in choosing the incorrect line approximately a third of the time. Further, the vast majority chose the same incorrect line as the confederates at least once. A small minority (less than 10%) agreed with the group every time they made an incorrect choice. Importantly, this effect was not replicated when the subjects were allowed to make their choice confidentially nor when they were tested alone. Asch (1956) interviewed the subjects afterward to gauge why they conformed with the group when they did (termed "yielding" or "compliant") – and why they didn't when they didn't (termed "independence"). Based on his overall findings, Asch (1956) hypothesized "independence requires the capacity to accept the fact of opposition without a lowered sense of personal worth... The compliant person cannot face this ordeal because he translates social opposition into a reflection of his personal worth" (pp. 51–52). As inherently social creatures, it may not be that surprising that we have a tendency to conform to those around us.

This pressure to conform is likely compounded when in the presence of an authority figure. Another famous – and controversial – study in the 1960s set out to test the power of authority. Stanley Milgram (1965, 1974) devised an experiment that had subjects perform the role of "teachers" in a supposed test of positive punishment on learning (see Chapter 4). In the presence of an experimenter (i.e., the authority figure), the subject "teachers" were to administer progressively more severe electrical shocks to the "learners" when they answered questions incorrectly. The subjects were not able to see the "learners," who were actually confederates of the study and not actually being shocked, but they could hear them clearly. The first shocks administered by the subjects were mild, perhaps not even eliciting a reaction from the "learner." As the level of the voltage progressed, the "learners" began to cry out and beg the subject to stop the experiment. If the subject asked the experimenter to discontinue, the experimenter told them they must continue.

To Milgram's surprise, most of the subjects continued to shock the "learners" despite their clear distress and pain. An astonishing 65% proceeded to the maximum shock level of 450 volts, which was labeled "Danger: Severe Shock." Additional trials varied the proximity of both the "learner" and the experimenter. Milgram (1965) found that the subjects were more likely to continue shocking despite the protests of the "learner" when they were farther away and could not be seen. This could mean it is easier to persist when one does not have to directly face the consequences of their actions. Additionally, the further removed the experimenter, the less likely the subject was to continue shocking the "learner" beyond their clear discomfort. Perhaps it is more difficult to ignore the commands of an authority figure when they are immediately present. This study is widely considered unethical by today's standards; researchers would no longer cause such distress to subjects without a clear and extensive benefit to the subject and society. However, Milgram's experiment in obedience to authority showed that most of us will obey an authority figure to an extent we might not be comfortable believing. While authority is necessary in many situations, such power should be wielded with great care and oversight.

Explaining Criminal Behavior

Hostile Attribution Bias

Two systematic reviews published in 2019 provided support for the connection between hostile attribution bias and aggressive behavior. Tuente and colleagues (2019) conducted a systematic review of studies of hostile attribution bias and aggression in adults. The authors were unable to complete a full statistical meta-analysis due to the lack of empirical research on the subject with adults. Given this dearth of research using adult samples, Tuente and her colleagues (2019) focused on two simple hypotheses: (1) that there is an association between hostile attribution bias and aggression in adults, and (2) that this association is stronger in samples known for aggressive behavior, such as criminal offenders. They were able to conclude that there is evidence to support a general link between hostile attribution bias and aggression in adult populations (i.e., support for their first hypothesis), but the relationship between these variables was not dependent on other characteristics of the population (i.e., no support for their second hypothesis).

The second review of research on hostile attribution bias (Verhoef et al., 2019) was able to conduct a more robust meta-analysis as it focused on the relationship between hostile intent attribution (the term used by these authors) and aggression in children. Many more studies have been done in this area using children as the population of interest. There was a large variation in the findings of the studies included in the meta-analysis, meaning some of that variation still needs to be explained. Nonetheless, Verhoef and colleagues (2019) were able to conclude that there is "an overall modest positive association between childhood HIA [hostile intent attribution] and aggression… As expected, the relation between HIA and aggressive behavior was found to be stronger in emotionally engaging situations" (pp. e536–e537).

Social Information Processing Theory

Smeijers and her colleagues (2020) conducted a systematic review of research integrating emotion and social information processing (i.e., the Lemerise & Arsenio model). They found that those who tend to experience heightened emotions and those who have difficulty understanding the emotions of others were more likely to experience hostile attribution bias, which impacts the steps of SIP. Their overall conclusion and suggestions for future research point to the likelihood of interactions among all of these variables: "it is very much likely that emotional experiences and emotion regulation skills have joint effects on distinct phases of SIP, perhaps with emotional experiences being more prominent at earlier stages, and emotion regulation skills becoming more important in subsequent stages" (Smeijers et al., 2020, p. 88; original citations removed).

Integrated Theories of Aggression

General Aggression Model

In 2002, Anderson and Bushman put forward an integrated model of aggression called the **general aggression model (GAM)**. The GAM combined several of the ideas and theories described in The Basics section of this chapter: schemas, cognitive neoassociation theory, and excitation transfer theory. Anderson and Bushman (2002) created a sort of flow chart (see Figure 5.2) of how someone moves through an interpersonal situation, which they called an **episode.** A single social encounter involves multiple such episodes and each one informs the next. There are three stages to each episode: inputs, routes, and outcomes. The **inputs** are the personal and situational factors that are present during an episode. Personal factors include traits, biological sex, beliefs, attitudes, values, long-term goals, and scripts. These personal factors form the lens through which the person views the situational factors. Situational factors include aggressive cues, provocation, frustration, pain/discomfort, drugs, and incentives. In line with the concepts of schemas and cognitive neoassociation theory, it is possible for different people to have different aggressive cues based on the different things that have been previously associated with aggression for them in the past.

These personal and situational inputs inform the present internal state of the person during the social encounter. The present internal state is comprised of three **routes**: cognition, affect, and arousal. They are called routes as they are the pathways through which the inputs are processed to lead to the outcomes of the episode. The cognitive route of the present internal state may consist of hostile thoughts and schemas, such as the hostile attribution bias. The affective route is the mood and emotions of the present internal state, as in the cognitive neoassociation model. Finally, the arousal route refers to the person's current

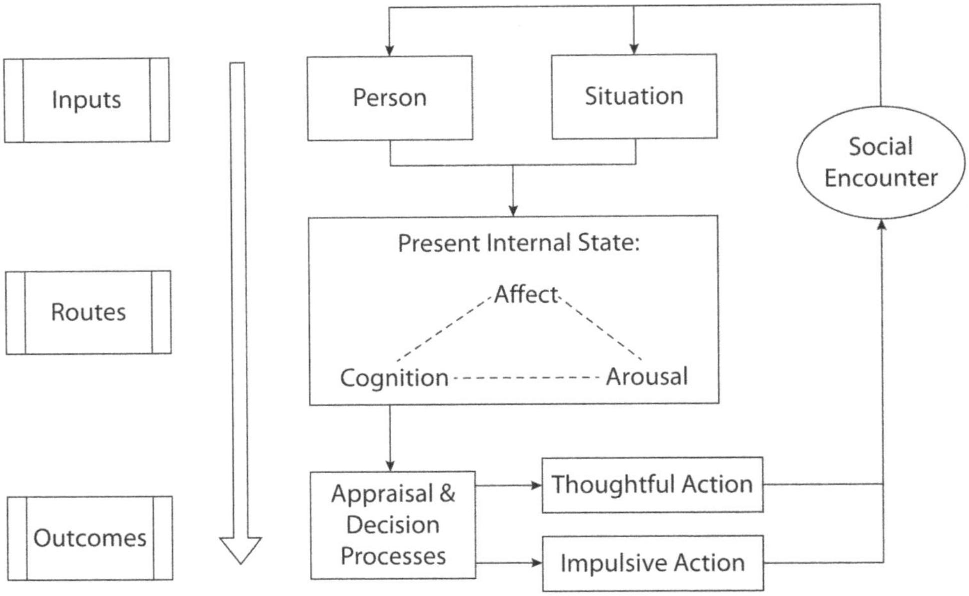

Figure 5.2 The General Aggression Model (Anderson & Bushman, 2002).

stimulation level; this may be due to the current inputs or perhaps a previous and unrelated episode, as in excitation transfer theory.

The final stage of an episode in the GAM is outcomes. **Outcomes** comprise the evaluation and decision-making processes, as well as the resulting chosen action, whether thoughtful or impulsive. The "appraisal and decision processes," as Anderson and Bushman call the beginning of the outcomes stage, entail an initial appraisal of the episode based on the inputs and routes. Reappraisal may occur during this stage, resulting in a more thoughtful action; however, an impulsive action is more likely. (Indeed, the GAM does not focus as much on non-aggressive outcomes, an issue remedied by the I^3 model described in the next section.) The chosen action then creates a new episode within the same social interaction, and the process begins again.

I^3 [I Cubed]

Finkel (2007) was interested in understanding why most couples do not resort to intimate partner violence (IPV). After all, every couple fights; what are the forces that prevent most of these fights from ending in violence? The I^3 (pronounced "eye cubed") model stands for **instigating trigger, impelling forces,** and **inhibiting forces.** The instigating trigger (or simply instigator) is the event that brings about the potential for IPV, such as an argument or disagreement. An impelling force (or impellor) is a factor that increases the chance of violence. And an inhibiting force (or inhibitor) is a factor that decreases the chance of violence.

Finkel (2007) began to construct his theory by categorizing the empirical risk factors for IPV (i.e., those risk factors that had been previously identified by research as correlated with IPV) by "the degree to which each of them (a) strengthens violence-impelling forces, (b) weakens violence-inhibiting forces, or (c) does both" (p. 195). He also distinguished between the sources of the risk factors: distal, dispositional, relational, and situational.

Table 5.1 Impelling and inhibiting risk factors for intimate partner violence (Finkel, 2007, p. 197).

Risk factors for strong violence-impelling forces		*Risk factors for weak violence-inhibiting forces*	
Distal	witnessing parental IPV; learned violence scripts; childhood abuse	Distal	cultural acceptance; poor IPV-relevant legal institutions
Dispositional	anger; attachment anxiety; dysthymia; borderline; narcissism; neuroticism; testosterone; genetics	Dispositional	low self-control; low empathy; psychopathy; low chivalry; beliefs about IPV consequences; genetics
Relational	contempt; dissatisfaction with power; poor communication; jealousy	Relational	low commitment; high partner dependence; weak communal feelings
Situational	environmental irritants: pain; physiological arousal; blameful attributions; aggression cues	Situational	alcohol; costs < benefits; blameful attributions; ego depletion; no fear of injury to self

Distal risk factors originate from the (sub)cultural, socioeconomic, and demographic world in which the person lives. **Dispositional risk factors** are those that stem from the individual's temperament, such as biological factors and general attitude. **Relational risk factors** are those interpersonal issues that are unique to the specific relationship at hand (in Finkel's research, this is the intimate partner relationship). Finally, **situational risk factors** are those "temporary cognitive, affective, and physiological experiences emerging from features of the current situation" (Finkel, 2007, p. 198). Finkel (2007) was able to categorize known risk factors for IPV into these categories as either impelling forces or inhibiting forces (see Table 5.1).

Complementary Theories

In a test of both GAM and I^3, Simmons and her colleagues (2022) point out that these two theories are quite complimentary to each other. Indeed, each stage of a GAM episode may be influenced by instigators, impellors, and inhibitors. Additionally, emotions can greatly alter the trajectory of a GAM episode as either impellors or inhibitors. In particular, Simmons and colleagues (2022) note that anger is often an impellor to aggressive behavior (I^3) and an affective route through which a GAM episode is processed. Future research is needed to fully explore the integration of the GAM and I^3 theories.

Deindividuation, Conformity, and the January 6th Capitol Insurrection

Paulus and Kenworthy (2022) used social-psychological theories to try to make sense of the breach of the United States Capitol building on January 6, 2021. This was the day that Congress was to certify the election of President Joe Biden and unseat President Donald Trump. Due to discredited reports, many Trump supporters believed that election fraud had caused their candidate to appear to have lost; they believed the election had been stolen. Tens of thousands of Trump supporters converged on Washington, DC for the so-called "Stop the Steal" rally. After the rally, thousands of attendees marched to the Capitol where the certification of the election was taking place. The vast majority likely intended a peaceful protest of the proceedings, which they believed were invalid. However, some members of the gathered group began forcibly breaking into the Capitol building. Only a fraction of those in attendance participated in the impending breach of the government building and still fewer engaged in direct violence. Nonetheless, the insurrection caused widespread fear, injuries, and even death at the US Capitol.

Deindividuation and conformity can be used to help explain why many normal citizens engaged in violence that day. Paulus and Kenworthy (2022) point out the fact that the vast majority of protestors did not enter the Capitol building is evidence that "there was not total mindless conformity" (p. 201). However, those who did participate in the insurrection may have felt caught up in the fervor of the large group of seemingly like-minded individuals. Indeed, Paulus and Kenworthy (2022) use the **social identity/deindividuation (SIDE**; Reicher et al., 1995) model to help explain the events of January 6th. Rather than the typical explanation of deindividuation leading to a diffusion of responsibility, SIDE argues that when individuals in a group share a social identity, they are more likely to conform their behavior to that of their associates. This is consistent with the belief that concern of social judgment underlies conformity. We are likely to be particularly worried about being negatively perceived by those with whom we self-identify and therefore more willing to forego our better judgment.

The Bystander Effect

Despite the dubious nature of the reports that prompted its initial study (see Box 5.2), the bystander effect has proven to be a robust phenomenon. An early meta-analysis by Latané and Nida (1981) found the bystander effect in a variety of situations ranging from non-emergency/general helping behavior (e.g., helping someone fix a flat tire) to emergency situations where all involved are in danger (e.g., evidence of an active fire). They also noted an inverse relationship between helping behavior and the number of bystanders present. This is consistent with a diffusion of responsibility explanation for the bystander effect, since the more people are around the more one may feel that someone else will intervene. However, they found the bystander effect to be *less* pronounced when the need for help was clearer and more immediate. This may be due to a lack of ambiguity as to whether help is needed. A more recent meta-analysis (Fischer et al., 2011) confirmed these findings, noting in addition that more dangerous emergency situations increased helping behavior (i.e., decreased bystander effect) and that people are more likely to help people they know.

Obedience to Authority and Conformity in Nazi-occupied Europe

The mass genocide of the Jewish peoples across Europe under the Nazi regime of the early twentieth century is an atrocity of which most are aware. What has puzzled the world ever since is how anyone could have participated in the killing of six million of their fellow human beings. Indeed, hundreds of "ordinary men" (soldiers and police were all male) took part in the orders to exterminate the Jewish people. Many in the decades since this tragedy have believed it was due to obedience to the authority of Adolf Hitler. Milgram himself devised his famous study to test this hypothesis, which he initially believed would be proven false (Milgram, 1974). Historians have come to partially embrace this perspective as well. Most notable is Christopher Browning (1992), whose book *Ordinary Men: Reserve Police Battalion 101 and the Final Solution in Poland* used Milgram's findings to help explain the point-blank-range shootings of over two million Jewish civilians by those seemingly just following orders.

However, like most things, the truth is likely not that simple. Many other historians and social psychologists point to several other factors that possibly contributed to "ordinary men" willingly committing mass murder (for a review see Overy, 2014). First, it was indeed willingly; many of those who were given orders to kill were also given the choice to take on other assignments instead (e.g., cooking for their fellow troops), and few of those who chose to step aside faced any official consequences for doing so. Instead, they faced social consequences. As demonstrated by the Asch experiments, humans tend to conform to those around them. This is especially true in the high-conformity settings of military and police forces. One does not want to be seen as not doing their part and forcing their comrades to bear the burden. We must also not forget the historical context. These men were not asked to commit murder out of the blue. For years prior, they participated in "escalating commitments" (Waller, 2007), whereby their agreement to successively more brutal acts made each step feel less horrible – until finally, they were willing to commit cold-blooded murder on a massive scale.

Summary

Social psychology can help us understand individual perspectives when people interact with others or act as part of a group. This discipline of psychology has long incorporated the role of thinking in our social interactions, as evidenced by the term social cognition. However, our emotions seem to play a large role in how we process our interpersonal interactions as well. This is demonstrated by the importance of anger in cognitive neoassociation theory, the addition of emotion to social information processing theory, the heightened experience of hostile attribution bias in emotional situations, and the affective route of the general aggression model. Learning how to regulate our emotions and recognize the emotions of others may lessen aggression and increase empathy. Such empathy and understanding may also help us to think twice before going along with a destructive crowd.

References

Asch, S. E. (1951). Effects of group pressure upon the modification and distortion of judgment. In H. Guetzow (Ed.), *Groups, leadership, and men* (pp. 177–190). Carnegie.

Asch, S. E. (1956). Studies of independence and conformity: A minority of one against a unanimous majority. *Psychological Monographs: General and Applied*, *70*(9), 1–70.

Agnew, R. (1992). Foundation for a general strain theory of crime and delinquency. *Criminology*, *30*, 47–88.

Anderson, C. A., & Bushman, B. J. (2002). Human aggression. *Annual Review of Psychology*, *53*, 27–51.

Barton, J., Vrij, A., & Bull, R. (2000). High speed driving: Police use of lethal force during simulated incidents. *Legal and Criminological Psychology*, *5*, 107–121.

Benjamin, A. J., Kepes, S., & Bushman, B. J. (2018). Effects of weapons on aggressive thoughts, angry feelings, hostile appraisals, and aggressive behavior: A meta-analytic review of the weapons effect literature. *Personality and Social Psychology Review*, *22*(4), 347–377.

Berkowitz, L. (1990). On the formation and regulation of anger and aggression: A cognitive-neoassociationistic analysis. *American Psychologist*, *45*(4), 494–503.

Berkowitz, L., & LePage, A. (1967). Weapons as aggression-eliciting stimuli. *Journal of Personality and Social Psychology*, *7*(2), 202–207.

Browning, C. R. (1992). *Ordinary men: Reserve police battalion 101 and the final solution in Poland*. Harper Collins.

Cook, K. (2014). *Kitty Genovese: The murder, the bystanders, the crime that changed America*. W. W. Norton & Co.

Crick, N. R., & Dodge, K. A. (1994). A review and reformulation of social information-processing mechanisms in children's social adjustment. *Psychological Bulletin*, *115*(1), 74–101.

Darley, J. M., & Latané, B. (1968). Bystander intervention in emergencies: Diffusion of responsibility. *Journal of Personality and Social Psychology*, *10*, 202–214.

Dodge, K. A. (1986). A social information processing model of social competence in children. In M. Perlmutter (Ed.), *The Minnesota symposium on child psychology* (Vol. 18, pp. 77–125). Erlbaum.
Dollard, J., Doob, L., Miller, N., Mowrer, O., & Sears, R. (1939). *Frustration and aggression.* Yale University Press.
Festinger, L., Pepitone, A., & Newcomb, T. (1952). Some consequences of de-individuation in a group. *Journal of Abnormal and Social Psychology*, *47*, 382–389.
Finkel, E. J. (2007). Impelling and inhibiting forces in the perpetration of intimate partner violence. *Review of General Psychology*, *11*(2), 193–207.
Fischer, P., Krueger, J. I., Greitemeyer, T., Vogrincic, C., Kasternmüller, A., Frey, D., Heene, M., Wicher, M., & Kainbacher, M. (2011). The bystander-effect: A meta-analytic review on bystander intervention in dangerous and non-dangerous emergencies. *Psychological Bulletin*, *137*(4), 517–537.
Gansberg, M. (1964). 37 who saw murder didn't call the police; apathy at stabbing of Queens woman shocks inspector. *The New York Times*, p. 1.
Huesmann, L. R. (1988). An information processing model for the development of aggression. *Aggressive Behavior*, *14*, 13–24.
Huesmann, L. R. (1998). The role of social information processing and cognitive schema in the acquisition and maintenance of habitual aggressive behavior. In R. G. Geen & E. Donnerstein (Eds.), *Human aggression: Theories, research, and implications for social psychology* (pp. 73–109). Academic Press.
Latané, B., & Darley, J. M. (1968). Group inhibition of bystander intervention in emergencies. *Journal of Personality and Social Psychology*, *10*, 215–221.
Latané, B., & Darley, J. M. (1970). *The unresponsive bystander: Why doesn't he help?* Appleton–Century–Crofts.
Latané, B., & Nida, S. (1981). Ten years of research on group size and helping. *Psychological Bulletin*, *89*, 308–324. https://doi.org/10.1037/0033-2909.89.2.308
Le Bon, G. (1896). *The Crowd. Tr. fr. the French*. T. Fisher Unwin.
Lemerise, E. A., & Arsenio, W. F. (2000). An integrated model of emotion processes and cognition in social information processing. *Child Development*, *71*, 107–118.
Manning, R., Levine, M., & Collins, A. (2007). The Kitty Genovese murder and the social psychology of helping: The parable of the 38 witnesses. *American Psychologist*, *62*(6), 555–562.
Merton, R. (1938). Social structure and anomie. *American Sociological Review*, *3*(5), 672–682. https://doi.org/10.2307/2084686.
Milgram, S. (1965). Some conditions of obedience and disobedience to authority. *Human Relations*, *18*(1), 57–75.
Milgram, S. (1974). *Obedience to authority: An experimental view*. Harper & Row.
Nasby, W., Hayden, B., & DePaulo, B. M. (1979). Attributional bias among aggressive boys to interpret unambiguous social stimuli as displays of hostility. *Journal of Abnormal Psychology*, *89*, 459–468.
Overy, R. (2014). "Ordinary men," extraordinary circumstances: Historians, social psychology, and the Holocaust. *Journal of Social Issues*, *70*(3), 515–530.
Paulus, P. B., & Kenworthy, J. B. (2022). The crowd dynamics and collective stupidity of the January 6 riot: Theoretical analyses and prescriptions for a collectively wiser future. *Group Dynamics: Theory, Research, and Practice*, *26*(3), 199–219.
Reicher, S. D., Spears, R., & Postmes, T. (1995). A social identity model of deindividuation phenomena. *European Review of Social Psychology*, *6*(1), 161–198.
Simmons, M., McEwan, T. E., & Purcell, R. (2022). A social-cognitive investigation of young adults who abuse their parents. *Journal of Interpersonal Violence*, *37*(1–2), NP327–NP349. https://doi.org/10.1177/0886260520915553
Smeijers, D., Benbouriche, M., & Garofalo, C. (2020). The association between emotion, social information processing, and aggressive behavior: A systematic review. *European Psychologist*, *25*(2), 81–91.
Solomon, J. D. (Director). (2015). *The witness* [Film]. FilmRise.
Tuente, S. K., Bogaerts, S., & Veling, W. (2019). Hostile attribution bias and aggression in adults—A systematic review. *Aggression and Violent Behavior*, *46*, 66–81.
Verhoef, R. E. J., Alsem, S. C., Verhulp, E. E., & De Castro, B. O. (2019). Hostile intent attribution and aggressive behavior in children revisited: A meta-analysis. *Child Development*, *90*(5), e525–e547.
Waller, J. (2007). *Becoming evil: Howe ordinary people commit genocide and mass killing*. Oxford University Press.

Zillman, D. (1971). Excitation transfer in communication-mediated aggressive behavior. *Journal of Experimental Social Psychology*, 7(4), 419–434.
Zillman, D. (1988). Cognition-excitation interdependencies in aggressive behavior. *Aggressive Behavior*, *14*, 51–64.
Zillman, D., Katcher, A. H., & Milavsky, B. (1972). Excitation transfer from physical exercise to subsequent aggressive behavior. *Journal of Experimental Social Psychology*, *8*, 247–259.
Zimbardo. (n.d.). *The Stanford prison experiment*. https://www.zimbardo.com/the-stanford-prison-experiment/
Zimbardo, P. G. (1970). The human choice: Individuation, reason, and order versus deindividuation, impulse, and chaos. In W. J. Arnold & D. Levine (Eds.), *Nebraska symposium on motivation, 1969* (pp. 237–307). University of Nebraska Press.

6 Personality Psychology

Introduction

While there are various takes on personality psychology, often from the perspectives of the other psychological disciplines (e.g., behavioral, developmental), this chapter will focus on trait-based personality psychology. This is the idea that there are a number of personality traits that define who we are and how we behave, with many scholars arguing that these personality traits can all fit into a handful of personality dimensions or continuums. In The Basics section, we will discuss the most common and empirically supported personality models (i.e., the five-factor model and HEXACO), as well as specific personality traits and personality disorders that have been associated with criminal behavior. The Explaining Criminal Behavior section of this chapter will explore the empirical evidence on whether and how personality traits lead to criminal behavior.

The Basics

Personality Assessment

In the psychology literature on personality, most research has focused on developing and perfecting ways to measure different personality constructs. The creation of these personality assessment tools dates back to the early twentieth century. In 1927, Kelley cautioned assessment creators about the **jangle fallacy**, a logical error made when a measure is presumed to capture a unique construct just because it is named differently than other measures. Around the same time (though it is difficult to know to whom the term should be credited), the similar term jingle fallacy was coined. The **jingle fallacy** refers to when two measures are named the same but in fact are measuring different constructs.

As we discuss various personality models, their corresponding assessment tools will also be covered. Keep an eye out for attempts to untangle jangle and jingle fallacies throughout the historical progression of our collective understanding of personality.

Lexical Method

When psychologists began studying the concept of personality traits, they began by examining the adjectives we use to describe ourselves and others. This is known as the **lexical method**, as it is based on a specific lexicon (i.e., the vocabulary of a language). To start, researchers compiled lists of adjectives and asked people to indicate the ones that they felt applied to themselves. The results were placed into a statistical model called factor analysis.

DOI: 10.4324/9781003250821-7

Factor analyses identified which adjectives were often found in the same individual. These distilled groupings of adjectives were assumed to represent broader categories in personality differences. Many studies using this method throughout the mid-twentieth century resulted in the identification of the five-factor model of personality.

The Five-Factor Model of Personality

The **five-factor model of personality (FFM)** is also sometimes referred to using the acronym OCEAN, which stands for its five personality dimensions. Each of the dimensions of FFM is a spectrum from high to low. Therefore, even though there are presumed to be only a small number of personality dimensions, the combination of highs and lows on the various dimensions creates a larger number of possible personality types. The O of the FFM stands for **Openness to Experience.** Someone can be very open to new ideas and experiences or more closed off and set in their ways. **Conscientiousness** is the C of OCEAN, with a person tending to be either highly diligent and meticulous or more careless and inattentive. The E stands for **Extraversion.** Someone high on the Extraversion scale is more outgoing and active, whereas someone low on the Extraversion scale is more introverted and quiet. The next FFM dimension is **Agreeableness.** The high end of the Agreeableness spectrum is characterized by cooperativeness and generosity, and the low end is more likely to be selfish and cold. Finally, the N stands for **Neuroticism.** The Neuroticism scale has traits like anxious and moody at the high end and traits such as stable and calm at the low end.

NEO Personality Inventory

Developed by Costa and McCrae (1985), the **NEO Personality Inventory (NEO-PI)** was specifically designed to measure the FFM. In fact, its name is an acronym for the Neuroticism, Extraversion, and Openness to Experience dimensions. Even so, the NEO-PI is designed to measure all five of the FFM personality dimensions. The current version, the NEO-PI-3, consists of 240 items. All versions of the NEO-PI include Likert-scale answer options as opposed to simply true or false. This means that for each item statement, respondents choose from five options ranging from strongly agree to strongly disagree.

The NEO-PI-3 contains six facet scales for each of the five personality domains of the FFM. Each of the facets is designed to capture a different aspect of each of the FFM dimensions. The facets of Openness are Fantasy, Aesthetics, Feelings, Actions, Ideas, and Values. The six facets of Conscientiousness are Competence, Order, Dutifulness, Achievement Striving, Self-Discipline, and Deliberation. The facet scales of Extroversion include Warmth, Gregariousness, Assertiveness, Activity, Excitement Seeking, and Positive Emotions. The Agreeableness domain includes the facets of Trust, Straightforwardness, Altruism, Compliance, Modesty, and Tender-Mindedness. Finally, the six facets of Neuroticism are Anxiety, Angry Hostility, Depression, Self-Consciousness, Impulsiveness, and Vulnerability. See Table 6.1 for a visual listing of the facets.

HEXACO

Although the FFM received much support in personality research, the twenty-first century brought a new grouping of dimensions. The collective work of Ashton, Lee, and their colleagues (2004) recognized that the FFM did not always translate well into other languages and cultures. When the lexical method was used to identify personality dimensions using

Table 6.1 NEO-Personality inventory facets (Costa & McCrae, 1985).

Openness	
1	Fantasy
2	Aesthetics
3	Feelings
4	Actions
5	Ideas
6	Values
Conscientiousness	
1	Competence
2	Order
3	Dutifulness
4	Achievement Striving
5	Self-Discipline
6	Deliberation
Extroversion	
1	Warmth
2	Gregariousness
3	Assertiveness
4	Activity
5	Excitement Seeking
6	Positive Emotions
Agreeableness	
1	Trust
2	Straightforwardness
3	Altruism
4	Compliance
5	Modesty
6	Tender-Mindedness
Neuroticism	
1	Anxiety
2	Angry Hostility
3	Depression
4	Self-Consciousness
5	Impulsiveness
6	Vulnerability

languages other than English, it seemed a six-dimension structure was the best fit rather than only five. Ashton and Lee (2007) named this new model **HEXACO,** both as an acronym for the six dimensions and for the classical Greek number six (i.e., *hexa*). There are many similarities between the FFM and HEXACO, with some reorganization (see Table 6.2)

The H of HEXACO stands for the **Honesty-Humility** personality dimension, which is perhaps the main difference from the FFM. Honesty-Humility ranges from personality descriptors such as sincere and fair-minded on the high end to greedy and hypocritical on the low end. **Emotionality** is the E of HEXACO and encompasses a spectrum of traits from sentimental and vulnerable to brave and independent. Ashton and Lee (2007) see similarities in Emotionality with both the Agreeableness and Neuroticism dimensions of the FFM. Next is X, which stands for **eXtraversion.** This is essentially the same dimension as the FFM, with the spectrum of traits ranging from outgoing and active to introverted and quiet. Also like the FFM, the A stands for **Agreeableness.** However, in the HEXACO model, Agreeableness

Table 6.2 Comparing the FFM and HEXACO models of personality.

The Five-Factor Model	*HEXACO*
Neuroticism	**Honest-Humility**
Anxiety	Sincerity
Angry Hostility	Fairness
Depression	Greed Avoidance
Self-Consciousness	Modesty
Impulsiveness	
Vulnerability	
Extroversion	**Emotionality**
Warmth	Fearfulness
Gregariousness	Anxiety
Assertiveness	Dependence
Activity	Sentimentality
Excitement Seeking	
Positive Emotions	
Openness	**Extroversion**
Fantasy	Expressiveness
Aesthetics	Social Boldness
Feelings	Sociability
Actions	Liveliness
Ideas	
Values	
Agreeableness	**Agreeableness**
Trust	Forgiveness
Straightforwardness	Gentleness
Altruism	Flexibility
Compliance	Patience
Modesty	
Tender-Mindedness	
Conscientiousness	**Conscientiousness**
Competence	Organization
Order	Diligence
Dutifulness	Perfectionism
Achievement Striving	Prudence
Self-Discipline	
Deliberation	
	Openness to Experience
	Aesthetic Appreciation
	Inquisitiveness
	Creativity
	Unconventionality

"excludes sentimentality and includes (lack of) anger" (Ashton & Lee, 2007, p. 152). As such, the Agreeableness spectrum of HEXACO ranges from tolerant and mild to stubborn and impatient. The C is also mostly unchanged from the FFM and still stands for **Conscientiousness.** Adjectives from the HEXACO Conscientiousness scale range from organized and diligent to negligent and irresponsible. Finally, **Openness to Experience** is the O of HEXACO and is much the same as the FFM with traits such as unconventional and innovative at one end of the spectrum and shallow and unimaginative at the other.

HEXACO Personality Inventory

After their discovery of six personality dimensions, Lee and Ashton (2004) set out to create an assessment tool to measure the new Honesty-Humility dimension and their reconceptualization of the other personality dimensions of the FFM. Each of the six dimensions of HEXACO contains four facets (see Table 6.2). The facets of the Honest-Humility dimension are Sincerity, Fairness, Greed Avoidance, and Modesty. The Emotionality dimension contains the facets of Fearfulness, Anxiety, Dependence, and Sentimentality. The facets of the Extroversion scale include Expressiveness, Social Boldness, Sociability, and Liveliness. Forgiveness, Gentleness, Flexibility, and Patience are the four facets of the Agreeableness dimension. Conscientiousness consists of the facets of Organization, Diligence, Perfectionism, and Prudence. Finally, the facets of Openness to Experience are Aesthetic Appreciation, Inquisitiveness, Creativity, and Unconventionality. The **HEXACO Personality Inventory** (**HEXACO-PI**) consists of 192 items that respondents rate on the same agreement Likert scale used for the NEO-PI. This number of items corresponds to eight items for each of the 24 total facets.

Impulsivity

As we have seen and will see throughout this chapter, impulsivity is commonly implicated in antisocial behavior. The neuroticism dimension of the NEO-PI-3 assessment tool to measure the FFM includes a facet called Impulsiveness. Several diagnostic criteria for the personality disorders most associated with antisocial behavior also include impulsiveness (more on personality disorders in the next section). It also makes some intuitive sense that someone who has trouble controlling their impulses is likely to run afoul of the law.

Having noticed a plethora of ways of conceptualizing impulsivity in the empirical literature, Whiteside and Lynam (2001) sought to better define impulsivity. They had hundreds of different people complete the same nine assessments commonly used in research to measure impulsiveness, including the NEO-PI (in its first version at that time). Additionally, they added several of their own questions to try to capture what is meant by impulsivity. They then used factor analysis to come up with four indicators of impulsivity: urgency, (lack of) premeditation, (lack of) perseverance, and sensation seeking. Using the acronym of these facets, Whiteside and Lynam (2001) created the impulsivity assessment **UPPS** from this work. The **negative urgency** facet is defined by difficulty resisting urges when in a negative affective state. Later recognizing difficulty resisting urges when in a *positive* affective state as well, the UPPS assessment was expanded to include **positive urgency**, creating the revised UPPS-P (Lynam et al., 2006). The **lack of premeditation** facet captures the fact that impulsive people tend not to think things through before they act. Similarly, **lack of perseverance** acknowledges the tendency of impulsive people to give up on tasks that they find boring or difficult. The final facet of this impulsiveness assessment, **sensation seeking**, "incorporates two aspects: 1) a tendency to enjoy and pursue activities that are exciting and 2) an openness to trying new experiences that may or may not be dangerous" (Whiteside & Lynam, 2001, p. 686).

Personality Disorders

The *Diagnostic and Statistical Manual of Mental Disorders* (DSM) is published by the American Psychiatric Association and is currently in its fifth edition (DSM-5). The DSM-5 provides definitions and diagnostic criteria for the multitude of mental disorders recognized by the American Psychiatric Association and defines a personality disorder as an "enduring pattern of inner experience and behavior that deviates markedly from the expectations of the individual's culture, is pervasive and inflexible, has an onset in adolescence or early adulthood, is stable over time, and leads to distress or impairment" (American Psychiatric Association, 2013, p. 645). There are 10 personality disorders with diagnostic criteria in the DSM-5, but here we will only discuss those that have been associated with criminal behavior: **antisocial personality disorder (APD)**, **borderline personality disorder (BPD)**, and **narcissistic personality disorder (NPD)**. See Table 6.3 for the full diagnostic criteria for each of these three personality disorders.

Antisocial personality disorder will be covered more in Chapter 7, as it is often used synonymously with psychopathy (though there are distinctions). Notice from Table 6.3 that many of the diagnostic criteria for APD relate specifically to trouble with the law and interpersonal aggression. Similarly, the diagnostic criteria for BPD include a number of items related to poor anger management and impulsivity. The relationship between the diagnostic criteria for NPD and criminal behavior is perhaps less straightforward. However, behavioral issues may stem from others not treating those diagnosed with NPD at the high level they believe they deserve.

Interestingly, all three of these personality disorders fall into Cluster B of personality disorders in the DSM-5, which notes that "[i]ndividuals with these disorders often appear dramatic, emotional, or erratic" (American Psychiatric Association, 2013, p. 646). Additionally, these personality disorders have a tendency to disregard how their actions affect others. Other authors have characterized Cluster B personality disorders as having "problems with emotion regulation, impulsivity and interpersonal conflicts" (Young et al., 2018, p. 706). Given these descriptions, it is not surprising that people with these personality disorders often end up in trouble with the law.

Explaining Criminal Behavior

FFM and Criminal Behavior

Decades of research and three meta-analyses have discovered which of the FFM dimensions and facets are most related to criminal behavior. Broadly speaking, the low end of the FFM dimensions of Agreeableness and Conscientiousness are the most observed among those prone to antisocial behavior. These two dimensions are negatively related to antisocial behavior, with those involved in aggressive and/or criminal behavior more likely to be lower in Agreeableness and lower in Conscientiousness. The negative end of the Agreeableness dimension has been referred to as antagonism. Whereas the negative end of the Conscientiousness dimension has been referred to as disinhibition.

The first meta-analysis to examine the FFM model of personality (and other personality models) and how it relates to antisocial behavior was conducted by Miller and Lynam in 2001. Since they did not exclusively look at the FFM model of personality, Miller and Lynam (2001) were only able to discuss correlations between the higher-order dimensions (i.e., *not* facets) represented by the OCEAN acronym. Nonetheless, they were able to demonstrate that traits related to Agreeableness and Conscientiousness, as defined by the FFM, were most related to aggression and antisocial behavior.

A decade later, another meta-analysis by Jones, Miller, and Lynam (2011) supported this result. Agreeableness and Conscientiousness were again significantly negatively related to aggression and antisocial behavior. They also found a small but significant positive correlation between Neuroticism and both aggression and antisocial behavior. Additionally, there was a small negative relationship between both Extroversion and Openness to Experience

Table 6.3 Diagnostic criteria for antisocial personality disorder, borderline personality disorder, and narcissistic personality disorder (American Psychiatric Association, 2013).

Antisocial personality disorder	*Borderline personality disorder*	*Narcissistic personality disorder*
A. A pervasive pattern of disregard for and violation of the rights of others, occurring since age 15 years, as indicated by three (or more) of the following:	A pervasive pattern of instability of interpersonal relationships, self-image, and affects, and marked impulsivity, beginning by early adulthood and present in a variety of contexts, as indicated by five (or more) of the following:	A pervasive pattern of grandiosity (in fantasy or behavior), need for admiration, and lack of empathy, beginning by early adulthood and present in a variety of contexts, as indicated by five (or more) of the following:
1 Failure to conform to social norms with respect to lawful behaviors, as indicated by repeatedly performing acts that are grounds for arrest. 2 Deceitfulness, as indicated by repeated lying, use of aliases, or conning others for personal profit or pleasure. 3 Impulsivity or failure to plan ahead. 4 Irritability and aggressiveness, as indicated by repeated physical fights or assaults. 5 Reckless disregard for safety of self or others. 6 Consistent irresponsibility, as indicated by repeated failure to sustain consistent work behavior or honor financial obligations. 7 Lack of remorse, as indicated by being indifferent to or rationalizing having hurt, mistreated, or stolen from another.	1 Frantic efforts to avoid real or imagined abandonment. (Note: Do not include suicidal or self-mutilating behavior covered in Criterion 5.) 2 A pattern of unstable and intense interpersonal relationships characterized by alternating between extremes of idealization and devaluation. 3 Identity disturbance: markedly and persistently unstable self-image or sense of self. 4 Impulsivity in at least two areas that are potentially self-damaging (e.g., spending, sex, substance abuse, reckless driving, binge eating). (Note: Do not include suicidal or self-mutilating behavior covered in Criterion 5.) 5 Recurrent suicidal behavior, gestures, or threats, or self-mutilating behavior. 6 Affective instability due to a marked reactivity of mood (e.g., intense episodic dysphoria, irritability, or anxiety usually lasting a few hours and only rarely more than a few days). 7 Chronic feelings of emptiness. 8 Inappropriate, intense anger or difficulty controlling anger (e.g., frequent displays of temper, constant anger, recurrent physical fights). 9 Transient, stress-related paranoid ideation or severe dissociative symptoms.	1 Has a grandiose sense of self-importance (e.g., exaggerates achievements and talents, expects to be recognized as superior without commensurate achievements). 2 Is preoccupied with fantasies of unlimited success, power, brilliance, beauty, or ideal love. 3 Believes that he or she is "special" and unique and can only be understood by, or should associate with, other special or high-status people (or institutions). 4 Requires excessive admiration. 5 Has a sense of entitlement (i.e., unreasonable expectations of especially favorable treatment or automatic compliance with his or her expectations).
B. The individual is at least age 18 years. C. There is evidence of conduct disorder with onset before age 15 years. D. The occurrence of antisocial behavior is not exclusively during the course of schizophrenia or bipolar disorder.		

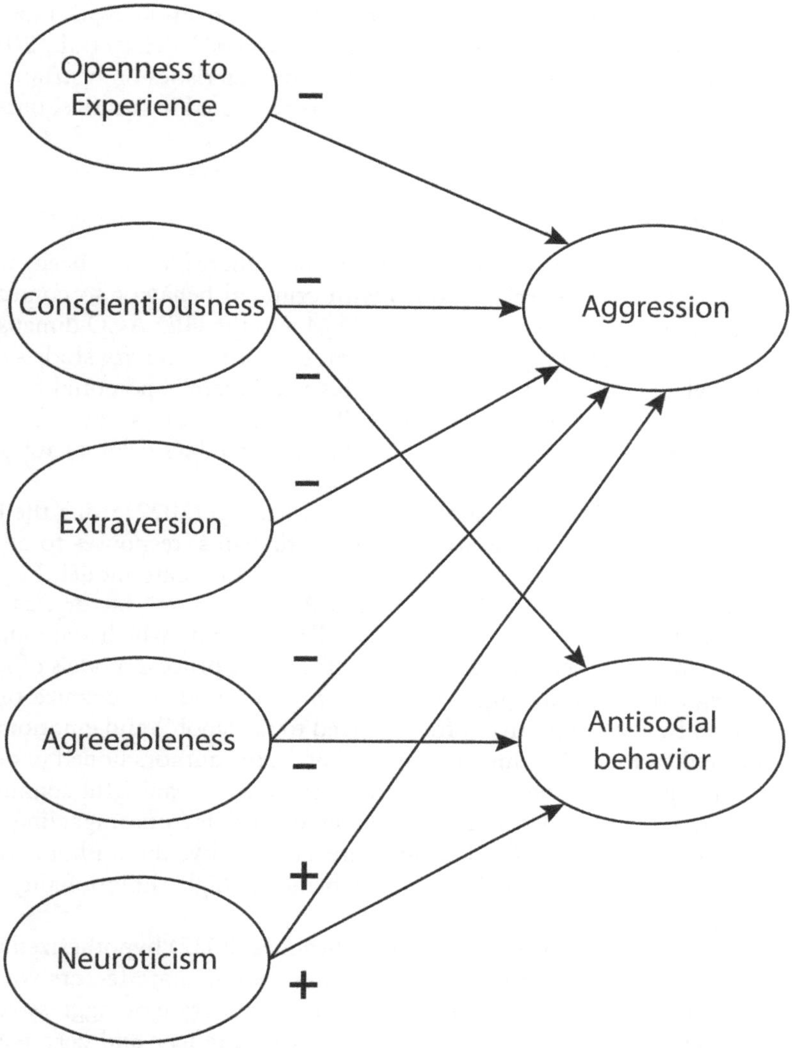

Figure 6.1 Correlations of FFM personality domains with aggression and antisocial behavior (Jones et al., 2011).

with aggression but not antisocial behavior. All 12 of the facets related to Agreeableness and Conscientiousness were negatively related to both aggression and antisocial behavior, lending even more support to the higher-order dimension correlations. Facets from the other dimensions that were found to be correlated with both antisocial behavior and aggression were angry hostility and impulsiveness from the Neuroticism dimension (all positively related) and warmth from the Extraversion dimension (negatively related). Figure 6.1 provides a visual depiction of these correlations.

Finally, and most recently, Vize and his colleagues (including Miller and Lynam) conducted an extensive meta-analysis in 2019. At the dimension or domain level, again Agreeableness and Conscientiousness were the most highly related (negatively) to antisocial behavior. Moreover, their "results show that Agreeableness' relations with most antisocial outcomes is about twice the magnitude of Conscientiousness'" (Vize et al., 2019, p. 73). These authors also examined the effect of personality characteristics on instrumental versus reactive forms of aggression and found Neuroticism to be related to reactive, but not instrumental, forms of aggression.

HEXACO and Criminal Behavior

Since the HEXACO model of personality is relatively new, there have not been enough studies examining these dimensions' relationships with criminal behavior to conduct a meta-analysis. Given the overlap between many of the FFM and the HEXACO dimensions, there have been meta-analyses including the HEXACO model *combined with* studies of the FFM model. However, when studies are compared in this way, there is potential for both jingle and jangle fallacies. Instead, in this section we will discuss a recent study specifically using only the HEXACO model that was not conducted by that model's original authors (to presumably avoid potential biases).

The study was conducted by van Gelder and his colleagues (2022) using the HEXACO-PI and virtual reality (VR) simulation to examine participants' responses to an immersive altercation scenario. The goal of the study was to test a trait-state model, based on both personality traits, as determined by the HEXACO-PI, and "state" factors, aspects of the immediate situation that may also affect response. To determine which state factors to examine, van Gelder and his colleagues (2022) drew from **dual-process models of information processing** and prior research on aggression. Dual-process models recognize that decision making is impacted by both cognitive (often referred to as "cool") and emotional (referred to as "hot") internal factors. Utilizing previous research, the authors honed in on perceived risk and anticipated guilt and shame as potentially the most meaningful cognitive factors, and anger and fear were hypothesized to be the emotional factors impacting aggression. While they used the full HEXACO-PI to measure personality, the authors were primarily interested in the dimensions of (low) Agreeableness, (high) Emotionality, and (low) Honesty-Humility.

Based on trait-state theories, van Gelder and colleagues (2022) hypothesized that certain personality traits would only impact aggression when certain state factors were also present. Specifically, they "predicted agreeableness to mainly operate on aggressive intentions via anger. Emotionality was hypothesized to operate via state fear and perceived risk, and honesty-humility through anticipated shame/guilt and perceived risk" (p. 421). The authors also made predictions regarding whether there would be direct effects of personality traits on state factors, and direct effects of both personality traits and state factors on aggression. See Figure 6.2 for a path model of these hypotheses (modified slightly from the original to exclude the tests of the VR model versus traditional written vignettes and to indicate significant findings). Only a few of these direct-effect hypotheses were *not* supported in their findings, and all of the indirect-effect hypotheses (i.e., personality traits combined with state factors impacting aggression) were statistically significant.

Impulsivity and Criminal Behavior

The relationship between trait impulsivity and antisocial behavior has been studied extensively. Since the UPPS was created using many other impulsivity assessment tools, Bresin (2019) was able to include in his meta-analysis of impulsivity and aggression studies which

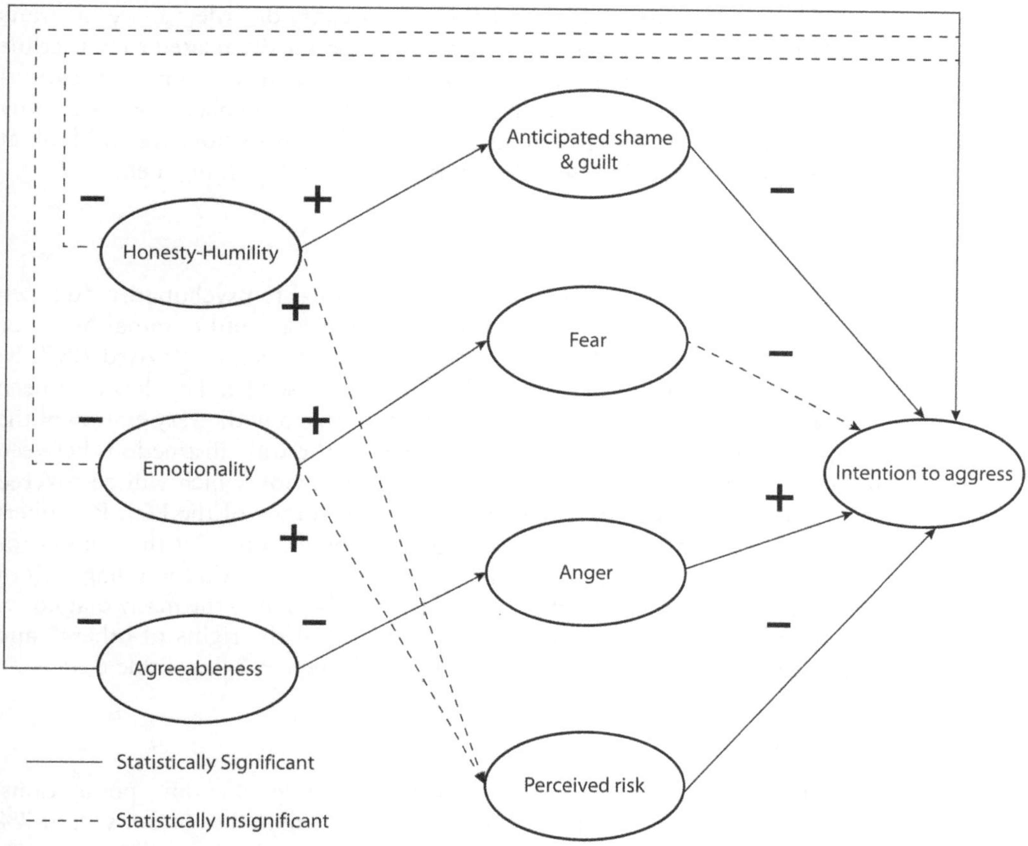

Figure 6.2 Path model and significant findings for van Gelder et al. (2022).

used many different assessments of impulsivity. The meta-analysis revealed that "all facets of impulsivity were significantly positively related to general and physical aggression" (Bresin, 2019, p. 136). However, the facets of negative urgency and lack of premeditation had stronger correlations with aggression than the other two main facets of the UPPS impulsivity model (i.e., sensation seeking and lack of perseverance). Though fewer studies included in the meta-analysis examined positive urgency, there was a similarly strong positive relationship between this facet of impulsivity and aggression. While these findings solidify the role of impulsivity in aggressive behavior, Bresin (2019) cautioned that impulsivity does not explain all variation in aggressive behavior. Interestingly, this meta-analysis also claims support for the I³ theory presented in Chapter 5.

Personality Disorders and Criminal Behavior

The meta-analysis discussed earlier that examined the FFM in relation to antisocial behavior (Vize et al., 2019) also claims that their "meta-analytic results help explain why more multidimensional clinical constructs like antisocial personality disorder, narcissistic personality disorder, and borderline personality disorder demonstrate relations with antisocial behavior outcomes" (p. 73). The authors assert that these three personality disorders share the traits of antagonism and disinhibition, and negative affectivity is specifically related to borderline personality disorder. They suggest that the fact that their meta-analysis found correlations between all three of these traits and antisocial behavior offers an explanation as to why these personality disorders are related to criminal behavior. In this section, we will look at the direct evidence of these personality disorders' relationship with criminal behavior.

Antisocial Personality Disorder

As mentioned previously, antisocial personality disorder is similar to psychopathy. So much so, that many studies of the relationship between these conditions and criminal behavior have relied on psychopathy as identified by the Psychopathy Checklist-Revised (PCL-R; Hare, 1993) rather than a diagnosis of antisocial personality disorder. This has also been linked to the fact that the diagnostic criteria for APD have changed with every edition of the DSM, making comparisons across time difficult. Nonetheless, there are distinctions between these two constructs and their relationship with antisocial behavior, which will be covered in more detail in Chapter 7. Suffice to say for now, that the author of the PCL-R, Robert Hare, pointed out that while 50% to 80% of the prison population meet the criteria for APD only approximately 15% of the prison population meets the criteria for a diagnosis of psychopathy (Hare, 2003 as cited in Ogloff, 2006). This may be due to the many diagnostic criteria for APD having a direct relationship with "violation of the rights of others" and "failure to conform to social norms with respect to lawful behaviors" (see Table 6.3).

Borderline Personality Disorder

Borderline personality disorder (BPD) is more prevalent among offending populations. Whereas the prevalence of BPD in the general population is estimated to be between 0.7% and 3.8%, the prevalence among those in prison or on probation is between 15% and 35% (Sebastian et al., 2019, p. 2). The connection between borderline personality disorder and antisocial behavior has been linked primarily to the fact that those diagnosed with BPD often have difficulty regulating their emotions and tend to act impulsively. These traits have been hypothesized to relate to reactive aggression specifically. However, the empirical research on these connections has been sparse. Further, the studies that have been done on the emotion dysregulation and impulsivity of BPD have provided mixed results. A systematic review of the limited research in this area (Lowenstein et al., 2016) found that emotion dysregulation was more important in predicting violent offending than impulsivity among those with BPD symptoms. In contrast, Wojciechowski (2021) found "the impulsivity that is generally characteristic of BPD was much more important for understanding violent offending risk related to BPD symptomology than was emotion dysregulation" (p. 2336). It is possible that the emotional dysregulation and impulsivity of those with BPD are intertwined in the sense that emotional dysregulation is potentially what causes impulsivity in BPD. Clearly, more research is needed in this area.

While little research has examined the connection between BPD and violence generally, much more research has looked at BPD and intimate partner violence (IPV). A meta-analysis examining IPV and personality disorders (Collison & Lynam, 2021) found both APD and BPD most strongly associated with IPV perpetration. Interestingly, this meta-analysis also found a significant and positive relationship between BPD and IPV *victimization*. Armenti and Babcock (2021) examined possible underlying causes for why BPD sufferers are more likely to engage in IPV. Perhaps not surprisingly, they discovered that the inter-relational difficulties those with BPD tend to have are key to understanding this relationship. Namely, rejection sensitivity, a hypervigilance to real and perceived rejection by close partners that is common in those with BPD, was found to be associated with an increased likelihood for physical and psychological abuse of an intimate partner.

Narcissistic Personality Disorder

A meta-analysis published in 2021 examined the correlation of various narcissistic types and traits with aggression (Kjærvik & Bushman, 2021). The authors examined different components of narcissism, as well as various levels of aggression, up to and including violence. Kjærvik and Bushman (2021) distinguish between grandiose narcissism and vulnerable narcissism, a distinction that will be further explained later in this chapter. Additionally, they examined an overarching characteristic of narcissism: entitlement. The meta-analysis found all three of these characteristics to be associated with aggression, further indicating that "the link between narcissism and aggression is not trivial in size" (Kjærvik & Bushman, 2021, p. 489). Narcissism was also related to all forms of aggression, with the correlation between narcissism and the highest form of aggression (i.e., violence) only slightly smaller than less serious forms of aggression. Further, they found that narcissistic traits need not reach the level for diagnosis of narcissistic personality disorder to be linked with aggression; even sub-clinical levels of narcissism were associated with increased aggression.

Kjærvik and Bushman (2021) also examined the merits of two theories used to explain the relationship between narcissism and aggression. The first is the **threatened egoism model** (Baumeister et al., 1996), which suggests that narcissists will become aggressive toward those whom they feel do not share the same high opinion that narcissists have of themselves, causing frustration and anger that may lead to reactive aggression. The second theory is the **status pursuit in narcissism model (SPIN**; Grapsas et al., 2020). This theory posits that a narcissist may use aggression preemptively to increase their status, which is more akin to instrumental aggression. The authors of the meta-analysis found support for both of these theories, stating that "individuals high in narcissism do not just aggress against others in an impulsive, hostile, and reactive manner. They also aggress against others in a cold, calculated, deliberate, instrumental, and proactive manner" (Kjærvik & Bushman, 2021, p. 490).

The Dark Triad: Narcissism, Machiavellianism, and Psychopathy

Narcissism, Machiavellianism, and psychopathy are highly related personality constructs which together are labeled the **Dark Triad**. Originally proposed by Paulhus and Williams (2002), there has been much debate as to whether or not the Dark Triad is a unique personality concept. Some have argued that the concepts can be captured using the FFM or HEXACO general models of personality, albeit concentrated at the more negative ends of those dimensions. Others have argued the Dark Triad can be further differentiated from a Vulnerable Dark Triad. Nonetheless, all of these traits have been linked with criminal behavior. Before we discuss the evidence for their ability to explain criminal behavior, let's first look at each of the three Dark Triad concepts.

Narcissism

The narcissism component of the Dark Triad of course relates to narcissistic personality disorder. However, Paulhus and Williams (2002) focused on sub-clinical narcissism, meaning there are narcissistic traits present but they do not rise to the level for an NPD diagnosis.

Therefore, the **narcissism** of the Dark Triad shares the same traits with narcissistic personality disorder but perhaps at a lower level.

Many studies have examined the constructs of the Dark Triad as compared to the FFM and HEXACO models. The findings of these studies can help us better understand narcissism as it relates to the more "normal" traits of these broader models of personality. A meta-analysis of studies comparing the Dark Triad to the FFM (O'Boyle et al., 2014) found "[t]he strong positive relation between narcissism and [FFM] extroversion relies primarily on assertiveness and excitement seeking, whereas positive emotions and warmth are negatively related" (p. 653). A more recent meta-analysis of studies examining the relationship between the HEXACO dimension of Honesty-Humility and the Dark Triad (Howard & Van Zandt, 2020) found the modesty facet of the Honesty-Humility dimension was strongly inversely related to narcissism. Therefore, in addition to the DSM criteria for NPD, we can say the traits of Dark Triad narcissism are high assertiveness and excitement seeking, and low modesty and warmth.

Machiavellianism

Machiavellianism is not found in the DSM-5. Rather it is a personality distinction based on the work of Nicolò Machiavelli in the sixteenth century. In Machiavelli's philosophical work *The Prince*, he advocated for royals to use any means necessary to stay in power. His ideas can be summed up as "the ends justify the means." For Machiavelli, simply remaining in power is a justifiable "end." And the "means" he advocated included murdering rivals! From this description alone, it is easy to see how Machiavellianism might be associated with criminal behavior.

However, **Machiavellianism** as a personality construct has evolved to include specific traits. As with narcissism, it can be instructive to look at how Machiavellianism relates to the FFM and HEXACO models. Many studies have found that Machiavellianism is inversely related to Agreeableness, meaning those who rate highly on Machiavellianism tend to rate low on Agreeableness. The creators of both HEXACO and the Dark Triad each found a small positive relationship between Neuroticism and Machiavellianism (O'Boyle et al., 2014). It has been suggested that the sincerity and fairness facets of the Honesty-Humility dimension are negatively related to Machiavellianism. The same meta-analysis cited above which looked specifically at the Honesty-Humility dimension (Howard & Van Zandt, 2020) found that indeed Machiavellianism is highly negatively correlated with Honesty-Humility as a whole. Finally, research has found that Conscientiousness is lower in those who are high in Machiavellianism.

Psychopathy

The overall concept of psychopathy will be covered in detail in Chapter 7. For now, suffice to say that there are some differences between psychopathy and antisocial personality disorder, despite these terms often being used interchangeably even in scholarly research. Psychopathy and Machiavellianism are the most highly correlated of the three Dark Triad personality constructs. Those high in psychopathy and those high in Machiavellianism are both very manipulative. However, psychopaths also tend to be more impulsive and callous than Machiavellians.

It will be instructive for the purposes of this chapter to look at psychopathy as compared to the FFM and HEXACO personality models. The meta-analysis that examined FFM traits compared to the Dark Triad (O'Boyle et al., 2014) found that psychopathy was negatively related to all facets of agreeableness. It was also found that psychopathy was negatively related to the Conscientiousness facets of deliberation, dutifulness, and self-discipline. Psychopathy was also found to be positively related to the Neuroticism facets of angry hostility and impulsiveness. In relation to the Honesty-Humility dimension of HEXACO, the meta-analysis by Howard and Van Zandt (2020) found psychopathy to be negatively related to all four facets of that dimension (i.e., sincerity, fairness, greed avoidance, and modesty).

Dark Triad Assessments

Though there have been attempts to design an assessment tool specifically for the Dark Triad, it is much more common for assessments of the three separate personality constructs to be used. Indeed, assessments for narcissism, Machiavellianism, and psychopathy had been in use long before Paulhus and Williams (2002) discovered a correlation among these three concepts. The assessments used most commonly in research on the Dark Triad are the **Narcissistic Personality Inventory (NPI)**, the **MACH-IV** for Machiavellianism, and the third version of the Self-Report of Psychopathy (SRP-III).

Created and validated by Raskin and Terry (1988), the NPI consists of 40 items that assess seven facets of narcissism: authority, exhibitionism, superiority, vanity, exploitativeness, entitlement, and self-sufficiency. Each item of the NPI contains two statements that are somewhat opposite of each other. Respondents must choose which of the two statements describes them better. The MACH-IV was created in 1970 by Christie and Geis and has respondents rate their agreement with 20 statements on a five-point Likert scale, from strongly agree to strongly disagree. The assessment's 20 items fall within one of three subscales related to morals, views, and tactics. Finally, the SRP-III was created as a self-report measure of psychopathy similar to the original Psychopathy Checklist-Revised (PCL-R). The original author of the PCL-R, Robert Hare, and one of the creators of the Dark Triad, Delroy Paulhus, were both involved in creating this assessment tool (Paulhus et al., 2009). The SRP-III contains 64 statements to which respondents rate their agreement on a five-point Likert scale. These items correspond to four subscales: interpersonal manipulation, callous affect, erratic lifestyle, and antisocial behavior. (See Chapter 7 for more on psychopathy, its various assessments, and a caution on self-reporting.)

The Vulnerable Dark Triad

Originally proposed by Miller and his colleagues in 2010, the **Vulnerable Dark Triad** addresses inconsistencies in the empirical research of the components of the original Dark Triad. First, there may be a distinction between grandiose narcissism and **vulnerable narcissism**. Grandiose narcissism is more aligned with the DSM diagnostic criteria for narcissistic personality disorder. Whereas, "[v]ulnerable narcissism reflects a more defensive and fragile grandiosity that may serve primarily as a mask for feelings of inadequacy" (Miller et al., 2010, p. 1532). Second, there is some empirical evidence to show that the two factors of the PCL-R (Factor 1 focusing on interpersonal and affective characteristics, and Factor 2 relating to social deviance) are not equally correlated with the other two Dark Triad components of Machiavellianism and narcissism. Given these findings and the interpersonally reactive characteristics of borderline personality disorder, Miller and his colleagues (2010) suggested that the Vulnerable Dark Triad consists of vulnerable narcissism, Factor 2 psychopathy, and BPD. They then suggest a variation of the original Dark Triad to include grandiose narcissism, Factor 1 psychopathy, and Machiavellianism.

Crime and the Dark Triad

Edwards, Albertson, and Verona (2017) examined the relationship between both the Dark Triad and the Vulnerable Dark Triad and adult criminal behavior. They found that the Dark Triad was related to general criminality, including violent crimes, and the Vulnerable Dark Triad was only related to crimes against property and drug offenses. These findings suggest that while both types of the Dark Triad are linked to criminal behavior, only the original Dark Triad is related to violent behavior. The authors provide a potential explanation for this: "Disinhibition and emotional reactivity [characteristic of both the Dark Triad and the Vulnerable Dark Triad] may not extend to physical violence, in the absence of [Dark Triad]-related callousness" (Edwards et al., 2017, p. 925). However, they also provide the caveat that the Dark Triad and Vulnerable Dark Triad traits could not explain all offending behavior. Therefore, other characteristics must also be implicated in criminal propensity.

Summary

This chapter has covered various personality constructs and how they may relate to antisocial behavior. Personality psychology as a discipline has focused primarily on the categorization of personality constructs and the creation of assessment tools for those categorizations. This has led to a plethora of models and measurements with which to examine criminal behavior. At the same time, the vast number of measures has potentially led to confusing and conflicting empirical evidence. Hopefully, the field of personality psychology will begin to focus on parsimony in its models and measurements. Once we have a better understanding of personality concepts, we will be better able to look at the potential positive and negative consequences of certain personality types.

References

American Psychiatric Association. (2013). *Diagnostic and statistical manual of mental disorders* (5th ed.). American Psychiatric Publishing, Inc.

Armenti, N. A., & Babcock, J. C. (2021). Borderline personality features, anger, and intimate partner violence: An experimental manipulation of rejection. *Journal of Interpersonal Violence*, *36*(5–6), NP3104–NP3129.

Ashton, M. C., & Lee, K. (2007). Empirical, theoretical, and practical advantages of the HEXACO model of personality structure. *Personality and Social Psychology Review*, *11*(2), 150–66.

Ashton, M. C., Lee, K., Perugini, M., Szarota, P., De Vries, R. E., Di Blas, L., Boies, K., & De Raad, B. (2004). A six-factor structure of personality-descriptive adjectives: Solutions from psycholexical studies in seven languages. *Journal of Personality and Social Psychology*, *86*(2), 356–366.

Baumeister, R. F., Smart, L., & Boden, J. M. (1996). Relation of threatened egotism to violence and aggression: The dark side of high self-esteem. *Psychological Review*, *103*(1), 5–33. https://doi.org/10.1037/0033-295X.103.1.5

Bresin, K. (2019). Impulsivity and aggression: A meta-analysis using the UPPS model of impulsivity. *Aggression and Violent Behavior*, *48*, 124–140.

Christie, R., & Geis, F. L. (1970). *Studies in Machiavellianism*. Academic Press.

Collison, K. L., & Lynam, D. R. (2021). Personality disorders as predictors of intimate partner violence: A meta-analysis. *Clinical Psychology Review*, *88*, 102047.

Costa, P. T., & McCrae, R. R. (1985). *The NEO personality inventory manual*. Psychological Assessment Resources.

Grapsas, S., Brummelman, E., Back, M. D., & Denissen, J. J. A. (2020). The "why" and "how" of narcissism: A process model of narcissistic status pursuit. *Perspectives on Psychological Science*, *15*(1), 150–172. https://doi.org/10.1177/1745691619873350

Hare, R. D. (1993). *Without conscience: The disturbing world of the psychopaths among us*. The Guilford Press.
Hare, R. D. (2003). *Manual for the Hare Psychopathy Checklist-Revised* (2nd ed.). Multi-Health Systems.
Howard, M. C., & Van Zandt, E. C. (2020). The discriminant validity of honesty-humility: A meta-analysis of the HEXACO, Big Five and Dark Triad. *Journal of Research in Personality*, *87*, 103982.
Jones, S. E., Miller, J. D., & Lynam, D. R. (2011). Personality, antisocial behavior, and aggression: A meta-analytic review. *Journal of Criminal Justice*, *39*(4), 329–337.
Kelley, E. L. (1927). *Interpretation of educational measurements*. World Book Co.
Kjærvik, S. L., & Bushman, B. J. (2021). The link between narcissism and aggression: A meta-analytic review. *Psychological Bulletin*, *147*(5), 477–503.
Lee, K., & Ashton, M. C. (2004). Psychometric properties of the HEXACO personality inventory. *Multivariate Behavioral Research*, *39*(2), 329–358. https://doi.org/10.1207/s15327906mbr3902_8
Lowenstein, J., Purvis, C., & Rose, K. (2016). A systematic review on the relationship between antisocial, borderline and narcissistic personality disorder diagnostic traits and risk of violence to others in a clinical and forensic sample. *Borderline Personality Disorder and Emotion Dysregulation*, *3*(14), 1–12. https://doi.org/10.1186/s40479-016-0046-0
Lynam, D. R., Smith, G. T., Whiteside, S. P., & Cyders, M. A. (2006). *The UPPS-P: Assessing five personality pathways to impulsive behavior (technical report)*. Purdue University.
Miller, J. D., Dir, A., Gentile, B., Wilson, L., Pryor, L. R., & Campbell, W. K. (2010). Searching for a vulnerable dark triad: Comparing factor 2 psychopathy, vulnerable narcissism, and borderline personality disorder. *Journal of Personality*, *78*(5), 1529–1564.
Miller, J. D., & Lynam, D. (2001). Structural models of personality and their relation to antisocial behavior: A meta-analytic review. *Criminology*, *39*(4), 765–798.
O'Boyle, E. H., Forsyth, D. R., Banks, G. C., Story, P. A., & White, C. D. (2014). A meta-analytic test of redundancy and relative importance of the Dark Triad and Five-Factor Model of personality. *Journal of Personality*, *83*(6), 644–664.
Ogloff, J. R. (2006). Psychopathy/Antisocial personality disorder conundrum. *Australian & New Zealand Journal of Psychiatry*, *40*(6–7), 519–528.
Paulhus, D. L., Neumann, C. S., & Hare, R. D. (2009). *Manual for the Hare Self-Report Psychopathy Scale*. Multi-Health Systems.
Paulhus, D. L., & Williams, K. M. (2002). The Dark Triad of personality: Narcissism, machiavellianism, and psychopathy. *Journal of Research in Personality*, *36*(6), 556–563.
Raskin, R., & Terry, H. (1988). A principal-components analysis of the narcissistic personality inventory and further evidence of its construct validity. *Journal of Personality and Social Psychology*, *54*(5), 890–902.
Sebastian, A., Retz, W., Tüscher, O., & Turner, D. (2019). Violent offending in borderline personality disorder and attention deficit/hyperactivity disorder. *Neuropharmacology*, *156*, 107565.
van Gelder, J., de Vries, R. E., van Sintemaartensdijk, I., & Donker, T. (2022). Personality pathways to aggression: Testing a trait-state model using immersive technology. *Criminology*, *60*(3), 406–428.
Vize, C. E., Collison, K. L., Miller, J. D., & Lynam, D. R. (2019). Using Bayesian methods to update and expand the meta-analytic evidence of the five-factor model's relation to antisocial behavior. *Clinical Psychology Review*, *67*, 61–77.
Whiteside, S. P., & Lynam, D. R. (2001). The Five Factor Model and impulsivity: Using a structural model of personality to understand impulsivity. *Personality and Individual Differences*, *30*(4), 669–689.
Wojciechowski, T. (2021). The dual mediating roles of impulsivity and emotion regulation of the borderline personality disorder-violence relationship: A structural equation modeling approach. *Journal of Forensic Sciences*, *66*(6), 2329–2339.
Young, C., Habarth, J., Bongar, B., & Packman, W. (2018). Disorder in the court: Cluster B personality disorders in United States case law. *Psychiatry, Psychology, and Law*, *25*(5), 706–723.

7 Psychopathy and Serial Murder

Box 7.1 Ted Bundy, the quintessential psychopathic serial killer

If you are not familiar with Ted Bundy and his crimes, there are myriad ways to learn about him, both old and new. Netflix has released two shows about him, one scripted (*Extremely Wicked, Shockingly Evil and Vile*) and one in the killer's own words (*Conversations with a Killer: The Ted Bundy Tapes*). And of course, the original tell-all book by Bundy's friend, Ann Rule, titled *The Stranger Beside Me*, written after his conviction but before his execution with numerous follow-up editions. For these reasons, we are going to dive right into why Ted Bundy is the quintessential psychopath.

By all accounts, Bundy was incredibly charming and manipulative. He was able to convince young women to help him with menial tasks, only for them to become his victims. Bundy was the inspiration for the kidnapping scene in *The Silence of the Lambs*. His lack of planning and follow through caused the love of his life to leave him. This is when some believe he began to target young brunettes with their long hair parted in the middle. Although his acquaintances saw him as emotionally stable, those who were closest to him knew he was also prone to outbursts of anger. He was able to escape jail twice. Due to his limited criminal history prior to the murders, some might call Bundy a "successful psychopath." Working as the prosecution's psychiatrist, Hervey Cleckley himself conducted an extensive interview and reviewed other accounts to diagnose Ted Bundy as a psychopath.

For more information on psychopathy and Ted Bundy (and serial murder more generally):

Hickey, E. W., Walters, B. K., Drislane, L. E., Palumbo, I. M., & Patrick, C. J. (2018). Deviance at its darkest. In C. J. Patrick (Ed.), *Handbook of psychopathy* (2nd ed.). The Guilford Press.

Introduction

What is a **psychopath**? You may think it is just something you call a serial killer or someone else who does unspeakable things. In reality, a psychopath must meet very specific criteria, and it is unlikely that every serial killer is a psychopath. True psychopaths are also quite rare; some estimate that approximately 1% of the general population may meet the criteria for a psychopathy diagnosis. In this chapter's The Basics section, we will explore the history

DOI: 10.4324/9781003250821-8

of the term, the groups of symptoms/traits, diagnostic tools, and the etiology of the disorder. In the Explaining Criminal Behavior section, we will learn the empirical evidence for psychopathy's link with violent behavior generally and its diagnostic use in assessing for risk of recidivism. The chapter concludes with a thorough look at what is empirically known about the phenomenon of serial murder and its connection to psychopathy.

The Basics

Cleckley's Mask of Sanity

Though others delved into the idea of a psychopathic personality, the grouping of traits that became known as psychopathy was popularized by Hervey Cleckley in 1941. His seminal work, *The Mask of Sanity*, describes many cases Cleckley encountered in his work in both psychiatric and general hospitals. The patients all exhibited similar symptoms/traits, but neither Cleckley nor his colleagues could put their finger on a diagnosis. It did not seem to fit existing diagnoses. More interestingly, once he became aware of the phenomenon, Cleckley began noticing these traits in people outside of the hospital setting. He found businessmen, scientists, and even psychiatrists exhibiting some of the same symptoms he had noted in hospitalized patients. The title of Cleckley's book alludes to what he found most interesting about these people. They seem to be wearing a "mask" that makes the casual observer think they are sane. A similar condition was noted by Pinel in the nineteenth century termed "mania without delirium" (Patrick, 2018). *The Mask of Sanity* identified 16 characteristics of Cleckley's as-yet-to-be-named psychopath, which can be found in Table 7.1.

Psychopathy, Sociopathy, and Antisocial Personality Disorder

Karpman's Primary and Secondary Psychopathy

One of the first to speculate that there are different versions of psychopathy was Karpman (1948). He distinguished between primary and secondary psychopathy. The **primary psychopath** is more calculating and calm in his deviance, whereas the **secondary psychopath** is more

Table 7.1 Characteristics identified by Cleckley in *The Mask of Sanity*.

1	Superficial charm and good "intelligence"
2	Absence of delusions and other signs of irrational thinking
3	Absence of "nervousness" or psychoneurotic manifestations
4	Unreliability
5	Untruthfulness and insincerity
6	Lack of remorse or shame
7	Inadequately motivated antisocial behavior
8	Poor judgment and failure to learn by experience
9	Pathologic egocentricity and incapacity for love
10	General poverty in major affective reactions
11	Specific loss of insight
12	Unresponsiveness in general interpersonal relations
13	Fantastic and uninviting behavior with drink and sometimes without
14	Suicide rarely carried out
15	Sex life impersonal, trivial, and poorly integrated
16	Failure to follow any life plan

Source: (Cleckley, 1941, pp. 338–339).

volatile and impulsive. Further, Karpman asserted that primary psychopathy stemmed from an innate lack of conscience. Secondary psychopathy, sometimes called sociopathy, results from a conscience that was not properly formed due to inept parenting. Due to the fact that the secondary psychopath has an underlying conscience that was merely improperly developed, Karpman believed this group could be rehabilitated by working to develop their conscience.

DSM's Antisocial Personality Disorder

The American Psychiatric Association included a diagnosis of **antisocial personality disorder** (APD) in their *Diagnostic and Statistical Manual of Mental Disorders*, third edition (DSM-III) in 1980. The current criteria for a diagnosis of APD, found in the fifth edition (DSM-5; American Psychiatric Association, 2013) can be found in Table 7.2.

Lykken's Primary (Psychopath) and Secondary (Sociopath) APD

Similar to Karpman, Lykken (1995) distinguishes between primary and secondary diagnoses. However, his starting diagnosis is APD. Lykken speculated that APD can be broken into two different categories, which he labeled psychopathy and sociopathy. The cause of **Lykken's psychopathy** is a genetically derived poor temperament. Even the best parents cannot instill a conscience in a psychopath. However, **Lykken's sociopath** fails to develop a conscience due to poor parenting, much like Karpman's secondary psychopath. Both Lykken and Karpman's distinctions can be summed up as "[Primary] Psychopaths are born; sociopaths [secondary psychopaths] are made."

Diagnostic Tools

Psychopathy Checklist

Given the considerable debate and confusion regarding what is truly meant by the term "psychopathy," many scholars began devising diagnostic tools to obtain a firmer grasp of

Table 7.2 Diagnostic criteria for antisocial personality disorder (American Psychiatric Association, 2013).

1. A pervasive pattern of disregard for and violation of the rights of others, since age 15 years, as indicated by three (or more) of the following:
    - a Failure to conform to social norms concerning lawful behaviors, such as performing acts that are grounds for arrest.
    - b Deceitfulness, repeated lying, use of aliases, or conning others for pleasure or personal profit.
    - c Impulsivity or failure to plan.
    - d Irritability and aggressiveness, often with physical fights or assaults.
    - e Reckless disregard for the safety of self or others.
    - f Consistent irresponsibility, failure to sustain consistent work behavior, or honor monetary obligations.
    - g Lack of remorse, being indifferent to or rationalizing having hurt, mistreated, or stolen from another person.
2. The individual is at least age 18 years.
3. Evidence of conduct disorder typically with onset before age 15 years.
4. The occurrence of antisocial behavior is not exclusively during schizophrenia or bipolar disorder.

the concept. The first and most well-known of these is Robert Hare's **Psychopathy Checklist.** Dr. Hare began working on a diagnostic tool for the psychopath after reading Cleckley's *The Mask of Sanity*. Through the years, Hare and his colleagues have developed The Psychopathy Checklist, the Psychopathy Checklist-Revised (PCL-R), Psychopathy Checklist-Screening Version (PCL-SV), and Psychopathy Checklist-Youth Version (PCL-YV). In his 1993 book *Without Conscience*, Hare (1993) explains in detail the criteria included in diagnosing a psychopath using his tools.

Hare's PCL-R has two "factors" with two "facets" each (see Table 7.3). Each of the 20 items on the checklist "loads" on one of these facets, with the exception of two items. Promiscuous Sexual Behavior and Many "Short-Term" Marital Relationships are indicators of psychopathy, according to Hare, but they are not correlated with any of the other criteria. Under Factor 1, interpersonal/affective, the first facet is interpersonal and the second facet is affective. Items on the interpersonal facet have to do with how the potential psychopath relates to others (recall some of Cleckley's characteristics that dealt with interpersonal relations). Items that load on the affective facet have to do with the potential psychopath's emotions or affect and how easily or well they show them. The facets under Factor 2 deal with social deviance. Items that load on facet 3 have to do with the potential psychopath's lifestyle – remember Cleckley's characteristics that indicate that psychopaths will not follow a life plan and are impulsive. Those are lifestyle characteristics. The type of items that load on facet 4, antisocial behavior and traits, can also be found in Table 7.3.

Diagnosing a psychopath is not to be taken lightly. The PCL-R and its siblings require training to conduct properly. The first part of the process is file review. Dr. Hare goes so far as to suggest not conducting a PCL-R if the file review cannot be done. Acquiring ample background information prior to interviewing the subject will allow for asking better questions and detecting deception. Also, it is important to get a feel for the person in a variety of contexts. It may also be helpful to interview those who know the subject. Next is the

Table 7.3 Factors, facets, and items on Hare's Psychopathy Checklist-Revised.

		1	Promiscuous sexual behavior
		2	Many short-term marital relationships
Factor 1: Interpersonal/Affective	Facet 1: Interpersonal	3	Glibness/Superficial charm
		4	Grandiose sense of self-worth
		5	Pathological lying
		6	Conning/Manipulative
	Facet 2: Affective	7	Lack of remorse or guilt
		8	Shallow affect
		9	Callous/Lack of empathy
		10	Failure to accept responsibility for own actions
Factor 2: Social Deviance	Facet 3: Lifestyle	11	Need for stimulation/Proneness to boredom
		12	Parasitic lifestyle
		13	Lack of realistic long-term goals
		14	Impulsivity
		15	Irresponsibility
	Facet 4: Antisocial	16	Poor behavioral controls/Aggressivity
		17	Early behavior problems
		18	Juvenile delinquency
		19	Revocation of conditional release
		20	Criminal versatility

interview with the subject themselves. It consists of 124 questions that cover a range of topics, such as education, employment, family and interpersonal relationships, and adolescent and adult antisocial behaviors. The purpose of the interview is not only to obtain information, but also to observe the person's interactional style and check for consistency in their responses. Finally, when scoring the PCL-R, each of the items is rated either a two, one, or zero. Rating an item a two means the person fits the item really well. It does not necessarily have to match perfectly, but it should fit in multiple contexts to warrant a score of two. If the item only matches somewhat or sometimes, or if there is conflicting information from the files versus the interview, a one can be scored for the item. If the item does not seem to apply at all, especially if the person seems to have the opposite trait, the item is scored a zero. Once everything is totaled up, a score of 30 or greater is needed for a diagnosis of psychopathy.

Comprehensive Assessment of Psychopathic Personality

Cooke, Hart, Logan, and Michie set out to design a test for psychopathy using plain language and thus created the **Comprehensive Assessment of Psychopathic Personality** (CAPP; Cooke & Logan, 2018). Despite the dominance of the PCL-R, Cooke and colleagues saw the need to simplify the terminology used to identify symptoms of psychopathy. After reviewing the literature and interviewing experts, they developed a list of symptoms commonly agreed upon within these sources. These symptoms were then broken down into their most basic "trait-descriptive adjectives" (Cooke & Logan, 2018). Each of the CAPP's 33 symptoms has three trait-descriptive adjectives (or phrases). Among these 33 symptoms, six domains were identified: attachment, behavioral, cognitive, dominance, emotional, and self.

Like the PCL-R, the CAPP requires file review and a **semi-structured interview**. Cooke and colleagues offer an abundance of suggestions for the semi-structured interview, including ways to control the interview, identify dishonesty, and strategically confront the interviewee on their lies. The rater must look for information or behavior indicative of the trait-descriptive adjectives used to identify each of the 33 symptoms. These symptoms are rated individually on a seven-point scale. The ultimate goal is not necessarily an exact diagnosis. Rather, things like treatment plans or facility placement are determined based on the degree each symptom is present and the degree to which the symptom affects prosocial functioning.

Self-Report Measures

There has been much interest in simplifying the assessment process for psychopathy. This has led to a number of psychopathy measures that rely solely on self-report, meaning the potential psychopath fills out a questionnaire themself. One problem is obvious: psychopaths lie. Sellbom and colleagues (2018) identified additional problems with asking a potential psychopath to self-evaluate. First, psychopaths have extreme difficulty self-evaluating; they do not see themselves as others see them. Second, any test of psychopathy will need to ask about experiences, or lack thereof, with emotions. If someone has never experienced an emotion, how will they truly know? Moreover, to get by in life, many psychopaths learn to fake emotions by observing others. However, this imitation is not likely to be entirely accurate. Even if a psychopath is not deliberately trying to lie, they are unlikely to be able to precisely evaluate themself on key components of psychopathy. A key feature of any self-report questionnaire, especially one designed to measure psychopathy, is validity scales. A **validity scale** is a group of questions designed to detect untruthfulness. With these embedded in the questionnaire, those administering the diagnosis can more easily spot those trying to throw the test.

Table 7.4 Factors, subscales, and example statements of the Psychopathic Personality Inventory-Revised (Lilienfeld & Andrews, 1996).

	1 Coldheartedness	"I have had 'crushes' on people that were so intense that they were painful." (False for a psychopath.)
Fearless Dominance (FD)	2 Social potency	"Even when others are upset with me, I can usually win them over with my charm."
	3 Fearlessness	"Making a parachute jump would really frighten me." (False for a psychopath.)
	4 Stress immunity	"I can remain calm in situations that would make many other people panic."
Self-Centered Impulsivity (SCI)	5 Machiavellian egocentricity	"I always look out for my own interests before worrying about those of the other guy."
	6 Rebellious nonconformity	"I sometimes question authority figures 'just for the hell of it.'"
	7 Blame externalization	"I usually feel that people give me the credit I deserve." (False for a psychopath.)
	8 Carefree nonplanfulness	"I often make the same errors in judgment over and over again."

PSYCHOPATHIC PERSONALITY INVENTORY

Lilienfeld and Andrews (1996) set out to develop a self-report measure of the personality characteristics of psychopathy, while deliberately avoiding the antisocial behavioral aspects of the diagnosis. They believed these personality characteristics to be the most important aspects of a true diagnosis over simply measuring someone's criminal propensity. Lilienfeld and Andrews developed the **Psychopathic Personality Inventory** (PPI) using psychopathy constructs from many of the original and leading theorists on the subject, relying mostly on Cleckley's original vision. After a revision in 2005, the Psychopathic Personality Inventory-Revised (PPI-R) ended up with 154 statements to be rated *False, Mostly False, Mostly True,* or *True.* As well as statements that captured the psychopathy constructs, validity measures were included to detect attempts at manipulations. Lilienfeld and colleagues identified eight subscales in their questionnaire, and subsequent research was able to group most of these subscales into two factors (see Table 7.4). The subscale *Coldheartedness* (e.g., "I have had 'crushes' on people that were so intense that they were painful," which a psychopath would rate *False*; all example statements from Lilienfeld & Andrews, 1996) did not correlate with the other subscales.

There appear to be similarities between the two PCL-R factors and the two PPI-R factors. Indeed, both PCL-R Factor 1 and PPI-R Self-Centered Impulsivity (SCI) appear to tap into the personality of the psychopath, whereas PCL-R Factor Two and PPI-R Fearless Dominance (FD) tend to measure a tendency for antisocial behavior. Some have argued that PCL-R Factor 2 is most similar to the Coldheartedness subscale (Hicks & Dislane, 2018), which is not correlated with the other PPI-R subscales and is not included in either of the PPI-R factors. Although the research is somewhat mixed, there is some evidence of a correlation between SCI and PCL-R Factor 1, as well as a correlation between FD and PCL-R Factor 2 (Hughes et al., 2013).

ELEMENTAL PSYCHOPATHY ASSESSMENT

Lynam and colleagues (2011) used personality traits from the five-factor model (FFM; see Chapter 6) that have been empirically correlated with psychopathy to create their **Elemental Psychopathy Assessment** (EPA). The EPA is a 178-item self-report questionnaire. These items are intended to measure the respondent on 18 subscales that are grouped into four factors. EPA Factor 1 is titled Antagonism and includes the subscales of distrust, manipulation, opposition, and callousness. EPA Factor 2, Emotional Stability, has unconcern, anger, and invulnerability as subscales. EPA Factor 3 is Disinhibition and has the subscales disobliged, impersistence, rashness, urgency (impulsiveness), and thrill seeking. Finally, EPA Factor 4, Narcissism, has the most subscales: self-assurance, dominance, self-contentment, arrogance, self-centeredness, and coldness.

TRIARCHIC PSYCHOPATHY MODEL

Patrick, Fowles, and Krueger (2009) set out to combine the ideas from all definitions of and diagnostic tools for psychopathy. Three main concepts within the psychopathic personality were identified: disinhibition, boldness, and meanness. They call their theory the **triarchic model of psychopathy**. The concept of disinhibition covered the aspects of the psychopathic personality related to impulsiveness and nonplanfulness. Boldness is a concept mostly derived from research on the PPI. It captures a psychopath's "capacity to remain calm and focused in situations involving pressure or threat, an ability to recover quickly from stressful events, high self-assurance and social efficacy, and a tolerance for unfamiliarity and danger" (Patrick et al., 2009, p. 926). Also similar to the PPI's coldheartedness concept, meanness encompasses the affective and interpersonal deficits of the psychopath. The 58-question self-report Triarchic Psychopathy Measure was created to measure the concepts of the triarchic psychopathy model.

Etiology

What makes a psychopath? Are they born or made? As noted earlier, Karpman and Lynam had similar ideas regarding different types of psychopathy based mostly on the cause of the disorder. These ideas have led to the common (mis)conception that psychopaths are born whereas sociopaths are made. Modern neuropsychology has mostly put an end to the idea of nature *versus* nurture. Time and again it has been proven that most human characteristics come from a mixture of biology and environment – both nature *and* nurture (see Chapter 2).

It seems psychopathy is no different. Adrian Raine is perhaps the leading scientist studying the etiology of psychopathy. His book with coauthor Andrea L. Glenn, *Psychopathy: An Introduction to Biological Findings and Their Implications*, covers the empirical evidence of several potential biological and environmental causes of psychopathy. The biological areas of psychopathy research are grouped into the source of the abnormality: genetic, hormonal, brain structure, and brain function. Just like nature and nurture, each of these areas of biology likely influence one another. But here is what we know so far about each of these areas individually.

Introduced in Chapter 2, behavioral genetics, the study of whether our genes influence our behavior, has contributed much to our understanding of psychopathy. Thanks to twin studies (see Chapter 2), scientists have found that psychopathic traits can be inherited from previous generations. The science of molecular genetics, the study of specific genes that influence various aspects of our being, is still in its infancy. And the answer to whether the genes for specific behaviors can be pinpointed is likely to be complicated. Molecular geneticists are finding that rarely does a single gene – or even a group of genes – directly cause any particular behavior or trait. Like most things, it is likely the interaction of multiple genes coupled with environmental factors that create who we are as a person. In fact, some research suggests that our environment – particularly early in life – can *alter* the expression of our genes.

The two hormonal culprits of psychopathic traits that have been studied are cortisol and testosterone. Higher levels of cortisol are indicative of a response to a stressful situation. Those with psychopathic traits have been found to have lower levels of cortisol. This may correspond with the psychopathic traits of fearlessness, disinhibition, and shallow affect. Testosterone is a male sex hormone, which may explain the overrepresentation of men with psychopathy. Additionally, many studies have found a link between high testosterone levels and traits or behaviors found in psychopathy, such as impulsivity, disinhibition, and lack of planning.

There is some evidence that the brains of psychopaths look and operate differently than those of the rest of us. The two most studied areas with the most consistent findings are the amygdala and the prefrontal cortex (see Chapter 2 for an overview of the brain). The amygdala, which is responsible for interpreting stimuli and regulating our emotional responses, may be under functioning and/or under developed (i.e., smaller) in psychopaths. What this means is that psychopaths may not be able to process information from their environment in an emotional way. This may contribute to their callousness, lack of empathy, and shallow affect. The prefrontal cortex is often considered the center of decision making and rational thought. It is what keeps our "reptilian brain" from acting on impulses. This area of the brain has been found to have much less gray matter in psychopaths. More specifically, the orbitofrontal area of the prefrontal cortex has recently been found to be both lower functioning and lacking in gray matter among psychopaths. Not surprisingly, the orbitofrontal region has been linked with the processing and understanding of emotions, both in ourselves and in others. This main function of this region of the brain means it also helps us understand the consequences of our actions and inhibit behaviors that may cause pain to ourselves or others. Research has also found a disconnect between the amygdala and orbitofrontal cortex of the brains of psychopaths, further impairing emotional processing. In short, the brains of psychopaths seem to be lacking in the areas responsible for understanding and processing emotions.

Glenn and Raine (2014) also discuss the environmental influences of psychopathy that researchers have discovered, including biosocial explanations of how the environment can influence our biology (see Chapter 2 for a full discussion of biopsychology and gene-environment interactions). "Emerging research suggests that environmental factors such as parenting, abuse, poverty, head injury, birth complication, nutrition, toxins, and a variety of other factors both within and outside the home many be associated with psychopathy" (Glenn & Raine, 2014, p. 146). Their book summarizes findings from the Cambridge Study in Delinquent Development (CSDD), a 40-year longitudinal study of 411 males – 304 of whom completed the PCL:SV at age 48. The CSDD found a correlation between adult psychopathy scores and both family conflict and inconsistent, severe childhood discipline. There is speculation that this correlation may be due to improper or unhealthy attachment between parent and child (see Chapter 4). Glenn and Raine (2014) point out that such early stress and/or trauma can cause the brain to permanently change the way it responds to stressful situations in the future.

Psychopathy in Youth

A diagnostic criterion for APD is that the subject must be 18 or older. Similarly, Hare initially advised that the PCL-R not be used to assess the behavior of children. Due to these factors, psychopathy has often not been used as a diagnosis for children or adolescents. Instead, the DSM diagnoses of **oppositional defiant disorder** (ODD) or **conduct disorder** (CD) are seen by some as precursors to a potential later diagnosis of psychopathy (or a DMS diagnosis of

Box 7.2 Was Columbine shooter Eric Harris a psychopath?

Even if you are not old enough to remember the massacre at Columbine High School in Littleton, Colorado on April 20, 1999, you have likely heard about it. Many people speculated at the time and since that the perpetrators, Eric Harris and Dylan Klebold, were seeking revenge for being bullied. Many believed that Harris and Klebold were part of the "Trench Coat Mafia," a group of kids who were teased for dressing in all black including long, black trench coats. According to Dave Cullen's book *Columbine*, the truth lies in the volatile mix of two personality types: a depressive and a psychopath.

Klebold was a typical teenager struggling with self-identity. He did not have a lot of friends, but he was not entirely an outcast either. He even had a date to prom. Harris, on the other hand, was somewhat popular. He was the cool rebel kid who got invited to parties. This may have been attributable to his charming swagger. The contents of Eric Harris's journal show other psychopathy characteristics.

Harris titled his journal "The Book of God." That is how he saw himself: as God. He believed he was superior to everyone else in every way – especially intellectually. In his journal, he admits to lying constantly just for the fun of deception. Harris had no long-term plans, apart from his year-in-the-making plan to attack his school. He relished in the planning. There was no sympathy at all for his future victims.

Supervisory Special Agent Dwayne Fuselier, the lead FBI agent on the Columbine investigation, was the first to suspect Eric Harris was a psychopath. A psychologist himself, Fuselier presented evidence of his diagnosis to a group of psychologists at a conference on school shooters organized by the FBI. Among those in attendance was Dr. Robert Hare. They all came to the consensus that Eric Harris had indeed been a psychopath.

For more on psychopathy and the massacre at Columbine High School: Cullen, D. (2009). *Columbine*. Twelve.

APD). ODD is characterized by a child who is often angry/irritable, argumentative/defiant, and vindictive. It is important to note that these symptoms must be pervasive and not directed solely at family members. The symptoms associated with CD are aggression toward people or animals, destruction of property, deceitfulness or theft, and serious violation of rules. Due to the lack of overlapping symptoms between either ODD or CD and traditional psychopathy symptoms, the DSM-5 added **conduct disorder with limited prosocial emotions** (CD+LPE). However, the addition of lack of remorse or guilt, callousness–lack of empathy, lack of concern about performance in important activities, and shallow or deficient affect (American Psychiatric Association, 2013) may still not accurately describe a fledgling psychopath. Scholars not committed to using DSM diagnoses have usually described youth who may have psychopathic tendencies as having callous-unemotional traits.

Noncriminal Psychopaths

Even though the symptoms of psychopathy make it seem that all psychopaths have criminal tendencies, there are noncriminal psychopaths. Scholars sometimes refer to these people as **successful psychopaths**. Although the definition of what is meant by "successful" varies, these psychopaths generally avoid criminal convictions and may even obtain high social status. Keep in mind that the absence of a criminal conviction does not necessarily mean these individuals do not engage in unethical and even illegal behavior. They are simply able to get away with it. Some are even able to find their way into careers that tend to value some of the traits that psychopaths possess. Babiak and Hare (2006) found that individuals in upper-level management positions in corporations are 3.5 times as likely to have psychopathic traits compared to the general population. Psychopathic traits such as being manipulative and charming may allow these successful psychopaths to weasel their way up the corporate ladder. Additionally, those who score high on the Fearless Dominance subscale of the PPI may be drawn to careers that offer risk taking, such as firefighting (Lilienfeld et al., 2014). There seems to be some indication that psychopathic traits may allow a few psychopaths to be successful rather than incarcerated.

Explaining Criminal Behavior

Psychopathy and Violence

Despite some evidence that a few psychopaths are "successful," research has shown a correlation between aggression and violent behavior and a psychopathy diagnosis. Aggression and violence can be classified in two ways: instrumental and reactive. **Instrumental violence** is premeditative and is a means to an end. It is "instrumental" in that it aids the person in gaining what they are truly after, often money or other material goods. **Reactive violence** is just that: a reaction to an immediate threat, real or perceived. Studies have shown that psychopaths are more likely than the general population to employ instrumental violence. This makes sense given their cold and calculating nature. However, there is some indication that psychopaths do engage in reactive violence as well. Some traits of psychopathy can cause seemingly unprovoked reactions from the psychopath. This has led some scholars to use the term "impulsively instrumental" to describe the aggressive behavior of some psychopaths (Porter et al, 2018).

In addition to physical violence, psychopathy is associated with relational aggression which often involves verbal threats and intimidation. Remember, psychopaths are willing to manipulate people in any way necessary to get what they want. Female psychopaths in particular turn to emotional and verbal abuse to control those who dare to get close to them. This often means their family members.

Psychopathy and Recidivism

Research has shown a correlation between PCL-R psychopathy (particularly Factor 2) and reoffending after release from incarceration. This and the relationship between psychopathy and aggressive, sometimes violent, behavior led the criminal justice system in some jurisdictions to rely on measures of psychopathy as assessments of an offender's risk to recidivate. The PCL-R has been the most often used measure of psychopathy for predicting recidivism. However, recent meta-analyses and the development of other risk assessment tools (see Chapter 13) have led to a decline in the use of the PCL-R in assessing risk for recidivism. In their meta-analysis, Rosenberg Larsen and colleagues (2020) found that Factor 1 items ("personality traits") were not predictive of recidivism, but Factor 2 "behavioral items" were. They argued that Factor 2 items are similar to other risk assessment tools made solely for assessing the risk of recidivism. Additionally, more recent risk assessment tools have been made to measure dynamic factors to determine changes in an offender's level of risk. Chapter 13 will more fully address the evolution of risk assessment tools.

Serial Murder

The definition of serial murder has evolved over the years, with most changes having to do with body count and a "cooling off period." While mass murders occur in a single event, the current FBI definition of serial murder is "[t]he unlawful killing of two or more victims by the same offender(s), in separate events" (Behavioral Analysis Unit, 2005, p. 9). There used to be a distinct category of multicide known as "spree murder." However, the only difference between a serial murderer and a spree murderer was the length of time between killings, known as the "cooling off period." Generally speaking, while a serial killer may go months without killing, a spree murderer commits his/her crimes in a matter of days or weeks. Without a clear consensus on the length of time necessary for the distinction, it was ultimately decided to do away with a separate "spree murder" category.

Are All Serial Murderers Psychopaths?

Now that you have a better understanding of what psychopathy actually is, hopefully, it is easier to see why not all serial killers are necessarily psychopathic. Not all of those who murder continuously are particularly charming, grandiose, or manipulative. Some serial killers have extensive and versatile criminal histories, and others compartmentalize their killings while leading otherwise "normal" lives. Lying is used mostly to conceal the crimes of some serial murderers, instead of the pathological lying of a true psychopath.

After reviewing the limited existing research and conducting PCL-R diagnoses of their own, Hickey and colleagues (2018) came up with a couple of conclusions regarding the juxtaposition of serial murder and psychopathy. They "hypothesize that only a small proportion of serial murderers are 'true psychopaths'" and "suggest that the main basis for a systematic association between the phenomenon of serial homicide and the diagnosis of psychopathy lies in the callous-unemotional (meanness) features represented in the Affective facet of the PCL-R" (p. 581).

Other Explanations for Serial Murder

There have also been other ideas offered to explain the crime of serial murder. Pettigrew (2020) analyzed one serial killer's confession using Sykes and Matza's (1957) techniques of neutralization (see Chapter 3). In 1993, Hale proclaimed learning theories (see Chapter 4) could explain serial murder with the subtitle "You too can learn to be a serial killer." Castle and Hensley (2002) took that idea and went so far as to say military training may teach serial murderers how to kill effectively. Atchison and Heide (2011) use a variety of criminological theories to make sense of the Manson "family" murders: labeling theory, general strain theory, and social learning theory. Then there is of course the MacDonald Triad, the idea that particular childhood behaviors – torturing animals, setting fires, and bed wetting, specifically – are predictive of future serial murder. Despite its proliferation, this trilogy of supposedly predictive behaviors has not been empirically supported (Parfitt & Alleyne, 2020).

Classifications of Serial Murder

Many scholars have sought to identify distinct groups of serial killers. Often these grouping are based on the killers' stated or presumed motivation for murdering multiple victims. Holmes and DeBurger (1985; later refined by Holmes & Holmes [2009] in their book *Serial Murder*) identified four types of serial murderer: visionary, mission-oriented, hedonistic, and power/control-oriented. The hedonistic type is further broken down into three more specific, pleasure-based motivations: lust, thrill, and comfort.

The visionary serial killer suffers from some form of mental illness, leading them to hear or see things that direct them to kill others. A common misconception is that David Berkowitz, the Son of Sam, was a visionary killer since he claimed his neighbor's dog told him to shoot people. However, this claim by Berkowitz was later recanted. The motivation for the mission-oriented serial killer is their belief that they are ridding the world of those they see as undesirable. An example of this type of killer is Gary Ridgway, the Green River Killer, who killed prostitutes. However, given that he often had sex with his victims prior to or while killing them, his disdain for prostitutes may be questionable. Killing is primarily a source of pleasure for the hedonistic serial killer. The exact source of this pleasure may vary, resulting in the subtypes of the hedonistic serial killer. Lust is perhaps the most common motivation for a serial killer. The hedonistic lust killer derives sexual pleasure from the murder itself or through necrophilia. A possible tie for the most common motivation for a serial killer is the thrill. The hedonistic thrill killer simply enjoys killing people. They get excited, though not necessarily sexually, from taking another's life. The primary motivation for the hedonistic comfort killer is gaining some comfort in life, usually money or other material gains. Finally, the power/control-oriented serial killer enjoys "playing God." Their motivation for killing is the complete domination of another human being. Invoking fear in their victims may be a part of the motivation as well.

Another serial killer typology based on presumed motivation came from the San Antonio Symposium, a meeting of homicide detectives and criminologists organized by the FBI's Behavioral Analysis Unit in 2005. It is clear that there is much overlap with the Holmes typology, with some nuanced additions. The following are the primary motivations of serial killers identified by those at the San Antonio Symposium:

- **Anger** is a motivation in which an offender displays rage or hostility toward a certain subgroup of the population or with society as a whole.
- **Criminal Enterprise** is a motivation in which the offender benefits in status or monetary compensation by committing murder that is drug, gang, or organized crime related.
- **Financial gain** is a motivation in which the offender benefits monetarily from killing. Examples of these types of crimes are "black widow" killings, robbery homicides, or multiple killings involving insurance or welfare fraud.
- **Ideology** is a motivation to commit murders in order to further the goals and ideas of a specific individual or group. Examples of these include terrorist groups or individual(s) who attack a specific racial, gender, or ethnic group.
- **Power/thrill** is a motivation in which the offender feels empowered and/or excited when he kills his victims.
- **Psychosis** is a situation in which the offender is suffering from a severe mental illness and is killing because of that illness. This may include auditory and/or visual hallucinations and paranoid, grandiose, or bizarre delusions.
- **Sexually-based** is a motivation driven by the sexual needs/desires of the offender. There may or may not be overt sexual contact reflected in the crime scene (Behavioral Analysis Unit, 2005, p. 18).

It is likely that these types intersect, with the same serial killer having multiple motivations. It should also be noted that the utility of these typologies has been questioned. One use of serial killer typologies may be to help apprehend an active serial killer. This was the goal of perhaps the most well-known serial murder dichotomy: organized versus unorganized. Indeed, this typology created by members of the Behavioral Science Unit within the FBI's Training Division was designed for criminal profiling, which will be fully covered in Chapter 9.

Summary

A psychopath has very specific characteristics. The correct means for diagnosing psychopathy are still being debated. What is certain is they are not like the rest of us, but they are not as "crazy" as people might think. Some psychopaths can be very successful in life, and not all serial killers are psychopaths. Serial killers are unique though. Despite attempts to classify types of serial killers, the truth may be that the motivation to murder multiple people may come from a combination of these "types." Though it is fascinating to try to understand both of these rare categories of individuals, it may ultimately be difficult to fully comprehend these complex people.

References

American Psychiatric Association. (2013). *Diagnostic and statistical manual of mental disorders* (5th ed.). American Psychiatric Publishing, Inc.

Atchison, A. J., & Heide, K. M. (2011). Charles Manson and the family: The application of sociological theories to multiple murder. *International Journal of Offender Therapy and Comparative Criminology*, *55*(5), 771–798.

Babiak, P., & Hare, R. D. (2006). *Snakes in suits: When psychopaths go to work*. HarperCollins.

Behavioral Analysis Unit. (2005). *Serial murder: Multi-disciplinary perspectives for investigators*. Federal Bureau of Investigation. https://www.fbi.gov/file-repository/stats-services-publications-serial-murder-serial-murder-july-2008-pdf

Castle, T., & Hensley, C. (2002). Serial killers with military experience: Applying learning theory to serial murder. *International Journal of Offender Therapy and Comparative Criminology*, *46*(4), 453–465.

Cleckley, H. M. (1941). *The mask of sanity*. The C.V. Mosby Company.

Cooke, D. J., & Logan, C. (2018). Capturing psychopathic personality: Penetrating the mask of sanity through clinical interview. In C. J. Patrick (Ed.), *Handbook of psychopathy* (2nd ed.). The Guilford Press.

Cullen, D. (2009). *Columbine*. Twelve.

Glenn, A. L., & Raine, A. (2014). *Psychopathy: An introduction to biological findings and their implications*. New York University Press.

Hale, R. L. (1993). The application of learning theory to serial murder or "you too can learn to be a serial killer." *American Journal of Criminal Justice*, *17*(2), 37–45.

Hare, R. D. (1993). *Without conscience: The disturbing world of the psychopaths among us*. The Guilford Press.

Hickey, E. W., Walters, B. K., Drislane, L. E., Palumbo, I. M., & Patrick, C. J. (2018). Deviance at its darkest. In C. J. Patrick (Ed.), *Handbook of psychopathy* (2nd ed.). The Guilford Press.

Hicks, B. M., & Drislane, L. E. (2018). Variants ("subtypes") of psychopathy. In C. J. Patrick (Ed.), *Handbook of psychopathy* (2nd ed.). The Guilford Press.

Hughes, M. A., Stout, J. C., & Dolan, M. C. (2013). Concurrent validity of the psychopathic personality inventory-revised and the psychopathy checklist screening version in an Australian offender sample. *Criminal Justice & Behavior*, *40*(7), 802–813.

Holmes, R. M., & DeBurger, J. E. (1985). Profiles in terror: The serial murderer. *Federal Probation*, *49*(3), 29–34.

Holmes, R. M., & Holmes, S. T. (2009). *Serial murder* (3rd ed.). SAGE.

Karpman, B. (1948). The myth of psychopathic personality. *American Journal of Psychiatry*, *103*, 523–534.

Lilienfeld, S. O., & Andrews, B. P. (1996). Development and preliminary validation of a self-report measure of psychopathic personality traits in noncriminal populations. *Journal of Personality Assessment*, *66*(3), 488–524.

Lilienfeld, S. O., Latzman, R. D., Watts, A. L., Smith, S. F., & Dutton, K. (2014). Correlates of psychopathic personality traits in everyday life: Results from a large community survey. *Frontiers in Psychology*, *5*, 740.
Lykken, D. T. (1995). *The antisocial personalities*. Routledge.
Lynam, D. R., Gaughan, E. T., Miller, J. D., Miller, D. J., Mullins-Sweatt, S., & Widiger, T. A. (2011). Assessing the basic traits associated with psychopathy: Development and validation of the Elemental Psychopathy Assessment. *Psychological Assessment*, *23*(1), 108–124.
Parfitt, C. H., & Alleyne, E. (2020). Not the sum of its parts: A critical review of the MacDonald Triad. *Trauma, Violence, & Abuse*, *21*(2), 300–310.
Patrick, C. J. (2018). Psychopathy as masked pathology. In C. J. Patrick (Ed.), *Handbook of psychopathy* (2nd ed.). The Guilford Press.
Patrick, C. J., Fowles, D. C., & Krueger, R. F. (2009). Triarchic conceptualization of psychopathy: Developmental origins of disinhibition, boldness, and meanness. *Development and Psychopathology*, *21*(3), 913–938.
Pettigrew, M. (2020). Confession of a serial killer: A neutralization analysis. *Homicide Studies*, *24*(1), 69–84.
Porter, S., Woodworth, M. T., & Black, P. J. (2018). Psychopathy and aggression. In C. J. Patrick (Ed.), *Handbook of psychopathy* (2nd ed.). The Guilford Press.
Rosenberg Larsen, R., Jalava, J., & Griffiths, S. (2020). Are Psychopathy Checklist (PCL) psychopaths dangerous, untreatable, and without conscience? A systematic review of the empirical evidence. *Psychology, Public Policy, and Law*, *26*(3), 297–311.
Sellbom, M., Lilienfeld, S. O., Fowler, K. A., & McCrary, K. L. (2018). The self-report assessment of psychopathy: Challenges, pitfalls, and promises. In C. J. Patrick (Ed.), *Handbook of psychopathy* (2nd ed.). The Guilford Press.
Sykes, G. M., & Matza, D. (1957). Techniques of neutralization: A theory of delinquency. *American Sociological Review*, *22*(6), 664–670.

Part Two

The Criminal Justice System

8 Mental Illness, Trauma, and Substance Use

Introduction

The first part of this textbook focused on explanations for criminal behavior derived from various psychological disciplines. However, if you ask a psychologist working with justice-involved populations, they would likely say the biggest psychological issues among their clientele are mental illness, trauma, and substance use. But do these issues cause criminal behavior? Or are they separate issues that happen to coincide with the things that can lead to criminal behavior? Throughout this chapter, we will see how the criminal justice system responds in the areas where mental illness, trauma, and substance use intersect with the law.

Mental Illness and Criminal Behavior

Mental illness has a long history of being criminalized. Throughout most of civilized history, symptoms of severe mental illness were instead thought to be symptoms of the dangerously supernatural, such as demonic possession or witchcraft. This fear of what was not yet well understood led to abhorrent treatment of the mentally ill, including executions. Those who were not killed were usually locked away, so as not to have to be dealt with. This often meant being warehoused in horrible conditions in jails, the predominate source of secure housing until the mid-nineteenth century.

In the 1840s, a future civil war nurse named Dorothea Dix came along to change this poor treatment of the mentally ill. Beginning in New England, she visited jails all over the country. Having witnessed the abuses of those with mental illness in these facilities, Dix advocated for separate institutions for the mentally ill who had no family able or willing to care for them. She and other advocates lobbied state legislatures, and the government-run psychiatric hospital was born. This movement of the mentally ill from jails to state-funded mental institutions is known as **transinstitutionalization**, since inmates/patients were being moved from one institution to another. Unfortunately, these new facilities were not well-run or well-funded, and the poor treatment of the severely mentally ill (SMI) continued into the twentieth century despite the efforts of Dix and other advocates.

Deinstitutionalization

The mid-twentieth century saw a push for equal rights for marginalized groups. While this time is most notably associated with the fight for civil rights for Black Americans, civil rights for those with mental illness were sought too. The continued maltreatment of the mentally ill housed in psychiatric institutions led to a new push to treat these individuals

DOI: 10.4324/9781003250821-10

on an out-patient basis in the community instead. It was believed that those with mental illnesses should be allowed to live in the community where they could live more independent lives with the help of community mental health centers for treatment of their mental illness. This was also seen as being more cost-effective for government funding, as the price of room and board for in-patient services left less money for quality treatment programs. The move of psychiatric patients out of in-patient hospitals and into the community, followed by the closure of many in-patient psychiatric facilities, is known as **deinstitutionalization.**

The intention of deinstitutionalization was an increase in community-based mental health centers to care for those discharged from the in-patient facilities. In 1963, Congress passed the **Community Mental Health Act (CMHA)** to build centers to deliver mental health care on an out-patient basis. With the promise of federal funding to establish the needed facilities in the community, the CMHA was perhaps the biggest driver in the closure of many state-run mental hospitals. However, only about half of the 1,500 community-based facilities called for in the legislation were ever built, and adequate funding, both initially and on-going, never materialized.

The promise of community-based treatment was also bolstered by the pharmaceutical boom of the mid-twentieth century. It was thought that drugs such as Thorazine, a powerful antipsychotic heavily marketed in the 1950s and 1960s, would make treating the SMI in the community easier. However, even if a "miracle drug" is prescribed, those with SMI have a tendency to stop voluntarily taking their medication causing them to **decompensate**, or experience a resurgence or worsening of the symptoms of their mental illness.

When someone with severe mental illness is on the proper medication, their symptoms lessen. This reduction of symptoms can cause someone to believe they are "better" and no longer need the medication. As anyone who has seen a pharmaceutical commercial knows, prescription medications often have unpleasant side effects. This combination of undesirable side effects and a feeling of symptom improvement – not to mention the high cost of prescription medications – are the reasons those with SMI sometimes stop voluntarily taking their medication. As mentioned, this causes them to decompensate, and the resurgence of disturbing symptoms can lead to involvement with the criminal justice system. The silver lining is that those sentenced to jail or prison will likely be administered their medication while incarcerated, leading to a renewed stabilization of symptoms. If they are released back into the community, they may again stop taking their medication, decompensate, and land back in jail. This is one of the many ways in which our criminal justice system tends to have a "revolving door."

The nail in the coffin for government-funded in-patient mental health institutions was the Supreme Court of the United States' (SCOTUS) ruling in *Wyatt v. Stickney* (1972). SCOTUS declared that those with mental illness have a "right to treatment," and that they were not getting such treatment in the asylums of the preceding century. Ironically, the "right to treatment" led to further deinstitutionalization that was not fully met with treatment facilities in the community. Therefore, the "right to treatment" led to even fewer treatment opportunities for those experiencing severe mental illness. It should be noted, and may not be surprising, that the negative effects of deinstitutionalization were disproportionately experienced by those with fewer financial resources to secure a bed in a private (i.e., not government funded) psychiatric in-patient facility.

Another ironic outcome of the deinstitutionalization movement was a sort of reverse transinstitutionalization. As the government-funded in-patient mental health institutions closed, and few government-funded out-patient facilities materialized, those with severe mental illness (and little money) were left with insufficient help. The disruptive and sometimes dangerous behavior of these individuals caused them to get "caught up" in the criminal justice system. As a result, jails and prisons saw an increase in inmates with severe mental illnesses. Deinstitutionalization has also been cited as one source of the mass incarceration boom during the second half of the twentieth century.

The inverse relationship of the population sizes of psychiatric hospitals and correctional institutions is not a new idea. The **Penrose hypothesis**, named for Lionel Penrose who first suggested it in 1939, states that as the population of one of these institutions decreases, the population of the other institution will increase. This has also been called the transinstitutionalization hypothesis. It has been well established that the number of people with a psychiatric diagnosis is far greater in correctional institutions than in the general public (Hall et al., 2019). The Penrose hypothesis places blame for this fact directly on deinstitutionalization; an increase in the numbers of inmates with mental illness was inevitable with the closing of state-funded mental institutions, according to the transinstitutionalization hypothesis. While this hypothesis makes some intuitive sense, it has not been empirically proven. This may be partly due to difficulty in isolating the effects of one variable in a complex system. And like many things in the social sciences, the truth likely involves more than just one factor (i.e., deinstitutionalization). As we will discuss later in this chapter, the so-called War on Drugs is also often implicated in the mass incarceration boom.

In 2011, Prins outlined the multiple likely reasons for the higher proportion of mental illness in correctional facilities. He noted that those opposed to the Penrose hypothesis suggest that the populations of SMI now in prisons and jails are demographically distinct from those who would have been housed in state-funded psychiatric institutions. While those who had previously lived their whole lives in mental institutions were predominately white and schizophrenic, the majority of correctional inmates with SMI are Black with myriad diagnoses. This means that "reinstitutionalization," or rebuilding more government-run mental health hospitals, would likely not alleviate the problem of SMI within correctional facilities.

Prins (2011) also cites a study of justice-system involvement within five years of release from a long-term psychiatric facility in London, England. Leff and his colleagues (2000) followed 700 patients released upon the closing of two mental hospitals near London and found that just 2.6% of them had a "recorded criminal incident" (Prins, 2011, p. 719) within five years, though some were responsible for multiple offenses. These findings are similar to at least three other studies tracking specific individuals after their release from psychiatric in-patient services in the USA (Erickson et al., 2008; McGrew et al., 1999; Rothbard et al., 1999). Even proponents of the Penrose hypothesis concede that some percentage of SMI could be served with adequate community-based care, with only a small portion needing long-term in-patient care. The main takeaway from this debate, according to Prins (2011), is that there is no one-size-fits-all approach to caring for SMI citizens.

Are People with Severe Mental Illness More Likely to Commit Crime?

The short answer to whether the public should be afraid of those with SMI is a resounding no. It seems as though, perhaps like the general population, only a small percentage of those with SMI commit violent acts. The vast majority of individuals with SMI are not violent or dangerous. In fact, research has shown that those with SMI are actually more likely to experience violent victimization than the general public (Latalova et al., 2014). In recent years, there has also been increased news coverage of incidents where someone with SMI experiencing serious symptoms was killed by police (more on this later in the chapter).

While the vast majority of those with severe mental illness do *not* commit violent crimes, there is reason to be concerned for the health and safety of both citizens with severe mental illness and others whom they encounter. The groups most at risk of experiencing psychiatric symptoms that lead to violence are those whose symptoms are hallucinatory, paranoid, and/or delusional, which are part of a group of symptoms known as **psychosis**. The diagnoses most associated with these symptoms are schizophrenia spectrum disorders and bipolar disorder. A meta-analysis conducted by Whiting and colleagues (2022) found that those with schizophrenia spectrum disorders were three times more likely than the general population to perpetrate a violent crime. This risk increased to 10 times more likely than the general population when the individual also had a substance use disorder. A longitudinal study on the effects of bipolar disorder on violent offending and a systematic review of previous studies on the topic also found an increase in risk for violence when bipolar individuals also had a substance use disorder diagnosis (Fazel et al., 2010). However, a more recent systematic review and meta-analysis on the connection between bipolar disorder and violence found no statistical difference in violent criminality when comparing those diagnosed with bipolar disorder to the general population (Verdolini et al., 2018).

To address these mixed findings, Lamberti and his colleagues (2020) examined existing literature on the subject to try to determine whether the relationship between psychosis, mania, and criminal behavior is causal (i.e., the psychosis or mania directly caused the criminal behavior). They came to five conclusions. First, psychotic or manic symptoms are rarely a direct cause of criminal behavior, but this is still an important fraction of the offending population. Second, those with SMI are more likely to experience other factors empirically associated with increased criminal behavior (factors known as criminogenic needs; see Chapter 13). Third, symptoms of psychosis and mania are likely to impact a person's ability to engage in and benefit from treatment programs. (This is known as responsivity and is also covered in more detail in Chapter 13.) Fourth, co-occurring psychosis/mania and chronic substance use may be a particularly criminogenic combination: "Substance use is known to be associated with medication nonadherence, emergence of psychotic and manic symptoms, and worsening of the course of illness among individuals with schizophrenia or bipolar disorder" (Lamberti et al., 2020, p. 195). Finally, the stigma associated with SMI may lead to escalated interactions with law enforcement and more restrictive management in correctional facilities. This stigma likely stems from media coverage of violent acts perpetrated by those with SMI (even though these are rare occurrences) and the insistence by the media and politicians that mass shootings are a result of SMI, even though this is also empirically rare (see Peterson et al., 2022).

Lamsma and her colleagues (2019) confirmed the increased risk of violence when those with SMI use a wide variety of substances. They also described several possible reasons for increased violence risk among SMI who regularly use substances. As will be discussed later in this chapter, the first reason is simply due to the psychological and physiological effects of substances of abuse and/or the effects of symptoms of withdrawal from these drugs. More specifically for SMI, the use of drugs not prescribed by a doctor may increase, alter, or worsen psychotic symptoms – not to mention the risk of producing any interaction effects with prescribed medications the person may be taking. This alludes to the final reason substance use may interact with SMI to increase the chances of violent behavior. "Individuals with problematic substance use are less likely to seek and adhere to treatment than those without these substance problems" (Lamsma et al., 2019, p. 2031).

Ways to Better Care for Those with Severe Mental Illness

Even though only a small percentage of those with SMI commit violent acts, the best place for those experiencing severe symptoms of mental illness is most likely not a correctional facility. Thankfully, research has identified interventions at each point in the criminal justice process (i.e., policing, courts, and corrections) to help those with SMI who find themselves involved with the justice system.

Policing

Given the news coverage in recent years of those experiencing a mental health crisis being killed by police, it is not surprising that police response models (PRMs) for handling citizens with SMI have been the subject of a lot of research. The **Crisis Intervention Team (CIT)** model has been the most implemented and the most studied PRM. CIT trains police officers to recognize symptoms of mental illness and de-escalate a crisis situation. CIT utilizes existing police officers selected to be specially trained to serve on the CIT; usually only a fraction of a department's force is trained to be on the CIT. Emergency dispatch personnel are also trained to assign calls for service which involve a mental health crisis to the CIT team of police officers. This training is extensive, time-consuming, and, therefore, expensive. A recent meta-analysis found that while CIT improved police understanding and sympathy for those experiencing a mental health crisis, the effects on outcomes for the citizen (e.g., decreased chance of arrest or use-of-force) were small (Seo et al., 2021).

The next most common PRM for handling mental-illness-related calls for service is some form of **co-response model**. These approaches involve on-call mental health professionals whom police can call when they arrive at a scene where one or more citizens appear to be in psychological distress. Unfortunately, this PRM increases response time to address the mental health crisis, as mental health professionals are not typically dispatched directly from emergency call centers. Despite this lag in response time, the meta-analysis by Seo and his colleagues (2021) found that co-response PRMs resulted in better outcomes than CIT and other models. This led the research team to conclude that "collaborations between mental health professionals and law enforcement officers in co-response models may be more effective in handling police encounters with the mentally ill than providing training to frontline officers" (Seo et al., 2021, p. 11). Indeed, diverting government funding from the police force to public mental health services (including mental health first responders) is one suggestion of the poorly named movement to "Defund the Police." Rather than the anti-police movement it is often made out to be, calls to defund the police are usually appeals to fund other government programs and services that *support* police officers in their interactions with SMI (albeit by taking funds away from police departments).

Courts

When someone with a mental illness commits a crime, they should be arrested like anyone else. However, an increasing number of special therapeutic courts have been put in place to divert certain populations from more punitive sanctions into treatment programs instead. So-called "problem solving courts" are in place for low-level drug offenders (drug courts; more later in this chapter), former military personnel (veterans courts), and those with mental health issues (mental health courts), to name a few. Mental health courts are covered more in Chapter 11. For now, suffice to say that there are good options for keeping those with SMI out of prison and accountable to community treatment programs.

Corrections

Inevitably, even if the above programs are implemented, some people with SMI will commit serious crimes and justifiably be sent to a correctional facility. As covered more thoroughly in Chapter 14, prison time need not be idle time, and most correctional facilities have rehabilitation programs. For those with SMI, being incarcerated can mean stable medication and therefore fewer or milder symptoms. However, there is intriguing new research that suggests that moral reasoning training may be beneficial for those with psychotic symptoms who have perpetrated violent acts.

A 2019 study by O'Reilly and his colleagues found that moral cognitions (i.e., ways in which we think about what is right and what is wrong) helped explain the connection between psychosis and violent behavior. This finding was further supported by an evaluation of Moral Reasoning Development Intervention (MRDI) with schizophrenics with a history of violence (Hsu & Ouyang, 2022). MRDI is a treatment program similar to Moral Reconation Therapy, covered in Chapter 3. Hsu and Ouyang (2022) not only found that MRDI decreased violent behavior, but that it "may have helped individuals with mental disorders strengthen their willpower to engage in self-care skills, improve interpersonal relationships, and promote decision-making for behavior changes" (p. 1183). However, much more research is needed, since this is a new area of study.

Trauma and Criminal Behavior

You may have heard the phrase "hurt people hurt people." This is not just a saying popularized on social media; there is empirical research that shows those who commit crimes and violence are much more likely to have trauma in their past (and present). In 2014, the Substance Abuse and Mental Health Services Association (SAMHSA) published a report outlining the concept of trauma and suggestions for working with people who have had one or more traumatic experiences, known as a trauma-informed approach.

What Is Trauma?

The first step in a trauma-informed approach is defining trauma. According to SAMHSA (2014),

> [i]ndividual trauma results from an *event*, series of events, or set of circumstances that is *experienced* by an individual as physically or emotionally harmful or life threatening and that has lasting adverse *effects* on the individual's functioning and mental, physical, social, emotional, or spiritual well-being (p. 7; emphasis in original).

The words italicized in the above definition are called the three "e"s of trauma (see Table 8.1). The first "e" is event, which refers to the fact that trauma is usually related to something that happened to the person. This could be a single event, such as surviving the terrorist attacks on

Table 8.1 The three "e"s of trauma (SAMHSA, 2014).

Event: The initial incident or circumstance which caused the trauma. This can be a single event, a series of events or a set of circumstances.
Experience: The subjective way an individual responds to an event. Everyone will not experience the same event in the same way.
Effects: The array of psychological and physiological responses to trauma. The effects of trauma also vary from person to person.

September 11, 2001. Or it could be a series of events, such as repeated child sexual abuse. An "event" could also be a traumatic set of circumstances, such as growing up and/or living in a community with a history of being over-policed (see Chapter 9). The second "e" refers to the individual's experience of the event. It is important to remember that experiences are subjective. This means that different people may "experience" the same event in different ways. An event that is experienced as traumatic for one person may not be felt as trauma by someone else. The way someone "experiences" trauma will lead to its "effects," the third "e." Adverse effects of trauma are relatively easy to identify, but may not be cognitively connected to the traumatic event(s). This is because the effects of trauma are also often unique to the individual. Some will experience adverse effects of trauma immediately and either ongoing or only for a short time. For others, the effects of trauma may not surface until years or decades after the event. SAMHSA (2014) gave some examples of the effects of trauma: "inability to cope with the normal stresses and strains of daily living; to trust and benefit from relationships; to manage cognitive processes, such as memory, attention, [and] thinking; to regulate behavior; or to control the expression of emotions" (p. 8). Adverse effects of trauma can also be the more severe symptoms associated with a diagnosis of post-traumatic stress disorder (PTSD), such as hypervigilance or seeming "jumpy," avoiding triggers, and even flashbacks or nightmares about the event (see Table 8.2 for the full diagnostic criteria for PTSD from the fifth edition of the *Diagnostic and Statistical Manual of Mental Disorders*).

Table 8.2 Diagnostic criteria for post-traumatic stress disorder (American Psychiatric Association, 2013, pp. 271–272).

A Exposure to actual or threatened death, serious injury, or sexual violence in one (or more) of the following ways:

1 Directly experiencing the traumatic event(s).
2 Witnessing, in person, the event(s) as it occurred to others.
3 Learning that the traumatic event(s) occurred to a close family member or close friend. In cases of actual or threatened death of a family member or friend, the event(s) must have been violent or accidental.
4 Experiencing repeated or extreme exposure to aversive details of the traumatic event(s) (e.g., first responders collecting human remains; police officers repeatedly exposed to details of child abuse). **Note:** Criterion A4 does not apply to exposure through electronic media, television, movies, or pictures, unless this exposure is work related.

B Presence of one (or more) of the following intrusion symptoms associated with the traumatic event(s), beginning after the traumatic event(s) occurred:

1 Recurrent, involuntary, and intrusive distressing memories of the traumatic event(s). **Note:** In children older than 6 years, repetitive play may occur in which themes or aspects of the traumatic event(s) are expressed.
2 Recurrent distressing dreams in which the content and/or effect of the dream are related to the traumatic event(s). **Note:** In children, there may be frightening dreams without recognizable content.
3 Dissociative reactions (e.g., flashbacks) in which the individual feels or acts as if the traumatic event(s) were recurring. (Such reactions may occur on a continuum, with the most extreme expression being a complete loss of awareness of present surroundings.) **Note:** In children, trauma-specific reenactment may occur in play.
4 Intense or prolonged psychological distress at exposure to internal or external cues that symbolize or resemble an aspect of the traumatic event(s).
5 Marked physiological reactions to internal or external cues that symbolize or resemble an aspect of the traumatic event(s).

(*Continued*)

Table 8.2 (Continued)

C Persistent avoidance of stimuli associated with the traumatic event(s), beginning after the traumatic event(s) occurred, as evidenced by one or both of the following:

1 Avoidance of or efforts to avoid distressing memories, thoughts, or feelings about or closely associated with the traumatic event(s).
2 Avoidance of or efforts to avoid external reminders (people, places, conversations, activities, objects, situations) that arouse distressing memories, thoughts, or feelings about or closely associated with the traumatic event(s).

D Negative alterations in cognitions and mood associated with the traumatic event(s), beginning or worsening after the traumatic event(s) occurred, as evidenced by two (or more) of the following:

1 Inability to remember an important aspect of the traumatic event(s) (typically due to dissociative amnesia, and not to other factors such as head injury, alcohol, or drugs).
2 Persistent and exaggerated negative beliefs or expectations about oneself, others, or the world (e.g., "I am bad," "No one can be trusted," "The world is completely dangerous," "My whole nervous system is permanently ruined").
3 Persistent, distorted cognitions about the cause or consequences of the traumatic event(s) that lead the individual to blame himself/herself or others.
4 Persistent negative emotional state (e.g., fear, horror, anger, guilt, or shame).
5 Markedly diminished interest or participation in significant activities.
6 Feelings of detachment or estrangement from others.
7 Persistent inability to experience positive emotions (e.g., inability to experience happiness, satisfaction, or loving feelings).

E Marked alterations in arousal and reactivity associated with the traumatic event(s), beginning or worsening after the traumatic event(s) occurred, as evidenced by two (or more) of the following:

1 Irritable behavior and angry outbursts (with little or no provocation), typically expressed as verbal or physical aggression toward people or objects.
2 Reckless or self-destructive behavior.
3 Hypervigilance.
4 Exaggerated startle response.
5 Problems with concentration.
6 Sleep disturbance (e.g., difficulty falling or staying asleep or restless sleep).

F Duration of the disturbance (Criteria B, C, D, and E) is more than 1 month.

G The disturbance causes clinically significant distress or impairment in social, occupational, or other important areas of functioning.

H The disturbance is not attributable to the physiological effects of a substance (e.g., medication, alcohol) or another medical condition.

Unfortunately, trauma is fairly common in the human experience. Most of us have experienced some form of trauma at some point in our lives. Interestingly, research has found that "trauma" need not be overly extreme to have negative effects. Childhood adversity and/or experiencing multiple different distressing events or circumstances throughout life (i.e., cumulative effects) can lead to a number of detrimental consequences for both mental and physical health. We turn now to research on these adverse childhood experiences or ACEs.

Adverse Childhood Experiences

Beginning in the 1980s, a group of researchers from Kaiser Permanente and the Centers for Disease Control and Prevention (CDC) conducted a robust study on the impact of various childhood experiences on a wide variety of adult health outcomes. The survey asked almost 20,000 patients about ten **adverse childhood experiences (ACEs)** which fit

Table 8.3 Ten adverse childhood experiences (ACEs; Hays-Grudo & Morris, 2020).

Abuse	1	Emotional abuse
	2	Physical abuse
	3	Sexual abuse
Neglect	4	Emotional neglect
	5	Physical neglect
Family dysfunction	6	Domestic violence
	7	Household substance use
	8	Household mental illness
	9	Parental separation or divorce
	10	Household criminality

into three categories: "*abuse*—emotional, physical, and sexual; *neglect*—emotional and physical; and *family dysfunction*—domestic violence, household substance use, household mental illness, parental separation or divorce, or household criminality" (Hays-Grudo & Morris, 2020, p. 5; emphasis in original; see Table 8.3). It was discovered that ACEs are unfortunately quite common; the original ACE study found that 52% of respondents had experienced at least one ACE (Felitti et al., 1998). Additionally, an increase in the number of different ACEs, known as cumulative ACEs, corresponds with an increase in negative outcomes. Research often cites four or more ACEs as the threshold of concern (Hughes et al., 2017). Two meta-analyses found significant increases in anxiety, depression, drug and alcohol abuse, adult violent victimization, and suicide attempts when four or more ACEs were reported (Hughes et al., 2017; Sahle et al., 2022). Criminal justice researchers have specifically explored the possible connection between ACEs and offending behavior.

ACEs and Offending

Perhaps unsurprisingly, most research on the effect of ACEs on offending has been conducted with juveniles. It has been assumed that ACEs would be most likely to affect behaviors close in time to when the trauma occurred: childhood. ACEs may have a long-term impact on behavior as well, but more research is needed on adult populations.

Due to the abundance of research on the effect of ACEs on juvenile offending, systematic reviews have been possible. Malvaso and her colleagues (2022) identified 124 studies from across the world to assess the prevalence of ACEs among juvenile delinquents. Results of this systematic review showed that almost 87% of youth involved in the justice system had experienced at least one ACE. The average number of ACEs reported across all included studies was 2.33, below the commonly mentioned four or more ACEs benchmark. However, the authors were able to determine that an average of 11.2% of juveniles across all studies experienced enough trauma symptoms to meet the diagnostic criteria for PTSD (see Table 8.2). Astridge and her colleagues (2023) also conducted a meta-analysis of 31 studies on the effects of ACEs on youth recidivism. They found that "a greater number of ACEs was associated with a 99.1% increase in the odds of youth reoffending" (Astridge et al., 2023, p. 11). Experiencing childhood neglect and/or physical abuse were specifically related to increased recidivism among juvenile offenders. The authors cite insecure attachment as a possible reason for this finding (see Chapter 3).

It is important to note that research has yet to determine a *causal* relationship between ACEs/trauma and offending or violent behavior. It is therefore possible that the life circumstances that increase the likelihood of trauma also increase the likelihood of offending behavior. One may not cause the other; instead, something else may be causing both. Further research is needed, particularly more longitudinal studies that can better investigate causal relationships between variables.

Trauma, Mental Illness, and Substance Use

The same meta-analysis that identified the four-ACEs threshold (Hughes et al., 2017) also reported a link between trauma, mental illness, and "problematic substance abuse" (p. e365). These three negative outcomes were most prevalent when cumulative ACEs were experienced. Hughes and her colleagues (2017) also pointed out the intergenerational implications of these negative outcomes, because they "can represent ACEs for the next generation (exposure to parental domestic violence, mental illness, and substance use)" (p. e365). Another recent meta-analysis conducted by Ranu and her colleagues (2022) found that not only can a history of ACEs help explain the variability in violence perpetration among SMI, but it is possible that ACEs can lead directly to SMI as well.

Substance Use and Criminal Behavior

We have seen much overlap in the issues of severe mental illness, trauma, and substance use already in this chapter. The empirical evidence has confirmed that these issues often co-occur in the same individual. Substance use in particular has long been common among those with trauma and/or severe mental illness as a form of "self-medication." This is particularly true for those also experiencing poverty, as they likely do not have access to quality physical and mental health care. People turn to street drugs as a last resort for relief of their suffering, whether mental or physical. Experiencing a combination of mental illness and substance use disorder is so common that it has a name: **dual-diagnosis.** You may also hear the terms comorbidity or co-occurring disorders. These terms are also used for other issues that occur together. However, they are most often referring to the co-occurrence of mental illness and substance use disorder as this combination is so common.

The War on Drugs

America began its War on Drugs in 1971, with then President Richard Nixon proclaiming "America's public enemy number one in the United States is drug abuse. In order to fight and defeat this enemy, it is necessary to wage a new, all-out offensive." Since this declaration, the United States government has spent over $1 trillion in fighting this war that most people not only see as a failure but as having caused immense harm to the American people. Grecco and Andrew Chambers (2019) go even further:

> [T]he core strategy of the War on Drugs, through punishing drug use and closely related behavior, represents Harm Amplification, where various primary and secondary damages associated with having the disease are deliberately compounded by the criminal justice system (e.g., via public humiliation, financial penalties, and incarceration), in hopes that this will motivate effort in the individual to abandon their addiction. (p. 7)

Grecco and Andrew Chambers (2019) also suggest that the War on Drugs worsened the Penrose effect. Given the prevalence of dual-diagnosis of a mental illness and substance use disorder, the authors propose that criminalizing drug use only increases the likelihood that those with SMI who self-medicate or otherwise use illicit substances will end up in the criminal justice system. Some may justify this by citing the data showing those with dual-diagnoses are more likely to be violent. However, the criminal-legal approach has done very little to *treat* these illnesses, perhaps understandably so since the criminal justice system is not equipped to provide psychiatric treatment. Nonetheless, problems for these individuals and society will persist if these issues are not properly treated.

Crime and Drug Use

The War on Drugs helped create the perception that illicit drug users are dangerous. Indeed, the idea that illicit drug markets and drug users themselves are a threat to society was touted as the reason for their criminalization and the harsh penalties for violating drug laws. In 1985, Paul Goldstein developed a framework to help empirically evaluate this claim. His seminal work outlined three ways in which illicit drugs may contribute to crime and violence.

The first way in which Goldstein (1985) proposed illicit drugs may lead to violent crime is **psychopharmacological violence.** Sometimes called the intoxication model, this refers to the psychological effect of the drug itself causing those who ingest it to behave violently. He noted that several studies in the 1960s and 1970s had already disproved this path from drugs to violence for at least two substances: opiates and marijuana. However, Goldstein (1985) left open the possibility that *withdrawal* from opiates may lead to symptoms conducive to violent behavior. He also suggested that those with substance use disorder may be more likely to become a *victim* of violent crime. Thirty years later in 2015, a qualitative study involving interviews with carjackers, some of whom were also chronic drug users, supported Goldstein's idea that drug use can lead to victimization: "The violent men we spoke with purposely targeted people they labeled as crackheads for robberies, but they also sought out such people for expressive violence" (Copes et al., 2015, p. 40).

A more recent systematic review of the research on psychopharmacological violence examined the effects of specific drugs as a pathway to violence. Tomlinson and her colleagues (2016) found that alcohol – the only fully legal substance studied – is highly associated with aggressive behavior, particularly intimate partner violence and sexual assault. Methamphetamine was the only other drug in their study to show a direct connection to psychopharmacological violence. The connections between violence and cannabis, cocaine, and opioid use appear to be mediated by other characteristics of the individual, such as impulsiveness and predisposition to aggression.

The second pathway from drugs to crime described by Goldstein (1985) is **economic compulsive violence.** This stems from a drug addict's need for money to buy more drugs. Two studies conducted in Canada found these first two pathways to be the most common explanation for the link between drug use and crime. A robust study using data from the 1990s found that 47% of the crimes committed in Canada were due to either being under the influence of drugs or alcohol or to obtain money to support an addiction (Pernanen et al., 2002). A small-scale replication of this study similarly found that "just over 42% of crime would probably not have occurred if the perpetrator had not been under the influence of or seeking alcohol or other drugs" (Young et al., 2021, p. 3202). Again, however, this more recent study also found that alcohol dependence was linked with more offending and more violent offending than any of the illegal drugs they studied. Because it is legal for adults to consume, alcohol use is inherently not as large a factor in the third pathway from substance use to crime first described by Goldstein (1985): systemic violence.

Systemic violence, sometimes referred to as the systemic model, refers to crime and violence that stem from the fact that most drugs of abuse must be sold and purchased on the black market. Goldstein (1985) provided examples of this pathway:

1 Disputes over territory between rival drug dealers
2 Assaults and homicides committed within dealing hierarchies as a means of enforcing normative codes
3 Robberies of drug dealers and the usually violent retaliation by the dealer or his/her bosses
4 Elimination of informers
5 Punishment for selling adulterated or phony drugs
6 Punishment for failing to pay one's debts
7 Disputes over drugs or drug paraphernalia
8 Robbery violence related to the social ecology of copping areas [open-air drug markets] (p. 497)

Quantitative empirical analyses of criminal enterprise are inherently difficult as the best sampling techniques (i.e., some form of random sampling) are not possible among clandestine populations, such as those involved in the illicit drug market. However, the same qualitative study cited above (Copes et al., 2015) found some support for the proliferation of violent crime in the black market. Their interviewees reported an expectation of violence in areas with high drug trafficking. They saw crime and violence as merely part of doing business.

The authors of the robust Canadian study mentioned earlier (Pernanen et al., 2002) identified a fourth pathway tied directly to the war on drugs. The **substance-defined model** captures those whose actions were labeled as criminal only because the law says that they were illegal. Legal scholars refer to this as ***mala prohibita***, which is Latin for "wrong because it is prohibited." In contrast, the other crimes described above are considered ***mala in se***, or "wrong in itself." The substance-defined model includes drug selling, drug possession, and drug use. Largely due to the systemic violence of the black market, it is often difficult to separate *mala prohibita* crimes from *mala in se* crimes related to illicit drugs. Additionally, it may be difficult to separate the substance-defined model from economic compulsive violence, since drug users may not come to the attention of police unless they commit a crime other than simply using or possessing an illicit substance. However, data from the Uniform Crime Reports (UCR) from 2021 indicates that 498,209 were arrested nationally for drug possession and 66,035 were arrested for drug sales or manufacturing.

Therapeutic Interventions

It is clear that simply criminalizing and punishing drug use has not only failed to alleviate the problem but in many cases has made it worse. Some have called for the decriminalization of illicit drugs and support harm reduction strategies, such as locations known as **supervised consumption facilities** where drug users can consume or inject drugs they have purchased under the supervision of health care workers to minimize deaths due to overdose. Decriminalization does not legalize drugs; rather, **decriminalization** simply removes criminal penalties for drug use and possession of small quantities for personal use, often replacing such penalties with citations and/or fines. Others suggest that drug use can be addressed through more therapeutic approaches to the criminal justice process. Within this approach, treatment programs should focus on the intersection of mental illness, trauma, and substance use.

Decriminalization and Harm Reduction

As was hopefully learned from the country's deinstitutionalization crisis of nearly a century ago, just decriminalizing drugs without other services in place will likely not work to reduce the problem of chronic substance use. Oregon recently embarked on a sort of real-time experiment when its citizens passed Measure 110 which decriminalized drug use and possession while also allocating money to increase or support existing treatment services. The measure passed in November 2020 and went into effect on February 1, 2021. While the change in policing approach was able to go into effect immediately, the extra funding for treatment services was bogged down by bureaucratic processes. According to Russoniello and his colleagues (2023), funding for the Behavioral Health Resource Networks, responsible for screening those who receive a citation (in exchange for waiver of the fine) and coordinating care, was not allocated until August 2022. Some of the additional grant money for new and expanded treatment services was approved by the state legislature in early 2021, but much more of the promised grant money is yet to be budgeted. Likely due to these implementation issues, overdose deaths drastically increased after decriminalization and Oregon's legislature recriminalized possession of small amounts of drugs for personal use in 2024. Russoniello and his colleagues (2023) caution against judging the Oregon experiment too harshly or too soon. It will take time and innovation to undo the War on Drugs. Hopefully, the lessons learned in Oregon will serve as guidance for other jurisdictions interested in a harm reduction approach for their citizens with a substance use disorder.

Despite concerns that supervised consumption facilities will bring more crime and disorder to the communities surrounding their locations, two systematic reviews of the research have not found this to be the case. There is no evidence that these services result in more crime or "drug use-related public nuisance" (Levengood et al., 2021, p. 746). Therefore, the potential benefits of these facilities far outweigh the potential costs. Supervised consumption facilities greatly reduce – often to zero – the number of overdose deaths, as well as providing access to treatment services for those ready to quit (Kennedy et al., 2017; Levengood et al., 2021).

Drug Courts

As mentioned earlier in this chapter, the past several decades have seen a rise in "problem solving courts." The first of its kind were drug courts. These therapeutic court systems are designed to divert those arrested for a low-level drug crime away from correctional facilities. Drug courts act as a form of community supervision with a focus on treatment. Participants are mandated to attend treatment programs and meet frequently with a supervision team that includes both criminal justice personnel (i.e., judge, probation officer) and substance use treatment workers. Unfortunately, a common criticism of drug courts is the quality of the available treatment programs.

A Syndemic Model of Treatment

After reading this chapter, it should be clear that substance use disorder is quite often comorbid with mental illness and trauma. However, treatment programs have historically focused on only one of these issues at a time. According to Grecco and Andrew Chambers (2019), "only 18% of addiction treatment programs and 9% of mental health-treatment programs are considered dual diagnosis capable" (p. 5). This has led many to advocate for a syndemic model of treatment. The word **syndemic** is short for synergistic epidemic and recognizes the prevalence with which certain diseases or issues co-occur and also influence each other. A systematic review of research on various treatment modalities found that cognitive behavioral therapies (CBT) were most effective in treating multiple diagnoses (Sabri et al., 2019; see Chapter 13 for more on CBT).

Summary

Mental illness, trauma, and substance use are incredibly common among justice-involved individuals for a variety of reasons. And these three issues are often found in the same people. But all of them are in fact matters for medical and mental health services, not the criminal justice system. Major reforms are needed in the way we treat these illnesses, and it is going to take time to reverse the harm caused by the War on Drugs. Renewed advocacy for these under- and mis-served populations gives hope for a better future where people suffering from mental illness, trauma, and/or substance use disorder are provided help instead of punishment.

References

American Psychiatric Association. (2013). *Diagnostic and statistical manual of mental disorders* (5th ed.). American Psychiatric Publishing, Inc.

Astridge, B., Wen Li, W., McDermott, B., & Longhitano, C. (2023). A systematic review and meta-analysis on adverse childhood experiences: Prevalence in youth offenders and their effects on youth recidivism. *Child Abuse & Neglect*, *140*, 106055.

Copes, H., Hochstetler, A., & Sandberg, S. (2015). Using a narrative framework to understand the drugs and violence nexus. *Criminal Justice Review*, *40*(1), 32–46.

Erickson, S. K., Rosenheck, R. A., Trestman, R. L., Ford, J. D., & Desai, R. A. (2008). Risk of incarceration between cohorts of veterans with and without mental illness discharged from inpatient units. *Psychiatric Services*, *59*(2), 178–183.

Fazel, S., Lichtenstein, P., Grann, M., Goodwin, G. M., & Långström, N. (2010). Bipolar disorder and violent crime: New evidence from population-based longitudinal studies and systematic review. *Archives of General Psychiatry*, *67*(9), 931–938.

Felitti, V. J., Anda, R. F., Nordenberg, D., Williamson, D. F., Spitz, A. M., Edwards, V., Koss, M. P., & Marks, J. S. (1998). Relationship of childhood abuse and household dysfunction to many of the leading causes of death in adults: The adverse childhood experiences (ACE) study. *American Journal of Preventative Medicine*, *14*(4), 245–258.

Goldstein, P. J. (1985). The drugs/violence nexus: A tripartite conceptual framework. *Journal of Drug Issues*, *15*(4), 493–506.

Grecco, G. G., & Andrew Chambers, R. (2019). The Penrose Effect and its acceleration by the war on drugs: a crisis of untranslated neuroscience and untreated addiction and mental illness. *Translational Psychiatry*, *9*(1), 320.

Hall, D., Lee, L. W., Manseau, M. W., Pope, L., Watson, A. C., & Compton, M. T. (2019). Major mental illness as a risk factor for incarceration. *Psychiatric Services*, *70*(12), 1088–1093.

Hays-Grudo, J., & Morris, A. S. (2020). *Adverse and protective childhood experiences: A developmental perspective*. American Psychological Association.

Hughes, K., Bellis, M. A., Hardcastle, K. A., Sethi, D., Butchart, A., Mikton, C., Jones, L., & Dunne, M. P. (2017). The effect of multiple adverse childhood experiences on health: A systematic review and meta-analysis. *Lancet Public Health*, *2*(8), e356–e366.

Hsu, M. C., & Ouyang, W. C. (2022). Effects of integrated Moral Reasoning Development Intervention for management of violence in schizophrenia: A randomized controlled trial. *Journal of Clinical Medicine*, *11*(5), 1169–1186.

Kennedy, M. C., Karamouzian, M., & Kerr, T. (2017). Public health and public order outcomes associated with supervised drug consumption facilities: A systematic review. *Current HIV/AIDS Reports*, *14*, 161–183.

Lamberti, J. S., Katsetos, V., Jacobowitz, D. B., & Weisman, R. L. (2020). Psychosis, mania and criminal recidivism: Associations and implications for prevention. *Harvard Review of Psychology*, *28*(3), 179–202.

Lamsma, J., Cahn, W., & Fazel, S. (2020). Use of illicit substances and violent behaviour in psychotic disorders: Two nationwide case-control studies and meta-analyses. *Psychological Medicine*, *50*(12), 2028–2033.

Latalova, K., Kamaradova, D., & Prasko, J. (2014). Violent victimization of adult patients with severe mental illness: A systematic review. *Neuropsychiatric Disease and Treatment*, *10*, 1925–1939.

Leff, J., Trieman, N., Knapp, M., & Hallmam, A. (2000). The TAPS project: A report on 13 years of research, 1985–1998. *Psychiatric Bulletin*, *24*(5), 165–168.

Levengood, T. W., Yoon, G. H., Davoust, M. J., Odgen, S. N., Marshall, B. D. L., Cahill, S. R., & Bazzi, A. R. (2021). Supervised injection facilities as harm reduction: A systematic review. *American Journal of Preventive Medicine*, *61*(5), 738–749.

Malvaso, C. G., Cale, J., Whitten, T., Day, A., Singh, S., Hackett, L., Delfabbro, P. H., & Ross, S. (2022). Associations between adverse childhood experiences and trauma among young people who offend: A systematic literature review. *Trauma, Violence, & Abuse*, *23*(5), 1677–1694.

McGrew, J. H., Wright, E. R., Pescosolido, B. A., & McDonel, E. C. (1999). The closing of central state hospital: Long-term outcomes for persons with severe mental illness. *Journal of Behavioral Health Services & Research*, *26*(3), 246–261.

O'Reilly, K., O'Connell, P., O'Sullivan, D., Corvin, A., Sheerin, J., O'Flynn, P., Donohoe, G., McCarthy, H., Ambrosh, D., O'Donnell, M., Ryan, Aisling, & Kennedy, H. G. (2019). Moral cognition, the missing link between psychotic symptoms and acts of violence: A cross-sectional national forensic cohort study. *BMC Psychiatry*, *19*, 1–24.

Pernanen, K., Cousineau, M., Brochu, S., & Sun, F. (2002). Proportions of crimes associated with alcohol and other drugs in Canada. Canadian Centre on Substance Abuse. https://www.ccsa.ca/sites/default/files/2019-04/ccsa-009105-2002.pdf

Peterson, J. K., Densley, J. A., Knapp, K., Higgins, S., & Jensen, A. (2022). Psychosis and mass shootings: A systematic examination using publicly available data. *Psychology, Public Policy, and Law*, *28*(2), 280–291.

Prins, S. J. (2011). Does transinstitutionalization explain the overrepresentation of people with serious mental illnesses in the criminal justice system? *Community Mental Health Journal*, *47*(6), 716–722.

Ranu, J., Kalebic, N., Melendez-Torres, G. J., & Taylor, P. (2022). Association between adverse childhood experiences and a combination of psychosis and violence among adults: A systematic review and meta-analysis. *Trauma, Violence, & Abuse*, *23*(5), 1677–1694.

Rothbard, A. B., Kuno, E., Schinnar, A. P., Hadley, T. R., & Turk, R. (1999). Service utilization and cost of community care for discharged state hospital patients: A 3-year follow-up study. *American Journal of Psychiatry*, *156*(6), 920–927.

Russoniello, K., Vakharia, S. P., Netherland, J., Naidoo, T., Wheelock, H., Hurst, T., & Rouhani, S. (2023). Decriminalizatoin of drug possession in Oregon: Analysis and early lessons. *Drug Science, Policy, and Law*, *9*, 1–16.

Sabri, B., Greene, C., & Lucas, G. M. (2019). A systematic review of comprehensive interventions for substance use: Focus on victimization. *Aggression and Violent Behavior*, *48*, 46–59.

Sahle, B. W., Reavley, N. J., Li, W., Morgan, A. J., Yap, M. B. H., Reupert, A., & Jorm, A. F. (2022). The association between adverse childhood experiences and common mental disorders and suicidality: An umbrella review of systematic reviews and meta-analyses. *European Child & Adolescent Psychiatry*, *31*, 1489–1499.

SAMHSA's Trauma & Justice Strategic Initiative. (2014, July). SAMHSA's concept of trauma and guidance for a trauma-informed approach. Retrieved, 27 April 2022, from https://ncsacw.acf.hhs.gov/userfiles/files/SAMHSA_Trauma.pdf

Seo, C., Bitna, K, & Kruis, N. E. (2021). Variation across police response models for handling encounters with people with mental illness: A systematic review and meta-analysis. *Journal of Criminal Justice*, *72*, 101752.

Tomlinson, M. F., Brown, M., & Hoaken, P. N. (2016). Recreational drug use and human aggressive behavior: A comprehensive review since 2003. *Aggression and Violent Behavior*, *27*, 9–29.

Verdolini, N., Pacchiarotti, I., Köhler, C. A., Reinares, M., Samalin, L., Colom, F., Tortorella, A., Stubbs, B., Carvalho, A. F., Vieta, E., & Murru, A. (2018). Violent criminal behavior in the context of bipolar disorder: Systematic review and meta-analysis. *Journal of Affective Disorders*, *239*, 161–170.
Whiting, D., Gulati, G., Geddes, J. R., & Fazel, S. (2022). Association of schizophrenia spectrum disorders and violence perpetration in adults and adolescents from 15 countries: A systematic review and meta-analysis. *JAMA Psychiatry*, *79*(2), 120–132.
Young, M. M., De Moor, C., Kent, P., Stockwell, T., Sherk, A., Zhao, J., Sorge, J. T., Farrell MacDonald, S., Weekes, J., Biggar, E., & Maloney-Hall, B. (2021). Attributable fractions for substance use in relation to crime. *Addiction*, *116*, 3198–3205.

9 Police and Public Safety Psychology

Introduction

Established in 1984, the Police and Public Safety section of American Psychological Association (APA) Division 18 (Psychologists in Public Service) states that members are "involved in the selection of employees, fitness for duty evaluations, critical incident stress debriefing, management of mental health programs, criminal investigative analysis (profiling) and hostage negotiations" (APA, n.d., para. 1). This chapter will present these activities in four sections: assessment, clinical intervention, operational support, and organization consultation. The section on assessment will cover psychologists' involvement in screening law enforcement applicants and fitness-for-duty evaluations. Clinical intervention includes the ways psychologists address the mental health concerns among police personnel. Operational support will cover the ways in which the expertise of psychologists can assist in policing, such as hostage negotiations, criminal profiling, and policing Black communities. Finally, organizational consultation is essentially industrial/organizational psychology applied to police departments, meaning psychologists assist in the way police officers work together.

Assessment

Psychologists have been involved in the selection of law enforcement personnel for over one hundred years. In 1916, the first widely-used intelligence test, the Stanford-Binet, was used by its creator Lewis Terman to study whether it predicted success among newly hired police officers in San Jose, California (Weiss & Inwald, 2018). Several government reports in the 1960s pushed for the use of a professional (i.e., a psychologist or psychiatrist) to screen law enforcement candidates, and by the 1990s the use of psychological assessments administered by trained professionals was a common hiring practice at nearly all law enforcement agencies.

Pre-Employment Psychological Screening

Not just anyone can be a police officer. Prior to an applicant being hired by a department, they are typically subject to screening processes to determine whether they will make a good law enforcement officer. The standards vary by jurisdiction, but they usually include a physical as well as psychological evaluation. The psychological evaluation will often involve an interview with a psychologist or psychiatrist and a written personality assessment. The most commonly used personality assessment for law enforcement pre-employment screening is a version of the **Minnesota Multiphasic Personality Inventory** (**MMPI**). Pearson Assessments offers the MMPI-2-RF Police Candidate Interpretive Report which "identifies potential

DOI: 10.4324/9781003250821-11

problems in 10 job-relevant domains: Emotional control and stress tolerance; Routine task performance; Decision-making and judgment; Feedback acceptance; Assertiveness; Social competence and teamwork; Integrity; Conscientiousness and dependability; Substance use; [and] Impulse control" (Pearson Assessment, n.d.). Whitman and her colleagues (2021) found support for using the MMPI and the cutoff scores suggested in its Police Candidate Interpretive Report when analyzed against the ten dimensions of the California Commission on Peace Officer Standards and Training standards: "Emotional Regulation and Stress Tolerance, Avoidance of Substance Use and Other Risk-Taking Behavior, Impulse Control and Attention to Safety, Assertiveness, Social Competence, Teamwork, Decision-Making and Judgment, Adaptability and Flexibility, Conscientiousness and Dependability, and Integrity and Ethics" (Whitman et al., 2021, p. 1169).

Fitness-for-Duty Evaluations

Fitness-for-duty evaluations (**FFDEs**) are similar to pre-employment screenings, but they are administered to those who have already been hired and may have been a law enforcement officer for some time. Once a police officer has been hired, there are a number of reasons the department may want to conduct another assessment to determine if they are still fit for the work or whether they are ready to return to work after an absence. Most notably, FFDEs should be administered after a police officer has been involved in a critical incident. A **critical incident** can be anything that might cause undue stress on those who were either directly or indirectly involved, such as an officer-involved shooting or the death of a fellow officer. (See the next section on Clinical Intervention for more on how psychologists can help following these incidents.) FFDEs can be helpful in determining whether an officer is ready to return to active duty right away, what services they should receive before returning to active duty, and if/when they are ready to return to active duty after a leave of absence.

Clinical Intervention

Critical Incident Stress and Post-Traumatic Stress Disorder

Being a police officer is extremely stressful. Police psychologists have long recognized the phenomenon of **critical incident stress syndrome** (**CISS**) following officer-involved shootings, hostage situations, and other "critical incidents." Though similar to post-traumatic stress disorder (PTSD), according to the Occupational Safety and Health Administration's (OSHA, n.d.) Critical Incident Stress Guide, "Post Traumatic Stress Disorder differs from critical incident stress by lasting longer than four weeks after the event triggering the emotional, mental or physical response."

Many departments offer **Critical Incident Stress Management** (**CISM**), which often consists of peer support. However, a particular model called **Critical Incident Stress Debriefing** (**CISD**; sometimes called the "Mitchell Model" for its creator Dr. Jeffrey Mitchell) calls for at least one mental health professional trained in CISD, along with at least one peer, to facilitate a small group discussion following a critical incident. The members of this small group should be only those directly affected by the event and share the same role. What this means is that only police officers present at the scene should be in the same small group for CISD. Other first responders on the scene (e.g., firefighters, emergency medical personnel) would need a separate session for their group. Peer support persons involved in the CISD should also be from the same profession and have training in CISM, if not CISD specifically.

Timing of a CISD session should be soon after the critical incident, but after allowing time for those involved to re-adjust to "reality." According to Mitchell and Everly (1997), "24 to 72 hours after the incident the small, homogenous group gathers for the CISD" (p. 3). The CISD group meeting takes about one to two hours and consists of seven phases: (1) introduction, (2) facts, (3) thoughts, (4) reactions, (5) symptoms, (6) teaching, and (7) reentry. In the introduction phase, the facilitators describe the process and note that participation is voluntary and confidential. The facts phase asks the participants to briefly describe what happened, with the main goal being to get people talking. Therefore, details are discouraged at this point. "The thought phase is a transition from the cognitive domain toward the affective domain" (Mitchell & Everly, 1997, p. 4) by asking participants to share their first thoughts on the scene. While the facts and thoughts phases give everyone a chance to speak by systematically going around the room (participants are free to decline to speak), the rest of the CISD is less formal. Mitchell and Everly (1997) call the reactions phase "the heart of CISD" (p. 4), with facilitators asking "What is the very worst thing about this event for you personally?" The symptoms phase, unsurprisingly, asks the group to share any symptoms they have experienced since the incident. During the teaching phase, facilitators validate any symptoms or responses that are normal to traumatic experiences. This education piece is important to assure participants that what they are experiencing is normal. The final phase of reentry provides a summary of the CISD experience and provides any additional information or directives. Refreshments are typically served after a CISD session to encourage participants to stick around for informal one-on-one discussions or referrals to more formal counseling. One to three additional follow-up check-ins by the CISD facilitators in the following weeks is recommended.

There is also a high likelihood of regularly experiencing and/or witnessing trauma on the job, resulting in complex or **cumulative post-traumatic stress disorder** (PTSD). The idea that prolonged or repeated exposure to traumas might result in complex PTSD was first put forward by Herman (1992). While not specifically recognized in the *Diagnostic and Statistical Manual of Mental Disorders* published by the American Psychiatric Association, the National Institute of Health has funded research on cumulative PTSD (Geronazzo-Alman et al., 2017) and the National Health Service in England has recognized complex PTSD as being "diagnosed in adults or children who have repeatedly experienced traumatic events, such as violence, neglect or abuse" (National Health Service, n.d.). Practicing **self-care** is important for all of us, but especially for those at risk of or already experiencing symptoms of PTSD. (See Box 9.1 for self-care recommendations.)

Unfortunately, the risks of not properly responding to the mental health needs of law enforcement are dire. Police suicide is a "quiet epidemic" (Dvorak, 2021, title). Blue H.E.L.P. is an organization dedicated to raising awareness and honoring all first responders who have taken their own lives. According to their statistics, compiled since 2017, over one hundred officers die by suicide each year. In 2018, that number was almost 200 (198). While not all individual struggles may be related to the job of law enforcement, offering support for those that are is important.

Operational Support

Hostage Negotiations

When a perpetrator has taken hostages, the stakes are very high for all involved. A **hostage negotiator** is someone who will communicate with the hostage taker to de-escalate the situation and hopefully reach a peaceful end. For safety and tactical reasons, the hostage

Box 9.1 Practicing self-care; Adapted from "Wise Choices" as part of the National Institute of Health's Emotional Wellness Toolkit (https://www.nih.gov/health-information/emotional-wellness-toolkit).

Be observant. Recognize signs of excessive stress. These include difficulty sleeping, being easily angered or irritable, feeling depressed, and low energy.

Schedule regular times for a relaxing activity.

- **Take some deep breaths.** Breathe in through your nose to a count of 4, hold for 1 second and then exhale through the mouth to a count of 5. Repeat often.
- **Enjoy a stroll.** As you walk, pay attention to your breath and the sights and sounds around you. If thoughts and worries enter your mind, note them but then return to the present.
- **Practice mindful eating.** Be aware of taste, textures, and flavors in each bite. Listen to when your body is hungry and full.
- **Do a body scan.** Bring your attention to how each part of your body is feeling. This can help you connect with your body.

Exercise regularly. Just 30 minutes per day of walking can help boost your mood and reduce stress.

Get enough sleep. Adults need about 7 or more hours of sleep per night. School-age children need 9–12 hours, while teenagers need 8–10 hours.

Set goals and priorities. Decide what must get done now and what can wait. Learn to say "no" to new tasks if you start to feel like you're taking on too much.

Build a social support network. Stay connected with people who can provide emotional support.

Show compassion for yourself. Note what you've accomplished at the end of the day, not what you've failed to do.

Remember your good deeds. Give yourself credit for the good things you do for others each day.

Forgive yourself. Everyone makes mistakes. Learn from what went wrong, but don't dwell on it.

Explore your beliefs about the meaning and purpose of life. Think about how to guide your life by the principles that are important to you.

Seek help. Talk to a health care provider if you feel unable to cope, have suicidal thoughts, or use drugs or alcohol to cope. If you or someone you know is in crisis, call the National Suicide Prevention Lifeline at 1-800-273-TALK (8255). Or text "HOME" to the Crisis Text Line at 741741.

negotiator is rarely a psychologist themselves. However, hostage negotiators should have training from a psychologist and there may be a psychologist on a broader hostage negotiation team within the department. This is because best practices involve the use of a number of strategies from psychology, such as active listening, modeling, and positive reinforcement. Additionally, mental health professionals will be better able to ascertain if the hostage taker may be suffering from a mental illness and how this might impact negotiation strategies.

One of the main goals in hostage situations is to keep the situation calm, which means keeping the hostage taker calm. This can be aided by the hostage negotiator modeling calm behavior and using active listening skills. The hostage taker most likely wants to be heard, first and foremost. Therefore, a "basic principle of negotiation is to listen twice as much as you talk" (Miller, 2005, p. 282). **Active listening** skills will help diffuse the situation. **Emotional labeling** gives a name to what the hostage taker is feeling, which normalizes it. **Paraphrasing** what the hostage taker is saying will show understanding. The hostage negotiator can keep the hostage taker talking to buy valuable time and gain more information by using mirroring, minimal encouragers, open-ended questions, and simply silence. **Mirroring** the last part of what the person said in the form of a question encourages the person to elaborate (e.g., "That made you mad?"). **Minimal encouragers** are common active listening interjections, such as "yeah" and "uh huh," that signal you are paying attention. And silence is powerful in active listening since the hostage taker will likely keep talking to fill the silence.

Of course, the ultimate goal in a hostage situation is a peaceful ending with minimal harm to the hostage(s). Every step toward this end, no matter how small, should be positively reinforced by the hostage negotiator. As covered in Chapter 4, behavior is best shaped by using positive reinforcement. When the hostage taker is positively reinforced for steps taken towards a peaceful resolution, they will be more likely to take more steps in that direction, ultimately leading to the surrender and freeing of the hostage(s).

Criminal Profiling

Perhaps the most popular topic in the intersection of psychology and criminal justice is **criminal profiling,** also known as offender profiling and psychological profiling. People are fascinated with the idea that we can determine the characteristics of an offender based on their victim(s) and crime scene(s) – thereby helping the police capture the perpetrator. But is this truly possible? Despite the proliferation of two models of criminal profiling, one started in the United States and one started in the United Kingdom, there are some who criticize the practice as being based on faulty underlying assumptions.

History

The public's fascination with getting inside the criminal mind may have begun with the fictional Sherlock Holmes and the very real case of Jack the Ripper. Both surfaced in the 1880s in England. Created by Sir Arthur Conan Doyle, Holmes was a private investigator with a knack for deduction. The brilliant Sherlock Holmes was able to use his own vast knowledge of how things work to make eerily accurate guesses as to the circumstances and individuals involved in a crime. We will see later in this section that deductive approaches to criminal profiling are sometimes referred to as "top-down."

Jack the Ripper committed his killing spree in the Whitechapel neighborhood of London in 1888, just a year after Conan Doyle debuted the character of Sherlock Holmes. Five brutal murders of prostitutes are commonly attributed to Jack the Ripper, though there could have been more. The terror the murders instilled in the area led to what is considered the first criminal profile. Dr. Thomas Bond provided police at the time with his assessment of the characteristics of the murders and what they might mean about the characteristics of the man who committed them. Unfortunately, the first criminal profile proved unhelpful to police, as Jack the Ripper was never caught and has still not been officially identified.

Stateside, the first criminal profile is often attributed to the case of the Mad Bomber in the mid-twentieth century. Dozens of bombs were left around New York City, many of them exploding causing serious injuries though thankfully no deaths. After well over a decade of terror, the New York Police Department enlisted the help of James A. Brussel, a psychiatrist. Brussel developed an almost comically specific profile of the man who had been dubbed the Mad Bomber. Most shocking was his assertion that the man would be wearing a buttoned, double-breasted suit when he was finally arrested. Despite the fact that police used the Mad Bomber's own writings to newspapers to identify him as George Metesky, it was the arrestee's attire that lives on in criminal profiling lore: a buttoned, double-breasted suit.

Federal Bureau of Investigation Model

The first group to formalize a process for criminal profiling were agents with the Federal Bureau of Investigation (FBI). Working in the newly formed Behavioral Sciences Unit (now called the Behavioral Analysis Unit), Special Agents John Douglas and Robert Ressler started by interviewing serial killers, such as Edmund Kemper and Ted Bundy, in an effort to understand their motivations and reasons for certain crime scene behaviors. Fans of the Netflix show *Mindhunter*, named for Douglas's book of the same title, are likely familiar with this early attempt to understand the criminal mind. From these interviews and other experience working on cases of serial crime, Douglas and Ressler gained specialized knowledge. In the years since, this specialized knowledge has been used to train others and consult on investigations throughout the country.

The **FBI approach to criminal profiling** is based on deductive reasoning from specialized knowledge, much the same way that Sherlock Holmes made his inferences. **Deductive reasoning** is the process of applying broad knowledge to a specific situation. Since the process of deduction takes wide knowledge and applies it to a narrow situation (i.e., a particular crime scene), using deduction for criminal profiling has sometimes been termed the **"top-down" approach**.

The most important aspect of identifying a serial offender is crime linkage. **Crime linkage** is the process of identifying similarities among separate crime incidents lending credence to the idea that they were all committed by the same perpetrator(s). The way the FBI model determines crime linkage is primarily through modus operandi (MO) and signatures. **Modus operandi** is the specific way in which a crime is committed. In a burglary, how is entry gained to the home? In a murder, what method is used to kill? The MO has to do with the necessary processes of the crime. The **signature**, on the other hand, is often superfluous to actions necessary to commit the crime. According to Douglas and colleagues (2013), the signature is a psychological element needed to fulfill the fantasy of the crime. While the MO can change and evolve as the offender gains experience, the signature will rarely change "at its core" (Douglas et al., 2013, p. 24).

Crime linkage and criminal profiling entail an intense examination of crime scenes. Douglas, Ressler, and their colleagues (2013) outlined their process of **Crime Scene Analysis**. It consists of six stages: (1) profiling inputs, (2) decision-making models, (3) crime assessment, (4) the criminal profile, (5) investigation, and (6) apprehension. The fifth and sixth stages are essentially out of the hands of the profiler and back in the hands of the police.

The **profiling inputs** stage includes collecting comprehensive case materials, background information on the victim, forensic information, and police reports. The profiler obtains detailed information about the crime scene. This includes the area outside the immediate crime scene, such as the feel of the surrounding neighborhood. It is also important to get as much information about the victim as possible. This means information about the victim when they were alive. Knowing who the victim was in life can reveal a lot about the perpetrator, such as how much risk they are willing to take and whether they may have a "type" of victim they will continue to go after. When obtaining forensic information, the profiler wants information from the crime scene, such as the type of weapon used and blood spatter analysis. They also want the autopsy report, with toxicology screens, estimated time and cause of death, photographs of wounds, and speculation on the sequence in which the wounds were received. Finally, profilers will want police reports, including large color photographs of the crime scene, aerial photographs, if possible, as well as maps of the area. Notice one thing that is not on the list of information from police: suspects. Profilers do not want to know anything about any possible suspects. They are just as susceptible to suggestion as the rest of us, and they do not want their analysis to be influenced by anything except the facts of the case and the scene.

According to the **decision-making models** stage, there are seven decision points in the process of creating a criminal profile: (1) homicide type and style, (2) primary intent of the murderer, (3) victim risk, (4) offender risk, (5) escalation, (6) time factors, and (7) location factors. The first decision point, **homicide type and style,** deals with the distinction between single murder, double murder, mass murder, spree murder, and serial murder. These distinctions were covered in more detail in Chapter 7. As for the **primary intent of the murderer**, Ressler and his colleague have three classifications of murderer: (1) criminal enterprise, such as a hitman or mobster; (2) emotional, selfish, or cause-specific, including self-defense, mercy killings (euthanasia), paranoid delusion, and mass suicides; and finally (3) killing to fulfill a sexual fantasy. (Recall from Chapter 7 that serial murder classification systems developed by Holmes & DeBerger and the San Antonio Symposium were discussed.) **Victim risk** has to do with factors such as age, occupation, lifestyle, physical stature, resistance ability, and location of the victim. These are considered in order to classify the victim as low, moderate, or high risk for victimization. **Offender risk** refers to the amount of risk the offender was willing to tolerate in committing their crime. This is related to victim risk in that taking a generally low-risk victim may incur a higher risk for the offender. The fifth key decision point is **escalation**. The profiler deduces from what he knows about the crime scene, the victim and the offender whether this offender is just beginning their murderous career, whether they have committed similar offenses before, and most importantly if they will do it again. **Time factors** include determining the length of time it would have taken to kill the victim, do anything else to or with the body, and dispose of the body. The amount of time the offender is willing to spend with the victim or at the crime scene will give an idea of their level of risk tolerance. Finally, **location factors** include where the victim was first approached (if known), where the crime occurred, and if the body was not found at the primary crime scene, where the body was dumped.

The **crime assessment** stage of crime scene analysis is when the profiler determines whether the offender is organized or disorganized. According to the FBI model of criminal profiling, an **organized** offender will leave a more organized crime scene (e.g., evidence of planning), and a **disorganized** offender will leave a more disorganized crime scene (e.g., leaving the murder weapon behind). Ressler and his colleagues had already been using this dichotomy in their profiling work but did not formalize the distinctions with research until 1986. It was then that Ressler and colleagues used data they had gathered from their work to test whether there was a correlation between what they were seeing at crime scenes and offender characteristics. See Table 9.1 for a summary of their findings. Since then, it has been acknowledged that the organized/disorganized dichotomy is more of a continuum with few offenders or crime scenes being at either extreme. This has led some to question the usefulness of the dichotomy in criminal profiling (see Canter et al., 2004).

Table 9.1 Organized versus disorganized crime scene and perpetrator characteristics (Ressler et al., 1986).

	Organized	*Disorganized*
Crime Scene Characteristics	Plan Use restraints Commit sexual acts with live victims Show or display control of victim Use a vehicle	Leave a weapon at the scene Position dead body Perform sexual acts on dead body Keep dead body Try to depersonalize the body Not use a vehicle
Perpetrator Characteristics	More intelligent Skilled in occupation Likely to think out and plan the crime Likely to be angry and depressed at the time of the murder Likely to have precipitating stress Likely to have a car in decent condition Likely to follow crime events in media Likely to change jobs or leave town	Low birth order children Come from a home with unstable work for the father Have been treated with hostility as a child Be sexually inhibited and sexually ignorant and to have sexual aversions Have parents with histories of sexual problems Have been frightened and confused at the time of the crime Know who the victim is Live alone Have committed the crime closer to home/work

The final stage in the FBI's criminal profiling process is of course the creation of the profile. The final **criminal profile** will describe the type of person who committed the crime and also how they might respond to common investigation techniques. This may include demographics, physical characteristics, habits, beliefs/values, pre-offense behavior, and post-offense behavior. Sometimes profilers have encouraged police to leak certain information to the public (sometimes false information) to entice the offender to come forward – or at least come out of hiding.

Investigative Psychology

David Canter and his colleagues have tested the various typologies of serial offending that have been put forward over the years, including the FBI's organized/disorganized dichotomy. It was found that when taking data from actual cases, very few fit neatly into only one category. A typology that cannot clearly distinguish between different offenders is likely of little use. Since the empirical evidence for the utility of existing criminal profiling techniques has been scarce, Canter has advocated using **inductive reasoning** or a **"bottom-up" approach** to criminal profiling. Rather than trying to apply broad concepts to specific crime scenes and criminals, an inductive approach uses existing data to try to ascertain empirical connections between crime scenes and the criminals who made them.

Canter has modeled his brand of criminal profiling on what he calls A → C, with A representing the offender's actions during and surrounding the crime and C representing the offender's characteristics. FBI criminal profiling has been criticized for providing information to police that is not very useful in actually identifying a suspect, such as "trouble with women." Therefore, Canter has advocated for Cs in his model to be actionable, "such as information about where the person might be living, his/her criminal history, age or domestic circumstances" (Canter, 2010, p. 239).

Investigative psychology has been called a coherent system of information retrieval, inference, and decision support (Canter, 2010). **Information retrieval** aids police officers in collecting relevant data from crime scenes. This not only helps law enforcement create better data for themselves, but it also provides better data for empirical tests of Canter's A → C model. More and better empirical tests will allow investigative psychologists to provide better inferences. **Inferences** are the criminal profiling part of investigative psychology. Finally, with better information retrieval leading to better inferences, investigative psychologists can provide police with **decision support**.

Criticisms

The most common criticisms of criminal profiling stem from the assumptions upon which these investigative techniques rely. The logical assumptions underlying criminal profiling have been termed the offender consistency hypothesis and the homology hypothesis.

The **offender consistency hypothesis** states that offenders behave consistently across their separate crimes. This can be thought of as *intra*-criminal similarities. The assumption on which criminal profiling relies is that a serial offender will behave similarly enough across their crimes that these similarities will be seen at the crime scenes they leave behind. But is this a reasonable assumption? Research in personality psychology tells us that people's behavior is related to the situation as well as their general personality characteristics (see Chapter 6). Given that someone's behavior is impacted by their immediate environment and the fact that a serial offender is likely to evolve in their MO (a likelihood recognized by even early criminal profilers), the offender consistency hypothesis may not be a good assumption upon which to rely.

Relatedly, criminal profiling relies on the assumption of *inter*-criminal differences. In order for the characteristics of an offender to be determined from their crime scene, we have to assume that different criminals behave differently. Otherwise, the same crime scene could be linked to many different offenders! This assumption needs further study. It is likely that different burglars, for example, use the same techniques to gain entry to a building which would lead to some similarities in their crime scenes. However, it is possible that some crime scene behaviors do differ between different offenders. It is important for the field of criminal profiling to empirically determine the uniqueness of crime scene behaviors.

The **homology hypothesis** states that an offender's behavior at their crime scene can be used to infer their overall personality and characteristics helpful to identify them. This is the central assumption of any attempt at criminal profiling. It is also the reasoning behind Canter's bottom-up, inductive reasoning approach. Historically, the homology assumption has been taken for granted rather than tested as a hypothesis should be. Investigative psychology's "coherent system" will hopefully lead to increased empirical evidence of the homology hypothesis, as well as specific crime scene behaviors that are empirically linked to specific offender characteristics.

Another common criticism of criminal profiling is the lack of empirical support. Some of this criticism was covered in the section on investigative psychology. But even the empirical support in Canter's inductive model is limited given the infancy of that approach. Given this particular criticism of criminal profiling, it is important to mention the lack of empirical evidence in other areas of forensic "science."

In 2009, the Committee on Identifying the Needs of the Forensic Science Community, convened by the National Academy of Sciences, issued their report (National Research Council, 2009). The committee concluded that a number of forensic identifications routinely admitted into criminal court proceedings were lacking in scientific basis, statistical evidence, and/or credible and established techniques of identification that limit human error.

For example, although it is commonly believed that no two fingerprints are alike, this has never been scientifically established. Further, the procedure commonly used in friction ridge analysis (the broader term that includes prints from palms and feet) contains numerous steps that rely on the judgment of the examiner, making the chances of a human error a grave possibility. And these are only the committee's concerns with a relatively well-established forensic science! The report also raised similar issues with tool mark and ballistics evidence, hair evidence, questioned document examination, burn pattern analysis, and forensic odontology. Despite the scientific community's concern with the validity of the forensic sciences, the admissibility of evidence and expert testimony typically rely on much lower standards (see Chapter 11). It is also important to note that while many of these techniques should be used with caution to make a "match," they can likely be safely used to exclude suspects.

Policing Black Communities

Historical Trauma

Understanding the contemporary relationship between police and Black communities cannot be decoupled from historical context. Policing in general in the United States evolved from practices that met the needs of distinct sections of early America. Most notably, a predominant task of police in pre-Civil War southern states was patrolling slaves. "Enslaved and freed Blacks lived in fear as slave patrols operated with impunity in subjecting Blacks to stops, searches, physical beatings, detentions, re-enslavement, and lynching" (Brown, 2019, p. 190). Even after the end of the Civil War made slave patrols moot, police were tasked with enforcing the racialized laws of Reconstruction and Jim Crow. In the United States, Black communities have always been policed differently.

Policing has historically been a practice "passed down" through generations due to most education and training happening internally within a department or police academy. Further, Jones-Brown (2007) argues that "policing in the United States is Pavlovian in nature" (p. 103). What she means is that through generations of inherited trainings and procedures, American police have been conditioned to associate Blacks – and young, Black males in particular – with criminality and danger. Recall from Chapter 4 that classical conditioning requires repeated non-pairings of the conditioned stimulus (e.g., young Black males) with the unconditioned stimulus (e.g., dangerous and criminal situation) for the extinction of the association. This is why Jones-Brown (2007) argues that "[t]o believe that nearly three and a half centuries of racialized law enforcement would disappear simply because the rules of engagement changed is to deny the importance and validity of the work of Pavlov and other behavioral scientists" (p. 104).

Contemporary Trauma

Laurencin and Walker (2020) outlined six ways in which the over-policing of Black communities impacts public health, including stress, anxiety, and trauma. The first is "violent confrontation with police that causes injury or death." Understandably, direct experience with injury or death at the hands of a public servant is traumatizing. Second, "police language that escalates a confrontation through micro-aggressions or macro-aggressions" can at the very least lead to distrust. The third way in which over-policing impacts public health in Black communities is through "sub-lethal confrontation[s] with police." A study of the mental health impacts of New York City's infamous stop-and-frisk policy (Geller et al., 2014) found that these interactions with police led to increased anxiety and even post-traumatic stress, with more intrusive stops leading to worse mental health effects. Laurencin and Walker's (2020) fourth way that over-policing can affect mental health is through "actual and/or perceived threat[s] from police." This can be understood as the stress and trauma of anticipating negative encounters with police due to having heard about or seen such negative encounters. Laurencin and Walker's final two points relate to the indirect effects of over-policing. Vicarious trauma can be experienced by "someone who has knowledge of or a relationship with an individual that has been mistreated or racially profiled." Finally, there can be mental health effects even if there is "no relationship with an unarmed individual who has been killed by police and the effects on the community." This drives the point home that Black individuals can have negative mental health effects from simply being exposed to media coverage of police violence against Black individuals.

Trauma-Informed Policing

Given the historical and contemporary context of policing in Black communities, it is important to remember that classical conditioning and passed-down "training" apply to these historically over-policed Black communities as well. Classical conditioning and intergenerational "training" have understandably led Black communities to be more fearful of police (see Pickett et al., 2022). Police officers must be sensitive to these facts when working in and with Black communities.

Trauma psychology can offer one approach – among many that are needed – to better police interactions with Black communities. The strategy of **trauma-informed policing** has recently been suggested as a response to research on the effects of adverse childhood experiences (ACEs; see Chapter 8). Trauma-informed policing should also realize the historical/generational and contemporary trauma over-policing has caused in Black communities. In fact, "realize" is the first R in the four keys to a trauma-informed approach presented by the Substance Abuse and Mental Health Services Administration (SAMHSA) and recommended by Laurencin and Walker (2020).

> A program, organization, or system that is trauma-informed *realizes* the widespread impact of trauma and understands potential paths for recovery; *recognizes* the signs and symptoms of trauma in clients, families, staff, and others involved with the system; and *responds* by fully integrating knowledge about trauma into policies, procedures, and practices, and seeks to actively *resist re-traumatization.*
>
> (SAMHSA's Trauma & Justice Strategic Initiative, 2014, p. 9, emphasis in original)

Police agencies need to be especially cognizant about the need to "resist re-traumatization" as they are the source of the trauma. Although implementing trauma-informed policing is challenging (SAMHSA's Trauma & Justice Strategic Initiative, 2014 provides principles and guidelines for utilizing a trauma-informed approach), it is an important component in healing the fractured relationship between police and Black communities.

Organization Consultation

Industrial/Organizational Psychology

The fourth and final area of police and public safety psychology is organization consultation. This is essentially the application of industrial/organizational psychology to police departments. **Industrial/Organizational (I/O) psychology** uses psychological principles to understand individual and group dynamics in a working environment. I/O psychologists work in any number of occupations to help employees work better together. In police work, the most common issue from I/O psychology is groupthink.

Groupthink – Cohesion, Loyalty and Stress

Pressure to conform is a common social psychology phenomenon (see Chapter 5). Irving Janis first used the word **groupthink** in a 1971 article in Psychology Today: "I use the term groupthink as a quick and easy way to refer to the mode of thinking that persons engage in when *concurrence-seeking* becomes so dominant in a cohesive ingroup that it tends to override realistic appraisal of alternative courses of action" (p. 84; emphasis in original). Although Janis (1971) first applied groupthink to military "fiascos," the concepts clearly apply to police investigations as well.

The central tenet of groupthink is group cohesion. The more cohesive the group, the more danger there is of groupthink. This is because group loyalty will get in the way of critical thinking. Members of a highly cohesive group will censor themselves both internally and externally. Janis (1971) presented the idea of **mindguards** as people within a cohesive group who will admonish any dissention from group members. This censorship eventually becomes internalized when members of the group begin to doubt their thoughts of disagreement, believing instead that other members of the group know best.

Group cohesion also leads to feelings of us versus them, the classic social psychological phenomenon of the ingroup and outgroup. This sense of loyalty to your in-group is another principle that can lead to groupthink. It contributes to self-censorship because members of the ingroup believe "we" must be right and "they" must be wrong.

Janis (1971) emphasized that not all highly cohesive groups will exhibit groupthink. But when the group faces a situation of immense pressure, groupthink is more likely. It is difficult to argue that investigating a crime and seeking justice for victims is not stressful. And police agencies can face even more pressure while investigating high-profile cases.

In his seminal article, Janis (1971) outlined eight symptoms of groupthink. The first is invulnerability. "Most or all of the members of the ingroup share an *illusion* of invulnerability that provides for them some degree of reassurance about obvious dangers and leads them to become overoptimistic and willing to take extraordinary risks" (p. 85; emphasis in original). The second symptom is rationale. Groups exhibiting groupthink are easily able to rationalize their decisions and to dismiss criticisms that arise internally or externally. This is in part due to the third symptom: morality. Due to their extreme group cohesion, those displaying groupthink believe their ingroup to inherently have the moral high ground. This may also be because of their belief in stereotypes of the outgroup, which is the fourth symptom of groupthink. Stereotypes of the outgroup will undoubtedly be negative. In addition to the outside pressure that can lead to groupthink, the fifth symptom of groupthink is pressure exhibited within the group. This is pressure to conform to the group's way of thinking. In fact, another symptom of groupthink is the aforementioned mindguards who exert this pressure to conform. This pressure to conform leads to the seventh symptom of groupthink: self-censorship, which is the internalization of conformity. When there is no one openly disagreeing with the group, the final symptom of groupthink is achieved: the appearance of unanimity. Box 9.2 provides an example of groupthink in action.

Rather than acting as mindguards, McGill (2017) suggests appointing a "devil's advocate" within the department. This person should be "a critical thinker and aware of both organizational and personal bias that may limit the ability of themselves or others to see

Box 9.2 Groupthink and the case of the Norfolk Four

On the night of July 7, 1997, Michelle Moore-Bosko was brutally raped and murdered in her own apartment. After her body was discovered the next day when her husband came home, police spoke with neighbors in the hope of obtaining leads. A friend of Michelle pointed the finger at a neighbor, Danial Williams. Williams was immediately brought in for questioning and denied any involvement. At 5 am, after having already been interrogated for eight hours, Detective Robert Ford was brought in to interrogate Williams. Known for being able to obtain confessions from suspects (more on the multiple false confessions in this case in Chapter 10), Ford was able to get Williams to confess to the murder of Ms. Moore-Bosko.

Then the DNA evidence from the scene came back; it did not belong to Williams. Instead of thinking they must have the wrong man, Norfolk police instead decided that Williams must have had an accomplice. They brought Williams's roommate, Joseph Dick Jr., in for questioning. Dick claimed to have been working aboard a Navy ship at the time of the murder, an assertion that was never investigated by police. Instead, Dick was interrogated by Ford and confessed to being involved in the murder. Later, when Dick's DNA did not come back as a match, Ford and a jail-house informant planted by investigators coerced Dick into identifying two more accomplices: Eric Wilson and Derek Tice. Both men confessed after being interrogated by Ford. However, DNA from neither Wilson nor Tice was a match. Tice then named three more accomplices after several more interrogation sessions over countless hours. John Pauley, Geoffrey A. Farris, and John E. Danser never confessed and were never tried for the rape and murder due to lack of evidence. None of these suspects' DNA matched that from the crime scene.

In February 1999, a letter surfaced from a man claiming to have raped and murdered Michelle Moore-Bosko. This letter had been sent by Omar Ballard to Michelle's friend who had initially suspected Williams. She had also suggested Ballard as a suspect at the time, as he had a history of violence toward women, but investigators ignored this part of her statement to them. When finally questioned by police, he immediately confessed to being the *sole perpetrator* in the crimes against Moore-Bosko. DNA also confirmed that Ballard had raped Michelle. Instead of believing him that he committed the crimes alone, Norfolk police and prosecutors put forward the case that Michelle Moore-Bosko was gang raped and murdered by eight men. Ballard did not know any of the original suspects, so police claimed that they all met in the parking lot of the apartment complex. According to Norfolk police and prosecutors, Ballard joined the other seven to assist in gaining access to the apartment. Crime scene evidence had shown no forced entry.

Groupthink had to be a powerful contributor in this case. Believing strongly in Ford's ability to obtain confessions, all involved in the investigation ignored evidence that did not support their theory of what happened to Michelle Moore-Bosko. Groupthink was so strong that police and prosecutors put forward a complicated and highly-unlikely scenario, rather than changing course when a simpler explanation presented itself. Williams, Dick, Tice, Wilson, and Ballard were all tried and convicted of the supposed gang rape and murder of Michelle Moore-Bosko.

the big picture" (McGill, 2017, para. 9). The point of having a devil's advocate is to bring potential issues with the current direction of an investigation (or any decision being made within the agency) to the forefront. Of course, this requires all others to be receptive to the points of dissention. It is important to recognize that dissent is not personal, but a necessary part of good decision making.

Summary

This chapter has covered police and public safety psychology, divided into four general areas: assessment, clinical intervention, operational support, and organizational consultation. Psychologists aid in the assessment of law enforcement officers via pre-employment screening and fitness-for-duty-evaluations. Clinical intervention by psychologists can help police officers manage stress and maintain good mental health. There are a number of ways in which psychologists can offer operational support to police departments, such as in hostage negotiations. Criminal profiling is another way in which psychological principles can provide operational support, but the current criminal profiling techniques are not without their critics. An understanding of trauma psychology may help bridge the gap between law enforcement and Black communities. And industrial/organizational psychologists can provide organizational consultation to police departments, especially in identifying and combating groupthink.

References

American Psychological Association. (n.d.). *Police and Public Safety*. https://www.apadivisions.org/division-18/sections/police?_ga=2.232046559.1792476548.1649183578-1911255244.1633791365)

Brown, R. A. (2019). Policing in American history. *Du Bois Review*, *16*(1), 189–195.

Canter, D. V., Alison, L. J., Alison, E., & Wentink, N. (2004). The organized/disorganized typology of serial murder: Myth or model? *Psychology, Public Policy, and Law*, *10*(3), 293–320.

Canter, D. V. (2010). Offender profiling. In Brown, J. M. & Campbell, E. A. (Eds.), *The Cambridge handbook of forensic psychology*. Cambridge University Press.

Douglas, J. E., Burgess, A. W., Burgess, A. G., & Ressler, R. K. (2013). *Crime classification manual: A standard system for investigating and classifying violent crime* (3rd ed.). Wiley.

Dvorak, P. (2021, August 9). Death by suicide among police is a quiet epidemic. It needs to be acknowledged. *The Washington Post*. https://www.washingtonpost.com/local/death-by-suicide-among-police-is-a-quiet-epidemic-it-needs-to-be-acknowledged/2021/08/09/c7dc2036-f941-11eb-9c0e-97e29906a970_story.html

Geller, A., Fagan, J., Tyler, T., & Link, B. G. (2014). Aggressive policing and the mental health of young urban men. *American Journal of Public Health*, *104*(12), 2321–2327.

Geronazzo-Alman, L., Eisenberg, R., Shen, S., Duarte, C. S., Musa, G. J., Wicks, J., Fan, B., Doan, T., Guffanti, G., Bresnahan, M., & Hoven, C. W. (2017). Cumulative exposure to work-related traumatic events and current post-traumatic stress disorder in New York City's first responders. *Comprehensive Psychiatry*, *74*, 134–143.

Herman, J. L. (1992). Complex PTSD: A syndrome in survivors of prolonged and repeated trauma. *Journal of Traumatic Stress*, *5*(3), 377–391. https://doi.org/10.1002/jts.2490050305

Janis, I. (1971). Groupthink. *Psychology Today*, 84–89.

Jones-Brown, D. (2007). Forever the symbolic assailant: The more things change, the more they remain the same. *Criminology & Public Policy*, *6*(1), 103–121.

Laurencin, C. T., & Walker, J. M. (2020). Racial profiling is a public health and health disparities issue. *Journal of Racial and Ethic Health Disparities*, *7*(3), 393–397.

McGill, J. (2017, March 7). *Cut the groupthink: Why police leaders need to play devil's advocate*. Police1. https://www.police1.com/chiefs-sheriffs/articles/cut-the-groupthink-why-police-leaders-need-to-play-devils-advocate-1QcFDHidYok1MLZy/

Miller, L. (2005). Hostage negotiation: Psychological principles and practices. *International Journal of Emergency Mental Health*, 7(4), 277–298.
Mitchell, J. T., & Everly, G. S. (1997). Critical incident stress debriefing (CISD). *An operations manual for the prevention of traumatic stress among emergency service and disaster workers* (2nd ed., Revised). Chevron Publishing Corporation.
National Health Service. (n.d.). *Complex PTSD - Post-traumatic stress disorder*. Retrieved, 12 April 2022, from https://www.nhs.uk/mental-health/conditions/post-traumatic-stress-disorder-ptsd/complex/
National Institute of Health. (n.d.). *Emotional Wellness Toolkit*. Retrieved, 12 April 2022, from https://www.nih.gov/health-information/emotional-wellness-toolkit
National Research Council. (2009). *Strengthening forensic science in the United States: A path forward*. National Academies Press.
Occupational Safety and Health Administration. (n.d). *Critical incident stress guide*. Retrieved, 12 April 2022, from https://www.osha.gov/emergency-preparedness/guides/critical-incident-stress#:~:text=Post%20Traumatic%20Stress%20Disorder%20differs,two%20days%20and%20four%20weeks.
Pearson Assessment. (n.d.). MMPI-2-RF Police Candidate Interpretive Report. Retrieved, 13 June 2022, from https://www.pearsonassessments.com/campaign/mmpi-2_rfpcir.html
Pickett, J. T., Graham, A., & Cullen, F. (2022). The American racial divide in fear of the police. *Criminology*, *60*(2), 291–320.
Ressler, R. K., Burgess, A. W., Douglas, J. E., Hartman, C. R., & D'Agostino, R. B. (1986). Sexual killers and their victims: Identifying patterns through crime scene analysis. *Journal of Interpersonal Violence*, *1*(3), 288–308.
SAMHSA's Trauma & Justice Strategic Initiative. (2014, July). SAMHSA's concept of trauma and guidance for a trauma-informed approach. Retrieved April 27, 2022, from https://ncsacw.acf.hhs.gov/userfiles/files/SAMHSA_Trauma.pdf
Weiss, P. A., & Inwald, R. (2018). A brief history of personality assessment in police psychology: 1916-2008. *Journal of Police and Criminal Psychology*, *33*, 189–200.
Whitman, M. R., Elias, L. S., Cappo, B. M., & Ben-Porath, Y. S. (2021). Criterion validity of MMPI-3 scores in preemployment evaluations for public safety candidates. *Psychological Assessment*, *33*(12), 1169–1180.

10 Psychology and Police Procedure

Introduction

In addition to those covered in Chapter 9, there are many more ways in which the field of psychology can help us understand the area of law enforcement. This chapter will cover the investigative topics of detecting deception and interrogating suspects, including the phenomenon of false confessions. But first, it will explore how our knowledge of how memory works can assist in interviewing witnesses, including the Cognitive Interview and advice for suspect identification.

Interviewing Witnesses

One of the first steps after securing the crime scene is to interview witnesses to the crime. The discipline of psychology has a lot to contribute to this important investigative task. This section will cover eyewitness memory and how to improve accurate recall of events and accurate identification of suspects.

Eyewitness Memory

Perhaps no topic at the intersection of criminal justice and psychology has been more researched than eyewitness memory. Despite psychological research on the fallibility of eyewitness memories dating back to the 1970s, it was not until the 1990s that people in the criminal justice system started paying attention. That is because exonerations using DNA evidence revealed that 69% of those wrongfully incarcerated were convicted primarily on eyewitness evidence (Innocence Project, 2020).

How Memory Works

Before we examine what can go wrong with eyewitness memory, and more importantly what police can do to improve accuracy, it will help to have a basic understanding of how memory works. There are three stages to our memory: encoding, storage, and retrieval. The **encoding** process simply consists of our taking in sensory information. Much of this process is unconscious, and our brains filter out a lot of "noise" (i.e., sensory information deemed unimportant or so familiar it is automatically understood).

The next step in the memory process is **storage**, first as short-term memory and then as long-term memory. **Short-term memories** are stored in the frontal lobe for an extremely short period of time, about 15–30 seconds. Without consolidation into long-term memory,

DOI: 10.4324/9781003250821-12

these memories are lost. Our short-term memory can only store about seven pieces of information at any one time. This is why memories need to either move on (to long-term memory) or out (forgotten).

The process of converting short-term memories into long-term memories is known as **consolidation.** Consolidation happens when the neural networks (see Chapter 2) associated with the memory are continually repeated through rehearsal or recall of the memory. There are two broad types of long-term memory: implicit and explicit. **Implicit long-term memories** are procedural, such as muscle memory. Whereas **explicit long-term memories** are more informational and also include two types: semantic and episodic. **Semantic long-term memories** are information without context, essentially general knowledge. **Episodic long-term memories** are information about an event that we experienced. Witnessing a criminal event results in episodic long-term memories.

Creating long-term memories requires the repeated firing of associated neurons. The more these neurons fire, the more associated they become. This allows them to become more stable than short-term memories. However, this does not mean that long-term memories are permanent or infallible. Over time, these neural pathways will weaken if they are not accessed during memory retrieval, the final step in the memory process.

The **retrieval** step of the memory process entails recalling a memory from where it is stored. In a way, you are bringing a long-term memory back into the forefront almost as if it is a new short-term memory. In fact, some psychologists believe that every time a long-term memory is accessed it must then be reconsolidated. Unfortunately, this repeated process of retrieval and reconsolidation leaves memories open to distortion. We will turn now to the number of ways our memories can be affected at every stage of the process.

What Can Affect Memory at Each Stage?

It is important for law enforcement to understand the things that can affect a witness's memory at each of these three stages. At the encoding stage, various environmental issues can impact how well we take in information in the first place. Things such as lighting conditions, distance, and obstructions will obviously affect a witness's ability to view the incident. Was it dark or was the incident obscured in shadow? How far away was the witness from the incident? Was there anything between the witness and the incident or perpetrator that may have impeded getting a good look? Additionally, how much attention did the witness pay to the incident or the perpetrator? And did they notice things were amiss right away? Often, we do not initially realize we are witnessing a crime and may not pay close attention to what seems to not be our business. Surprisingly, even the simplest disguise can impact what a witness believes they are seeing. Law enforcement should assess these variables when interviewing witnesses.

Of particular interest when assessing the accuracy of a witness's memory is the amount of stress they were under during the incident. Research has shown that experiencing stress can impact the encoding process. Morgan and his colleagues (2004) demonstrated this by testing the memories of soldiers during survival training in mock prisoner-of-war camps. They found that a significant number of soldiers were unable to later recognize their perpetrator, even though the physical confrontations lasted more than 30 minutes.

The most well-documented occurrence of stress impacting memory encoding is called **weapon focus** (not to be confused with the weapons effect discussed in Chapter 5). When a weapon is present, our focus is naturally drawn to this threat to our personal safety. As such, we pay less attention to the identifying features of the perpetrator. This phenomenon is so well established that studies of eye movements from as long ago as the 1970s have demonstrated this phenomenon (e.g., Antes, 1974). A meta-analysis concluded that the effect of weapon focus impedes the identification of the person holding the weapon (Steblay, 1992).

Another characteristic that affects the memory encoding of a witness to a crime is the race of the perpetrator. Ample research has demonstrated that people have a difficult time noticing distinguishing features on the faces of races other than their own. This has come to be known as **own-race bias.** Scholars are still unsure exactly why this occurs, but there is general agreement that it stems from a lack of experience with other-race faces as compared to own-race faces. For the most part, we are more likely to be familiar with a variety of faces of our own race allowing us to focus on more distinguishing features of a new face of our own race. Whereas our general unfamiliarity with other-race faces makes it difficult for us to recognize unique facial features.

Once encoded, time is the biggest enemy of memory storage. Recall that the storage of memories occurs due to neural networks. These networks very much operate on a "use it or lose it" principle. The longer the amount of time that a memory is stored without being accessed via the retrieval process, the weaker these neural networks become. Eventually, the neurons cease to be connected at all, resulting in one way in which memories are forgotten. This is not good news for law enforcement when they are not able to interview witnesses immediately following the crime. This too must be taken into consideration by law enforcement when interviewing witnesses.

The process of memory retrieval is where law enforcement officers can have the most impact on eyewitnesses – either in aiding or hindering accurate memory retrieval. There are two broad types of information officers seek from eyewitnesses: what they saw and who they saw.

Usually, the first step in interviewing a witness to a crime is to ascertain what they saw happen. Law enforcement must be aware of the phenomenon of **memory conformity.** This is the tendency for us to change our memory to conform to what we hear from others. This tendency is most prominent in relation to the memories of those closest to us. Studies have found that people are most apt to change their memories to conform to what their spouse says they saw. But the phenomenon can occur when comparing what we saw with anyone else's recollection. This is why officers often seek to separate eyewitnesses as soon as possible and why they are also interviewed separately.

How an eyewitness interview is conducted is highly influential on memory. In a series of early studies by Elizabeth Loftus (1975) and her colleagues in the 1970s, the researchers demonstrated the impact of the wording of questions on eyewitness memory. For example, subjects who were asked if they saw *the* broken headlight were more likely to report having seen it than those asked if they saw *a* broken headlight (Loftus & Zanni, 1975). Additionally, when the presence of a barn was subtly mentioned in a question posed following the viewing of a video, subjects recalled seeing a barn in the video when questioned one week later. There was no barn in the video (Loftus & Palmer, 1974). While there is some debate as to whether these leading questions actually impact the *content* of one's memory, the findings of these studies are important for how law enforcement questions eyewitnesses.

The Cognitive Interview

The **Cognitive Interview** (CI) has become the gold standard to increase accuracy when interviewing eyewitnesses. According to Fisher and Geiselman (2010), "[t]he elements of the CI are organized around three basic psychological processes: cognition, social dynamics, and communication" (p. 322). Originally, the CI consisted of four mnemonics, or memory-enhancing techniques: (1) report everything, (2) reinstate the context, (3) describe events from a different perspective, and (4) recall events in reverse order. After further use and research, four more standards were added: (5) rapport building, (6) witness controls the interview, (7) witness-compatible questioning, and (8) mental or guided imagery.

Report Everything

It is important that interviewers instruct eyewitnesses to report everything they can remember, even if it seems unimportant or contradicts something they have already stated. It should be noted that any contradictions should be recorded by the interviewer to follow up on later; the free flow of information from the eyewitness should not be interrupted (see *Witness controls the interview*). Not only have the most trivial of details broken cases but recalling everything may lead to other memories resurfacing. However, it is just as important that eyewitnesses be told not to speculate or guess and that it is okay to say "I don't know." Speculation may engage a different part of the brain, hindering accurate recall.

Reinstate the Context

It will be easier for the eyewitness to accurately recall the event if they mentally put themselves back there. Eyewitnesses should be encouraged to close their eyes while remembering the incident. The physiological, cognitive, and emotional states they were in at the time should be evoked. As such, interviewers should promote the remembering of emotions as well as factual information. It may also be helpful for the eyewitness to draw the scene.

Describe Events from a Different Perspective

In order to elicit additional memories, it is beneficial to have the eyewitness describe the events from a different perspective. This can be from a different vantage point or as if they were in a different emotional state. For example, if they were fearful at the time of the incident, the interviewer can ask the eyewitness to imagine being calmer as they mentally recall the events. This technique would take place after the initial free recall of events in their original context as a way to draw out more details.

Recall Events in Reverse Order

Another way to extract further details after the initial recall is to ask the eyewitness to remember the events in reverse order. This technique leads to increased accuracy of recall due to the limitation it places on the influence of prior knowledge. Often our brains will fill in gaps in our memories using pre-existing ideas. For example, if someone has an image in their mind that a robber would wear a ski mask, their brain may put a ski mask on the robber even if they did not really see one. Since our brains are not used to thinking of things in reverse order, we are less likely to fill in details that were not actually there.

Rapport Building

The interviewer should take the time to establish a rapport with the eyewitness. This can be as simple as empathizing with what the eyewitness has just gone through. Explain to them why their story is important. Throughout the interview, use active listening skills without interrupting. An eyewitness who feels heard and respected will have an easier time recalling accurate information.

Witness Controls the Interview

Allowing the eyewitness to control the interview is probably the most difficult part of CI for veteran officers. The typical police interview is led by the officer asking closed-ended questions and interrupting the eyewitness with more pointed questions about what they are saying. This not only prompts the eyewitness to keep quiet until they are asked more questions but actually leads to less accurate recall of information. The interviewer should instruct the eyewitness to give a free-flowing narrative of what they remember. The eyewitness is, after all, the one with all of the information. The interviewer may prompt the eyewitness using open-ended questions. Notes can be taken during the eyewitness's story to circle back to important points with further open-ended questioning. This technique is superior to interrupting the free flow of information from the eyewitness.

Witness-Compatible Questioning

Good listening skills are important to ensure witness-compatible questioning. When the interviewer asks questions, which should be done sparingly in a CI, they should be relevant to the place the eyewitness currently is within their memory of the event. This means that if the eyewitness is currently discussing what they remember about the victim, any questions should be about the victim. This is not the time for the interviewer to ask questions about the perpetrator. Some officers may find this difficult, especially if they do not believe information about the victim is most important to the case. However, changing the focus of the eyewitness's current memory recollection will not provide the most accurate information.

Mental or Guided Imagery

When prompting an eyewitness to recall further detail, it helps to encourage the eyewitness to recall things from various sensory perspectives. Prompts such as, "what do you remember hearing as the perpetrator left the scene?" or "Think about the vehicle the perpetrator got into as he left," encourage the eyewitness to search their memory through multiple pathways which may stimulate additional recall.

Once the eyewitness has completed their narrative and all follow-up prompts have been addressed, the interviewer should provide a formal summary and conclusion to the interview. It is important that the interviewer summarize for the eyewitness what they have heard them say during the interview. This will allow for corrections to the official record and may even prompt additional memory recall. The interview process should conclude with a reiteration of empathy and sincere appreciation of the witness's cooperation and hard work. See Table 10.1 for a suggested structure for a CI.

Eyewitness Identification

The lineup is the most common method used by law enforcement for eyewitness identification of a perpetrator. Lineups can be in person or via a pack of photos, however, it is far more common these days that photo lineups are used. According to Wells and Olson (2003), there are four categories of research on the ways law enforcement personnel can affect the

Table 10.1 Suggested structure of the Cognitive Interview (Griffiths & Milne, 2010, as cited in Paulo, Albuquerque & Bull, 2013, p. 194).

1	Greet and rapport
2	Explain the aims of the interview
3	Initiate a free report (using context reinstatement technique and open-ended questions)
4	Questioning (using report everything and witness-compatible questioning)
5	Varied and extensive retrieval (using different perspectives and temporal orders)
6	Investigatively important questions (now the interviewer can introduce topics, even though the witness didn't yet mention these, if they are crucial for the investigation)
7	Summary
8	Closure
9	Evaluation (evaluating obtained information and interviewers' performance)

identification by an eyewitness of a perpetrator in a lineup: "instructions, content, presentation method, and behavioral influence" (p. 285).

Instructions

One of the most important findings to come out of eyewitness identification research is including in the instructions that the perpetrator *may not be present* in the lineup. In an effort to help catch the bad guy, eyewitnesses have a strong desire to choose *someone* from the lineup. Without proper instructions that the perpetrator may not be present, the eyewitness may feel that choosing no one is unhelpful to the investigation. In an effort to combat this tendency, law enforcement will often ask the eyewitness how confident they are in their selection. While this is a good step toward accuracy, confidence is not immune to influence. Research has shown that eyewitnesses may be only somewhat confident at the time of their initial identification, but upon repeated exposure to the person they initially identified, they become more and more confident. Any features of the actual perpetrator can actually be *replaced* in the eyewitness's memory by the face they identified in the lineup (See Box 10.1). This will likely lead the eyewitness to be more confident over time and perhaps willing to state that they are certain on the witness stand at trial. Further research has demonstrated that time to identification is a better predictor of accuracy. This makes sense since someone will more quickly point out a perpetrator if they truly remember seeing them. If an eyewitness spends time considering the various people in the lineup, they are likely engaging in **relative judgment** of the faces. This means they are probably using comparisons among those present in the lineup and a process of elimination to come to their final identification. Research has shown that this process leads to more false identifications since there is no guarantee that the perpetrator is actually present in the lineup. The content and presentation method of the lineup can also increase the use of **absolute judgment** rather than relative judgment.

Content

The content of the photo lineup is important for lessening the likelihood of false identifications. When constructing a photo lineup, law enforcement will include their suspect along with other photos known as **fillers**. Who is included as a filler is very important for accurate identification. It requires a delicate balance between similarity and dissimilarity. The fillers should be similar enough to the suspect that the suspect does not stand out. If the fillers do not at least somewhat resemble the suspect, the tendency to use relative judgment will be

Box 10.1 The case of Jennifer Thompson and Ronald Cotton

In the middle of the night in July 1984, Jennifer Thompson awoke to a man in her bedroom with a knife to her throat. The man was in her home for thirty minutes before she was able to escape. During her ordeal, Thompson was determined to remember details about her rapist, determined to be able to help police find him if she lived.

Within hours of her rape, Thompson worked with detectives to create a composite sketch. That sketch led to a suspect: Ronald Cotton. Cotton was first put into a six-pack photo lineup. While not a double-blind administration and presented simultaneously, police did tell Thompson that it was okay to not select someone from the lineup. But Thompson was determined to catch the guy who had done this to her. After studying the photos for five minutes, she selected a man from the lineup saying she was sure he was her attacker. Days later, she was brought in to try to identify her rapist in a physical lineup. Even though the investigators again assured her it was okay to say he was not there or that she was unsure, Thompson felt mounting pressure to make an identification. She ended up again selecting Ronald Cotton. This made her even more confident that she had identified the right man. Police proceeded with prosecuting Cotton, and with Thompson's confident identification on the stand, he was convicted and sentenced to life plus 50 years in prison.

While in prison, he met Bobby Poole. They looked so much alike that correctional officers often confused them. Then other inmates heard Poole bragging that he had committed the crimes for which Cotton was convicted. This won Cotton a second trial, but Thompson's testimony that he was her rapist again earned him a conviction. In fact, Thompson was incensed that anyone would think she would not remember the face from the most horrible night of her life. Ronald Cotton's face was the one she saw in her nightmares.

Thompson believed Cotton was her rapist until DNA proved her wrong. She was filled with guilt at the news. In 1995, Cotton was exonerated. Thompson asked for his forgiveness, which he granted. They are now good friends, together raising awareness of faulty eyewitness memory. You can read more about their case in their co-authored memoir *Picking Cotton*.

heightened – and easier. However, the fillers should not be so similar that the suspect simply blends in with the fillers and makes it extremely difficult for an eyewitness to make any choice at all. This becomes especially important when the eyewitness is of a different race than those in the lineup. When choosing fillers for a photo lineup, law enforcement must be careful about who is included.

Presentation Method

The presentation method of the photo lineup can affect the manner in which the eyewitness selects the alleged perpetrator. As previously mentioned, it is better for the eyewitness to use absolute judgment over relative judgment. The way in which the lineup is presented to the eyewitness can greatly impact their manner of judgment. The **simultaneous lineup**, in which all photos are presented to the eyewitness at once, promotes the use of relative judgment.

This is because all of the photos are presented together and easily compared. The **sequential lineup**, in which the photos are presented to the eyewitness one at a time, forces the eyewitness to use absolute judgment in determining whether or not each photo looks like the perpetrator whom they saw. Therefore, law enforcement should use sequential lineups when seeking an eyewitness identification.

Behavioral Influence

Finally, we look at how law enforcement behavior can influence eyewitness identifications. When presenting an eyewitness with a photo lineup, officers may consciously or unconsciously provide feedback to the eyewitness based on their selection. First, the person presenting the photo lineup should not pressure the eyewitness to make a selection. In fact, based on the discussion of instructions, the eyewitness should be *discouraged* from making a selection if they are unsure. Second, if and when the eyewitness does make a selection, it should not be indicated in any way whether or not they made the "right" choice. This may be harder than it sounds. Even if the officer does not overtly indicate their approval or disapproval of the eyewitness's selection, they may make a subconscious signal of their feelings. Research has shown that this can have a profound effect on eyewitness confidence in their selection. Thankfully, there is an easy solution to this problem. It is best practice to have an officer unfamiliar with the case administer the photo lineup, known as **double-blind lineup administration.** This way it is not possible for subconscious influence on the eyewitness's decision, because the person administering the lineup has no knowledge of whether their choice is "right" or "wrong."

Interrogating Suspects

Perhaps the most widely used method in investigations is the **Reid Technique** of Interviewing and Interrogation. It was created in the 1940s and 1950s by a former polygraph examiner working in Chicago, John E. Reid. The Reid Technique consists of three stages: factual analysis, the Behavioral Analysis Interview, and the accusatory interview. **Factual analysis** consists of assessing evidence to identify persons of interest to interview. The **Behavioral Analysis Interview** (BAI) offers suggestions for determining whether an interviewee is innocent or guilty. The process of the BAI consists of asking neutral baseline questions, followed by a series of investigative and behavior-provoking questions. This process is intended to provide cues to the investigator as to the likelihood of the interviewee's guilt via deception detection. Finally, someone deemed likely to be guilty due to perceived deception during the BAI will then undergo the **accusatory interview**, discussed later in this chapter.

Detecting Deception

Humans are bad at detecting deception. Most studies indicate that even with training in various techniques, people cannot spot a lie much better than guessing. However, some techniques are better than others. And given the importance of lie detection in criminal investigations, understanding what are and are not good indicators of deception is important.

First, we will look at what are not good indicators of deception. Unfortunately, the indicators that are taught in the Reid Technique are not good indicators of deception. (It should be noted that proponents of the Reid Technique have criticized research on its effectiveness as misunderstanding the goal of detecting "lies" with its true goal of detecting "liars"; Horvath et al., 2008.) Nonverbal cues, such as avoiding eye contact, are commonly brought up in Reid Technique trainings as an indication that the suspect is lying. Research has found that not only are these nonverbal cues not good indicators of deception, but relying on them can lead to false confessions. In studies by Kassin and his collaborators (Kassin & Fong, 1999; Meissner & Kassin, 2002), those trained to detect deception using nonverbal cues had higher confidence in their abilities despite not actually being better at spotting liars. Relying on nonverbal cues is also problematic due to varying norms across cultures. For example, some cultures consider eye contact to be rude or disrespectful. Also, due to the widespread belief that certain nonverbal cues indicate deception, good liars will deliberately try to mimic behavior expected of a truth-teller.

What *has* research found to be correlated with deception? A meta-analysis of deception-detection studies by DePaulo and her colleagues (2003) discovered that liars tell less detailed and less rational tales. Those who are lying tend to offer fewer details than those who are telling the truth. False stories have inconsistencies and are less plausible or logical than true stories. These findings lend credence to the technique of cognitive lie detection.

Cognitive Lie Detection

Not to be confused with cognitive interviewing (described earlier in the chapter), **cognitive lie detection** is all about increasing **cognitive load**. It is premised on the idea that lying is cognitively difficult, due to having to keep one's story straight and monitoring believability. Therefore, someone who is telling the truth should have no problem telling their story under increased cognitive load. But a liar may slip up when put under cognitive pressure.

Cognitive lie detection offers three techniques to increase cognitive load. One, ask the person to tell their story in the reverse order. This not only increases cognitive load as it is a difficult task for both the truth-teller and the liar, but a liar is less likely to have rehearsed their story backward. Two, ask for more details or listen for the amount of detail offered. Due to having to remember a false story, liars will typically not provide a lot of details and will have more difficulty making up details on the spot. The difficulty in spontaneous fabrication leads to the third suggestion of cognitive lie detection: ask unexpected questions. Having rehearsed their story beforehand, deceivers will have prepared for certain types of questions. Throwing them off with unexpected questions will result in verbal cues to deception that are more reliable, such as increased response time.

Interrogation Techniques

Once police believe they have narrowed in on a suspect, that suspect is subjected to a special type of interview called an **interrogation**. There are two broad styles of interrogation: accusatory and information gathering.

Accusatory Interrogation Styles

Accusatory styles of interrogation have a long tradition in Western law enforcement. You may have heard the phrase the "**third degree.**" This was a term used in the early twentieth century to describe interrogation tactics that would now be considered torture. The fourteenth edition of *Encyclopedia Britannica* described the third degree as "not only the use of physical violence, but also such forms of torture as depriving a prisoner of food, drink, sleep and toilet facilities and the prolonged and uninterrupted interrogation of him when exhausted, suffering and broken down by such deprivations" (1929; as cited in Keedy, 1937, footnote 3). Keedy (1937) noted that many police officers of the day denied using such tactics. Nonetheless, the Supreme Court of the United States (SCOTUS) banned the use of such physical force and violence to obtain confessions in *Brown v Mississippi* (1936). Since then, police have turned to psychological manipulation in their interrogation of suspects.

As noted earlier, the Reid Technique is the most widely used method of interrogation today. There are nine steps in this accusatory method of interrogation, most of which entail minimizing and maximizing techniques. **Minimizing techniques** include offering excuses or neutralizations and suggesting, but not promising, leniency (such leniency rarely happens after confession). **Maximizing techniques** include inflating the amount and veracity of evidence against the suspect and suggesting that cooperation is the only way out of the situation. Other steps of the Reid Technique of interrogation (i.e., step three, handling denials, and step four, overcoming objections) instruct interrogators to push past denials and objections made by the person being interrogated. Supporters of the Reid Technique believe "[a]n innocent person will not allow such denials to be cut off" (Inbau et al., 2013, p. 188). However, there is no empirical evidence to support such assertions. In fact, as we will see in the later section on false confessions, the Reid Technique of interrogation indeed helps police obtain confessions – both true and false.

Information Gathering Interrogation Styles

Contrary to the accusatory interrogation style, the **information gathering interrogation style** seeks to gather information rather than elicit a confession. This style focuses on rapport building and being truthful with the accused. The approach is very similar to the Cognitive Interview (CI) commonly reserved for cooperative witnesses. But allowing the suspect to provide their side of the story, uninterrupted, allows for opportunities to catch them in lies and inconsistencies – especially when coupled with strategic use of evidence. Strategic use of evidence will be discussed in detail after a review of a common model of information gathering interrogation, the PEACE model.

PEACE MODEL

In the early 1990s, the United Kingdom (UK) began the development of what has become the standard for information gathering interrogation techniques. The **PEACE model** stands for: Planning and preparation; Engage and explain; Obtain an Account; Closure; Evaluation.

The initial step of planning and preparation is seen as important by all investigators, no matter their preferred interrogation style. Planning involves mentally gathering the necessary information for the interrogation. This includes information on the crime incident, including evidence already obtained and evidence still needed, as well as information about the suspect to be interrogated. Preparation conveys the need to prepare the physical aspects of the interrogation, such as the interrogation room and any equipment needed. Planning and preparation may seem obvious, but they are incredibly important first steps in an information gathering interrogation.

The engage and explain step in the PEACE process is all about rapport building. Being clear and reasonably accommodating from the very beginning will lead to more information gathering. The interrogator should ensure that the subject is comfortable and their basic needs are met (e.g., providing a beverage). In addition to basic rapport building, it is important that the interrogator explain exactly what is going on to the subject. Why are they here? What do officers want to know? If charges have been filed, what are they? Being open and honest about the situation will go a long way to building trust and rapport. It may also appease hostile or uncooperative subjects.

An important step of information gathering interrogation techniques is allowing the subject to provide their account of what happened without interruption. In the case of a suspect interrogation, this can be seen as "giving them the rope to hang themselves with." Listening skills are crucial at this stage. The interrogator should listen closely to the subject's account and make note of any inconsistencies. Once the subject has concluded their full account, clarifying questions can be asked. These should be open-ended questions designed to get the subject talking again. Only once a full account has been provided and clarified by the subject should the interrogator begin questioning the inconsistencies in the narrative. This should not be accusatory. Inconsistencies should simply be brought up, allowing the subject to clarify or change their story. How inconsistencies are addressed by the subject will either clear them up or provide more rope, so to speak.

Upon completion of the bulk of the interrogation, it is important to summarize what the subject has said and provide information on the next steps. Summarizing the subject's account, including any clarifications and changes made, is crucial to ensuring that the report is correct and making the subject feel fully heard. This summary process also serves as a final offering to add anything to the narrative. The subject should then be informed of what to expect next, including whether they may be asked to provide additional interviews.

The final step of the PEACE model involves not only evaluating the information that was provided by the subject of the interview but also reflecting on the quality of the interview. The narrative provided by the subject should be evaluated based on other evidence in the case. Similarly, existing evidence in the case should be evaluated based on the subject's narrative. This constant re-evaluation of all evidence and information related to a case will ensure that information gathering is the primary goal of the process. Additionally, officers should be willing to reflect on and evaluate their own performance. Seeking to constantly improve their techniques will lead to growth in their abilities as an interviewer and interrogator.

Strategic Use of Evidence

Evidence that has already been obtained can be used strategically to confront suspects with inconsistencies in their established narrative. This **strategic use of evidence** (SUE) aids in detecting deception. According to the PEACE technique, the person being interrogated should not be told about any existing evidence until they are locked into a narrative. Only then can evidence be strategically used to elucidate aspects of the suspect's narrative that do not make sense. Withholding knowledge of evidence allows for easier deception detection, as a truthful person's narrative should not contradict other solid evidence. As such, investigators should be careful to understand the veracity of existing evidence.

False Confessions

Through high-profile exonerations, more people have become aware of the phenomenon of **false confessions.** Using the case of the Norfolk Four (see Box 10.2) to illustrate, Leo and Davis (2010) identified seven ways in which false confessions that lead to wrongful convictions can be explained through common psychological processes. These are misleading specialized knowledge, tunnel vision/confirmation biases, motivational biases, emotion,

Box 10.2 False confessions: A continuation of the case of the Norfolk Four

You may have noticed in the first discussion of the Norfolk Four (see Box 9.3 in Chapter 9) that only five of the eight men implicated in Michelle Moore-Bosko's rape and murder confessed to committing the crimes. These were the Norfolk Four (Danial Williams, Joseph Dick Jr., Eric Wilson, and Derek Tice) and the self-confessed sole perpetrator, Omar Ballard. Although there was physical evidence against Ballard (his DNA was found at the crime scene), the Norfolk Four were convicted based on their confessions alone. How did this happen?

The main interrogator in the case, Detective Robert Ford, was described by many as a "bulldog." He relentlessly pursued confessions from suspects and was known for obtaining them. The reasons these men confessed to crimes they did not commit can be explained in three categories: exhaustion, lies, and intimidation.

Exhaustion: As is common in interrogations, the men were in the interrogation room for a long time. In Williams's first interrogation, he was left waiting for an hour and a half before being interrogated for eleven hours, until 7 am. He had not eaten since 9 am the previous morning. Dick was interrogated for nine hours before his initial confession (all confessions needed to be revised as more people were implicated). Wilson was interrogated for ten hours, also overnight. Tice was interrogated for nine hours.

Lies: All four false confessors were lied to about failing their respective polygraphs. Interrogators also lied to Williams about an eyewitness seeing him leaving Bosko's apartment around the time of the murder. Dick was falsely told that his alibi did not check out. In fact, investigators never even attempted to confirm Dick's alibi.

Intimidation: Ford told all four of the false confessors that they would be given the death penalty if they did not confess. According to Leo and Davis (2010), Dick was also threatened with physical violence prior to his confession. Also, "Wilson later testified that he would have falsely confessed to anything... to get away from Detective Ford" (Leo & Davis, 2010, p. 15).

With the exception of the alleged threat of physical violence, the above tactics are all perfectly legal. However, many jurors are not told of the circumstances under which someone confessed to a crime. And many people believe that no one would confess to something they did not do. Without proper context and an understanding of the phenomenon of false confessions, juries will continue to convict innocent people.

institutional influences, inadequate and/or misleading relevant knowledge and beliefs, and progressively constricting relevant information.

Misleading Specialized Knowledge

A confession is much more credible if it contains information that only the perpetrator would know. This is why police often withhold certain information from the press in high-profile cases. Some knowledge needs to be kept "special" so investigators will know when they have the right person. But what if this specialized knowledge is consciously or subconsciously leaked to a suspect during interrogation? This is what Leo and Davis (2010) called **misleading specialized knowledge** (MSK). It is misleading because it was not knowledge that the suspect actually had prior to interrogation. How could this happen? "Motivational biases among police may combine with genuine failures of memory to obscure the true source of MSK, even as early as during the interrogation, and as late as after the suspect has definitively been proven innocent" (Leo & Davis, 2010, p. 28).

Tunnel Vision/Confirmation Biases

While psychologists see tunnel vision and confirmation bias as distinct phenomena, they combine within the criminal justice system to encourage false confessions and wrongful convictions. **Tunnel vision** is the tendency to focus our attention on one thing to the exclusion of all others. Athletes might call it being "in the zone." But when this happens in a criminal investigation, it can lead to confirmation bias. There may be various reasons an investigator homes in on a certain suspect. But if they develop tunnel vision, they may subconsciously see all other evidence in light of their belief that the suspect is guilty (i.e., confirmation bias). Erroneous cues to deception taught by the Reid Technique can exacerbate this effect. And accusatory interrogation techniques in general typically rely on the assumption that the suspect is guilty. Ironically, a confession (coerced or otherwise) is also subject to confirmation bias. Rather than question the integrity of the confession, investigators see it as further proof of their existing belief in the suspect's guilt.

Motivational Biases

The psychological concepts of motivated cognition and goal pursuit explain our tendency to focus our attention on what we are motivated to achieve. In this way, our motivations and goals can lead to tunnel vision. Many criminal justice actors are motivated both internally and externally to solve a case quickly and ensure a conviction. Indeed, professional reputations are often based on case closures and convictions – not to mention the public pressure in high-profile cases. Even the person being interrogated is motivated by their goals. Their initial goal is to assert their innocence. Interrogation techniques are often designed to wear away at this goal and replace it with the goal of minimizing the consequences. When a person being interrogated is factually innocent, they may falsely confess to meet a new goal of escaping the harsh interrogation.

Psychological phenomena such as cognitive dissonance, groupthink (covered in Chapter 9), and simple pride can lead to an increased commitment to previously stated beliefs. Simply put: people do not like to admit they were wrong. **Cognitive dissonance** is an uncomfortable state in which your stated beliefs contradict new information or circumstances. When faced with cognitive dissonance, we must either change our belief (i.e., admit we were wrong) or dismiss the new information as somehow flawed. Groupthink and pride can certainly impact which of these paths we choose, often causing us to double down on our existing beliefs and dismiss information to the contrary. This is also an example of confirmation bias.

Emotion

Stress, fear, and anger all come into play in a criminal investigation, all of which can contribute to false confessions and wrongful convictions. The stress and fear induced in the suspect during an interrogation can contribute to them making a confession to escape the interrogation and/or more severe punishment. This is indeed the goal of an accusatory interrogation. But when the suspect is innocent, stress and fear can lead to false confessions. The investigators are likely also feeling anger and stress, having witnessed the aftermath of a crime and feeling the pressure to solve it. These emotions can contribute to the investigator having tunnel vision and becoming susceptible to confirmation bias.

Institutional Influences

As noted earlier, there are often institutional pressures to close cases and convict defendants. These pressures are often coupled with financial restrictions limiting or directing the path of the case. The vast majority of police departments do not have access to all of the fancy forensics we see on television. These financial limitations may increase the pressure for investigators to secure a confession and may also affect their bias towards believing it.

Inadequate and/or Misleading Relevant Knowledge and Beliefs

Most people are not aware of the dangers of false confessions. In fact, most people probably believe that an innocent person would never confess to a heinous crime that they did not commit. This includes police officers, prosecutors, defense attorneys, judges and jurors. Investigators have the added disadvantage of possibly receiving *misinformation* on the risk of false confessions. Although the Reid Technique included a chapter on "Distinguishing between True and False Confessions" (Inbau et al., 2013, p. 339) in their training manual beginning in 2001, the discussion largely downplays the likelihood of someone confessing to a crime they did not commit. Further, proponents of accusatory interrogation techniques usually do not acknowledge that these techniques can elicit false confessions. Inaccurate beliefs about the human ability to correctly detect deception also affect judgments of the legitimacy of confessions, from police to jurors.

Progressively Constricting Relevant Information

The very nature of the criminal justice system funnels information and evidence. Police have the broadest pool of evidence to sift through. The judgments made by investigators regarding all of that initial information filter the information that is received by subsequent actors in the criminal justice system. As such, potentially exonerating information may not even make its way to attorneys, judges, and jurors. Evidence that a confession may be false may be included in "all evidence regarding the initial interactions of police with the suspect, all evidence relevant to probable cause for targeting the suspect (including leads to other suspects), and all evidence regarding the interrogation itself" (Leo & Davis, 2010, p. 46). This information may be found in police reports and recordings of interrogations. Reports are limited by the information included – or more importantly not included. Although recording interrogations is recommended by myriad professional organizations, it is still not required in all 50 states. Even when interrogations are fully video recorded, research has shown that the focus of the angle can affect perceptions of confession credibility (see Lassiter & Lindberg, 2010).

Types of False Confessions

Saul Kassin is inarguably the leading scholar on false confessions. He began researching them in the early 1980s, long before DNA exonerations would prove them a huge cause of wrongful convictions. In 1985, Kassin and Wrightsman articulated three types of false confessions: voluntary, coerced-compliant, and coerced-internalized.

Voluntary False Confessions

"A **voluntary false confession** is a self-incriminating statement that is offered without external pressure from the police" (Kassin, 1997, p. 225). This type of false confession is perhaps most baffling – until you consider the possible reasons. The most relatable reason one might volunteer a false confession is to protect a friend or family member. A psychological need for attention may be another reason someone would choose to confess to something they did not do. Indeed, it is a symptom of several personality disorders, with histrionic personality disorder being the most likely to cause someone to falsely confess.

Coerced-Compliant False Confessions

"**Coerced-compliant confessions** occur when a suspect confesses in order to escape or avoid an aversive interrogation or to gain a promised reward" (Kassin, 1997, p. 225). This type of false confession is probably the easiest to understand and perhaps the most common. The goal of accusatory interrogations is to elicit a confession; the process is coercive by design. And given what psychology has taught us about deference to authority (see Chapter 5), coerced-compliant false confessions seem obvious.

Coerced-Internalized False Confessions

"**Coerced-internalized confessions** are those in which an innocent person – anxious, tired, confused, and subjected to highly suggestive methods of interrogation – actually comes to believe that he or she committed the crime" (Kassin, 1997, p. 226). Suggestibility, minimization, and false evidence all play into coerced-internalized confessions. Common techniques used in accusatory interrogations can lead a suggestible but innocent person to fully believe that they committed a crime that they did not commit. Investigators routinely offer minimizations such as, "Maybe you blacked out," to push back on suspect denials. Convincing the suspect that there is an abundance of evidence against them or that they failed a polygraph test are also common tactics in an accusatory interrogation. These techniques have been known to lead highly suggestible people to internalize a false confession.

Groups Most Vulnerable to Falsely Confessing

Various sources point to juveniles and those with mental impairments as highly suggestible and most susceptible to falsely confessing (see Kassin et al., 2010 for an overview). First, these groups are overrepresented among exonerees who were wrongfully convicted due to false confessions. Research in developmental psychology has shown that juveniles are "cognitively and psychosocially less mature than adults – and that this immaturity manifests in impulsive decision making, decreased ability to consider long-term consequences, engagement in risky behaviors, and increased susceptibility to negative influences" (Kassin et al., 2010, p. 19). Low IQ (below 70) has been linked with increased suggestibility due to "tendencies to rely on authority figures for solutions to everyday problems; please persons in authority; seek out friends; feign competence; exhibit a short attention span; experience memory gaps; lack impulse control; and accept blame for negative outcomes" (Kassin et al., 2010, p. 21). There is some research that suggests those with certain mental illnesses may be at increased risk of making false confessions, though more research is needed regarding which specific disorders are more vulnerable. Despite these special populations being more susceptible to and overrepresented among false confessors, the majority of false confessions are given by adults of average intelligence and mental health. Therefore, anyone could fall victim to coercive interrogation tactics.

Summary

This chapter covered various topics where psychology intersects with police procedures. We learned the ways in which our fallible memories can cause problems in eyewitness statements and identifications and ways to improve these crucial investigative tools. Issues surrounding another investigative tool, interrogation, were presented, including the ways traditional interrogation techniques can lead to false confessions. Information gathering models of interrogation are more psychologically sound, making them less likely to cause false confessions. We also learned that humans are horrible lie detectors, but cognitive lie detection techniques may help.

References

Antes, J. R. (1974). The time course of picture viewing. *Journal of Experimental Psychology*, *103*(1), 62–70.

Brown v Mississippi, 6297 U.S. 278 (1936).

DePaulo, B. M., Lindsay, J. L., Malone, B. E., Muhlenbruck, L., Charlton, K., & Cooper, H. (2003). Cues to deception. *Psychological Bulletin*, *129*(1), 74–118.

Horvath, F., Blair, J. P., & Buckley, J. P. (2008). The behavioral analysis interview: Clarifying the practice, theory and understanding of its use and effectiveness. *International Journal of Police Science and Management*, *10*(1), 101–118. https://doi.org/10.1350/ijpsm.2008.10.1.68

Fisher, R. P., & Geiselman, R. E. (2010). The cognitive interview method of conducting police interviews: Eliciting extensive information and promoting therapeutic jurisprudence. *International Journal of Law and Psychiatry*, *33*(5-6), 321–328.

Griffiths, A., & Milne, R. (2010). The application of cognitive interview techniques as part of an investigation. In C. A. Ireland & J. M. Fisher (Eds.), *Consultancy and advising in forensic practice: Empirical and practical guidelines* (pp. 71–90). BPS Blackwell.

Inbau, F. E., Reid, J. E., Buckley, J. P., & Jayne, B. C. (2013). *Criminal interrogation and confessions* (5th ed.). Jones & Barlett Learning.

Innocence Project. (2020, April 15). *How Eyewitness Misidentification Can Send Innocent People to Prison.* https://innocenceproject.org/how-eyewitness-misidentification-can-send-innocent-people-to-prison/

Kassin, S. M. (1997). The psychology of confession evidence. *American Psychologist*, *52*(3), 221–233.

Kassin, S. M., Drizin, S. A., Grisso, T., Gudjonsson, G. H., Leo, R. A., & Redlich, A. D. (2010). Police-induced confessions: Risk factors and recommendations. *Law and Human Behavior*, *34*(1), 3–38.

Kassin, S. M., & Fong, C. T. (1999). "I'm innocent!": Effects of training on judgements of truth and deception in the interrogation room. *Law and Human Behavior*, *23*(5), 499–516.

Kassin, S. M., & Wrightsman, L. S. (1985). Confession evidence. In S. M. Kassin & L. S. Wrightsman (Eds.), *The psychology of evidence and trial procedure* (pp. 67–94). Sage.

Keedy, E. R. (1937). The third degree and legal interrogation of suspects. *University of Pennsylvania Law Review And American Law Register*, *85*(8), 761–777.

Lassiter, G. D., & Lindberg, M. J. (2010). Video recording custodial interrogations: Implications of psychological science for policy and practice. *The Journal of Psychiatry & Law*, *38*(1-2), 177–192.

Leo, R. A., & Davis, D. (2010). From false confession to wrongful conviction: Seven psychological processes. *The Journal of Psychiatry & Law*, *38*(1/2), 9–56.

Loftus, E. F., & Palmer, J. C. (1974). Reconstruction of automobile destruction: An example of the interaction between language and memory. *Journal of Verbal Learning and Verbal Behavior*, *13*(5), 585–589.

Loftus, E. F. (1975). Leading questions and the eyewitness report. *Cognitive Psychology*, *7*(4), 560–572.
Loftus, E. F., & Zanni, G. (1975). Eyewitness testimony: The influence of the wording of a question. *Bulletin of the Psychonomic Society*, *5*, 86–88.
Meissner, C. A., & Kassin, S. M. (2002). "He's guilty!": Investigator bias in judgements of truth and deception. *Law and Human Behavior*, *26*(5), 469–480.
Morgan, C. A., Hazlett, G., Doran, A., Garrett, S., Hoyt, G., Thomas, P., Baranoski, M., & Southwick, S. M. (2004). Accuracy of eyewitness memory for persons encountered during exposure to highly intense stress. *International Journal of Law and Psychiatry*, *27*(3), 265–279.
Paulo, R. M., Albuquerque, P. B., & Bull, R. (2013). The enhanced cognitive interview: Towards a better use and understanding of this procedure. *International Journal of Police Science & Management*, *15*(3), 190–199.
Steblay, N. M. (1992). A meta-analytic review of the weapon focus effect. *Law and Human Behavior*, *16*(4), 413–424.
Wells, G. L., & Olson, E. A. (2003). Eyewitness testimony. *Annual Review of Psychology*, *54*, 277–295.

11 Psychologist as Court Expert

Introduction

Psychologists assist in the criminal courtroom in a number of ways. Marion and her colleagues (2019) distinguish "between the anticipatory process of expert work and actual expert testimony events" (p. 319). Much of the work of psychologists in the courtroom falls into the anticipatory process, but psychologists occasionally take the stand as well. This chapter will cover this work and other topics at the intersection of psychology and the criminal court, from the insanity defense to mental health courts to what it means to be an "expert" in the eyes of the court. But first, we will discuss the assessment and restoration of criminal competency.

Criminal Competency Evaluations

One of the most important tenets of due process is that the defendant understands the proceedings and is able to assist in their own defense. In psycholegal terms, this is known as **adjudicative competency**. Ideally, a person accused of committing a crime should be competent at every important stage of the criminal justice process. Any court actor (i.e., prosecution, judge, and defense) can raise the question of adjudicative competence. Not surprisingly, the issue is most often raised by the defense. Psychologists and psychiatrists have been asked to assess competency to waive Miranda rights, competency to waive counsel (to proceed *pro se)*, competency to be sentenced, and competency to be executed, among many others. The most common competency evaluation requested is **competency to stand trial.**

Competency to Stand Trial

While the idea that a defendant must be competent to stand trial was inherited from English Common Law, it was in 1960 that the Supreme Court of the United States (SCOTUS) identified and codified what it means to be competent to stand trial. This is known as the ***Dusky* standard,** as *Dusky v. United States* (1960) stated that a defendant should have "sufficient present ability to consult with his lawyer with a reasonable degree of rational understanding" and "a rational as well as factual understanding of the proceedings against him" (p. 402). This has also been called the *Dusky* three-prong standard due to the three components of the ability to (1) rationally consult with counsel, (2) rationally understand proceedings, and (3) factually understand proceedings.

Although competency evaluations are commonly conducted by psychologists or psychiatrists, it is important to note that a diagnosed mental illness is not necessary or sufficient to

DOI: 10.4324/9781003250821-13

be deemed incompetent to stand trial (or any other question of competency). This means that just because someone is diagnosed with a mental illness does not automatically mean they are adjudicatively incompetent. Likewise, a defendant does not have to have a diagnosed mental illness to be judged incompetent. Adjudicative competence is a legal distinction, not a medical or psychological one.

Many psychologists who conduct competency evaluations do so without the use of any assessment instrument. The evaluating psychologist will often request various records (e.g., criminal, medical, psychological, educational) to use as supplementary information to an interview with the defendant. Such information can be used to help determine whether the defendant is malingering. **Malingering** is when someone fakes or exaggerates a condition in order to benefit themselves in some way. In the case of competency to stand trial, psychologists must be on the lookout for a defendant who is only pretending to not understand legal proceedings. However, as we will see in the section on restoring competency, it may actually not be in the defendant's best interest to fake incompetence.

How much evidence is necessary for a defendant to be judged incompetent? In *Cooper v. Oklahoma* (1996), SCOTUS ruled that a defendant's competence should be judged by the preponderance of evidence. **Preponderance of evidence** means that there is more evidence than not that a defendant is incompetent (greater than 50%). This standard is typically used in civil cases rather than criminal cases, and it is a much lower standard than that needed to convict someone of a crime (i.e., beyond a reasonable doubt). This lower standard speaks to the importance placed on due process within our criminal justice system; we would rather err on the side of caution than be too strict in assessing a defendant's competence.

Assessment Tools

Similar to risk assessment tools in corrections (see Chapter 13), there has been a drive in the last 30 years to create objective measures of competency to stand trial. Using assessment tools that have been researched and tested can be beneficial in providing more impartial results than relying on professional opinions based on un- or semi-structured interviews and supplementary information. Two such tools for assessing competency to stand trial will be reviewed here: the MacArthur Competence Assessment Tool – Criminal Adjudication (MacCAT-CA) and the Evaluation of Competency to Stand Trial – Revised (ECST-R).

MacArthur Competence Assessment Tool – Criminal Adjudication

The **MacArthur Competence Assessment Tool – Criminal Adjudication** (MacCAT-CA) was developed by the MacArthur Foundation Research Network on Mental Health and the Law (Otto et al., 1998). The aim was to evaluate each of *Dusky's* three prongs, so the MacCAT-CA has three sections: Understanding, Reasoning, and Appreciation. The Understanding and Reasoning sections are based on a vignette (i.e., story) that is read to the defendant. The Appreciation section asks competency-related questions regarding the defendant's own case. The Understanding section asks factual legal questions about the case in the vignette. This section also tests the defendant's ability to be restored to competency. If they do not test well on the initial questions, they are provided a brief lesson on the relevant concepts and asked to paraphrase this information back to the evaluator. The intent of this is to gauge the defendant's ability to learn the factual knowledge required by *Dusky*. The Reasoning section of the MacCAT-CA again uses the vignette to ask the defendant questions regarding what the defendant in the vignette should do at different decision-making points in the legal process. This section is intended to measure the defendant's ability to assist their counsel in their own defense. Finally, the Appreciation section shifts the focus away from the vignette and onto the defendant's own legal case. The defendant is asked questions to ascertain how well they understand and appreciate their own legal situation. This is meant to test the rational-understanding prong of the *Dusky* standard.

Evaluation of Competency to Stand Trial – Revised

The **Evaluation of Competency to Stand Trial – Revised** (ECST-R) was first published in 2004 by Rogers, Tillbrook, and Sewell. Like the MacCAT-CA, the ECST-R was created to specifically test for the three-prong *Dusky* standard. The authors consulted with legal experts to ensure the items on the ECST-R would align with the *Dusky* standards. It also includes a specific test for malingering and is the only competency-to-stand-trial assessment instrument to do so. The ECST-R has three subscales that exactly match the *Dusky* three-prong standard: Factual Understanding of the Courtroom Proceedings (FAC), Rational Understanding of the Courtroom Proceedings (RAC), and Consult with Counsel (CWC). Interspersed in these three subscales are questions that explicitly test for malingering, resulting in an Atypical Presentation (ATP) subscale. The administration style of the ECST-R is a semi-structured interview with a few structured questions. Unlike the MacCAT-CA, the ECST-R focuses mostly on the defendant's knowledge of and experience with their own case.

Restoration of Competency

If it is decided that a defendant is incompetent to stand trial, they will be ordered into treatment to restore their competency. The trial cannot continue until the defendant has been restored to competence. Restoration treatment should focus on the underlying condition that has led to legal incompetence. This is usually a mental illness and/or lack of knowledge or understanding of the legal processes. When the underlying cause is a mental illness, the defendant may be provided medication. When the underlying cause is a lack of knowledge or understanding, legal education will likely be the restoration treatment. When necessary, both medication and education are used. Regardless of the treatment protocol, most jurisdictions provide competency treatment in an inpatient setting, often at state-run psychiatric hospitals.

There are two important constitutional concerns regarding competency restoration, both of which have been addressed by SCOTUS. The first is the indefinite nature of the time it will take to restore someone to competency. The Constitution protects the right of citizens to a speedy trial (Sixth Amendment) and restricts loss of liberty without due process (Fifth Amendment). This issue was partially addressed in *Jackson v. Indiana* (1972). The second constitutional concern around the restoration of competency is whether the state can forcibly medicate a citizen against their will. This issue was addressed in *Sell v. United States* (2003).

Jackson v. Indiana (1972)

When we, as a country, began institutionalizing defendants to attempt to restore them to competency, there were no rules or guidelines for how long the defendant would remain in competency restoration treatment. Despite several doctors indicating that it was unlikely Jackson could be restored to competency, the state of Indiana committed him to a psychiatric hospital to undergo treatment in an attempt to restore him to competency. The case was ultimately heard by SCOTUS, which ruled that a defendant could not be "held more than the reasonable period of time necessary to determine whether there is a substantial probability that he will attain competency in the foreseeable future" (*Jackson v. Indiana*, 1972,

p. 716). If it is determined that the defendant cannot be restored to competency, the state must go through civil commitment procedures to keep the defendant institutionalized. While SCOTUS has not defined a "reasonable period of time," many states have implemented their own limits.

Sell v. United States (2003)

As noted, when the underlying cause of a defendant's incompetency is a mental illness, the treatment to restore competency is likely to be medication. Sell, who had been diagnosed with a delusional disorder and previously diagnosed schizophrenic, refused medication to restore him to competency to stand trial in his fraud and attempted murder cases. SCOTUS held that the Constitution permits the Government to involuntarily administer antipsychotic drugs to render a mentally ill defendant competent to stand trial on serious criminal charges if: the treatment is medically appropriate, is substantially unlikely to have side effects that may undermine the trial's fairness, and, taking account of less intrusive alternatives, is significantly necessary to further important governmental trial-related interests (*Sell v. United States*, 2003, p. 167).

Therefore, defendants can be forcibly medicated to restore competency as long as the stipulations laid out by SCOTUS are met. Specifically, the medication must be appropriate to treat the diagnosed illness; any side effects of the medication will not further compromise the defendant's ability to participate in his/her own defense, and all other avenues to restore competency are insufficient. A recent case of competency restoration is described in Box 11.1.

Box 11.1 The competency restoration of Jared Loughner

On January 8, 2011, United States Representative Gabrielle Giffords was holding an informal town hall meeting with her constituents outside of a grocery store in Tucson, AZ. No one knew that Jared Loughner was planning to shoot the Congresswoman. Loughner arrived with a 9mm handgun and began firing into the crowd. He left six people dead and 14 more injured, including Representative Giffords who was shot in the head but miraculously made a full recovery. The gunman was tackled by witnesses and held until police arrived. Loughner was charged in federal court with dozens of counts of murder and attempted murder of federal employees.

By May 2011, it had become clear to the court that Loughner may not be competent to stand trial. After being evaluated by two professionals, it was determined that he was incompetent to proceed with his trial. He was also diagnosed with paranoid schizophrenia, but Loughner refused medication. A series of rulings and appeals led to the conclusion that while he did not meet the criteria for forcible medication under *Sell v. United States* (2003), the staff at the federal prison hospital could medicate him if he was deemed a danger to himself or others. Perhaps unsurprisingly, such a determination was made, and the prison began giving Loughner antipsychotic drugs against his will. More than a year after his initial competency evaluations, it was determined by the court that Loughner was now competent to stand trial. On August 7, 2012, he pleaded guilty to avoid the death penalty and will spend the rest of his life in federal prison. However, given his diagnosis, he is currently housed at the Federal Medical Center in Rochester, MN, which is run by the Federal Bureau of Prisons.

Competency Services Crisis

According to Gowensmith (2019), competency evaluation and restoration services are in crisis. The work of forensic psychologists over the past several decades has produced more effective competency evaluations and competency restoration processes. However, Gowensmith argues that because these services exist in a system that is bogged down with increasing referrals, both efficiency and effectiveness must be valued. In other words, the field needs to work to find quicker ways to effectively evaluate and restore competency. This is, of course, because it is a violation of the defendant's constitutional rights to be held in custody for extended periods of time *prior to* being convicted of a crime. However, long wait times have become increasingly the case for those defendants referred for competency evaluations and those on inpatient waitlists to be restored to competency. Most often these pre-adjudication defendants are housed in county jails while they wait. It is likely a matter of time before SCOTUS rules that these wait times are unconstitutional, as they did with the indefinite hospitalization of those attempting to be restored to competency in *Jackson.*

Gowensmith (2019) offers several potential solutions to the competency services crisis. The first is to create and validate shorter competency evaluation instruments, including checklists and screening tools. Another suggestion is to increase the number of qualified personnel to administer competency evaluations by expanding training beyond just psychologists and psychiatrists. Increasing the use of outpatient restoration services, rather than inpatient services that often have long waitlists, is another proposition offered by Gowensmith. Mandating shorter wait times is something he suggests with caution, as often quicker turnaround results in compromised validity. More promising may be Gowensmith's proposal of increased use of diversion programs, such as mental health courts, for misdemeanor offenders who may be incompetent to stand trial.

Mental Health Courts

Over the last 30 years, many jurisdictions have created what have collectively been called **specialty courts** or **problem-solving courts.** They are called problem-solving courts because they are intended to take a non-adversarial approach to solving problems that often lead individuals into trouble with the law. They are focused on the treatment of the problem, which is seen as the underlying cause of criminal behavior in some cases. **Mental health courts** are one type of specialty court that are used to divert defendants with mental illnesses away from the adversarial court process and into treatment for their mental illness. These courts are not a get-out-of-jail-free card! Treatment programs are often rigorous and are mandatory for those defendants who choose mental health court over traditional court procedures. Periodic meetings with a mental health court judge ensure that the defendant is on track and committed to their treatment protocol. If they fail to complete the requirements laid out by the mental health court, they will be returned to the traditional court system to face their original charges. If they successfully complete the treatment requirements, in many jurisdictions the case against them will be dismissed and possibly expunged from their record. As mentioned, specialty courts are voluntary options given to defendants who meet certain criteria. Often, these diversion programs are offered to defendants charged with lower-level crimes who are part of the target population (e.g., mentally ill individuals for mental health court or chronic drug users for drug court).

The Insanity Defense

No discussion of the intersection of psychology and the court system would be complete without including the insanity defense. **Insanity** is not a psychological term; it is a legal term. There is no diagnosis of "insanity" in the fifth edition of the *Diagnostic and Statistical Manual of Mental Disorders* (DSM-5). Instead, the legal term "insane" refers to the defendant's mental state at the time the alleged crime was committed. Whereas competency has to do with the defendant's mental state at a certain time during criminal justice procedures (e.g., competency to stand trial considers the defendant's mental state at the time of trial), insanity has to do with the defendant's mental state when they were allegedly committing the crime for which they are being tried. Therefore, insanity is retrospective by its very nature.

A plea from a defendant of **Not Guilty by Reason of Insanity** (NGRI) is not accepted in all jurisdictions. Courts in some states will accept a plea of **Guilty but Mentally Ill** (GBMI) instead. This distinction reflects the public's uneasiness with someone "getting away with" a crime due to mental illness. However, the practical differences between the two pleas are minimal. Both a defendant who is found NGRI and a defendant who is found GBMI will likely spend the rest of their life (or a considerable portion of it) in a secure facility. Somewhat ironically, those convicted GBMI are less likely to get the psychological treatment they need as they are usually sent to the same prisons as any other convicted offender rather than a secure mental health facility, as is typically the case with those found NGRI.

Defining Insanity

There are two Latin phrases that pertain to determining a person's guilt in a crime: *actus reus* and *mens rea*. ***Actus reus*** refers to the criminal act itself; it must be proven that the defendant indeed committed an act that is against the law. ***Mens rea***, or "guilty mind," is a bit more complicated to determine. The concept of *mens rea* encompasses both knowledge that the act was wrong/illegal and the defendant's intention to go through with the act despite the knowledge of its wrongfulness. This intention may be determined to be absent if the defendant is coerced into the act. Self-defense is an example where *actus reus* is present but *mens rea* is absent. Often in self-defense cases, it is clear or admitted that the defendant committed the crime, but it is argued that the defendant did not have a "guilty mind" when committing the act. Instead, it is argued that they were coerced into committing the crime out of fear that the victim was about to cause them immediate bodily harm. An NGRI defense often also acknowledges that a crime was committed (*actus reus*). What is more difficult to determine is whether the defendant's mental state at the time of the alleged offense constitutes an absence of *mens rea*.

Until the mid-twentieth century, American jurisdictions used the **M'Naghten rule** to determine whether a defendant was insane at the time of their alleged offense. In 1843, Daniel M'Naghten intended to assassinate the Prime Minister of the United Kingdom (UK), Sir Robert Peel. Instead, he fatally shot Edward Drummond, Peel's secretary. M'Naghten was found not guilty due to his defense that he suffered paranoid delusions that the government was out to kill him. Even though M'Naghten spent the rest of his life confined in the infamous Broadmoor psychiatric hospital, the public – and Queen Victoria – demanded standards be established so that no one would "get away with" a crime ever again.

The House of Lords of the UK Parliament established the following:

> That if the accused was conscious that the act was one which he ought not to do; and if the act was at the same time contrary to law, he is punishable. In all cases of this kind the jurors ought to be told that every man is presumed to be sane, and to

> possess a sufficient degree of reason to be responsible for his crimes, until the contrary be proved to their satisfaction: and that to establish a defence [*sic*] on the ground of insanity, it must be clearly proved that at the time of commiting [*sic*] the act the party accused was labouring [*sic*] under such a defect of reason, from disease of the mind, as not to know the nature and quality of the act he was doing, or as not to know that what he was doing was wrong.
>
> (*M'Naghten's Case* 1843 10 C & F 200)

Three criteria were established here: (1) the burden of proof of insanity is on the defense (rather than on the prosecution as with the burden of proof of guilt), (2) the defendant must have been suffering a "defect of reason" or "disease of the mind" at the time the crime was committed, and (3) that this "defect of reason" or "disease of the mind" caused the defendant to not know what they were doing or to not know that the act was wrong. The M'Naghten rule is sometimes known as the right/wrong test due to this last criterion. It is also sometimes called the cognitive test, as it focuses on the cognitive elements of knowing and understanding. The M'Naghten rule, or a slight variation of it, is still used today in many US jurisdictions.

The mid-twentieth century brought a widening of the criteria for the insanity defense. *Smith v. United States* (1954) added a volitional or irresistible impulse standard to the M'Naghten criteria, which was also included in the 1962 American Law Institute (ALI) Test. The somewhat controversial volitional or **irresistible impulse test** states that a person can be found insane if at the time that they committed the criminal act, they were unable to control themselves due to a "mental disease or defect." This criterion is sometimes referred to as the "policeman at the elbow" standard, which implies that the impulse was so irresistible that the defendant would have still committed the act even if the police were actively observing it happen. The ALI Test, which in addition to adding the irresistible impulse test also expanded the criterion for the effects of "mental disease or defect" to "lacks substantial capacity" (as opposed to total inability), is still used in some American jurisdictions today. One of the major areas of controversy with this standard is whether or not someone under the influence of a chemical substance could be found insane due to not being able to control their impulses.

The second expansion of the insanity defense in the mid-twentieth century was with the *Durham* rule, named for *Durham v. United States* (1954). The ***Durham* rule** is often referred to as the product rule, as its only standard is that the act was a "product of [i.e., solely caused by] mental disease or mental defect." Perhaps due to the broad nature of this lone criterion, the *Durham* rule was overturned for use in federal court in 1972 (United States v. Brawner, 1972) and is only used in New Hampshire today.

Perhaps the largest overhaul of the insanity defense came after the trial of John Hinckley Jr. in 1982 for his attempted assassination of President Ronald Reagan (and severe wounding of others). Hinckley claimed that his actions were an attempt to impress actor Jodi Foster, and he was found NGRI and sentenced to treatment in a psychiatric hospital. This case catapulted the insanity defense into the national spotlight and citizens did not like it. Congress responded with the **Insanity Defense Reform Act** (IDRA) in 1984. The IDRA removed the irresistible impulse test of some standards and placed the burden of proof of insanity firmly on the defense. Additionally, the IDRA barred expert **"ultimate issue" testimony**. This means that if or when an expert is called to the witness stand regarding the sanity of the defendant, they cannot explicitly testify regarding their opinion of the defendant's meeting of the legal standard of sanity. They may only testify as to their professional opinion regarding the defendant's mental illness and/or mental capacity at the time of the crime. The "ultimate issue" of whether or not the defendant was legally insane must be left to the judge or jury.

Astute readers will notice that the IDRA standards are very similar to the M'Naghten rule. Thus, the insanity defense underwent a similar twentieth-century trajectory as American correctional ideals (see Chapter 13); the insanity defense was broadened in the mid-twentieth century only to once again become stricter in the "tough on crime" era that began in the 1970s and 1980s.

Assessing Insanity

As with competency evaluations, psychologists or other mental health professionals are usually employed to assess whether a defendant was legally insane at the time of their offense. Given the varying definitions of insanity across jurisdictions, the mental health professional tapped to evaluate the defendant should have knowledge of the local standard. According to Zapf and her colleagues (2013), three sources are typically used when evaluating a defendant's sanity:

1 An interview with the defendant;
2 Traditional and/or forensic assessment instruments; and
3 Third-party information, including but not limited to collateral reports, witness statements, victim statements, police reports, and records of various sorts (i.e., mental health, treatment, school, medical, crime scene) (p. 324).

There are two forensic assessment instruments designed specifically for determining insanity at the time of the offense: the Mental State at the Time of the Offense Screening Evaluation (MSE; Slobogin et al., 1984) and the Rogers Criminal Responsibility Assessment Scales (R-CRAS; Rogers, 1984). Both instruments were created in the early 1980s, and only the R-CRAS has been extensively studied. Given the complicated nature of assessing the mental state of someone during a past event, the use of any assessment instrument should only be a supplement to the other two sources of information.

It should come as no surprise that both criminal competency (i.e., mental state at the time for which competency is being questioned) and criminal responsibility (i.e., sanity at the time of the offense) are often questioned for the same defendant. This can lead to real complications in assessing both of these designations. Recall that when someone is deemed incompetent, they are often placed on medication to restore their competency. This medicated state can alter the assessment of sanity at the time of the offense. This issue was somewhat addressed in *Riggins v. Nevada* (1992) when SCOTUS ruled that a defendant pleading NGRI has the right to have the jury or judge see them in a non-medicated state. Nonetheless, evaluators of a defendant's sanity must be aware of whether and how recently the defendant may have been medicated for their mental illness.

Prevalence of the Insanity Defense

Despite the controversy surrounding the insanity defense, it is used much less often than many people think and is successful even more infrequently. The oft-cited statistic that less than 1% of defendants enter a plea of NGRI and that of those, only 26% succeed in being acquitted by reason of insanity came from an eight-state study funded by the

National Institute of Mental Health (NIMH) after the IDRA passed in 1984 (Callahan et al., 1991). Needless to say, these data should be updated. Hopefully, data will be more accessible in our current digital age. Callahan and her colleagues had to manually search through paper court dockets to gather their data! Perhaps this extensive work has deserved to be continually cited over many decades. Nonetheless, updated research should be conducted.

Testifying in Court

As mentioned in the introduction to this chapter, Marion et al. (2019) describe two phases of a psychologist's involvement in legal proceedings: the anticipatory process and the expert testimony event. They note that the vast majority of a psychologist's work comes before a case goes to trial. Indeed, most cases never even go to trial, and yet psychological expertise can be utilized in deciding how a case is handled. The anticipatory process can be thought of as data collection and analysis, with the expert testimony event being a presentation of the psychologist's findings. Psychologists may also testify due to their expert knowledge of issues related to the case, such as eyewitness memory or the hyperarousal of someone with post-traumatic stress disorder (PTSD). When a psychologist does take the stand, they are evaluated the same way as other expert witnesses.

Expert Witness Standards

What makes someone an "expert"? In the American courtroom, it is the trial judge who makes the final determination. However, some guidelines have been provided over the years: *Frye v. United States* (1923), the Federal Rules of Evidence in 1975, and the *Daubert* trilogy in the 1990s. Although these guidelines were created for the federal court system, many states have aligned their standards with the federal courts over the years.

Frye v. United States (1923)

In 1923, *Frye v. United States* was presented before SCOTUS regarding whether an early type of lie detection test should be admitted as evidence. The justices ruled that for scientific evidence to be admissible in a trial, the scientific knowledge on which that evidence is based must be generally accepted by the scientific community at large. This led to the ***Frye* standard** becoming known as the "general acceptance" standard of expert testimony. Those even somewhat familiar with scientific inquiry will recognize the difficulty with this standard. "General acceptance" is a relatively high threshold in the scientific community, as our collective understanding is almost constantly evolving. The *Frye* standard was excluding new scientific evidence that had not yet reached "general acceptance."

Rule 702 of the Federal Rules of Evidence

SCOTUS began drafting the Federal Rules of Evidence in the 1970s, and the rules were enacted into law by Congress in 1975. The Federal Rules of Evidence govern the admissibility of various kinds of evidence in federal criminal and civil trials. Rule 702 provides guidelines for expert testimony intended to loosen the restrictions of the *Frye* standard. SCOTUS proposed amendments to Rule 702 (and other Federal Rules of Evidence) and Congress passed them into law in 2023. These amendments added a preponderance of the evidence standard for the criteria and clarification that it is the expert's opinion that is being evaluated. Rule 702, with recent amendments indicated in italics and strikethrough, states:

> A witness who is qualified as an expert by knowledge, skill, experience, training, or education may testify in the form of an opinion or otherwise if *the proponent demonstrates to the court that it is more likely than not that*:
>
> (a) The expert's scientific, technical, or other specialized knowledge will help the trier of fact to understand the evidence or to determine a fact in issue;
> (b) The testimony is based on sufficient facts or data;
> (c) The testimony is the product of reliable principles and methods; and
> (d) The expert*'s opinion reflects a reliable application of* ~~has reliably applied~~ the principles and methods to the facts of the case.

Thus, **Rule 702 of the Federal Rules of Evidence** dictates that expert testimony should be admitted to trial if the preponderance of the evidence indicates it accurately applies information obtained via the scientific method and will help the trier(s) of fact to better understand aspects of the case. Therefore, the focus of Rule 702 was the reliability of the expert testimony, rather than the stricter general acceptance standard of *Frye*.

Daubert Trilogy

Despite the loosening of the standard for admitting expert testimony by the Federal Rules of Evidence, some jurisdictions were still using *Frye's* general acceptance standard. One such case was a civil case brought by the Daubert family against Merrell Dow Pharmaceuticals in which the Dauberts claimed that a prescription medication manufactured by Merrell Dow was the cause of their children's birth defects. Both sides had experts willing to testify that scientific studies had either shown or not shown a link between the drug and birth defects. However, the expert testimony of the Daubert's witnesses was deemed to not meet "general acceptability." In 1993, the case was heard by SCOTUS which unanimously ruled that the general acceptability standard was outdated and should no longer be considered a requirement by federal courts. The SCOTUS decision in *Daubert v. Merrell Dow Pharmaceuticals* (1993) outlined four criteria for judges to consider when deciding to admit expert testimony:

1 Is it based on theories or ideas that can be empirically tested? And if so, have the theories or ideas been empirically tested?
2 Have the theories or ideas been published in any peer-reviewed journals?
3 What is the error rate for the studies that have been conducted on the theories or ideas?
4 Has the theory, ideas, or technique on which the expert testimony is based obtained general acceptance in its scientific field?

That last guideline may have stood out to you. Indeed, it is the same "general acceptance" standard from *Frye v. United States* (1923)! SCOTUS ruled in *Daubert* that "general acceptance" is a reasonable standard for a judge to use, but it should not be the only standard used. Essentially, if there is general acceptance of an idea within the scientific community, it is safe to say that it should be admitted in a court of law. However, the *absence* of such general acceptance does not preclude admission of the expert testimony when the other standards are met.

Daubert has been criticized for requiring judges to have more knowledge of the scientific process than is part of their traditional education in law school. Given the wide range of topics presented by expert testimony, it is possible and likely that different judges may rule differently on the admissibility of the same expert testimony. This has led to the term "gatekeeper" to refer to a judge's role in expert testimony; it is ultimately up to the discretion of the judge to decide whether or not a specific expert's testimony should be presented at trial. The effect of these potential inconsistencies was addressed in *General Electric v. Joiner* (1997), which is considered part of the ***Daubert* trilogy**. SCOTUS held in this case that appellate courts may only hear appeals of the admission of expert testimony when there is an allegation of abuse of discretion in the judge's admission decision. This limited the number of cases that can be appealed due to differing opinions of the legitimacy of the expert testimony.

The third SCOTUS case included in the *Daubert* trilogy is *Kumho Tire Company v. Carmichael* (1999). In this case, SCOTUS clarified that an expert does not have to be a traditional scientist for the *Daubert* standards to apply. This had direct implications for the admissibility of expert testimony by clinical psychologists, who usually do not conduct scientific research. SCOTUS ruled that one can be an expert even if they do not conduct the scientific research themselves. Despite this broad view of who can be considered an expert, the gatekeeper's role of whether or not expert testimony can be heard during a trial is solely held by the presiding judge. (See Box 11.2 for a case of dubious expert testimony.)

Box 11.2 The occult expert in the West Memphis Three case

In 1993, at the height of the nation's fear of devil-worshipping rituals dubbed the "Satanic Panic," the bodies of three eight-year-old boys, Steven Branch, Christopher Byers, and Michael Moore, were found naked and hogtied in a wooded area of West Memphis, TN. The manhunt was immediate and the pressure to solve the case was high. Less than a month later, police interrogated 17-year-old Jessie Misskelley Jr., who had an IQ of 72, which led to a confession that he, Jason Baldwin, and Damien Echols had killed the three boys. Despite the dubious nature of the confession (see the discussion of false confessions in Chapter10), all three teenagers were charged in the crime.

Police believed that the murders were part of a ritual sacrifice to the devil. To bolster their case, the prosecution sought to present expert testimony from a so-called occult expert, Dr. Dale Griffis. The defense objected to Griffis's testimony being admitted due to the nature of his education. In 1983, Griffis received both his Master's degree in criminal justice and his PhD in "nontraditional group activity" from Columbia Pacific University (CPU), a correspondence university. It had taken him three years to complete both degrees, during which time he attended no classes. Judge David Burnett denied the defense's motion, saying, "I'm not sure in Arkansas or any other state that you have to have any kind of degree to be an expert in a particular field. If you can demonstrate knowledge, education, experience, and training in the field, you could have a third-grade education – if you have other education, experience, and training that qualifies you as an expert. So I'm not persuaded at all about your argument about a mail-order PhD." Dr. Griffis was allowed to testify and all three defendants were ultimately convicted of murder.

In 1997, three years after the convictions of Damien Echols, Jason Baldwin, and Jessie Misskelley, the California Bureau for Private Postsecondary and Vocational Education denied reapproval of CPU's right to grant degrees. When the university's administrators appealed the decision, the appellate court judge determined that CPU was too lenient with their expectations for a doctoral degree. However, all degrees issued *prior to* 1997 are still considered valid.

Summary

Psychologists and the field of psychology have a lot to offer in courtroom proceedings. It is important to due process that any defendant be competent to understand the procedures involved in being accused of a crime and be able to assist in their own defense. Often such competency is hindered by a mental illness, which means restoring a defendant to competency often requires forced medication – a controversial topic. In addition to the debate over whether or not someone should be forcibly medicated by the state, the overburdened system leads to long wait times for competency services. More often than not, defendants spend this time waiting in jail, which is a constitutional concern. Mental health courts may be able to address these issues. Although it is a legal term, the insanity defense is informed by psychology in determining *mens rea,* or whether the defendant possessed a "guilty mind" at the time of the alleged crime. And when psychologists are asked to testify in court, the same admissibility rules apply to them as to other "experts" put on the witness stand.

References

Callahan, L. A., Steadman, H. J., McGreevy, M. A., & Clark Robbins, P. (1991). The volume and characteristics of insanity defense pleas: An eight-state study. *Journal of the American Academy of Psychiatry and the Law Online*, *19*(4), 331–338.

Cooper v. Oklahoma, 517 US 348 (1996).

Daubert v. Merrell Dow Pharmaceuticals, 509 US 579 (1993).

Durham v. United States, 214 F.2d 862 (D.C. Cir. 1954).

Dusky v. United States, 362 US 402 (1960).

Frye v. United States, 293 F. 1013 (D.C. Cir. 1923).

General Electric v. Joiner, 52 US 136 (1997).

Gowensmith, W. N. (2019). Resolution or resignation: The role of forensic mental health professionals amidst the competency services crisis. *Psychology, Public Policy, and Law*, *25*(1), 1–14.

Insanity Defense Reform Act of 1984, 18 U.S.C.S. § 17 (1984).

Jackson v. Indiana, 406 US 715 (1972).

Kumho Tire Company v. Carmichael, 526 US 137 (1999).

Marion, S., Kaplan, J., & Cutler, B. (2019). Expert testimony. In N. Brewer, & A. Bradfield Douglass (Eds.), *Psychological science and the law*. The Guilford Press.

M'Naghten's Case 1843 10 C & F 200.

Otto, R. K., Poythress, N. G., Nicholson, R. A., Edens, J. F., Monahan, J., Bonnie, R. J., Hoge, S. K., & Eisenberg, M. (1998). Psychometric properties of the MacArthur Competence Assessment Tool – Criminal Adjudication. *Psychological Assessment*, *10*(4), 435–443.

Riggins v. Nevada, 504 U.S. 127 (1992).

Rogers, R. (1984). *Rogers Criminal Responsibility Assessment Scales (R-CRAS) and test manual.* Psychological Assessment Resources.

Rogers, R., Tillbrook, C. E., & Sewell, K. W. (2004). *Evaluation of competency to stand trial-revised (ECST-R)*. Psychological Assessment Resources.

Sell v. United States, 539 US 166 (2003).

Slobogin, C., Melton, G. B., & Showalter, C. C. (1984). The feasibility of a brief evaluation of mental state at the time of the offense. *Law and Human Behavior*, *8*, 305–320.

Smith v. United States, 348 US 147 (1954).

United States v. Brawner, 471 F.2d 969 (D.C. Cir. 1972).

Zapf, P. A., Golding, S. L., Roesch, R., & Pirelli, G.. (2013). Assessing criminal responsibility. In Weiner, I. B., & Otto, R. K. (Eds.) *The handbook of forensic psychology*. John Wiley & Sons, Inc.

12 Psychology of the Jury

Introduction

The vast majority of criminal cases are resolved through **plea bargaining**, where the defendant agrees to plead guilty to a lesser charge and/or for a lesser sentence than they would face going to trial. Though they do not happen often, a trial by a jury of one's peers is enshrined in the United States Constitution. Among other rights related to being accused of a crime, the Sixth Amendment guarantees our right to a trial "by an impartial jury of the State and district wherein the crime shall have been committed." As we will see in this chapter, ensuring that this right is not violated is no easy task.

In this chapter, you will learn the basics of a jury and how it is chosen. This will include a discussion of the ways that attorneys consult with psychologists and other social scientists during jury selection – and whether or not they should. We will then turn our attention to the jury itself by examining the psychology of juror decision making and the deliberation process. Finally, the need for psychological assistance for jurors who have served in a traumatic case will be discussed.

What Is a Jury?

A **jury** is a group of people selected from the community where the alleged crime took place. These individuals will listen to evidence of guilt, presented by the prosecution, and innocence, presented by the defense, during a criminal trial. After closing arguments are made by both sides, the jury will proceed to **deliberation**. Here, the individuals will weigh the facts of the case against the charges brought by the prosecution. This process is intentionally secretive to allow jurors the freedom to discuss any relevant information without outside influence. Deliberation can last a short time or as long as it takes to reach a unanimous verdict (see Box 12.1). If the jurors believe that no further deliberation will result in unanimity, the result is a **hung jury**. In this case, the prosecution has the choice to bring charges against the defendant again with a whole new trial process.

Although the term jury may conjure the image of *12 Angry Men* (Lumet, 1957), the reality of juries in America can be very different. First, not all juries consist of 12 individuals. In some jurisdictions, as few as six people can make up a jury. The United States Supreme Court ruled in *Ballew v. Georgia* (1978) that a jury of fewer than six members violates the due process clauses of the Sixth and Fourteenth Amendments. Despite the allowance of smaller juries, most juries still consist of 12 individuals. The film *12 Angry Men* (Lumet, 1957) was released at a time when jurors were just that: white men. Women were

DOI: 10.4324/9781003250821-14

Box 12.1 Unanimous verdicts

Unanimous verdicts have not always been required in American criminal trials. In fact, Louisiana and Oregon did not require unanimous verdicts until the Supreme Court of the United States (SCOTUS) required it in 2020 (*Ramos vs. Louisiana*). Since federal criminal trials do require a unanimous verdict, SCOTUS ruled via the Due Process Clause of the 14th Amendment that states must also require a unanimous verdict in criminal cases.

not allowed to serve on juries in all 50 states until 1968 (Mississippi was the last). Even though Black Americans have technically been allowed to serve on juries since the Supreme Court of the United States (SCOTUS) ruled in 1880 that excluding them violated the Fourteenth Amendment (*Strauder v. West Virginia*, 1880), they have often been systematically excluded. This is still a problem to this day, as we will see in the upcoming section on the venire and voir dire process.

As noted in the introduction to the chapter, jury trials are exceedingly rare. "Between March 2019 and March 2020, guilty pleas accounted for nearly 98% of criminal convictions in federal courts, where data are most reliable" (Evans, 2021). In a survey conducted by Diamond and Salerno (2020), half of judges (50%) and most defense attorneys (85%) blamed mandatory minimum sentencing laws for making pleading to a lesser charge or sentence attractive to defendants. Though this may be unjust, some amount of plea bargaining is necessary to avoid our judicial system grinding to a halt. There would never be enough time for every defendant to seek a full trial by jury.

Venire and Voir Dire

The jury selection process is somewhat complex. Eligible jurors are called to appear for what is called the **venire**. The judge, prosecution, and defense attorneys ask questions of potential jurors in a process called **voir dire** (pronounced *vwar deer*). Potential jurors can be eliminated from the venire in two ways: a **challenge for cause** and a **peremptory challenge.** To challenge the inclusion of a juror for cause, it must be demonstrated that the person would not be able to remain impartial in their assessment of the trial facts. A peremptory challenge is the removal of a juror from the venire without a reason given. Both the defense and prosecution are only allowed a certain number of peremptory challenges. In an adversarial court system, the idea is that when both sides are allowed to exclude potential jurors, the result will be an impartial jury.

SCOTUS has placed some limitations on peremptory challenges. In *Batson v. Kentucky* (1986), SCOTUS ruled that jurors cannot be eliminated from the venire solely based on their race. Since peremptory challenges normally do not require a reason, the defense must raise the question. Once disputed, the prosecution must present a reason for the exclusion that is not based on race. The presiding judge has the ultimate say in whether or not the peremptory challenge was racially motivated, but it has been relatively easy for prosecutors to come up with a seemingly innocuous justification for their challenge. In *J.E.B. v. Alabama ex rel T.B.* (1994), SCOTUS barred the same discrimination (with the same loophole) against female jurors in the venire.

Scientific Jury Selection

Chapter 11 presented many of the ways in which psychologists serve as consultants and experts in legal proceedings. Another one of these ways is in applying psychological principles and methods to the voir dire process. First used in the 1970s, **Scientific Jury Selection** (SJS) is so named because instead of relying on the lawyer's experience and intuition, SJS uses data and empirical knowledge in evaluating potential jurors. This data is obtained by the trial consultant in any number of ways, such as conducting focus groups and polling the community from which the venire is drawn, developing surveys for prospective jurors, and creating **shadow juries** who listen to the trial and can be asked their opinions of the evidence as the trial progresses.

Though many people make their livings as trial consultants, and there was even a prime-time television show on the subject (*Bull*), there is little evidence that SJS influences trial outcomes. Even worse, there are ethical dilemmas with the practice. Trial consultants are not inexpensive, so only those who can afford it have access to SJS. It further creates a sense of unfairness since the primary intention of SJS is a favorable jury rather than the constitutionally required impartial jury (i.e., the Sixth Amendment). To alleviate these concerns, Coughlan (2019) suggests that trial consultants should be hired by the court rather than one side or the other. She further suggests that the field should require licensure and regulation. Currently, anyone can advertise themselves as a trial consultant who uses SJS and be hired by either the defense or the prosecution as such. Coughlan (2019) argues that state licensure and other regulations will increase credibility by requiring educational standards and ethical conduct.

Evidence Presented in Court

Once the jury is selected, the trial begins. The prosecution will present evidence of guilt, and the defense will present evidence of innocence. There are two categories of evidence: circumstantial and direct. **Circumstantial evidence** points to the *circumstances* in which the crime occurred and requires jurors to make a logical inference connecting the defendant with the crime or crime scene. As such, a defendant may be placed at the scene of the crime due to circumstantial evidence, such as lack of alibi, motive, and DNA or fingerprints found at the scene. **Direct evidence** is someone *directly* indicating that the defendant committed the crime, which means no inference is necessary. Direct evidence can come from the defendant in the form of a confession or an eyewitness to the crime. According to surveys of professionals in the legal system (Schwietzer & Nunez, 2018), the following are the most common types of evidence used in criminal trials: "crime-scene pictures, witness to the crime, diagrams of injuries, police officer expert testimony, forensic expert testimony, weapon, fingerprints, maps, audio confession, and video confession" (p. 441).

Notice that DNA is missing from this list. This is because, contrary to many fictional crime shows, most crimes do not include typical DNA evidence (e.g., bodily fluids, hairs, skin cells). In the early days of popular fictional crime shows, court professionals worried about a "**CSI effect.**" They believed jurors expected forensic evidence, particularly DNA evidence, in every case, whether or not that expectation was reasonable. Prosecutors in particular worried that without such evidence, juries would not convict. Though the "CSI effect" became common vernacular, the truth is most jurors are able to distinguish reality from fantasy. While there may have been a minor "CSI effect" in the very early days of fictionalized-crime programming such as the CSI franchise, the vast majority of jurors understand that each crime will have different types of evidence.

But which types of evidence are most influential in juror decision making? Intuitively, eyewitness testimony and confessions seem the most reliable. The fallibility of these types of evidence was discussed at length in Chapter 10. In this chapter, we will focus on whether and why jurors find eyewitness testimony and confessions to be compelling evidence of guilt.

Eyewitness Testimony

Because most people do not understand how memory works, eyewitness testimony may seem very reliable to a juror. Research has shown that the most important aspect of this type of testimony is eyewitness confidence. If a witness identifies the defendant with a high level of confidence, jurors often believe them. Unfortunately, confidence is actually a very poor predictor of accuracy. Both of these juror tendencies stem from the same psychological phenomenon: **truth bias**. Humans are very likely to believe what people tell them, particularly when it is perceived that the person has no motive to lie. When coupled with a lack of understanding of the fallibility of eyewitness memory, jurors will believe eyewitness testimony.

Confession Evidence

It is very hard for us to imagine confessing to something that we did not do. Due to the **fundamental attribution error**, also known as correspondence bias, it is even harder for us to imagine someone else being a victim of circumstances (e.g., a coerced confession). The fundamental attribution error is our inclination to believe that things that others do are a matter of their character, whereas things that we do are a matter of circumstances. We *attribute* the causes of our behavior to things outside of our control and the causes of others' behavior to things within their control. Therefore, even if someone understands the concept of coerced confessions, psychologically they are still likely to negate the effects of the situation (i.e., interrogation) on a defendant's confession.

Juror Decision Making and Jury Deliberation

The group decision making process of deliberation involves both social and cognitive psychology. Using principles from cognitive psychology, we will first examine how individual jurors evaluate the presentation of evidence during trial. Then we will use social psychology to understand how the dynamics of a group influence jury deliberations and decision making.

Cognitive Psychology

A common concept in cognitive psychology is **cognitive load**. This refers to the limited ability of the brain's working memory to simultaneously process multiple things at the same time. Our individual brains vary in their ability to perform this juggling act. Some people's cognitive processing is overloaded more easily than others. When we are under high cognitive load, our overly taxed working memory will fall back on more automatic information processing, such as schemas.

Schemas

The various ideas that individual jurors bring into the courtroom must be examined. Through our personal experiences, we all have come to view the world and other people in a certain way. Mental shortcuts are created in our brains to help us process and manage the bombardment of sensory information we receive all the time. **Schemas** are types of mental shortcuts. Schemas are ideas and impressions we have about ourselves (**self schemas**), people with certain characteristics (**person schemas**), specific roles people take on (**role schemas**), and events that reoccur with some frequency (**event schemas**). Event schemas are also known as scripts since you can imagine something you have seen play out several times as if it were scripted.

All of these types of schemas are relevant to the role of a juror. If a juror has a self schema that they are an empathetic person, they may be more inclined to focus on the different points of view of the various people involved in the case. A juror with a person schema that Black men are violent will have a hard time believing a Black man's defense that he would never assault someone. Testimony of law enforcement officials will be more believable to a juror with a role schema that police officers are trustworthy and honest. And someone with a script that traffic stops are benign encounters will not understand why a Black man would be nervous upon being pulled over.

These are of course just examples. Hopefully, you can see how these cognitive shortcuts will impact how a juror views what is presented at a trial. Making things more difficult is the fact that we all can have different schemas and scripts due to our different life experiences. This means that different jurors are likely to interpret trial evidence differently. In fact, schemas cause us to overlook information that does not fit our existing schemas and to focus instead on information that confirms our existing schemas. This is called **confirmation bias.** Confirmation bias is also what causes the **perseverance effect** of schemas. This is the tendency for schemas to persist even in the face of contradictory evidence because confirmation bias tends to block that contradictory evidence from even registering! This phenomenon is known as **bias assimilation.** New information is evaluated as true or relevant based on whether or not it fits our existing schema. Information that does not *assimilate*, or conform, to our existing schemas is judged to be less true or relevant.

Astute attorneys can take advantage of schemas through priming and framing. **Priming** is the recency and frequency with which a particular schema is activated. The more recently and frequently a schema has been activated, the more likely that schema is to be applied to the current information. Given our original examples of the types of schemas, an attorney prosecuting a Black man for assault may attempt to prime a person's schema that Black men are violent by making references to Black male violence throughout the trial. **Framing** is often utilized when presenting character information about a defendant or witness. Again using examples from earlier in this chapter, an attorney may attempt to activate a role schema that police officers are trustworthy and honest by asking a police officer on the stand questions regarding the noble reasons they chose to become a police officer.

Individual Juror Decision Making

Humans are not computers. Computers process information in a unidirectional way: information is input, then integrated, and finally a conclusion is reached. Humans, on the other hand, process information bidirectionally in a feedback loop and consider information holistically rather than piecemeal. Each new piece of information is integrated with other pieces of information into our overall understanding of a situation. Our overall understanding of a situation also influences our interpretation of new information, affecting whether and how that information is integrated into our overall understanding. Further, any shift in our overall understanding will cause us to reevaluate previous information in a way consistent with our new overall understanding.

Our brains are attempting to construct a coherent story with the information we have been given. These concepts have been applied to juror decision making via two similar models: **Pennington and Hastie's story model** (1986) and **Simon's coherence-based reasoning** (2004).

THE STORY MODEL

Pennington and Hastie (1986) posited that jurors construct a narrative while observing evidence presented during a trial. This process consists of three parts: story construction, verdict category establishment, and story classification. To assist in finding the best story fit, each of these parts is directed by four certainty principles: coverage, coherence, uniqueness, and goodness-of-fit (Pennington & Hastie, 1992).

During the **story construction** phase, jurors use the evidence presented along with their own knowledge (and schemas) of human behavior and interaction to begin to develop an understanding of what they believe actually happened. Initially, multiple possible stories begin to emerge. The certainty principles of coverage and coherence will help determine which story is believed by the juror. A story's **coverage** refers to whether it accounts for all of the evidence presented. **Coherence** is broken out into three types: consistency, completeness, and plausibility. A story is judged as coherent if it does not contain any inconsistencies, is a complete narrative without holes, and makes sense (is plausible) given the juror's understanding of how the world works. A juror's confidence in their story construction is governed by the **uniqueness** principle. If more than one possible story is judged to be coherent and provide coverage of the evidence presented, then neither story is unique, and confidence in both is diminished.

Verdict category establishment comes at the end of the presentation of evidence. This phase of the story model is simply when jurors learn the details of their verdict options. This information is provided by the judge but may be influenced by the juror's preconceived ideas of the meaning of various legal terms. Jury instructions will be discussed later in the chapter.

The final step in the story model, **story classification**, involves the comparison of the juror's constructed story against the possible verdict categories. The certainty principle of **goodness-of-fit** is applied here. Given the legal standard of "beyond a reasonable doubt," a juror's constructed story must have a high goodness-of-fit for the juror to be confident in a guilty verdict.

COHERENCE-BASED REASONING

Simon (2004) and his colleagues expanded the story model by utilizing cognitive consistency theories to recognize the bidirectional feedback loop in human reasoning. Humans do not process information in a linear fashion. This is particularly true when we are faced with complex and sometimes unclear information, such as when serving on a jury. When striving to make sense of complicated and seemingly contradictory information, our brains seek coherence. A juror's decision is coherent when the juror believes it fits with the evidence presented. This can be likened to the story model's goodness-of-fit certainty principle. However, criminal trials rarely present a totality of evidence that is unambiguous. To make sense of all the information presented, coherence-based reasoning says that we will judge the veracity of newly presented evidence based on how coherent it is with our emerging story. When presented with strong evidence that contradicts our understanding of what happened, we may alter that overall understanding. When we do so, we will reevaluate all previously presented information in this new light. According to Simon (2004), this circular process happens largely unconsciously in our brain's effort to construct a coherent narrative.

Box 12.2 Moral reasoning and jury nullification

Kohlberg's moral development theory was discussed at length in Chapter 3, but it has relevance to a particular trial phenomenon: jury nullification. Though jurors are not specifically told of this option (*United States v. Dougherty*, 1972), it is possible for a jury to return a verdict of not guilty simply due to disagreement with the law or how it was applied. Recall from Chapter 3 that the upper levels of Kohlberg's moral development theory deal with conventional and post-conventional reasoning. In the stages of conventional reasoning, people tend to believe in conformity and that those who violate established laws and norms should be penalized. Jury nullification would not seem a reasonable option to jurors whose moral development is at these middle stages. To be willing to defy laws and legal precedent, jurors must have developed to at least stage five of Kohlberg's scale. At this stage, the need for a social contract is understood, but the flexibility of that social contract is paramount. Jury nullification is an exercise in that flexibility.

As the trial progresses, **coherence shifts** will happen as the juror becomes more and more entrenched in their constructed story. Jurors will become more confident in the information that fits their narrative in their unconscious effort at coherence. As the juror's constructed story becomes solidified, they may even change their view of evidence previously deemed untrustworthy or irrelevant if it ends up fitting with their current narrative. Coherence shifts show that jurors view evidence holistically rather than individually. Simon (2004) and his colleagues were also able to show that this process happens in real time, rather than as after-the-fact justifications for a decision.

Obviously, there are a lot of cognitive-psychological influences on individual juror decision making. But individual jurors do not make decisions alone; they must deliberate with other jurors. And due to coherence shifts in each juror's story classification, there can easily be conflicting yet strong opinions in the deliberation room. We turn now to social psychology to help us understand the jury deliberation process.

Social Psychology

Deliberation Styles

While the specific processes can vary, Hastie and his colleagues (1983) identified two styles of jury deliberation: verdict-driven and evidence-driven. A **verdict-driven jury** is likely to poll jurors early and often to see how close they are to consensus on a verdict. Individual opinions are made known to the group, and each side will then attempt to persuade the other. This will likely include references to evidence and testimony; however, no attempt is made to exhaustively review the information presented during the trial. **Evidence-driven juries**, on the other hand, often review the evidence and testimony in totality in an attempt to agree on a coherent story. This process can be seen as "constructing a collective reality" (Gavin, 2014, p. 311). Similar to the story model described above, the verdict must fit the agreed-upon narrative (i.e., story classification). As such, juror polls are often not taken until after the story is constructed.

Jurors in both of these deliberation styles will be subjected to social psychological influences, namely **normative influence** and **informational influence.** Given the different focus of the discussions in the two styles, verdict-driven juries may be more likely to be influenced by social norms and evidence-driven juries may be more likely to be influenced by the information that is discussed. "Normative influence stems from a desire to feel included by others and avoid standing apart from the rest of the group" (Devine, 2012, pp. 152–153). Since verdict-driven deliberation includes frequent, public polling, pressure to conform may be more strongly felt. Conversely, informational influence is persuasion by information, as the name implies. While jurors are persuaded by the facts of the case regardless of deliberation style, informational influence is likely to be weighted more strongly in evidence-driven deliberation.

Group Polarization and Groupthink

Despite these different deliberation styles, it is highly likely that the verdict favored by most jurors' pre-deliberation will be the ultimate verdict of the jury. This can be explained by the concept of **group polarization.** Social psychology research has found that when like-minded people converse they become more extreme on the opinion with which the majority originally agreed. Sunstein (2000) has explained this phenomenon in two ways. First, we have a desire to be liked by others and to think of ourselves highly as well. When in a room full of people with whom you mostly agree, the veracity of the arguments by those firmer in their opinions will lead you to want to agree with them even more. This will occur not only because you want to be liked by them, but also because you will feel justified in your initial leanings. And the more confident you are in your opinion, the more likely you are to voice it. This leads to the second reason for group polarization. If the majority of people share the same opinion, that will be the argument most heard by others. This is simple odds. Even if not all those in the room choose to share their opinion, most of those who do will voice the majority opinion. And hearing most people voicing the opposite opinion will also stifle the few dissenters who may be in the room.

Group polarization can also be explained by the idea of groupthink (Janis, 1971). The concept of groupthink was fully explained in Chapter 9 with regard to police investigations and is perhaps most applicable there. Juries are, after all, not nearly as cohesive a group as police officers, and group cohesion is a central tenet of groupthink. But there is considerable pressure on juries and jurors, another feature that may lead to groupthink. The concepts of self-censorship that lead to false senses of unanimity may also be present in jury deliberations.

Jury Instructions

After closing arguments and before deliberation begins, the judge will provide instructions to the jury. These basic instructions are sometimes called **standard instructions, pattern instructions,** or **guidance instructions.** Whether they are provided in writing or orally to the jury varies by jurisdiction, as does the information included in the instructions. In general, however, several pieces of important legal information are included in standard jury instructions, such as the definitions of the charges against the defendant and the jury's verdict options. Standard instructions also include a reminder that the defendant is innocent until proven guilty by the prosecution and that the level of that proof must be "**beyond a reasonable doubt.**"

The ability of the jurors to understand their task using the instructions provided by the judge has been heavily researched. In an attempt to hinder future appeals, judges often choose to include legal language in their instructions to the jury. However, the inability of most jurors to understand such "legalese" led to a push for **plain language jury instructions.** Plain language instructions may unfortunately be less precise or contain language that may have a different meaning for some jurors. Interestingly, many studies have found that jurors who did not receive any instruction understood important information as well as, if not better than, those jurors who received instructions. This may seem surprising until you recall the prominence of schemas.

Gordon (2013) pointed out that many jurors have existing schemas around legal concepts. These schemas are not necessarily based on legal reality. In order to create new and accurate schemas for the concepts relevant to the case, Gordon (2013) makes several suggestions. Primarily, "if courts incorporated a more neutral, pre-trial explanation of the law, this neutral and legally correct information would also have a priming and framing effect, creating and activating appropriate schemas and allowing jurors to better weigh the evidence from both sides" (p. 674). Here, Gordon (2013) is advocating for all instructions to occur *prior to* the beginning of the trial, rather than after all evidence is presented. Not only would this have a "priming and framing effect" for legally correct schemas, but it would fit with the story model of juror decision making. If the explanations of charges and associated verdict choices were presented before jurors were exposed to evidence and testimony, their emerging stories would be more likely to conform easily to their legal verdict options. Gordon (2013) also advocates for jurors being instructed to "create plausible explanations for both—or all—sides before coming to a decision" (p. 676). This may also reduce group polarization.

Curative Instructions

Judges can also provide instructions to jurors in an attempt to curb the effects of biases. Such jury instructions are known as **curative instructions** since they are attempting to *cure* the biases. (They are also sometimes known as admonitions or limiting instructions.) Curative instructions are commonly used to combat pretrial publicity and statements or evidence ruled inadmissible. But can a judge really instruct a juror to negate information they have already heard or seen? Despite rulings by the Supreme Court (see Box 12.3), basic principles of psychology say no.

Ironic process theory, reactance theory, the perseverance effect and coherence-based reasoning can all help explain why curative instructions may be ineffective. **Ironic process theory** says that telling someone to *not* think about something tends to have the opposite effect

Box 12.3 Curative jury instructions: You can't unring a bell, but what are we to do?

The Supreme Court of the United States (SCOTUS) has at times acknowledged that telling jurors to disregard information to which they have already been exposed is a "naïve assumption" (*Krulewitch v. United States*, 1949, p. 453). But SCOTUS has also repeatedly noted that our legal system must rely on the assumption that jurors will follow the instructions they are given. For example, when delivering a deciding opinion, Justice Scalia wrote, "The rule that juries are presumed to follow their instructions is a pragmatic one, rooted less in the absolute certitude that the presumption is true than in the belief that it represents a reasonable practical accommodation of the interests of the state and the defendant" (*Richardson v. Marsh*, 1987, p. 211).

(e.g., "don't think of a white bear"). Similarly, **reactance theory** has shown that people generally do not like to be told what they cannot do. Feeling as though they are not allowed to deliberate freely may prompt jurors into defiance. In fact, Kassin and Sommers (1997) found this to be especially true when jurors believed the evidence was inadmissible due to a legal technicality. The perseverance effect, applied earlier in the chapter to schemas, can also be applied to beliefs related to inadmissible evidence. Evidence, once presented, gets folded into a juror's overall understanding of the case (see the story model). This cognitive process cannot be undone due to belief perseverance. Coherence-based reasoning can also explain the ineffectiveness of curative instructions, especially if the inadmissible evidence is coherent with the jurors' story of what happened.

Juror Stress

The concepts of vicarious trauma and secondary traumatic stress were discussed at length regarding the mental health of law enforcement officers in Chapter 9. For jurors, these types of trauma and stress may arise from serving on juries for particularly violent crimes. Lonergan and her colleagues (2016) reviewed all previous studies of juror stress. They found that overall jurors who were exposed to graphic crime scene images and highly emotional witness testimony were more likely to experience symptoms of depression, secondary traumatic stress, or other anxiety disorders, though very few jurors reached a diagnostic level of symptoms. Jurors are also subjected to primary stress. "In the vast majority of survey studies, factors associated with jury deliberations and decision-making, such as tension between jurors, deciding on a verdict or the death penalty, fear of making a mistake, and being sequestered, were the most prominent sources of stress" (Lonergan et al., 2016, p. 57). Not all jurors report symptoms of stress, anxiety, or depression. Female jurors and jurors with a personal history of trauma were more likely to be negatively affected by jury service. Therefore, mental health problems stemming from being a juror appear to be most prevalent among women with existing trauma serving on juries for violent crimes with difficult verdict decisions.

Although this is a small subset of all jurors, interventions should be in place to mitigate any negative effects of this civic duty. Indeed, some jurisdictions provide **post-verdict debriefing.** These debriefing sessions typically consist of group meetings that offer support and awareness of symptoms of anxiety and depression. The presiding judge is often the one to decide whether or not debriefing will be offered and is also usually the person to lead the group. Lonergan and her colleagues (2016) suggested that debriefing should always be led by a clinician who understands the symptoms and is qualified to offer advice for coping with stress and vicarious trauma.

Summary

Jury service is a civic duty. We all have the potential to be called and selected to serve. This chapter reviewed the ways psychologists can assist in the jury selection process. But without educational standards or a code of ethics, the field of jury consulting is open to criticism. Also explored in this chapter was the impact of different types of evidence on the trial outcome, including the psychological reasons jurors may be particularly compelled by eyewitness testimony and confessions. Cognitive and social psychology has helped explain both individual juror decision making and the jury deliberation process – and their downfalls. The stressful and traumatic nature of certain trial evidence and procedures leaves jurors vulnerable to mental health issues, which can be mitigated if post-verdict debriefing sessions are offered.

References

Ballew v. Georgia, 435 U.S. 223 (1978).
Batson v. Kentucky, 476 U.S. 79 (1986).
Coughlan, S. M. (2019). The (im)partial jury: A trial consultant's role in the venire process. *Brooklyn Law Review*, *84*(2), 671–702.
Devine, D. J. (2012). *Jury decision making: The state of the science*. NYU Press.
Diamond, S. S., & Salerno, J. M. (2020). Reasons for the disappearing jury trial: Perspectives from attorneys and judges. *Louisiana Law Review*, *81*(1), 119–163.
Evans, E. (2021, February 17). *Jury trials are disappearing. Here's why*. Injustice Watch. https://www.injusticewatch.org/news/2021/disappearing-jury-trials-study/
Gavin, H. (2014). *Criminological and forensic psychology*. SAGE.
Gordon, S. (2013). Through the eyes of jurors: The use of schemas in the application of "plain language" jury instructions. *Hastings Law Journal*, *64*(3), 643–677.
Hastie, R., Penrod, S. D., & Pennington, N. (1983). *Inside the jury*. Harvard University Press.
Janis, I. (1971, November). Groupthink. *Psychology Today*, *5*(6), 84–89.
J.E.B. v. Alabama ex rel T.B., 511 U.S. 127 (1994).
Kassin, S. M., & Sommers, S. R. (1997). Inadmissible testimony, instructions to disregard, and the jury: Substantive versus procedural considerations. *Personality and Social Psychology Bulletin*, *23*(10), 1046–1054.
Krulewitch v. United States, 336 U.S. 440 (1949).
Lonergan, M., Leclerc, M., Descamps, M., Pigeon, S., & Brunet, A. (2016). Prevalence and severity of trauma- and stressor-related symptoms among jurors: A review. *Journal of Criminal Justice*, *47*, 51–61.
Lumet, S. (Director). (1957). *12 Angry Men* [film]. Orion-Nova Productions.
Pennington, N., & Hastie, R. (1986). Evidence evaluation in complex decision making. *Journal of Personality and Social Psychology*, *51*(2), 242–258.
Pennington, N., & Hastie, R. (1992). Explaining the evidence: Tests of the story model for juror decision making. *Journal of Personality and Social Psychology*, *62*(2), 189–206.
Ramos vs. Louisiana, 590 U.S. ___ (2020).
Richardson v. Marsh, 481 U.S. 200 (1987).
Schwietzer, K., & Nunez, N. (2018). What evidence matters to jurors? The prevalence and importance of different homicide trial evidence to mock jurors. *Psychiatry, Psychology and Law*, *25*(3), 437–451.
Simon, D. (2004). A third view of the black box: Cognitive coherence in legal decision making. *The University of Chicago Law Review*, *71*(2), 511–586.
Strauder v. West Virginia, 100 U.S. 303 (1880).
Sunstein, C. R. (2000). Deliberative trouble? Why groups go to extremes. *The Yale Law Journal*, *110*(1), 71–119.

13 Psychology of Behavior Change

Introduction

In 1974, Martinson published a now-famous article in which he argued that "nothing works" to rehabilitate criminal offenders. He was referring to his assessment that the correctional treatment programs of the preceding years had not led to reductions in re-offending. While many pointed out that Martinson's assessment was flawed, politicians seized the moment to enact decades of "tough on crime" policies. This push against correctional rehabilitation prompted researchers to examine what types of interventions *did* lead to reductions in recidivism. The field of corrections now embraces the principles of effective intervention, including the use of cognitive-behavioral and social learning treatment programs, as evidence-based ways to reduce offending.

The Risk-Need-Responsivity Model

Donald A. Andrews and James Bonta are world-renowned scholars in the application of psychology to the field of corrections. Together they created the principles of effective intervention, including the Risk-Need-Responsivity (RNR) model. This section will cover the core components of the RNR model (for thorough coverage of all 15 principles of effective intervention, see Bonta & Andrews, 2016), as well as the history of assessing risk of recidivism and tools to address responsivity issues. The section concludes with a recent addition to the RNR model: the fidelity principle.

The Risk Principle

The first principle of effective intervention is the **risk principle.** Corrections professionals have long tried to assess offenders' risk to the community by determining their likelihood of recidivating. **Recidivism** simply means committing another crime or reoffending. But the risk principle is more than just determining someone's risk of recidivism; it also outlines what should and should not be done once an offender's risk level is determined. This section will review the history of risk assessment and classification and conclude with recommendations of the risk principle.

Risk Assessment and Risk Factors

The history of risk assessment is typically thought of in generations. The **first-generation risk assessments** relied on the judgment of corrections professionals. These judgments were

DOI: 10.4324/9781003250821-15

made based on experience rather than research and were therefore subjective. The subjective nature of first-generation risk assessments left much room for error and manipulation.

This led to the development of the **second-generation risk assessments** which used an actuarial method. Actuarial assessments get their name due to their use of research and statistics to provide a formula for assessing the risk of recidivism. Therefore, many of these risk assessment "tools" allowed the assessor to essentially check boxes as to whether or not a particular factor associated with recidivism was present in the person being assessed. This both eliminated the need for an experienced professional and provided an objective "risk score." The problem with second-generation risk assessments was that they only measured static risk factors, such as criminal history. **Static risk factors** are so named because they cannot be changed. No amount of rehabilitation can go back in time to change someone's criminal history. If we want to assess the effectiveness of rehabilitation efforts, we need to measure risk factors that can change.

Third-generation risk assessments added dynamic risk factors to the actuarial method. **Dynamic risk factors** are things that can change and are also referred to as criminogenic needs. Much research was conducted between the second- and third-generation risk assessments. This research led to a general consensus that there are eight factors most associated with criminal behavior (see Table 13.1). All eight risk factors are known as the Central Eight, but the first four risk factors are such strong predictors of criminal behavior that they are called the Big Four.

The **Big Four risk factors** are (1) antisocial attitudes, (2) antisocial associates, (3) history of antisocial behavior, and (4) antisocial personality. Antisocial attitudes refer to patterns in thinking that encourage criminal behavior. Antisocial associates are friends and/or family who engage in antisocial behavior. History of antisocial behavior includes criminal history and other past antisocial behaviors, such as regularly behaving aggressively toward others. Antisocial personality refers to personality traits that may make one prone to criminal behavior, such as impulsiveness (see Chapter 6).

Together with the Big Four, the **Central Eight** adds (5) family/marital problems, (6) difficulty in school/work, (7) no prosocial leisure activities, and (8) chronic substance use. Family/marital problems can be related to criminal behavior by limiting support systems. Difficulty in school/work removes the main prosocial activity one has in their life. No prosocial leisure activities can either mean one has *antisocial* leisure activities or they have a lot of idle time ("idle hands are the devil's workshop"). While chronic substance use does increase the risk for criminal activity, Chapter 8 explains the varied reasons for this association.

Notice that criminal history (i.e., "history of antisocial behavior") is still included even though it is a static risk factor. The goal of third-generation risk assessments was not to ignore factors that are highly correlated with criminal behavior just because they cannot be changed, but to include (and focus on) those correlates that can be targeted for change. This

Table 13.1 The Big Four and Central Eight risk factors.

The Big Four	1	Antisocial attitudes
	2	Antisocial associates
	3	History of antisocial behavior
	4	Antisocial personality
The Central Eight	5	Family/Marital problems
	6	Difficulty in school/work
	7	No prosocial leisure activities
	8	Substance abuse

focus has become more prominent in **fourth-generation risk assessments** that include a case planning approach (more on this in *The Need Principle* section).

It should also be noted that some have called for a return to professional judgment with **Structured Professional Judgment** (SPJ) risk assessment tools (Douglas, 2019). These tools may provide the best of both worlds by allowing professionals to use their judgment to provide a more individualized assessment while still using a structured tool to measure evidence-based correlates of criminal behavior.

Dosage

An important part of Andrews and Bonta's risk principle is not just measuring someone's risk for recidivism with a valid risk assessment tool but also using that information to determine the proper dosage of treatment. **Dosage** refers to the frequency and duration of treatment. The risk principle states that treatment dosage should be based on risk level. Higher-risk individuals should receive a higher dose of treatment, and those with the lowest risk may not need treatment at all. In fact, the risk principle further dictates that people with low risk should not be in treatment with people who are high risk. One reason for this recommendation is that the dosage will be incorrect for some in such mixed groups. Another reason to not include low-risk people in the same treatment group as high-risk people is it forces the low-risk people to associate with higher-risk people. Remember that one of the Big Four risk factors is antisocial associates. Therefore, bringing together people of varying risk levels may actually increase the risk levels of those who were initially low risk. Additionally, correctional treatment programming requires people to take time away from other activities. For those with a low-risk level, those other activities are more likely to be prosocial in nature, such as work or school. Requiring people to take time away from prosocial activities to attend a treatment program with higher-risk individuals is simply not a good idea. In short, putting low-risk individuals into intensive treatment programs may do more harm than good.

The Need Principle

The second principle of the RNR model is the **need principle**. Recall that the third-generation risk assessments began focusing on correlates of criminal behavior that could be changed. Andrews and Bonta refer to these dynamic risk factors as criminogenic needs. **Criminogenic needs** are the dynamic risk factors from the Central Eight that are targeted for change. Those involved with the justice system likely have many other needs as well. Some may be struggling with secure housing, mental health issues, or motivation. Helping people with these **noncriminogenic needs** can be important, as we will learn in the next section on the responsivity principle. However, focusing treatment on criminogenic needs will have the biggest impact on recidivism.

This is why fourth-generation risk assessments include case planning tools. **Case planning** involves structuring treatment programming around someone's highest criminogenic need areas. Someone whose risk assessment indicates antisocial attitudes as a high criminogenic need area should be placed in treatment designed to address this area specifically (more on these types of programs later in the chapter), whereas someone for whom chronic substance use is a high-need area should be placed in a drug treatment program. Remember from the risk principle that people should be placed in treatment based on their overall risk level. The need principle indicates that we should also focus treatment on the person's highest criminogenic need areas (i.e., the dynamic risk factors with the highest score).

The Responsivity Principle

The **responsivity principle** is all about how to best bring about behavior change. It is divided into two types: general responsivity and specific responsivity. The **general responsivity principle** states that treatment programs based on empirically proven psychological science should be used for corrections populations, specifically cognitive-behavioral therapies and modalities based on social learning theories. The second half of this chapter is devoted to a review of these programs. The **specific responsivity principle** says that treatment and treatment delivery should be matched to the person's learning style and that barriers to participation in treatment should be removed. Barriers to treatment can include learning styles, learning disabilities, mental health issues, time, transportation, and motivation.

Motivation to change is obviously a difficulty when working with those who have been mandated by the courts to participate in treatment. Motivation is a dynamic noncriminogenic need that relates heavily to specific responsivity. Therefore, motivation to change can change. To help increase someone's motivation to change, it is helpful to understand the stages of change.

Stages of Change

The **stages of change** were first articulated by Prochaska and DiClemente (1984) in their transtheoretical model of behavior change through therapy. Through years of research and application, the model has evolved into five stages: pre-contemplation, contemplation, preparation/determination, action, and maintenance. Often these stages are depicted in a circle (see Figure 13.1) in recognition that progression through the stages of change is not always linear and one can enter or leave the circle at any stage.

During the **pre-contemplation stage** of change, the person is not even considering or perhaps even thinking about changing their behavior. They may not see a problem with their behavior or they simply may not want to change. When the person progresses to the **contemplation**

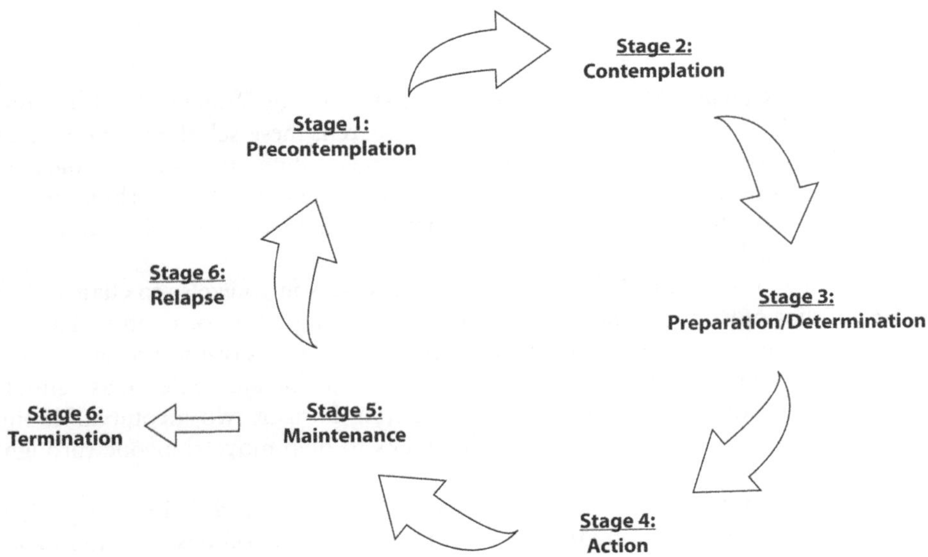

Figure 13.1 Stages of change.

stage, they acknowledge a need or desire to change their behavior. They are merely thinking about the possibility of change at this point; they may not feel ready to change. People may stay in one of these first two stages for a very long time, and some may stay here forever.

When in the **preparation stage** of change, the person is seriously considering taking steps toward changing their behavior and may have already taken small steps or made attempts to change. They have become determined to change their behavior, which is why this stage is sometimes referred to as the determination stage. Once they feel fully prepared, they will enter the action stage of change. This is the stage that is often most recognized by those surrounding the person and can sometimes be mistaken for a complete change. However, the **action stage** is simply when the person begins making clear and substantial efforts to modify their behavior. After the person has taken consistent action to change their behavior for about six months, they have moved into the **maintenance stage**. From the outside, it may seem like the change is complete at this point. However, Prochaska et al. (1992) said that "maintenance is a continuation, not an absence, of change" (p. 1104). The maintenance stage may be the most difficult as one continuously works to avoid relapsing to their old behavior.

Sometimes a sixth stage is included to acknowledge that behavior change can be extremely difficult to sustain. To capture this, the sixth stage is referred to either as "relapse" or "termination." The original work on the transtheoretical model was with addictive behaviors, hence the term "relapse." But it should be recognized that changing any behavior is difficult to maintain (how's your latest new year's resolution going?), and lapsing back into our old patterns is human nature. So, the sixth stage of relapse is one that is usually visited repeatedly. The termination stage is used to indicate that the person has maintained their behavior change for long enough that they have settled into a new way of being. Their old behaviors are no longer even tempting to them.

Understanding the stages of change is helpful for corrections professionals. But understanding where someone is at in their motivation to change their behavior will not necessarily facilitate behavior change. Motivational Interviewing was developed to help guide people through the stages of change.

Motivational Interviewing

Motivational Interviewing (MI) was developed in the 1980s by William R. Miller and Stephen Rollnick. Throughout the years of use and research, these scholars have refined this person-centered approach to eliciting behavior change, culminating in their most recent book (Miller & Rollnick, 2013) and trainings. If you are interested in working in the field of corrections, MI is a highly valuable training that you might seek out. Here, only an overview will be provided.

One of the key ideas within MI is that we cannot force someone else to change their behavior. Recall that most people are likely in the pre-contemplation or contemplation stage of change. They are possibly aware of the negative consequences of their behaviors but are ambivalent about changing. Miller and Rollnick (2013) define ambivalence as "simultaneously wanting and not wanting something, or wanting both of two incompatible things" (p. 6). It is this ambivalence to change that MI seeks to help move someone through to a definitive decision to change.

First, it is important to understand the spirit of MI. Miller and Rollnick (2013) name four components of the spirit of MI: partnership, acceptance, compassion, and evocation (see Table 13.2). **Partnership** is intended to remind practitioners that they are simply the facilitators and that their clients will be doing the heavy lifting. A key guideline for this

Table 13.2 The spirit of Motivational Interviewing (Miller & Rollnick, 2013).

1	Partnership
2	Acceptance
	Absolute worth
	Accurate empathy
	Autonomy support
	Affirmation
3	Compassion
4	Evocation

is that the clinician should do less than half of the talking. **Acceptance** has four "A"s: absolute worth, accurate empathy, autonomy support, and affirmation. **Absolute worth** is a reminder that every person has worth regardless of their actions. **Accurate empathy** reminds the practitioner to seek to correctly understand their client's circumstances and point of view. **Autonomy support** is a cue to recognize that people make their own decisions about how to live their lives. And **affirmation**, an important component of MI, encourages validation of "the person's strengths and efforts" (Miller & Rollnick, 2013, p. 19). **Compassion** was newly added to the spirit of MI in the most recent edition of the book. It is a reminder that the practitioner is there to serve the needs and benefits of the client, not their own. It was deemed a necessary addition by the authors, as one could remain faithful to the other elements of the spirit of MI (partnership, acceptance, and evocation) while also remaining self-serving. Essentially, the element of compassion is a reminder that MI is not about manipulating someone to do what you want them to do. Finally, **evocation** drives home the idea that the MI practitioner is a facilitator of behavior change. Every person has within them the desire and tools to change for their own betterment. The MI practitioner's job "is to evoke it, to call it forth" (Miller & Rollnick, 2013, p. 21).

In the third edition of their book, Miller and Rollnick (2013) describe the process of MI in four "stair steps" (see Figure 13.2): engaging, focusing, evoking, and planning. As indicated by the stair-step model, each step underlies and serves as the foundation for the remaining steps. The first step in the MI process is engaging. **Engaging** is the first step in any helping relationship whereby the practitioner and client establish a rapport and trust. Since MI is client-centered, the client must feel safe and comfortable talking and sharing. Once the client is engaged, the next step of MI is **focusing**. Since the client should be doing most

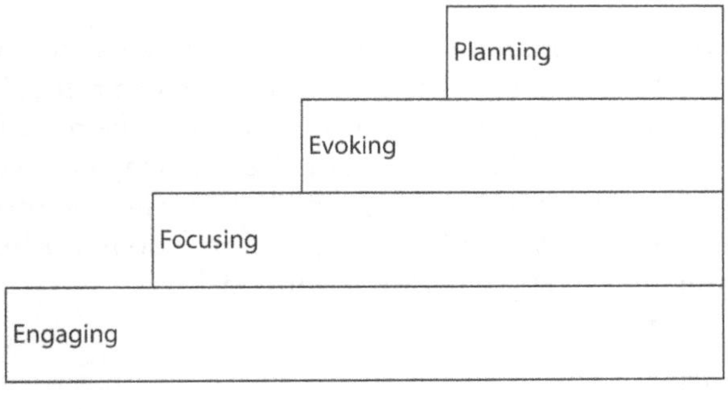

Figure 13.2 The four "stair steps" of motivational interviewing (Miller & Rollnick, 2013, p. 26).

of the talking, it is the job of the MI practitioner to focus the client's thoughts and desires in the direction of change. An important concept from MI is the idea of "change talk." The focusing step narrows in on and enhances the client's change talk. The next step of **evoking** "involves eliciting the client's own motivations for change, and it has always been at the heart of MI" (Miller & Rollnick, 2013, p. 28). Motivational Interviewing is about helping a person talk themselves into changing their behavior. The final step of the MI process, **planning**, is where the rubber meets the road. It is unfortunately where most attempts at eliciting behavior change begin and end. However, MI recognizes that a lot of thinking and motivating must precede any plan for action. Without the engaging, focusing, and evoking steps, any planning will be difficult to follow. Miller and Rollnick even note that if the first three steps are facilitated effectively, the client may not even need help with the planning step. However, it is important to remember that change is extremely difficult, and as indicated in the stages of change, "relapse" is extremely likely. It is the job of the MI practitioner to recognize this and assist the client through the steps again and again.

The Fidelity Principle

The fidelity principle was added to the RNR model when it was discovered that some correctional programs claiming to adhere to the risk, need, and responsivity principles did not see drops in recidivism. Some of the programs actually seemed to *increase* recidivism. What could be wrong? Previous research and principles in psychology have shown that the RNR model should bring about positive behavior change. Gendreau and Andrews (1996) created the Correctional Program Assessment Inventory (CPAI) to assess whether programs were indeed adhering to the principles of effective intervention. It was found that just because a correctional agency *said* they were using programming that fit the RNR model, it did not mean that these programs were being implemented as they were intended. The quality of program delivery is crucial. If you are given a recipe for a cake, but you do not properly follow the recipe, you will not end up with a great cake. Some correctional programs were not being implemented with integrity to their recipe. Thus, the fidelity principle was born!

The **fidelity principle** (sometimes called the program integrity principle) states that correctional programming that meets the principles of effective intervention must be implemented with integrity to its design. In short, follow the recipe. There are three suggestions for ensuring program fidelity: (1) leadership and staff buy in, (2) initial and ongoing training, and (3) process evaluations conducted by an outside agency.

Leadership and Staff Buy in

Change often comes from the top, but the rank-and-file workers who will be delivering the programming must also believe in it. When a new program or protocol is implemented, the leadership must believe in it in order to effectively "sell" it to the rest of the staff. Managers and supervisors must "buy in" to the program, or else they may not even want to try to sell it. More importantly, the staff who are charged with delivering the program material must "buy in" to what they are delivering. If leadership and staff do not believe that the program will be effective, they are less likely to deliver it with fidelity.

Initial and Ongoing Training

Staff must be properly trained in a specific program modality if they are expected to implement the program with fidelity. Initial training of staff should be conducted by someone who has been trained to accurately and effectively deliver the training. Many well-established correctional programs offer official "training of trainers" to ensure that those who are training end-user staff are doing so with integrity. Periodic ongoing training is also necessary to refresh staff on the proper implementation of the program.

Process Evaluations

Process evaluations, such as the CPAI, should also be conducted periodically. A **process evaluation** is a method of research that uses observation of program delivery and interviews with staff and clients to confirm that a program is being implemented as it was designed. It is important that these process evaluations are conducted by a group not directly affiliated with the agency being evaluated. This will ensure that there are no conflicts of interest when comparing the observations of the evaluators to the intentions and requirements of the program being assessed.

Correctional Treatment

As mentioned in the previous section of this chapter, the general responsivity principle indicates that treatments to reduce recidivism should have a track record of effective behavior change. Perhaps no form of treatment has been more effective at producing change across a wide variety of behaviors than cognitive-behavioral therapy.

Cognitive-Behavioral Treatment

The crux of **cognitive-behavioral treatment** (CBT) is the thought-behavior link. Indeed, cognition is really a fancy word for thoughts. Many of us do not realize just how much our thoughts impact our actions. The **thought-behavior link** states that our actions are driven by what and how we are thinking. If someone cuts us off in traffic, and we think "what a jerk; how dare they do that to me," we will be more likely to drive aggressively in retaliation. If instead we think, "maybe that person has an emergency and they need to get somewhere quickly," we will be more likely to continue to drive calmly. This is because our thoughts often impact our emotions as well. In the original scenario where we imagined having more negative thoughts, these negative thoughts would likely make us angry, leading to our more aggressive driving. Most people believe it is external factors (e.g., the other person's driving) that cause our emotions. While external factors may have *some* impact on our emotions and actions, how we choose to *think* about those external factors have a much greater impact on us. The University of Cincinnati Corrections Institute created a worksheet, called the Behavior Chain, that illustrates this concept (see Figure 13.3; University of Cincinnati Corrections Institute, 2008–2024).

The **Behavior Chain** (Figure 13.3) is designed to be used by probation officers with their clients on probation. On the top of the worksheet is a space to write the situation. The situation is an external event over which the client had no control. In the example provided in the previous paragraph, the situation would be getting cut off in traffic. The next box to be completed using the Behavior Chain is the thoughts box. This is where the client writes down all the thoughts that they had the moment the situation occurred. Next is the feelings box, which is a space to write the feelings that came up in the moment. The client may not realize at this time that their feelings are impacted by their thoughts. The whole process happens so fast that most of us believe it is the external situation that is directly causing our thoughts and feelings. This is ok; the control we have over our thoughts and feelings

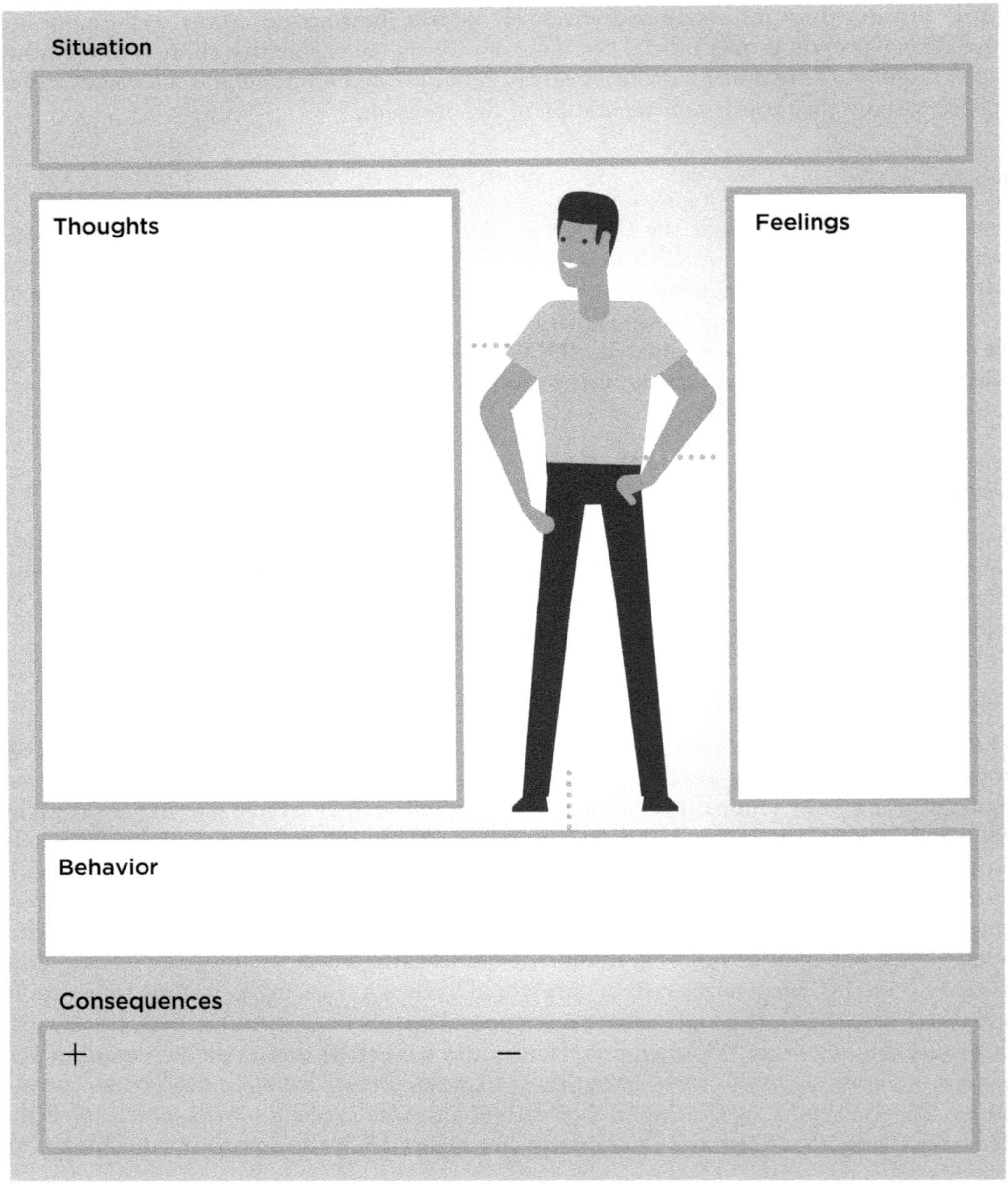

Figure 13.3 Behavior Chain worksheet. Figure reproduced with permission from University of Cincinnati Corrections Institute. Copyright 2008–2024 by the University of Cincinnati.

will become clearer during the following cognitive restructuring phase, discussed in the next paragraph. The box on the Behavior Chain worksheet labeled "Behavior" is where the client will write what action they took following the situation. In the example in the previous paragraph, the action might be "aggressively driving to get back in front of the driver who cut me off." Finally, the Behavior Chain entails listing both the positive and negative consequences of this action. There are positive consequences to negative actions, and it's important to honestly explore these as they are what is likely sustaining the negative thoughts and actions. For example, if you think "what a jerk; how dare they do that to me" when someone cuts you off and then drive aggressively to get back in front of them, the positive consequences will probably be a sense of vindication or perhaps "winning." What will emerge from exploring both the positive and negative consequences of negative thoughts and actions is that there are often more or worse negative consequences than positive ones. Recognizing this can help boost motivation to change.

The first step in CBT is recognizing that our thoughts control our actions (i.e., the thought-behavior link). And we have control over our own thoughts. It may not seem this way, as many of us do not think about thinking. We are in the habit of letting our thoughts come into our heads unabated and unchecked. **Cognitive restructuring** is the process by which one learns to slow down their thinking and choose to alter their thought patterns toward more positive outcomes. This is the second step in CBT. Once one understands the thought-behavior link, they can then begin to retrain their brain to have more positive thoughts. This is not easy! It requires paying attention to your thoughts in the moment you are having them. Often, this is a very stressful moment in time, when habits like to take over. How do we learn new habits? Through repetition and practice. The Behavior Chain can be used as a cognitive restructuring tool by completing a second worksheet on the same situation and brainstorming positive thoughts to replace the negative thoughts. It is then important to practice these new thoughts through modeling and role playing so they will be more likely to surface in a difficult situation.

Another important part of CBT is cognitive and social skills practice. Any skills teaching and practice involve the social-psychological learning components of modeling, role playing and positive reinforcement. Recall from Chapter 4 that **modeling** is when someone demonstrates something to another person by doing it themselves. In the context of CBT, the treatment provider (e.g., probation officer or CBT facilitator) will walk through the steps of the cognitive or social skill in front of the client. Then the client will be asked to role play the skill. **Role playing,** in this context, is when the person who is learning a new skill practices going through the steps of the skill in a benign situation (i.e., with the treatment provider and not in the middle of a stressful situation). The treatment provider then provides feedback to the client using plenty of positive reinforcement. Recall again from Chapter 4 that positive reinforcement is the most powerful for eliciting behavior change. **Cognitive skills,** such as the Behavior Chain outlined above, are skills around restructuring thinking patterns to achieve more positive outcomes. **Social skills** are the myriad skills needed to interact appropriately and positively with others, such as having a difficult conversation or responding to someone else's emotions. Repeated practice of new cognitive and social skills in a nonthreatening context (i.e., with a treatment provider) using modeling, role playing and positive reinforcement, as well as repeated practice in real-world situations when the client is ready, is needed to form new habits.

Group Treatment

While cognitive and social skills can be taught one-on-one, with a probation officer for example, many structured CBT programs are conducted in a group setting. Obviously, treating a group is more efficient than treating each individual. Group treatment settings have other benefits as well, including learning from and reinforcing each other's behavior change. However, not all groups are created equally, so facilitators must encourage positive interactions among members. One prominent issue in any group therapy setting is confidentiality. When sensitive topics are discussed within the group, it is important to emphasize the supportive intent of group treatment that would be undermined by sharing discussions outside the group.

The following are descriptions of a selection of CBT group treatments often used in corrections.

Thinking for a Change

Possibly the most prominent group CBT program in corrections is **Thinking for a Change** (T4C). Created by the National Institute of Corrections (Bush et al., 1997), T4C has been shown to effectively reduce recidivism (Lowenkamp et al., 2009). A T4C group meets once per week for one to two hours for a total of 22 weeks or more, depending on the number of social skills covered. The first eleven weeks of the curriculum are devoted to the ideas of cognitive restructuring. Various social skills are taught during the remaining weeks. The curriculum can be tailored and extended based on the social skills needed most by the participants, but the T4C curriculum suggests skills related to others' feelings, stressful conversations, anger management, and problem solving. The skill of problem solving is intended to be presented across six consecutive weeks due to its complexity and vast application. T4C facilitators are required to be trained to deliver the program with fidelity and proper use of the CBT modalities of modeling, role playing, and positive reinforcement.

Aggression Replacement Training

Originally designed for children and adolescents by Glick and Goldstein (1987) and Goldstein and Glick (1994), **Aggression Replacement Training** (ART) has been used as an anger management program for violent offenders of all ages. There are three components to ART: Skillstreaming, Anger Control Training (ACT), and moral education. Each of these three parts is designed to be delivered in a group setting once per week for ten weeks, for a total of 30 weeks for the entire ART program. **Skillstreaming** is what ART calls its social skills training. There are 50 specific prosocial skills provided by ART, divided into six groups: beginning social skills, advanced social skills, skills for dealing with feelings, alternatives to aggression, skills for dealing with stress, and planning skills. The next section of ART, **Anger Control Training (ACT)** was borrowed from Feindler, Marriott, and Iwata (1984). Participants are asked to keep a "hassle log" of situations that aroused their anger and their response to those situations using the following steps: identifying external triggers, identifying internal cues (e.g., increased heartrate, clenched jaw), using thoughts to remain calm (i.e., cognitive restructuring), using anger-control methods taught in ART (e.g., counting to ten, peaceful visualizations), and self-evaluation. The final component of ART is **moral education,** based on the idea from Kohlberg's moral development theory (see Chapter 3) that exposure to thoughts and ideas of a higher stage of moral development will increase one's own moral stage. As such, ART's moral education consists of evaluating various moral dilemmas in the group setting.

Rehabilitating Juveniles with Conduct Problems

Multisystemic Therapy

The lives of juveniles are characterized by several interweaving contexts, namely home/family, school, peers, and community. Sometimes (perhaps often) they act and react differently depending on with which of these multiple "systems" they are currently interacting. If you think back to your younger years, you will probably recall acting quite differently around your parents than you did around your friends. These various "systems" can also affect one another. It is the recognition of the interaction of these multiple systems that prompted the development of **multisystemic therapy (MST)** by Henggeler and his colleagues (1986). MST is a family-based therapy designed to work with the juvenile and their family in the home, rather than in a residential setting. There is no set curriculum; instead, a licensed and trained family therapist works closely with the family on their goals. "MST includes problem-focused interventions within the family as well as within peer, school, and other systems as needed" (Henggeler et al., 1992, p. 955). These interventions are determined by the therapist and often include cognitive-behavioral therapies. Perhaps it is this lack of consistent curricula and varying intended outcomes (i.e., the families' goals) that has led to the mixed empirical findings on the effectiveness of MST. A meta-analysis conducted by van de Stowe and colleagues (2014) found modest but significant effects on recidivism as a specific outcome. They also found that MST may not work as well for older children and non-white families.

Functional Family Therapy

Developed by Alexander and Parsons (1982), **Functional Family Therapy (FFT)** is a family-based therapy that is slightly more structured than MST. FFT has six distinct phases of treatment, but the specific interventions (often based in cognitive-behavioral theories), like MST, are tailored to the assessed needs of the child and their family. The first phase of FFT, engagement, is when the therapist creates trust, rapport, and buy-in from both the child and the family. In the second "motivation" phase, interpersonal dynamics within the family are identified to ensure all participants are on the same page and ready to get to work. The therapist delves deeper into the family's ways of interacting, particularly with the child whose behavior led to the initial referral to FFT, in the relational assessment phase. This assessment allows the therapist to identify targets for intervention in the fifth phase, the behavior change phase. In the behavior change phase, the child and their family members are taught techniques and skills for better interpersonal relationships. The sixth and final phase, generalization, consists of demonstrating the other areas of their lives where these techniques and skills can be utilized, thereby empowering autonomy from the therapist. These phases of FFT are intended to provide both a clear structure as well as a clear end to the providers' work with the family.

Summary

This chapter covered how principles from psychology have improved the way we rehabilitate those who have exhibited antisocial behavior. Although it was once believed that no treatments could be effective at rehabilitating criminal offenders, years of research have led to a recognition that behavioral change is possible with the right interventions and processes. The RNR model lays the foundation for how to reduce future offending behavior. Fourth-generation risk assessments allow for specific case planning to target dynamic criminogenic needs. Understanding the stages of change and using techniques like MI can help corrections practitioners motivate their clients to change their negative behavior. And specific treatment programs based on cognitive-behavioral and social-learning principles can indeed reduce recidivism when they are implemented with fidelity.

References

Alexander, J., & Parsons, B. V. (1982). *The anatomy of family therapy: Functional family therapy*. Brooks/Cole Publishing Company.

Bonta, J., & Andrews, D. A. (2016). *The psychology of criminal conduct* (6th ed.). Routledge.

Bush, J., Glick, B., & Taymans, J. (1997). *Thinking for a change: Integrated cognitive behavior change program*. National Institute of Corrections.

Douglas, K. S. (2019). Evaluating and managing risk for violence using structured professional judgment. In Polaschek, D. L. L., Day, A., & Hollin, C. R. (Eds.) *The Wiley International Handbook of correctional psychology*. John Wiley & Sons, Incorporated.

Feindler, E. L., Marriott, S. A., & Iwata, M. (1984). Group anger control training for junior high delinquents. *Cognitive Therapy and Research*, *8*(3), 299–311.

Gendreau, P., & Andrews, D. A. (1996). *Correctional program assessment inventory (CPAI)* (6th ed.). University of New Brunswick.

Glick, B., & Goldstein, A. P. (1987). Aggression replacement training. *Journal of Counseling and Development*, *65*(7), 356–362.

Goldstein, A. P., & Glick, B. (1994). Aggression replacement training: Curriculum and evaluation. *Simulation & Gaming*, *25*(1), 9–26.

Henggler, S. W., Melton, G. B., & Smith, L. A. (1992). Family preservation using multisystemic therapy: An effective alternative to incarcerating serious juvenile offenders. *Journal of Consulting and Clinical Psychology*, *60*(6), 953–961.

Henggeler, S. W., Rodick, J. D., Bordin, C. M., Hanson, C. L., Watson, S. M., & Urey, J. R. (1986). Multisystemic treatment of juvenile offenders: Effects on adolescent behavior and family interaction. *Developmental Psychology*, *22*(1), 132–141.

Lowenkamp, C. T., Hubbard, D., Makarios, M. D., & Latessa, E. J. (2009). A quasi-experimental evaluation of thinking for a change: A "real-world" application. *Criminal Justice and Behavior*, *36*(2), 137–146.

Martinson, R. (1974). What works? Questions and answers about prison reform. *The Public Interest*, *35*, 22–54.

Miller, W. R., & Rollnick, S. (2013). *Motivational interviewing: Helping people change* (3rd ed.). Guilford.

Prochaska, J. O., & DiClemente, C. C. (1984). *The transtheoretical approach: Crossing the traditional boundaries of therapy*. Dow Jones Irwin.

Prochaska, J. O., DiClemente, C. C., & Norcross, J. C. (1992). In search of how people change: Applications to addictive behaviors. *American Psychologist*, *47*(9), 1102–1114.

University of Cincinnati Corrections Institute. (2008-2024). *Behavior chain tool*. University of Cincinnati. https://cech.uc.edu/about/centers/ucci.html

van der Stouwe, T., Asscher, J. J., Stams, G. J. J. M., Deković, M., & van de Laan, P. H. (2014). The effectiveness of Multisystemic Therapy (MST): A meta-analysis. *Clinical Psychology Review*, *34*(6), 468–481.

14 Psychology in Prison

Introduction

Prison is not a pleasant place. It can be downright dangerous for everyone who must spend time there, both inmates and staff. Psychologists often work in prisons as part of both mental health services and rehabilitation efforts. This is undoubtedly a difficult job given the environment in which the psychologists' clients are living. These clients most likely import, or bring with them, mental health and behavioral issues when they enter prison. But there are also deprivations that an inmate experiences while incarcerated that may induce or exacerbate mental health issues. This chapter will cover the role of psychologists in prison and psychological ideas that can help explain the effects of the prison environment on both inmates and staff.

Psychologists in Prison

Historically, there have been five main reasons we punish people for disobeying the law: retribution, deterrence, incapacitation, rehabilitation, and restoration. **Retribution** encompasses the idea of "just deserts;" we punish people because they deserve it for the wrong they have done. **Deterrence** relies on positive and negative punishment (see Chapter 4) to dissuade people from committing crimes, both as an example to others (general deterrence) and as a lesson for the one being punished (specific deterrence). **Incapacitation** is intended to simply remove the offender from society so that they cannot cause harm to the general population while they are incarcerated. **Rehabilitation** has become a focal point in recent years, seeking to change the convict's future behavior to conform with the rules of society. Finally, **restoration** strives to not only rehabilitate the offender but to repair the broken relationships between the perpetrator, the victim, and society at large.

Behavioral psychology tells us that reinforcements are better than punishments at eliciting behavior change (see Chapter 4). As seen in the previous chapter, these psychological principles can help prompt behavior change for those already involved in the justice system. These principles also tell us that the traditional approaches to corrections (i.e., punishments and threats of punishment) may not be psychologically sound ways to gain conformity to laws or even prison rules.

Correctional psychology, the application of psychology to criminal justice correctional systems, is part clinical psychology and part industrial/organizational (I/O) psychology. This is especially true for psychologists working in an institutional correctional facility, rather than in community corrections. As we learned in Chapter 8, many inmates have mental illnesses that correctional psychologists can help to manage. Psychologists working in correctional settings also help to rehabilitate offenders through implementing and monitoring

DOI: 10.4324/9781003250821-16

treatment programs, as covered in Chapter 13. A background in clinical and/or counseling psychology is important for these tasks. However, correctional psychologists often assist in the operation of the jail or prison as well, including critical incident stress management for those working in the prison and assisting in inmate placement decisions. Therefore, an understanding of I/O psychology is also important for psychologists working in a correctional setting. In fact, a survey of correctional psychologists found that "interdepartmental communications/relationships were tapped almost daily" (Magaletta et al., 2007, p. 11). Correctional psychologists often wear many hats and work in a setting unique among clinical/counseling psychologists. As such, Magaletta and his colleagues (2007) have been using their continued research to help develop standards in correctional psychology for training and hiring practices.

Psychological Effects of Imprisonment

Adjustment to Prison Life

Being sentenced to prison is a huge life change. Adjusting to life in prison requires navigating both official and unofficial rules, which are often strict and violations are harshly punished. How well a new inmate adjusts to prison life depends on a number of factors, but becoming accustomed to this way of living will make the reentry process (covered later in this chapter) even more difficult. There is also debate as to whether the negative aspects of life behind bars are a result of the deprivations of prison or the importation of antisocial ideals.

Institutionalization/Prisonization

Given the strict confines and rigid routine of the prison environment, it is not surprising that new inmates must adjust to life on the inside. Donald Clemmer was the first to call this adjustment process "prisonization" back in 1958. The process has also been referred to as **institutionalization.** Craig Haney, who was the lead author of the famous Stanford Prison Experiment (see Box 14.1), described seven psychological adjustments that happen in institutionalization: dependence on institutional structure and contingencies; hypervigilance, interpersonal distrust, and suspicion; emotional over-control, alienation, and psychological distancing; social withdrawal and isolation; incorporation of exploitative norms of prison culture; diminished sense of self-worth and personal value; and post-traumatic stress reactions to the pains of imprisonment (Haney, 2002).

Part of institutionalization is learning both the official and unofficial rules of prison life. Both of these sets of rules can become so engrained that they affect individuals on a psychological level. Indeed, some have argued that institutionalization can be criminogenic (i.e., lead to future/further offending). The official rules are put forth by prison administrators; the unofficial rules are enforced by other inmates. But where do the unofficial rules come from? There are generally two schools of thought: deprivation and importation.

Deprivation

In 1958, Gresham Sykes first identified what he termed the **pains of imprisonment.** These pains are the result of various deprivations inherent to imprisonment. Some argue that the frustration inmates feel due to these deprivations results in the prison subculture (i.e., unofficial rules) which leads to the harmful and dangerous environment within prisons.

Box 14.1 The Stanford Prison Experiment

Craig Haney has been a life-long critic of the harsh realities of life in prison. This may have stemmed from his involvement in the Stanford Prison Experiment in 1971, which used random assignment of roles in a simulated prison environment. The Stanford Prison Experiment was conceived of by Dr. Phillip Zimbardo, with three psychology students assisting: W. Curtis Banks and David Jaffe, in addition to Haney.

The study consisted of a simulated prison environment built in the basement of the psychology building at Stanford University. Volunteers were solicited and, after mental health screenings, were randomly assigned to be either a prisoner or a guard. Those assigned to be prisoners were "arrested" by real police officers and brought to the makeshift prison. Nine guards worked in eight-hours shifts, with three guards to a shift. The nine inmates were not allowed to leave and were housed three to a six-by-nine-foot "cell." They were supposed to be incarcerated for two weeks; the experiment was ultimately canceled on the sixth day.

The only instructions the guards were given was to not let the inmates escape. How they decided to maintain order was up to them, as long as they did not inflict physical harm. Overnight the first night, the prisoners decided to rebel by barricading themselves in their cells. The second day of the experiment saw the guards retaliate by breaching the cells using a fire extinguisher, removing the inmates' clothing and mattresses, and placing who they determined to be the leaders of the rebellion in solitary confinement (a two-by-two-foot closet). Building on the us-versus-them mentality, the guards devised ways to pit the inmates against each other by sewing doubt as to which of the inmates might be working as an informant. The rebellions and retaliations continued to escalate over the next few days, with Zimbardo himself admitting later that he got psychologically caught up in his role as prison superintendent and forgetting this was an experiment of his own making. Even though several "inmates" had experienced mental breakdowns (with one being released from the experiment by Haney) and the guards were clearly intensifying their tactics, it was not until colleagues of Zimbardo questioned the ethics of what the experiment had become that he decided to finally end it after only five full days.

The Stanford Prison Experiment is considered by many to be the most unethical psychology experiment in history. Given the now stricter regulations on research, which partially stemmed from this experiment, it is not possible to replicate it. Scholars also question whether the methodology was sound enough to trust the results (Le Texier, 2019). Despite these criticisms, the Stanford Prison Experiment remains one of the most well-known experiments on the effects of imprisonment – on both inmates and guards. And given Haney's continued calls for prison reform, methodological concerns notwithstanding, it left a lasting impression on those involved.

Essentially, inmates end up using violence and intimidation as a way to exert some control in their lives that are now deprived of basic human rights and a sense of self identity. Sykes (1958) named five pains of imprisonment: deprivation of liberty, deprivation of goods and services, deprivation of heterosexual relationships, deprivation of autonomy, and deprivation of security.

Some of these pains of imprisonment are obvious and intended, while others are byproducts of life in a secure facility. **Deprivation of liberty** is an obvious consequence of imprisonment; inmates are not free. But Sykes's deprivation of liberty extends to the limitation of freedom of movement within the prison as well. Inmates are also deprived of their freedom to make decisions for themselves. This is Sykes's **deprivation of autonomy**, in that an inmate's life is solely dictated by the rules of the prison. Similarly, the **deprivation of goods and services** stems from this loss of choices. For example, inmates are limited in what they can buy and possess, what they can wear, and when and who cuts their hair. While the phrase "**deprivation of heterosexual relationships**" is outdated, the pain associated with the loss of intimate partnerships is not. Prisoners are utterly isolated and alone (even more so when in solitary confinement, which is covered later in this chapter). Finally, **deprivation of security** is an ever-present source of anxiety for most prisoners. Violence in prison is a daily possibility. Most inmates develop strategies for preventing victimization, which may include being the aggressor. It is easy to see how this might contribute to a violent, criminogenic culture in prison.

Importation

The **importation model of adjustment** to the prison environment was put forward by Irwin and Cressey in 1962. The central idea of this model is that inmates bring with them (i.e., "import") into prison a host of attitudes and behaviors that contribute to the harshness of prison life. This model was put forth as a direct contrast to the idea that the "pains of imprisonment" are what cause the severity of the prison environment.

Irwin and Cressey (1962) described two deviant subcultures among prisoners. The first they called the "thief subculture." This group relies upon what they learned from their criminal lifestyle on the streets to navigate prison life. Truly, this group "imports" their attitudes, beliefs and behaviors. The second deviant subculture is referred to by Irwin and Cressey (1962) as the "convict subculture." Both of these deviant subcultures follow traditional "criminal codes," such as no snitching, but the convict subculture adheres to these rules as a matter of practicality rather than as an inherent value system. However, the end result is much the same: a prison subculture that relies on the same rules as criminal life on the outside.

As with many dichotomies, the true source of the consequences of life in prison is likely *both* importation and deprivation. In the section on reentry later in this chapter, we will discuss the ramifications of prison life for the vast majority of inmates who are eventually released back into society.

Solitary Confinement

The reality of prison is that there must be a process for separating inmates from each other for protection and punishment. This is the purpose of **solitary confinement**. Within most prisons, there is a separate area where inmates are housed in individual cells for 22 to 24 hours a day, being released only occasionally for physical exercise and/or showering. Some inmates are placed in solitary confinement for short periods of time, while others spend their entire sentence there. Some other names given to this practice are administrative segregation, restrictive housing, segregated housing unit (SHU), and protective custody. These more benign-sounding names may be an attempt to give the public the perception that the practice is also benign, meaning it does not cause harm. The Vera Institute of Justice compiled a list of common misconceptions about solitary confinement to set the record straight (Shames et al., 2015; see Box 14.2).

Box 14.2 Vera Institute of Justice: Common misconceptions of solitary confinement (Shames et al., 2015)

Misconception #1: Conditions in segregated housing are stark but not inhumane
While the Supreme Court of the United States has indicated that solitary confinement does not violate the Eighth Amendment to the US Constitution prohibiting cruel and unusual punishment, the United Nations has consistently pushed for abdication of the practice.

Misconception #2: Segregated housing is reserved only for the most violent
Inmates can find themselves in solitary confinement for a number of reasons, including rule infractions and for their own protection from other inmates.

Misconception #3: Segregated housing is used only as a last resort
Corrections institutions are encouraged to use sanction grids that outline proportional punishments for various infractions to ensure solitary confinement is only used as a last resort.

Misconception #4: Segregated housing is used only for brief periods of time
It is not unusual for inmates to spend years and even decades in solitary confinement, sometimes having more time added for rule violations.

Misconception #5: The harmful effects of segregated housing are overstated and not well understood
The psychological science behind why solitary confinement is harmful is sound.

Misconception #6: Segregated housing helps keep prisons and jails safer
Institutions that have begun limiting their use of solitary confinement have not experienced a spike in violence in the general population of the prison.

Misconception #7: Segregated housing deters misbehavior and violence
Research has not found a deterrent effect in the use of solitary confinement, and some research shows it may increase misbehavior and violence.

Misconception #8: Segregated housing is the only way to protect the vulnerable
Alternative communal housing with special programming is a better option to protect vulnerable inmates.

Misconception #9: Safe alternatives to segregated housing are expensive
While there may be initial costs associated with establishing safe alternatives, solitary confinement is more expensive in the long run.

Misconception #10: Incarcerated people are rarely released directly to the community from segregated housing
Without a step-down model and reentry planning, inmates have been and will be released directly from solitary confinement into the community.

There have been concerns about prolonged seclusion in psychiatric settings since the 1950s. But it was in the 1980s when Grassian started applying this psychiatric research to prison settings. In 1983, Grassian conducted a qualitative, exploratory study with inmates in solitary confinement at the maximum-security prison in Walpole, MA. He observed a cluster of psychiatric symptoms which he later termed "**SHU syndrome**" after observing a similar phenomenon at Pelican Bay State Prison in California (Grassian, 2006). The symptoms of SHU syndrome include hyperresponsivity to external stimuli; perceptual distortions, illusions, and hallucinations; panic attacks; difficulties with thinking, concentration, and memory; intrusive obsessive thoughts/emergence of primitive aggressive ruminations; overt paranoia; and problems with impulse control.

Since Grassian's time, empirical research on whether or not solitary confinement leads to adverse psychological symptoms has been mixed. From the studies that have been conducted, it is unclear whether prisoners who have experienced the isolation and sensory deprivation of solitary confinement indeed experience more negative psychological effects than those in the general prison population. This is not really surprising, since it is incredibly difficult to disentangle the psychological effects of imprisonment in general from the particular psychological effects of solitary confinement specifically. In fact, a recent study found that any inmate with significant mental health issues is at risk for psychological decline whether they have experienced solitary confinement or not (Walters, 2018). Further, myriad factors may influence how a specific person responds to isolation. Magaletta and his colleagues have even suggested an "ecological model of segregation," recognizing that interacting personal, contextual, and process factors combine to impact how one is affected by solitary confinement (as cited in Clements et al., 2007, pp. 925–926). Given this lack of consensus in the empirical literature, this section will instead focus on the psychological principles behind why we might believe that solitary confinement has negative side effects: **social isolation** and **sensory deprivation**.

Social Isolation and Sensory Deprivation

Humans, and most mammals, are social creatures who require sensory stimuli to understand and navigate our world. When humans are deprived of these things, they will not only experience psychological distress, but their brains' neurons and neural pathways (see Chapter 2) may even be "rewired." Studies on mice and primates have shown a neurological effect of social isolation. Primates and rodents who have experienced social isolation show disruption of neural pathways in the limbic system and prefrontal cortex. Recall from Chapter 2 that the limbic system is involved in emotion regulation and the prefrontal cortex is responsible for higher-level thinking and decision making. Therefore, not only does social isolation impact cognitive and behavioral functioning, but it does so in ways that may be most detrimental to systems that can mitigate antisocial behavior.

Solitary confinement may also affect the inmates' senses in negative ways. Humans require sensory stimulation to understand our world. When the information we are receiving from our senses is limited or unusual, the neural pathways once used to process more normal sensory conditions will weaken and adapt. Inmates in solitary confinement are often exposed to only artificial light over which they have no control. Indeed, lights are often left on 24/7, which may cause inmates confusion and disruptions in circadian rhythms (i.e., sleep-wake cycle). Perhaps most damaging is the lack of physical touch from other human beings. Worse still, the only human touch or even interactions experienced by many housed in solitary confinement is during violent cell extractions used to enforce inmate compliance.

Perhaps unsurprisingly, these conditions can be even more detrimental for inmates with mental health issues. Indeed, many incarcerated individuals suffer from mental illnesses (see Chapter 8). Symptoms of mental illness can be made worse in isolation, causing inmates to decompensate, meaning lose any gains they may have made in controlling their mental health symptoms through therapy and/or medication. Further, those with mental health problems are more likely to end up in solitary confinement, due to their inability to conform to the rules of prison or a lack of another place to house the mentally ill whose behaviors may be deemed "disruptive."

A study conducted by Walters (2022) examined some of these interaction effects and provided a possible additional reason for the mixed empirical findings for any kind of SHU syndrome. Using longitudinal data from previous research on the psychological effects of solitary confinement, Walters (2022) specifically focused on the person-level factors of state versus trait anxiety and externalizing coping mechanisms (i.e., seeking distractions from outside oneself, such as acting impulsively) versus internal coping mechanisms (i.e., retreating inward, such as depression). **State anxiety** refers to the experience of anxiety in the face of situational stressors. Whereas, **trait anxiety** is a more generalized experience of anxiety across a variety of situations. Walters (2022) argued that the prolonged situational stressors of solitary confinement (i.e., state anxiety) may lead to more chronic anxiety in the form of trait anxiety, especially for those with predominately externalizing coping skills. He makes the assumption, though not an unfounded one, that inmates as a group tend to have more externalizing coping mechanisms. The case is made that inmates placed in solitary confinement will experience state anxiety that they may be unable to properly cope with using their usual externalizing coping skills. This inability to properly cope with the state anxiety experienced in solitary confinement may be a reason only some experience deleterious psychological effects. Indeed, Walters's (2022) study used inmates without previous mental health issues to compare the psychological effects of both solitary confinement and general population housing. He found that most inmates, especially those with good internal coping skills, did not report symptoms of SHU syndrome, but a minority of the inmates he studied did experience psychological decompensation. Walters (2022) concluded that "SHU syndrome is not solely a function of being placed in restrictive housing but involves a complex person x situation interaction" (p. 39). More research is needed on these interaction effects, but it might lead to screening tools to prevent those at most risk for developing SHU syndrome from being placed in solitary confinement.

Alternatives to Long-Term Solitary Confinement

Given that the psychological risks of solitary confinement seem to outweigh the benefits, perhaps it is time for correctional facilities to rethink their use of solitary confinement. The Vera Institute of Justice (Shames et al., 2015) published an explanation of the misconceptions about solitary confinement (see Box 14.2). Along with correcting these misconceptions, they provided recommendations for limiting the psychological impact of the practice on inmates. The publication highlighted institutions that have implemented step-down approaches to getting inmates out of solitary confinement. Similar to the problem-solving courts covered in Chapter 11, these step-down programs have those in solitary confinement progress through phases, getting closer and closer to returning to the general population with the successful completion of each phase. The authors also applaud and encourage the use of **sanction grids**, which recommend less severe repercussions for less severe behavior and reserve more punitive punishments, such as solitary confinement, for the most severe and/or prolonged behavior. Also advocated are frequent reviews of those inmates in solitary confinement and incentive programs that allow them to earn their way out of solitary confinement. These reforms are intended to limit the amount of time someone spends in solitary confinement. Inmates in solitary confinement should also still have access to both rehabilitative and mental health treatments, and perhaps more care should be provided in these units. There are also examples of institutions that have implemented separate communal housing units for those ordinarily placed in solitary confinement for "protective custody." Since these individuals are generally non-violent, housing them together but away from inmates who might do them harm is a much better alternative to solitary confinement. Finally, inmates should never be released directly from solitary confinement into the outside world. The step-down approaches described above can help ensure that those close to release are not in isolation just prior to doing so. A greater focus on the reentry process in general will be discussed later in this chapter.

PTSD/Post-Incarceration Syndrome

Stemming from Herman's (1992) work on complex post-traumatic stress disorder (PTSD) first mentioned in Chapter 9, Liem and Kunst (2013) explored whether there may be a distinct subtype of PTSD unique to those who have experienced long-term incarceration. They termed this **post-incarceration syndrome,** or PICS. They conducted in-depth interviews with a number of parolees who had been released from prison after serving a "life" sentence. (In many jurisdictions, an inmate can be paroled after serving a certain amount of their life sentence, unless otherwise indicated at sentencing.) Liem and Kunst (2013) found that there seem to be some symptoms above and beyond those associated with typical PTSD (see Table 14.1).

The additional PICS symptoms identified by Liem and Kunst (2013) fall into three categories: institutionalized personality traits, social/temporal alienation, and social-sensory disorientation. The symptoms of institutionalized personality traits are difficulties in trusting others, engaging in intimate relationships, and making decisions. Under the umbrella of social/temporal alienation are the symptoms of feelings of not belonging in social settings and feeling that good things can be taken away at any moment. Spatial disorientation and difficulty interacting socially are symptoms in the category of social-sensory disorientation. Notably, Liem and Kunst (2013) found the symptoms of social-sensory disorientation even in parolees who had *not* experienced solitary confinement. This may help further explain the difficulty in empirically isolating the effects of solitary confinement from the effects of imprisonment more generally.

Table 14.1 Liem & Kunst's post-incarceration syndrome (PICS).

Symptoms of PTSD *plus:*
Institutionalized personality traits
Difficulty trusting others
Difficulty engaging in intimate relationships
Difficulty making decisions
Social/temporal alienation
Feelings of not belonging in social settings
Feeling that good things can be taken away at any moment
Social–sensory disorientation
Spatial disorientation
Experiencing difficulty in interacting socially
Present even in those *without* experience in solitary confinement

In 2019, Piper and Berle conducted a meta-analysis on studies that assessed post-incarceration PTSD. They note that there is a lack of quality research on the topic, especially on whether there are potentially traumatic events (PTEs) unique to the prison environment and controlling for the effect of traumas experienced prior to incarceration. Based on the research they reviewed, incarcerated individuals are more likely than the general public to have experienced PTEs and symptoms of PTSD even prior to incarceration, which may increase vulnerability to PTEs while incarcerated. Piper and Berle (2019) also note that interpersonal traumas, such as physical violence and coercion, are more common in prison than traumatic incidents that do not involve interactions with others, such as accidents. They divide the concept of coercion further into direct coercion and indirect coercion. Direct coercion is applied through physical force or threat of physical force. But Piper and Berle (2019) state that more commonly, inmates experience indirect coercion due to "their experience of living in a threatening environment, controlled by fear and intimidation" (p. 856). Interestingly, their meta-analysis revealed that the length of time incarcerated was not associated with PTSD symptoms. Rather than being directly linked to the amount or severity of the experienced PTEs, PTSD or PICS may be more likely to occur in those who are most vulnerable for reasons we do not yet fully understand.

Reentry

The vast majority of inmates will eventually return to the community. Prior to the twenty-first century, this process of **reentry** was largely ignored. Released inmates were sent back into the community with nothing more than what they came to prison with, plus any money left on their books and/or enough money to take a bus or taxi to the nearest city (most prisons are in rural areas). Clearly, little thought was given to where these newly freed people would go, what they would do, and where they would live. The only message: "Don't come back." But the lack of support in the reentry process set released inmates up for failure rather than success in remaining crime-free.

We learned in Chapter 13 that behavior change is hard, but with support it can be achieved and sustained. Those reentering the community after a period of time in prison have additional challenges impacting their likelihood of **desistance**, especially if they were convicted of a felony. Felons in the United States are saddled with restrictions to their freedom that continue after they are released from prison and have "paid their debt to society." These additional restrictions are known as **collateral consequences**. For example, laws have been enacted that restrict a felon's ability to vote, participate in government assistance programs, including financial aid for education and housing, and obtain some professional licenses. Further, many employers will ask whether an applicant has been convicted of a felony directly on their employment applications, which very likely prevents ex-felons from even getting an interview. Recognition of the unfairness of this application question, usually accompanied by a checkbox, led to the start of the Ban the Box movement in 2003.

Pains of Desistance

In the spirit of Sykes and Matza's pains of imprisonment, Nugent and Schinkel (2016) outlined the pains of desistance. To do so, they described three types of desistance: act desistance, identity desistance, and relational desistance. These categories recognize desistance as a process. The first step in the process is **act desistance**, the ceasing of committing criminal acts. At this stage, the person may not yet self-identify as someone who does not commit crimes. When they do begin to see themselves this way, they have moved into **identity desistance.** However, it may take some time before others trust that they have truly changed their behavior, what Nugent and Schinkel call **relational desistance.** Relational desistance is further subcategorized based on the closeness of the relationship. Micro-level relational desistance refers to those closest to the individual believing they will no longer commit crimes. Meso-level relational desistance is when the person's broader community sees them as having given up criminal behavior. Finally, macro-level relational desistance is how the person is seen by society at large. Given our previous discussion of the Ban the Box movement, this example from Nugent and Schinkel (2016) is particularly apt: "For example, while employers are situated on the meso-level, the prevalent way in which criminal records are dealt with in recruitment decisions would be on the macro-level" (p. 570).

Through interviews with offenders released from prison after various lengths of incarceration, Nugent and Schinkel (2016) identified three pains of desistance: isolation and loneliness, goal failure, and lack of hope. The **pain of isolation and loneliness** is primarily tied to attempted act desistance. As we learned in Chapter 13, antisocial peers are a risk factor for offending behavior. To avoid recidivating, many of those released from prison will cut ties with their antisocial friends. Often, this leaves them with few, if any, prosocial friends with whom to spend time. Further, those who have experienced institutionalization may find isolation preferable to the hustle and bustle of the outside world.

The **pain of goal failure** is typically associated with the goal of obtaining employment. As noted earlier in the discussion of collateral consequences, finding gainful employment can be difficult for someone with a criminal record. If their criminal career had been a source of income, it is likely that the type of legitimate employment attainable by ex-offenders would bring in considerably less money. Indeed, Nugent and Schinkel (2016) found that the young men they interviewed also longed for the status that their criminal identities provided them. Given the difficulty of macro-level relational desistance, it is unlikely they will achieve a similar level of status in the noncriminal world.

It is likely that the first two pains of desistance lead to the third and final one: the **pain of hopelessness.** Again, behavior change is difficult for everyone. Desistance from criminal behavior is made even more difficult due to the restrictions that are placed on those with a criminal record (i.e., collateral consequences). These pains of desistance make identity desistance and relational desistance arduous, and it may begin to feel impossible. A source of support suggested by Nugent and Schinkel (2016) is the idea of **co-desistance,** a kind of support group similar to those used in addiction recovery. In addition to general support for enduring the pains of desistance, a co-desistance group could also provide networking for employment and prosocial recreational activities. Given the success of this model in addiction recovery, co-desistance is a promising concept that needs further research.

Reentry Process Theory

Durnescu's (2018) reentry process theory identified stages of prisoner reentry, similar to the stages of change discussed in Chapter 13 but with a specific focus on the process of reentry. The first stage was labeled **prerelease anticipation.** During this stage, inmates are still incarcerated but their release date is in sight. While they feel a sense of lost time as they anticipate their reunion with friends and family, "almost all participants at the time of release express a super-optimistic view over their successful reintegration" (p. 2203). The first two weeks post-release are referred to as the **recovery and reunion stage.** This stage was markedly different depending on the support system the person had upon release. Durnescu (2018) observed three levels of support based on how many were present to greet the person leaving prison. Some releasees had many family members and friends meet them at the gate, while others were met with only one or a few close family members and/or friends to pick them up. Unfortunately, there are some instances in which those who are released from prison are met with no support system at all.

The remainder of the first month post-release (weeks three and four) Durnescu (2018) called the **activation stage**. This is when releasees are actively looking for employment to provide for themselves and their families. Given the previous discussion regarding the pain of goal failure and collateral consequences, it is not surprising that those without a support system struggle more than those who may have already achieved some micro-level relational desistance. The activation stage is also characterized by the realities of life post-release setting in after the joys of the recovery and reunion stage fade.

The final stage of reentry process theory as outlined by Durnescu (2018) is either consolidation or relapse. If a releasee finds themselves on the right path with a positive support network, they will likely enter the **consolidation stage**. They will settle into a new, crime-free life. To use Nugent and Schinkel's (2016) term, they have achieved identity desistance. However, for those experiencing the pain of hopelessness, going back to their life of crime may seem the only – or at least easiest – option. Instead of the consolidation stage, these individuals return to criminal behavior in what Durnescu (2018) calls the **relapse stage**.

Second Chance Act

Corrections agencies began focusing on the reentry process around the turn of the twenty-first century. Rehabilitation efforts now often include increased focus on planning for eventual reentry and **wrap-around services**, meaning addressing all of the person's needs including continued support in the community upon release. The federal government recognized the need for an increase in these reentry-focused services by passing the **Second Chance Act** in 2007, which increased federal funding for corrections agencies looking to start, maintain, or expand their prisoner reentry programs. Increased attention and funding to the reentry process will help those seeking to change their lives for the better.

Correctional Officer Mental Health

Inmates are not the only people psychologically impacted by the conditions in correctional facilities. Similar to research on the inmate experience, research has uncovered a number of stress-inducing factors related to working in a correctional facility. Indeed, some of the same things that cause stress for inmates can also be stressful for guards, such as the risk of violence and witnessing violence, limited natural light, and excessive noise. In addition, Evers and colleagues (2020) note occupational stressors, such as "poor communication between administration, limited autonomy, exclusion from decision-making processes, little opportunity for promotion, underutilization of knowledge and skills, and lack of positive recognition" (p. 4). Like police officers (see Chapter 9), correctional officers are at risk of developing cumulative or complex PTSD due to repeated exposure to PTEs. Providing emotional and psychological support to correctional officers may also be met with the same "macho" culture as seen with police officers. The first step in changing this culture is to offer psychological services in these settings.

Support Services for Correctional Employees

There are several support services already being offered to correctional employees in some facilities. As with most employers in the twenty-first century, many prisons offer Employee Assistance Programs (EAPs) to their workers. However, these call-center-style support services are often the same as those used for other job types so the unique stressors of working in a secure facility with offenders are not always understood by the EAPs. Many prisons also use Critical Incident Stress Management (CISM) programs similar to those used for police officers. Recall from Chapter 9 that CISM protocols are meant to be reactive, rather than proactive, meaning the intervention happens after a critical incident. While it is important to have reactive structures in place, more proactive solutions are needed as well.

Proactive measures for correctional officer mental health include ongoing programming and hiring practices. Just as with police officers, psychoeducation programs that teach employees positive coping skills and stress management should be available to those working in a correctional setting. When hiring correctional officers, facilities should look for people who have a rehabilitation focus toward the job, rather than simply a punitive focus. A 2004 meta-analysis by Dowden and Tillier found that having a rehabilitation focus was correlated with less reported stress among correctional officers. It may also be beneficial to screen correctional employees for resiliency to stress (Konyk & Ricciardelli, 2022).

Summary

This chapter has focused on psychologists in prison and the psychological effects of the prison environment. Psychologists working in a secure correctional facility often utilize both clinical psychology, to assist the inmates and industrial/organizational psychology, to assist the staff. In helping inmates, they have their work cut out for them given the many documented and potential psychological effects of imprisonment and the additional psychological effects likely experienced by those in solitary confinement. However, there are alternatives to the harsh realities of solitary confinement. And attention to the potentially traumatic events experienced by both inmates and guards can help address post-traumatic stress symptoms. Perhaps most importantly for broader society, progress has been made in improving the reentry process for inmates released from prison. Better reentry services will help the vast majority of the inmates who are eventually released back into society to remain crime-free.

References

Clements, C. B., Althouse, R., Ax, R. K., Magaletta, P. R., Fagan, T. J., & Wormith, J. S. (2007). Systemic issues and correctional outcomes: Expanding the scope of correctional psychology. *Criminal Justice and Behavior*, *34*(7), 919–932. https://doi.org/10.1177/0093854807301561

Clemmer, D. (1958). *The prison community*. Rinehart.

Dowden, C., & Tellier, C. (2004). Predicting work-related stress in correctional officers: A meta-analysis. *Journal of Criminal Justice*, *32*(1), 31–47. https://doi.org/10.1016/j.jcrimjus.2003.10.003

Durnescu, I. (2018). The five stages of prisoner reentry: Toward a process theory. *International Journal of Offender Therapy and Comparative Criminology*, *62*(8), 2195–2215. https://doi.org/10.1177/0306624X17706889

Evers, T. J., Ogloff, J. R. P., Trounson, J. S., & Pfeifer, J. E. (2020). Well-being interventions for correctional officers in a prison setting: A review and meta-analysis. *Criminal Justice and Behavior*, *47*(1), 3–21. https://doi.org/10.1177/0093854819869975

Grassian, S. (1983). Psychopathological effects of solitary confinement. *American Journal of Psychiatry*, *140*(11), 1450–1454.

Grassian, S. (2006). Psychiatric effects of solitary confinement. *Washington University Journal of Law & Policy*, 22, 325–383.
Haney, C. (2002). The psychological impact of incarceration: Implications for post-prison adjustment [paper presentation]. National Institutes of Health conference, *From prison to home: The effect of incarceration and reentry on children, families and communities, Washington DC.* https://webarchive.urban.org/UploadedPDF/410624_PyschologicalImpact.pdf
Herman, J. L. (1992). Complex PTSD: A syndrome in survivors of prolonged and repeated trauma. *Journal of Traumatic Stress*, 5(3), 377–391. https://doi.org/10.1002/jts.2490050305
Irwin, J., & Cressey, D. R. (1962). Thieves, convicts and the inmate culture. *Social Problems*, *10*(2), 142–155.
Konyk, K., & Ricciardelli, R. (2022). Tough lessons: Pathways toward correctional officer resilience and growth. *Traumatology*. Advance Online Publication. https://doi.org/10.1037/trm0000408
Le Texier, T. (2019). Debunking the Stanford Prison Experiment. *American Psychologist*, *74*(7), 823–839. https://doi.org/10.1037/amp0000401
Liem, M., & Kunst, M. (2013). Is there a recognizable post-incarceration syndrome among released "lifers"? *International Journal of Law and Psychiatry*, *36*(3–4), 333–337. https://doi.org/10.1016/j.ijlp.2013.04.012
Magaletta, P. R., Patry, M. W., Dietz, E. F., & Ax, R. F. (2007). What is correctional about clinical practice in corrections? *Criminal Justice and Behavior*, *34*(1), 7–21. https://doi.org/10.1177/0093854806290024
Nugent, B., & Schinkel, M. (2016). The pains of desistance. *Criminology & Criminal Justice*, *16*(5), 568–584.
Piper, A., & Berle, D. (2019). The association between trauma experienced during incarceration and PTSD outcomes: A systematic review and meta-analysis. *The Journal of Forensic Psychiatry & Psychology*, *30*(5), 854–875. https://doi.org/10.1080/14789949.2019.1639788
Shames, A., Wilcox, J., & Subramanian, R. (2015). *Solitary confinement: Common misconceptions and emerging safe alternatives*. Vera Institute of Justice. https://www.vera.org/publications/solitary-confinement-common-misconceptions-and-emerging-safe-alternatives
Sykes, G. (1958). *The society of captives: A study of a maximum security prison*. Princeton University Press.
Walters, G. D. (2018). Checking the math: Do restrictive housing and mental health need add up to psychological deterioration? *Criminal Justice and Behavior*, *45*(9), 1347–1362. https://doi.org/10.1177/0093854818780177
Walters, G. D. (2022). Separate roles for state and trait anxiety in the formation of SHU syndrome: Testing a moderated mediation hypothesis. *The Prison Journal*, *102*(1), 25–46. https://doi.org/0.1177/00328855211069142

Glossary

Absolute judgment Deciding the authenticity of something without comparing it to other options.

Absolute worth A reminder to the Motivational Interviewing (MI) practitioner that every person has worth regardless of their actions, as part of the acceptance spirit of MI.

Acceptance A part of the spirit of Motivational Interviewing (MI) consisting of absolute worth, accurate empathy, autonomy support, and affirmation.

Accurate empathy A reminder to the Motivational Interviewing (MI) practitioner to seek to correctly understand their client's circumstances and point of view, as part of the acceptance spirit of MI.

Accusatory interrogation An interrogation style common in Western law enforcement for centuries that involves directly confronting the suspect about their guilt.

Accusatory interview The final stage of the Reid Technique involving the interrogation of someone deemed likely to be guilty due to perceived deception during the Behavioral Analysis Interview.

Acquisition The initial process of creating the conditioned stimulus and conditioned response in classical conditioning.

Act desistance The ceasing of committing criminal acts.

Action stage The fourth stage of change when the person begins making clear and substantial efforts to modify their behavior.

Activation stage The third and fourth weeks after release from incarceration, when the realities of post-release life begin to set in, which are often spent actively looking for employment.

Active listening A range of listening skills that indicate to the speaker that you are truly listening to what is being said.

Actuarial assessment Assessment tool that was developed using research and statistics to determine a level of risk of recidivism.

Actus reus One of two criteria for establishing guilt that refers to proving that the defendant committed the criminal act for which they are charged.

Adjudicative competency A tenet of due process of law by which a defendant must be able to understand any criminal proceedings against them and be able to assist in their own defense at all stages of the criminal justice process.

Advantageous comparisons One of Bandura's moral disengagements under the category of minimizing the immoral nature of the behavior by comparing the behavior to acts that seem even more immoral.

Adverse childhood experiences (ACEs) Negative events in childhood that have been empirically associated with a wide variety of negative outcomes in adulthood.

Affirmation A reminder to the Motivational Interviewing (MI) practitioner to validate their client's strengths and efforts, as part of the acceptance spirit of MI.

Aggression Any behavior intended to inflict some kind of harm (e.g., physical, emotional) upon another against their will.

Aggression Replacement Training An anger management program based on cognitive-behavioral principles created for violent offenders by Goldstein and Glick.

Agreeableness One of the personality dimensions of both the Five-Factor Model and HEXACO model of personality with characteristics ranging from cooperative and generous at the high end to selfish and cold at the low end, though there are some differences in the two models.

Alleles Variations in genotypes which impact genetic expression (phenotype).

Amygdala A structure in the limbic system of the brain thought to be the primary emotional center, dysfunctions of which are frequently implicated in violent behavior.

Anger Control Training A component of Aggression Replacement Training (ART) where participants are asked to keep a "hassle log" of situations that aroused their anger and their response to those situations.

Antisocial behavior Behavior that violates social norms or expectations, including breaking rules that are not necessarily laws.

Antisocial personality disorder (APD) A disorder listed in the *Diagnostic and Statistical Manual of Mental Disorders*, fifth edition (DSM-5) that is similar, but not identical, to psychopathy.

Anxious attachment style One of two insecure attachment styles in attachment theory characterized by a heavy reliance on others for a sense of safety.

Appealing to higher loyalties One of Sykes and Matza's techniques of neutralization used to justify antisocial behavior by claiming loyalty to something seen as more important than the law and whose interests or ethics conflict with current legal standards.

Attention The first stage of social cognitive theory which requires the observer to pay attention to the model of the behavior.

Attribution of blame One of Bandura's moral disengagements under the category of minimizing the worth of the victim by attributing blame for the crime to the victim; this is unfortunately common in many sexual assault cases.

Autonomous morality The second and final stage of Piaget's moral development theory which can only begin after a child has reached the formal operational stage of Piaget's cognitive development theory when abstract reasoning is possible. Also known as moral relativism due to the ability to consider the unique aspects of different situations.

Autonomy support A reminder to the Motivational Interviewing (MI) practitioner to recognize that people make their own decisions about how to live their lives, as part of the acceptance spirit of MI.

Autonomy versus shame and doubt The second stage of Erikson's psychosocial development theory thought to take place primarily between ages one and three. Caregivers' negative reactions to a toddler's attempts at independence will cause the child to doubt their ability to care for themselves.

Avoidant attachment style One of two insecure attachment styles in attachment theory characterized by a lack of trust in most other people.

Behavior Chain A worksheet developed by the University of Cincinnati Corrections Institute designed to teach the thought-behavior link and aid in cognitive restructuring.

Behavioral Analysis Interview The initial interview stage of the Reid Technique that offers suggestions for determining whether an interviewee is innocent or guilty by asking neutral baseline questions followed by a series of investigative and behavior-provoking questions and gauging their verbal and nonverbal responses.

Beyond a reasonable doubt The standard of proof in a criminal trial; a jury must find a defendant guilty only if there is no reasonable doubt as to their guilt.

Bias assimilation The psychological phenomenon by which new information is evaluated as true or relevant based on whether or not it fits our existing ideas or schemas.

Big Four risk factors The four factors most highly correlated with recidivism, namely antisocial attitudes, antisocial associates, history of criminal behavior, and antisocial personality.

Biopsychology The study of the psychological effects of biological processes, including behavioral neuroscience, behavioral endocrinology, evolutionary psychology, and behavioral genetics.

Borderline personality disorder (BPD) A personality disorder, characterized by criteria related to poor anger management and impulsivity, that has been associated with antisocial and aggressive behavior.

Bottom-up approach An inductive approach to criminal profiling that uses existing data to try to ascertain empirical connections between crime scenes and the criminals who made them.

Bystander effect The phenomenon of individual inaction in helping behavior when in the presence of many others.

CAPP semi-structured interview A specific interview style developed for use with the Comprehensive Assessment of Psychopathic Personality (CAPP) that provides suggestions for handling the difficult aspects of interviewing a potential psychopath, such as identifying deception.

Case planning Structuring treatment programming around someone's highest criminogenic need areas; an integral part of a fourth-generation risk assessment.

Central Eight risk factors The eight factors most highly correlated with recidivism, namely the Big Four plus family/marital problems, difficulty in school/work, no prosocial leisure activities, and substance abuse.

Central nervous system The half of the nervous system containing the brain and spinal cord.

Certainty of punishment One of the requirements of effective deterrence theorized by early philosophers and supported by research in behavioral psychology which suggests that punishment must be guaranteed to follow the criminal behavior to be an effective deterrent.

Challenge for cause A method of removing a juror from the venire due to a stated reasonable belief that said juror cannot be impartial.

Chromosomes Structures in each cell of the body that contain our DNA; half of our 46 chromosomes come from each parent.

Circumstantial evidence Evidence presented in a trail that points to the circumstances surrounding a crime or crime scene and requires a logical inference connecting the defendant with the crime or crime scene.

Classical conditioning A process of learning by associating a neutral stimulus with a reflexive, unconscious (unconditioned) stimulus and response.

Clinical judgment A test of an individual's moral development stage consisting of an evaluation by a professional, such as a psychologist.

Co-Desistance A support group for ex-offenders, similar to those used in addiction recovery.

Coerced-compliant false confession When an innocent suspect confesses in order to escape or avoid an aversive interrogation or to gain a promised reward.

Coerced-internalized false confession When an innocent person actually comes to believe that he or she committed the crime, often due to anxiety, fatigue, confusion, and highly suggestive methods of interrogation.

Cognitive disequilibrium A state of instability in one's worldview caused by that view being challenged by others who see things differently.

Cognitive dissonance An uncomfortable state in which your stated beliefs contradict new information or circumstances.

Cognitive distortions Patterns in thinking that help to neutralize any guilt or shame that might be felt for negative or antisocial behaviors, sometimes called thinking errors.

Cognitive Interview The gold standard interview process to increase accuracy when interviewing witnesses that consists of eight memory-enhancing techniques.

Cognitive lie detection A method of lie detection that involves increasing the cognitive load of the interviewee making it more likely for someone who is lying to slip up.

Cognitive load The limited ability of the brain's working memory to simultaneously process multiple things at the same time.

Cognitive neoassociation theory A modification of the frustration-aggression hypothesis which states that negative affective is the true underlying cause when frustration leads to aggression and situations that trigger schemas associated with negative affect and/or aggression will increase the odds of aggression.

Cognitive restructuring The process by which one learns to slow down their thinking and choose to alter their thought patterns toward more positive outcomes.

Cognitive skills Skills around restructuring thinking patterns to achieve more positive outcomes.

Cognitive-behavioral treatment Therapies based on cognitive and behavioral psychology that have been empirically proven to lead to behavior change.

Coherence shift A phenomenon in Simon's coherence-based reasoning model of juror decision making when a juror's story construction may continually change (shift) based on new information provided during trial and previous information is reevaluated based on the new narrative.

Coherence One of the certainty principles of Pennington and Hastie's story model that is broken into three types (consistency, completeness, and plausibility); a story is judged as coherent if it does not contain any inconsistencies, is a complete narrative without holes, and makes sense (is plausible) given the juror's understanding of how the world works.

Collateral consequences Additional restrictions placed on those with a criminal record even after they are released from prison that are the result of laws, not community supervision requirements of parole.

Community Mental Health Act (CMHA) The law passed by Congress in 1963 to build centers to deliver mental health care on an out-patient basis.

Compassion A part of the spirit of Motivational Interviewing (MI) intended to remind practitioners that they are there to serve the needs and benefits of the client, not their own.

Competency to stand trial The most common adjudicative competency questioned by the courts leading to evaluations often performed by psychologists or psychiatrists.

Complex post-traumatic stress disorder Also known as cumulative post-traumatic stress disorder, this condition can be the result of repeated and/or prolonged exposure to traumatic events.

Comprehensive Assessment of Psychopathic Personality (CAPP) A case planning tool developed using everyday language to describe the symptoms of psychopathy.

Concrete operational stage The third stage of Piaget's cognitive development theory, from age seven until roughly 11, when children learn their perspectives are possibly different from others. Children at this stage are also able to logically think about concrete things.

Condemnation of the condemners One of Sykes and Matza's techniques of neutralization used to justify antisocial behavior by claiming that everyone breaks the law and those condemning such behavior are hypocrites whose opinions should not be trusted.

Conditioned response The result of classical conditioning where a once neutral stimulus now elicits the same response as the unconditioned stimulus with which it was repeatedly paired.

Conditioned stimulus In classical conditioning, a once neutral stimulus that has been repeatedly paired with an unconditioned stimulus.

Conduct disorder (CD) A childhood disorder listed in the *Diagnostic and Statistical Manual of Mental Disorders*, fifth edition (DSM-5) and characterized by aggression towards people or animals, destruction of property, deceitfulness or theft, and serious violation of rules

Conduct disorder with limited prosocial emotions (CD+LPE) A diagnosis added to the *Diagnostic and Statistical Manual of Mental Disorders* (DSM) to capture traits indicative of a young psychopath, including lack of remorse or guilt, callousness–lack of empathy, lack of concern about performance in important activities, and shallow or deficient affect.

Confederate Someone who pretends to not be involved in an experimental study but is in fact an integral part of it.

Confirmation bias Our psychological tendency to overlook information that does not fit into our preexisting ideas and to focus instead on information that confirms our preexisting ideas.

Conformity The tendency for humans to follow others when they are part of a group, even if they think the group consensus is wrong.

Confounding variables Influences that affect the things we are trying to study, often unbeknownst to the researchers.

Conscientiousness One of the personality dimensions of both the Five-Factor Model and HEXACO model of personality with characteristics ranging from highly diligent and meticulous at the high end to more careless and inattentive at the low end.

Consolidation stage One of two possible final stages of Durnescu's (2018) reentry process theory characterized by settling into a new, crime-free life.

Consolidation The process of converting short-term memories to long-term memories caused by the repetition of the neural networks associated with the memory through rehearsal or recall of the memory.

Contemplation stage The second stage of change when the person acknowledges a need or desire to change their behavior.

Contingency management systems Ways of managing behavior using operant conditioning.

Continuous reinforcement A reinforcement schedule in operant conditioning whereby a reinforcement is provided every time the desired behavior is performed.

Control variables Measurements used by researchers to attempt to constrain their influence on what is being studied.

Conventional morality The second level of Kohlberg's moral development theory that contains stages three and four. Assumed to be the level of moral development for most adults.

Co-response model A policing response to a mental health crisis where the responding officer(s) call in mental health professionals to assist on scene.

Correctional psychology The application of psychology to criminal justice correctional systems that is part clinical psychology and part industrial/organizational (I/O) psychology, including any punishment and/or rehabilitative efforts.

Cortisol A hormone produced by the adrenal glands that is primarily responsible for stress response.

Coverage One of the certainty principles of Pennington and Hastie's story model; the amount of the evidence presented that fits with an emerging story.

Crime assessment The third stage of Crime Scene Analysis when the profiler determines whether the offender is organized or disorganized.

Crime linkage The process of identifying similarities among separate crime incidents lending credence to the idea that they were all committed by the same perpetrator(s).

Crime Scene Analysis The process of FBI criminal profiling that consists of six stages: (1) profiling inputs, (2) decision making models, (3) crime assessment, (4) the criminal profile, (5) investigation, and (6) apprehension. The fifth and sixth stages are essentially out of the hands of the profiler and back in the hands of the police.

Criminal profile The fourth stage of Crime Scene Analysis and the output that is turned over to law enforcement for the final two stages of FBI criminal profiling. The final criminal profile will describe the type of person who committed the crime and also how they might respond to common investigation techniques.

Criminal profiling Also known as offender profiling and psychological profiling, an investigative technique whereby characteristics of an offender are determined based on their victim(s) and crime scene(s).

Criminogenic needs Dynamic risk factors from the Central Eight that are targeted for change.

Criminology The study of crime and criminal behavior.

Crisis Intervention Team (CIT) A police response model to address calls for service which involve a mental health crisis that trains a select team of officers who respond to all mental health calls.

Critical Incident Stress Debriefing (CISD) A specific model of critical incident stress management (CISM) sometimes called the "Mitchell Model" for its creator Dr. Jeffrey Mitchell.

Critical Incident Stress Management (CISM) Protocols followed by many departments following critical incidents that often consist of peer support.

Critical incident stress syndrome (CISS) A condition experienced after a critical incident with symptoms similar to post-traumatic stress disorder but more short-lived (less than four weeks).

Critical incident An event during the line of duty that might cause undue stress on those who were either directly or indirectly involved, such as an officer-involved shooting or the death of a fellow officer.

CSI effect A belief by some court actors, which has not been empirically supported, that fictionalized-crime programming has affected the expectations of jurors.

Cumulative post-traumatic stress disorder Also known as complex post-traumatic stress disorder, this condition can be the result of repeated and/or prolonged exposure to traumatic events.

Curative instructions Jury instructions given by the judge meant to alleviate sources of bias, such as pretrial publicity or inadmissible evidence; also known as evidentiary instructions, admonitions, or limiting instructions.

Dark Triad A grouping of personality constructs (i.e., narcissism, Machiavellianism, and psychopathy) theorized to co-occur in people prone to various forms of antisocial behavior.

***Daubert* trilogy** Three cases heard by the Supreme Court of the United States regarding the admissibility of expert testimony, including *Daubert v. Merrell Dow Pharmaceuticals* (1993), *General Electric v. Joiner* (1997), and *Kumho Tire Company v. Carmichael* (1999).

***Daubert v. Merrell Dow Pharmaceuticals* (1993)** A landmark case where the Supreme Court of the United States outlined criteria for assessing the admissibility of expert testimony.

Decision making models The second stage of Crime Scene Analysis that consists of seven decision points: (1) homicide type and style, (2) primary intent of the murderer, (3) victim risk, (4) offender risk, (5) escalation, (6) time factors, and (7) location factors.

Decision support The part of investigative psychology that uses the other two parts (i.e., information retrieval and inferences) to assist police in their investigations.

Decompensate The experience of a resurgence or worsening of symptoms of mental illness often experienced when patients stop taking prescribed medication.

Decriminalization An approach to drug laws which removes criminal penalties for drug use and possession of small quantities for personal use, often replacing such penalties with citations and/or fines.

Deductive reasoning The process of applying broad knowledge to a specific situation.

Definitions In criminological theory, the beliefs and attitudes one holds.

Dehumanizing One of Bandura's moral disengagements under the category of minimizing the worth of the victim by thinking of them as sub-human or inhuman.

Deindividuation The loss of a feeling of oneself as separate from the group with which they identify or of which they are currently a part.

Deinstitutionalization The move of psychiatric patients out of in-patient hospitals and into the community, followed by the closure of many in-patient psychiatric facilities.

Deliberation The confidential process by which a jury discusses the facts of a case as presented at trial and decides as a group whether or not the defendant is guilty of the charges brought against them.

Denial of injury One of Sykes and Matza's techniques of neutralization used to justify antisocial behavior by saying it has not truly caused irreparable harm to the victim.

Denial of responsibility One of Sykes and Matza's techniques of neutralization used to justify antisocial behavior where the person positions themselves as a helpless victim of circumstances beyond their control.

Denial of the victim One of Sykes and Matza's techniques of neutralization used to justify antisocial behavior where the victim is portrayed as the initial perpetrator deserving of revenge.

Deoxyribonucleic acid (DNA) The most basic building block in our bodies, a kind of assembly and operations manual.

Deprivation of autonomy One of Sykes's pains of imprisonment; inmates are not able to make most decisions for themselves.

Deprivation of goods and services One of Sykes's pains of imprisonment; inmates are not able to freely choose what to goods to buy or services to patronize.

Deprivation of heterosexual relationships One of Sykes's pains of imprisonment; inmates are isolated from loved ones and are often not allowed intimate relationships.

Deprivation of liberty One of Sykes's pains of imprisonment; inmates are not free and their freedom of movement within the facility is further restricted.

Deprivation of security One of Sykes's pains of imprisonment; inmates are subjected to the near constant threat of violence.

Desistance The act of ceasing criminal behavior.

Deterrence One of the five main reasons for punishing people for disobeying the law; it relies on positive and negative punishment to dissuade people from committing crimes, both as an example to others (general deterrence) and as a lesson for the one being punished (specific deterrence).

Developmental psychology A branch of psychology focused on how humans gain certain basic human knowledge and skills throughout their lives.

Diathesis-stress model A theory of gene-environment interaction which posits that our specific genes may make us more vulnerable to adverse environmental conditions.

Differential association In criminological theory, the difference between the number of positive and the number of negative influences with whom one associates; also the name of the full theory proposed by Sutherland.

Differential association-reinforcement A criminological theory put forward by Burgess and Akers that expands on differential association theory by recognizing that we are also reinforced for different behaviors by the different associates in our lives.

Differential reinforcement In criminology, the idea that we are reinforced for different behaviors by the different associates in our lives.

Differential susceptibility model A theory of gene-environment interaction which suggests that our genes effect how sensitive we are to our environments.

Diffusion of responsibility (moral disengagement) One of Bandura's moral disengagements under the category of minimizing personal responsibility for the behavior whereby someone shares responsibility for their actions with their co-conspirators.

Diffusion of responsibility (social psychology) The feeling when acting as part of a group that the consequences of our actions are distributed among group members making the individual feel less accountable.

Direct evidence Evidence presented at trial that directly indicates that the defendant committed the crime, typically either eyewitness testimony or a confession.

Disorganized attachment style An attachment style in attachment theory characterized by an inconsistent reaction to the strange situation experiment and uncertainty about whom to trust.

Disorganized offender Part of the well-known organized/disorganized dichotomy of FBI criminal profiling, whereby inferences are made about the offender based on elements of the crime scene. Disorganized offenders will leave a more disorganized crime scene.

Displacement of responsibility One of Bandura's moral disengagements under the category of minimizing personal responsibility for the behavior by placing the blame for one's actions on someone else in a position of authority.

Displacement A Freudian defense mechanism characterized by taking out negative emotions on someone or something other than the cause of the negative emotion, usually when that cause is unavailable or seemingly inappropriate to attack.

Dispositional risk factor In the I^3 model, risk factors for violence that stem from the individual's temperament, such as biological factors and general attitude.

Distal risk factor In the I^3 model, risk factors for violence that originate from the (sub)cultural, socioeconomic, and demographic world in which the person lives.

Distortion of consequences The only one of Bandura's moral disengagements under the category of minimizing the consequences of the behavior by arguing to oneself and others that no real harm came to the supposed victim.

Dizygotic The scientific term for fraternal twins due to the fertilization of two (di) eggs (zygotes).

Dopamine A neurotransmitter that causes us to experience pleasure, which is why it is associated with learning and motivation.

Dosage The frequency and duration of treatment.

Double-blind lineup A lineup presentation method whereby an officer unfamiliar with the case administers the photo lineup.

Dual-diagnosis Also called comorbidity or co-occurring disorders, the presence of two clinical diagnoses in the same person most commonly used with mental illness and substance use disorder.

Dual-process models of information processing Models of decision making which recognize that decision making is impacted by both cognitive and emotional internal factors.

Due process The requirement of specific and thorough processes to be followed prior to depriving a citizen of life or liberty.

***Durham* rule** Also known as the product rule, a standard for assessing insanity at the time of an alleged crime that only asks whether the act was a "product of [i.e., solely caused by] mental disease or mental defect."

***Dusky* standard** Named for *Dusky v. United States* (1960) in which the Supreme Court of the United States identified the criteria for evaluating a defendant's competency, and also called the *Dusky* three-prong standard for the three components of ability to (1) rationally consult with counsel, (2) rationally understand proceedings, and (3) factually understand proceedings.

Dynamic risk factors Risk factors for recidivism that can be changed, such as antisocial attitudes.

Economic compulsive violence The idea that those addicted to drugs will commit crimes to acquire money or drugs to support their addiction.

Ego integrity versus despair The eighth and final stage of Erikson's psychosocial development theory thought to take place in the final years of our lives when we reflect on our contributions to the world.

Elemental Psychopathy Assessment (EPA) A self-report questionnaire used to diagnose psychopathy across four factors: Antagonism, Emotional Stability, Disinhibition, and Narcissism.

Emotionality A dimension of the HEXACO personality model with characteristics ranging from sentimental and vulnerable at the high end to brave and independent at the low end.

Emotional labeling In active listening, giving a name to what the speaker seems to be feeling, which normalizes it.

Encoding The first stage in our memory process that simply consists of our taking in of sensory information.

Engaging The first step in the Motivational Interviewing process, and any helping relationship, whereby the practitioner and client establish a rapport and trust.

Episode An interpersonal situation in the General Aggression Model, many of which may occur in a single encounter.

Episodic long-term memories Explicit long-term memories about an event we experienced, such as witnessing a crime.

Epistasis The scientific word for gene-gene interactions, or genes that affect other genes.

Escalation One of the decision points in the second stage of Crime Scene Analysis when it is determined whether the perpetrator has done this before and whether they will do it again.

Eugenics The weeding out of undesirable genetic traits through barbaric interventions such as castration and extinction.

Euphemistic labeling One of Bandura's moral disengagements under the category of minimizing the immoral nature of the behavior by calling the behavior something different so that it does not sound as bad or so that one's behavior seems justified.

Evaluation of Competency to Stand Trial – Revised A structured assessment tool designed to evaluate a defendant's competency resulting in four subscales: three subscales that align with the *Dusky* three-prong standard and one subscale intended to test for malingering.

Event schema Also known as a script, ideas and impressions we have about events that reoccur with some frequency.

Evidence-driven jury A style of jury deliberation in which all evidence and testimony is considered to create an agreed upon story of what happened, and individual jurors are typically not polled until this story is constructed.

Evocation A part of the spirit of Motivational Interviewing (MI) intended to remind practitioners that their job is to evoke their client's own desires and tools for change.

Evoking The third step of the Motivational Interviewing (MI) process and the heart of MI whereby the practitioner elicits the client's own motivations for change.

Excitation transfer theory A theory of aggression which states that because emotional and physiological arousal do not immediately dissipate, such excitation can be transferred to subsequent encounters unrelated to the original source of the arousal.

Executive functions A collection of higher-level processes of the brain, such as decision making, self-control, planning, and regulating emotional responses.

Explicit long-term memories A type of long-term memory associated with information, which has two types: semantic and episodic.

Extinction In classical and operant conditioning, when a previously learned behavior ceases due to having not been paired with the unconditioned stimulus (classical) or not receiving reinforcement (operant) for some time.

Extraversion One of the personality dimensions in both the Five-Factor Model and HEXACO model of personality with characteristics ranging from more outgoing and active at the high end to more introverted and quiet at the low end.

Factual analysis The first stage of the Reid Technique consisting of assessing evidence to identify persons of interest to interview.

False confession When someone admits to taking part in a crime when they in fact did not.

FBI criminal profiling A "top-down" approach to criminal profiling developed by agents at the Federal Bureau of Investigation's Behavioral Sciences Unit (now called the Behavioral Analysis Unit) that uses deductive reasoning from specialized knowledge.

Fear conditioning A behavioral learning response that inhibits behavior that has been associated with the experience of fear in the past.

Fidelity principle A newly added principle of effective intervention (RNR model) that states that correctional programming that meets the principles of effective intervention must be implemented with integrity to their design.

Fight-flight-freeze-or-fawn response A term for our biological responses to perceived external threats: fight the threat; flee from the threat; freeze, unable to respond immediately; or try to mitigate the threat by appeasing the source (fawn).

Fillers Photos/people in a line up other than the suspect.

First-generation risk assessment Offenders' risk for recidivism based solely on the judgement of corrections professionals.

Fitness-for-duty-evaluation (FFDE) Evaluations of currently employed police officers to determine whether they are still fit for the work and/or whether they are ready to return to work following an absence due to administrative leave.

Five-Factor Model of Personality (FFM) A widely used and widely accepted model of personality consisting of the five personality dimensions of Openness to Experience, Conscientiousness, Extraversion, Agreeableness, and Neuroticism.

Fixed interval reinforcement A reinforcement schedule in operant condition whereby a reinforcement is delivered only after a certain amount of time, as long as the desired behavior was completed at least once during that time.

Fixed ratio reinforcement A reinforcement schedule in operant condition whereby a reinforcement is provided only after the desired behavior has been repeated a specific number of times.
Focusing The second step of the Motivational Interviewing (MI) process whereby the practitioner focuses the client's thoughts and desires into the direction of change.
Forensic psychology Any application of psychology to the courtroom and its processes.
Formal operational stage The fourth and final stage of Piaget's cognitive development theory from age 11 through adulthood. The hallmark of this stage is abstract reasoning needed for moral development.
Fourth-generation risk assessment Offenders' risk for recidivism assessed using an actuarial method with a focus on the Central Eight risk factors and the inclusion of case planning based on assessed criminogenic needs.
Framing The activation of a schema by presenting new information in the context of that schema.
Frustration-aggression hypothesis The idea that feelings of frustration lead to increased chances of aggressive behavior.
***Frye* standard** Named for *Frye v. United States* (1923) and also known as the general acceptance standard, a standard for evaluating expert evidence whereby the scientific knowledge on which that evidence is based must be generally accepted by the scientific community at large.
Functional Family Therapy A family-based therapy for justice-involved youth that is structured into six distinct phases of treatment, intended to provide a clear structure and also a clear end to the provider's work with the family.
Fundamental attribution error Also known as correspondence bias, the inclination for people to believe that things that others do are a matter of their character, whereas things that they themselves do are a matter of circumstances.
Gene-environment interaction The understanding that and study of the ways our environment impacts our genes and gene expressions and vice versa; the complex outcomes of nature *and* nurture.
General aggression model (GAM) A series of stages explaining how interpersonal situations can become aggressive which integrates several existing theories of aggression.
General deterrence In line with observational learning, the idea in criminal justice that others who see someone punished for a crime will be less likely to commit that crime themselves.
General responsivity principle The part of the responsivity principle of effective intervention that states that correctional treatment programs should be based in empirically proven psychological science, specifically cognitive-behavioral therapies and modalities based on social learning theories.
General strain theory Agnew's expansion of Merton's strain theory which noted that there are many sources of stress and frustration that may lead to aggression and antisocial behavior.
Generativity versus stagnation The seventh stage of Erikson's psychosocial development theory thought to take place primarily between ages 40 and 65. A person may become stagnant and unproductive without a sense of legacy and contributions to society that will outlast them.
Genes Sections of DNA responsible for the construction and maintenance of our bodies, as well as our individual traits and characteristics.
Genotype The physical sequence of genes.
Goodness-of-fit One of the certainty principles of Pennington and Hastie's story model; how well a juror's story fits within the given verdict categories.
Group polarization A social psychology phenomenon whereby a discussion among like-minded people leads to more extreme opinions among the group.
Groupthink A social psychological phenomenon where group cohesion, group loyalty and stress can contribute to a lack of differing ideas and opinions within the group.
Guidance instructions A set of instructions given by the judge to the jury explaining the charges against the defendant, the verdict options, and reminders of the concepts of innocence until proven guilty and beyond a reasonable doubt; see also pattern instructions and standard instructions.
Guilty but Mentally Ill An alternative to Not Guilty by Reason of Insanity in some jurisdictions concerned with someone being found not guilty due to their mental state at the time of the crime.
Heredity The passing on of characteristics from one generation to the next.
Heritability estimates Techniques used in twin and adoption studies to approximate the impact of our genes on our traits and behavior.
Heteronomous morality The first stage of Piaget's moral development theory when children ages five to ten understand what is right and wrong based only on whether or not an action will be punished by an authority figure. Also known as moral realism.

HEXACO Personality Inventory (HEXACO-PI) A personality assessment specifically designed to measure the personality dimensions of the HEXACO model.

HEXACO An updated personality model developed using the lexical method across multiple languages leading to six personality dimensions rather than five.

Homicide type and style One of the decision points in the second stage of Crime Scene Analysis that deals with the distinction between single murder, double murder, mass murder, spree murder and serial murder.

Homology hypothesis A logical assumption underlying any attempt at criminal profiling that states that an offender's behavior at their crime scene can be used to infer their overall personality and characteristics helpful to identifying them.

Honesty-Humility A personality dimension unique to the HEXACO personality model which includes characteristics ranging from sincere and fair-minded at the high end to greedy and hypocritical at the low end.

Hormones Chemical messengers that originate in the endocrine system and are transported via the bloodstream.

Hostage negotiator Someone who will communicate with the hostage taker to de-escalate the situation and hopefully reach a peaceful end.

Hostile attribution bias Also known as hostile intent attribution, the tendency to perceive ambiguous social cues as having a hostile intent.

Hung jury A jury that is unable to come to a unanimous decision even after considerable effort to do so.

I^3 model Pronounced "eye cubed," a model of violent and nonviolent interpersonal interactions that consists of an instigating trigger, impelling forces, and inhibiting forces.

Identity desistance When one no longer sees themselves as someone who commits crime.

Identity versus role confusion The fifth stage of Erikson's psychosocial development theory thought to take place primarily between ages 12 and 18. To develop a healthy sense of identity, adolescents should be permitted to explore different ways of interacting with the world via their own choices.

Impelling force Also called an impellor, a factor that increases the chance of violence in the I^3 model.

Implicit long-term memories A type of long-term memory associated with procedures, such as muscle memory.

Importation model of adjustment An idea put forward by Irwin and Cressey (1962) that inmates bring with them (i.e., "import") into prison a host of attitudes and behaviors that contribute to the harshness of prison life.

Incapacitation One of the five main reasons for punishing people for disobeying the law; simply removing the offender from society so that they cannot cause harm to the general population while they are incarcerated.

Inductive reasoning The process of compiling data from specific cases to infer more general principles that can later be applied to other specific cases.

Industrial/Organizational psychology A branch of psychology that uses psychological principles to understand individual and group dynamics in a working environment.

Industry/competence versus inferiority The fourth stage of Erikson's psychosocial development theory thought to take place primarily between ages three and 12. Caregiver(s) reactions to the child's accomplishments in school will impact whether the child feels competent or inferior.

Inferences The criminal profiling part of investigative psychology.

Information retrieval A part of investigative psychology that aids police officers in collecting relevant data from crime scenes.

Informational influence Persuasion by information rather than social pressure; present in all jury deliberations, but perhaps given more weight in evidence-driven deliberation.

Information-gathering interrogation An interrogation style that seeks to gather information (rather than elicit a confession) by building rapport and being truthful with the accused.

Inhibiting force Also called an inhibitor, a factor that decreases the chance of violence in the I^3 model.

Inhibition One of three roles of executive functions that steps in to inhibit an initial, perhaps emotional, response to stimuli.

Initiative versus guilt The third stage of Erikson's psychosocial development theory thought to take place primarily between ages three and six. Children begin to assert themselves during play with other children, and a delicate balance is required by caregivers to encourage this leadership without letting the assertiveness give way to aggression.

Inputs The first stage of the General Aggression Model consisting of the personal and situational factors that are present during an episode.

Insanity Defense Reform Act A law enacted by Congress in 1984 after the successful use of Not Guilty by Reason of Insanity (NGRI) by the man who attempted to assassinate President Ronald Reagan.

Insanity A legal, not psychological, term relating to a defendant's mental state at the time the alleged crime was committed.

Instigating trigger Also called an instigator, the event that brings about the potential for violence in the I^3 model.

Institutionalization Also called prisonization, an umbrella term for the psychological processes that occur as an inmate adjusts to life in prison, such as learning the official and unofficial rules.

Instrumental aggression/violence Aggression or violence that is premeditated and often a means to an end, aiding the person in gaining what they are truly after, often money or other material goods.

Instrumental-relativist orientation The second stage of Kohlberg's moral development theory where judgments of morality are still based on external rewards and punishments, but it is understood that different people will reward and punish different things.

Interpersonal concordance The third stage of Kohlberg's moral development theory when people begin to internalize the morality of what is judged by the majority of society as right and wrong. Also referred to as the "good boy/girl" orientation due to the focus on being seen as a good person by others.

Interrogation A special type of police interview used on those suspected of committing a crime.

Intimacy versus isolation The sixth stage of Erikson's psychosocial development theory thought to take place primarily between ages 18 and 40. Developing close, committed relationships with other adults at this time will lead to a sense of love and belonging.

Investigative psychology A coherent system of information retrieval, inference, and decision support.

Ironic process theory A theory in psychology that says that telling someone to not think about something tends to have the opposite effect (e.g., "don't think of a white bear").

Irresistible impulse test Also known as the "policeman at the elbow" test, a somewhat controversial criterion added to the M'Naghten criteria in some jurisdictions to assess insanity at the time of an alleged crime.

Jangle fallacy A logical error made when a measure is presumed to capture a unique construct just because it is named differently than other measures.

Jingle fallacy A logical error when two measures are named the same, but in fact are measuring different constructs.

Jury A group of people selected from the community where the alleged crime took place who will hear evidence presented at trial and deliberate among themselves to render a verdict as to whether or not the defendant is guilty of the charges brought against them.

Karpman's primary psychopath A distinction made by Karpman in 1948, the primary psychopath is more calculating and calmer in his deviance stemming from an innate lack of conscience.

Karpman's secondary psychopath A distinction made by Karpman in 1948, secondary psychopathy, sometimes called sociopathy, results from a conscience that was not properly formed due to inept parenting resulting in a more volatile and impulsive person.

Lack of Perseverance A facet of the UPPS impulsivity assessment tool which acknowledges the tendency of impulsive people to give up on tasks that they find boring or difficult.

Lack of Premeditation A facet of the UPPS impulsivity assessment tool which captures the fact that impulsive people tend not to think things through before they act.

Lateralization The differing functions and structures of the right and left hemispheres of the brain.

Law and order orientation The fourth stage of Kohlberg's moral development theory characterized by strict obedience to the laws of society without question.

Law of effect The idea that a behavior is likely to be repeated when it is followed by a positive consequence and is unlikely to be repeated if it is followed by a negative consequence.

Lexical method A method used to determine personality traits by examining the adjectives we use to describe ourselves and others.

Limbic system A collection of structures in the center of the brain thought to be responsible for our emotions, memory, pleasure, reward response, and much more.

Location factors One of the decision points in the second stage of Crime Scene Analysis when the various locations related to the homicide are considered, including where the victim was first approached (if known), where the crime occurred, and if the body was not found at the primary crime scene, where was the body dumped.

Lykken's psychopathy Similar to Karpman's primary psychopath and stemming from a diagnosis of antisocial personality disorder (APD), Lykken's psychopathy is caused by a genetically derived poor temperament.

Lykken's sociopathy Similar to Karpman's secondary psychopath and stemming from a diagnosis of antisocial personality disorder (APD), Lykken's sociopathy is caused by the failure to develop a conscience due to poor parenting.

M'Naghten rule Also known as the right/wrong test or cognitive test, the criteria still used in many United States jurisdictions for determining whether a defendant was insane at the time of their alleged crime

MacArthur Competence Assessment Tool – Criminal Adjudication A structured assessment tool designed to evaluate a defendant's competency using three sections that align with the *Dusky* three-prong standard.

Machiavellianism Named for a sixteenth-century philosopher who advocated that the ends justify the means, one of the personality constructs of the Dark Triad characterized by low agreeableness, low conscientiousness, low honesty-humility, and high neuroticism.

MACH-IV An assessment tool to measure Machiavellianism which includes three subscales related to morals, views, and tactics.

Maintenance stage The fifth stage of change when the person has taken consistent action to change their behavior for about six months.

Mala in se Latin for "wrong in itself."

Mala prohibita Latin for "wrong because it is prohibited."

Malingering When someone fakes or exaggerates a condition in order to benefit themselves in some way.

Maximizing technique A method of the Reid Technique's accusatory interview involving inflating the amount and veracity of evidence against a suspect and suggesting that cooperation is the only way out of the situation.

Memory conformity The tendency to change our memory to conform to what we hear from others, especially those closest to us.

Mens rea One of two criteria for establishing guilt that refers to the "guilty mind" of the defendant whereby they knew the act for which they are charged is wrong and went through with the act despite this knowledge.

Mental health courts A type of specialty or problem-solving court used to divert defendants with mental illnesses away from the adversarial court process and into treatment for their mental illness.

Meta-analysis A study of studies using specific research methods and statistics to reach an overall conclusion on a topic based on the results from many studies.

Mindguards People within a cohesive group who will admonish any dissention from group members.

Minimal encouragers In active listening, short interjections, such as "yeah" and "uh huh," that signal you are paying attention.

Minimizing technique A method of the Reid Technique's accusatory interview involving offering excuses or neutralizations and suggesting, but not promising, leniency.

Minnesota Multiphasic Personality Inventory-Revised-Restructured Form (MMPI) The most commonly used law enforcement pre-employment screening tool.

Mirroring In active listening, repeating the last part of what the speaker just said in the form of a question, which encourages the person to elaborate.

Misleading specialized knowledge Information about the crime or crime scene known only to the police and true perpetrator that is consciously or subconsciously leaked to a suspect during an interrogation.

Modeling When someone demonstrates something to another person by doing it themselves.

Models In social learning theory and social cognitive theory, the people whom we observe and imitate.

Modus operandi (MO) The specific way in which a crime is committed, including methods and processes.

Molecular genetics The study of the sections of DNA that make up our genes and identifying what those genes do.
Monoamine oxidase A (MAOA) gene A gene responsible for regulating levels of dopamine and serotonin that has been linked to aggressive behavior, particularly for those who also experienced childhood maltreatment.
Monozygotic The scientific term for identical twins due to the sharing of a single (mono) egg (zygote).
Moral education A part of Aggression Replacement Training (ART) based on Kohlberg's moral development theory that consists of evaluating various moral dilemmas in a group setting.
Moral justification One of Bandura's moral disengagements under the category of minimizing the immoral nature of the behavior that reframes the supposed moral transgression into a moral virtue by justifying a means to an end.
Moral Reconation Therapy A correctional treatment program designed around Kohlberg's moral development theory.
Motivation The fourth and final stage of social cognitive theory which states that the observer must have sufficient motivation to continue to repeat the imitated behavior.
Motivational Interviewing A person-centered approach to eliciting behavior change developed by Miller and Rollnick.
Multisystemic therapy A family therapy for justice-involved youth and their families that recognizes that juveniles' lives exist in multiple separate but interdependent systems (i.e., family, school, peers, and community).
Narcissism As characterized by the Dark Triad, a personality construct consisting of potentially sub-clinical levels of narcissistic personality disorder criteria, as well as high assertiveness and excitement seeking, and low modesty and warmth; also known as grandiose narcissism.
Narcissistic personality disorder A personality disorder, characterized by criteria related to an inflated sense of self-worth, that has been associated with antisocial and aggressive behavior.
Narcissistic Personality Inventory (NPI) An assessment tool to measure narcissistic traits which includes seven facets: authority, exhibitionism, superiority, vanity, exploitativeness, entitlement, and self-sufficiency.
Natural selection The evolutionary process whereby members of a species with characteristics best suited for survival are able to pass on those characteristics to their offspring, whereas those members of a species whose characteristics are not well suited for their current environment will be unable to procreate, due to early death or simply lack of mates.
Need principle A principle of effective intervention (RNR model) that states that correctional treatment should target dynamic risk factors, also known as criminogenic needs.
Negative punishment Something pleasant that is subtracted or taken away to discourage an undesired behavior.
Negative reinforcement Something unpleasant that is subtracted or taken away to encourage a desired behavior.
Negative urgency A facet of the UPPS impulsivity assessment tool defined by difficulty resisting urges when in a negative affective state.
NEO Personality Inventory (NEO-PI) A personality assessment specifically designed to measure the personality dimensions of the Five-Factor Model.
Nervous system Considered the human operations center, it is responsible for information processing and communication throughout the body.
Neural pathways Networks of neurons created by repeated use of those neurons together; the more they are used, the more prominent they become.
Neurons Cells that use neurotransmitters to share information around the body and initiate other processes.
Neuroticism One of the personality dimensions of the Five-Factor Model of personality with characteristics ranging from anxious and moody at the high end to traits such as stable and calm at the low end.
Neurotransmitters Chemical messengers that originate in the nervous system and travel through the body via neurons and their neural pathways; there are over 100 different neurotransmitter chemicals.
Neutral stimulus In classical conditioning, something which does not elicit a response on its own.
Noncriminogenic needs Things a person may need but are not empirically related to recidivism, such as secure housing, mental health treatment, and motivation.

Nonviolent crime Crime that does not usually cause immediate, physical harm to another.

Normative influence The drive to conform to the majority due to the desire to feel included rather than isolated; likely more commonly felt in verdict-driven juries with frequent, sometimes public polling.

Not Guilty by Reason of Insanity (NGRI) In many jurisdiction, the plea entered when the question of the defendant's mental state at the time of their alleged offense is raised.

Obedience and punishment The first stage of Kohlberg's moral development theory where judgments of morality are based solely on rewards and punishments from external sources, namely parents or caregivers.

Offender consistency hypothesis A logical assumption underlying any attempt at criminal profiling that states that offenders behave consistently across their separate crimes.

Offender risk One of the decision points in the second stage of Crime Scene Analysis when the offender's tolerance of the risk of getting caught is categorized as low, moderate, or high.

Openness to Experience One of the personality dimensions of both the Five-Factor Model and HEXACO model of personality with characteristics ranging from being very open to new ideas and experiences at the high end to more closed off and set in one's ways at the low end.

Operant conditioning A process of learning from the consequences (both positive and negative) that come from our behavior.

Oppositional defiant disorder (ODD) A childhood disorder listed in the *Diagnostic and Statistical Manual of Mental Disorders*, fifth edition (DSM-5) and characterized by a child who is often angry/irritable, argumentative/defiant, and vindictive towards many people, including those outside their family.

Organized offender Part of the well-known organized/disorganized dichotomy of FBI criminal profiling, whereby inferences are made about the offender based on elements of the crime scene. Organized offenders will leave a more organized crime scene.

Outcomes In the General Aggression Model, the evaluation and decision-making processes, as well as the resulting chosen action, whether thoughtful or impulsive.

Own-race bias The psychological phenomenon whereby people have a difficult time noticing distinguishing features of faces of races other than their own.

Pain of goal failure One of Nugent and Schinkel's (2016) pains of desistance; those trying to create a prosocial life for themselves, such as gaining legitimate employment, often face setbacks in attaining these goals.

Pain of hopelessness One of Nugent and Schinkel's (2016) pains of desistance; the difficulties and setbacks faced by former offenders trying to lead a prosocial life may lead to a sense that a crime-free lifestyle is impossible to achieve.

Pain of isolation and loneliness One of Nugent and Schinkel's (2016) pains of desistance; those trying to desist from criminal behavior may remove themselves from temptations of certain friends and/or social situations.

Pains of imprisonment First identified by Sykes (1958), deprivations inherent to imprisonment that may lead to psychological distress and maladjustment.

Paraphrasing In active listening, repeating back to the speaker what they have just said using your own words.

Partnership A part of the spirit of Motivational Interviewing (MI) intended to remind practitioners that they are simply the facilitators and their client will be doing the heavy lifting.

Pattern instructions A set of instructions given by the judge to the jury explaining the charges against the defendant, the verdict options, and reminders of the concepts of innocent until proven guilty and beyond a reasonable doubt; see also guidance instructions and standard instructions.

PEACE model A specific information-gathering interrogation technique created in the United Kingdom.

Pennington and Hastie's story model A theory of juror decision making that says jurors construct a narrative based on the evidence presented at trail and classify that story into the available verdict categories based on the four certainty principles of coverage, coherence, uniqueness, and goodness-of-fit.

Penrose hypothesis Also called the transinstitutionalization hypothesis, the idea that as the population of either prisons or psychiatric hospitals decreases, the population of the other institution will increase; named for Lionel Penrose who first suggested it in 1939.

Peremptory challenge A limited option for both the prosecution and defense to remove a juror from the venire without having to provide a reason, except if the opposing attorney questions whether the challenge is racially motivated.

Peripheral nervous system The half of the nervous system containing the complex system of neurons responsible for relaying information between the other parts and systems of the body and the central nervous system.

Perseverance effect A byproduct of confirmation bias, the tendency to adhere to ideas or schemas even in the face of contradictory evidence.

Person schema Ideas and impressions we have about people with certain characteristics.

Phenotype The way our genes are expressed within our bodies and to the world.

Phenotypic plasticity The biological phenomenon of different phenotypes emerging from the same genotype.

Plain language jury instructions The result of removing legalese from jury instructions that may leave more room for error in interpretation.

Planning The fourth and final step of Motivational Interviewing (MI) whereby the practitioner helps the client make specific plans for changing their behavior.

Plasticity The ability to be reshaped and reformed.

Plea bargaining Through an offer made by the judge or prosecution, the defendant agrees to plead guilty to a lesser charge and/or for a lesser sentence than they would face going to trial.

Pluralistic ignorance The tendency to believe others see things in the opposite way that you do.

Police psychology Any intersection of psychology and the field of law enforcement.

Positive punishment Something unpleasant that is added or given to discourage an undesired behavior.

Positive reinforcement Something pleasant that is added or given to encourage a desired behavior.

Positive urgency A facet of the revised UPPS-P impulsivity assessment tool defined by difficulty resisting urges when in a positive affective state.

Postconventional morality The third level of Kohlberg's moral development theory that contains stages five and six. Few people are believed to reach this level.

Post-Incarceration Syndrome Proposed by Liem and Kunst (2013), a possibly distinct subtype of PTSD unique to those who have experienced long-term incarceration.

Post-verdict debriefing A meeting of the jury after the verdict has been delivered to discuss the emotional impact of the case and offer coping strategies, often led by the judge or a clinician.

Pre-contemplation stage The first stage of change when the person is not even considering or perhaps even thinking about changing their behavior.

Preconventional morality The first level of Kohlberg's moral development theory that contains the first the first two stages of the theory.

Prefrontal cortex The area of the frontal lobe directly behind the forehead known for a collection of higher-level processes called executive functions.

Preoperational stage The second stage of Piaget's cognitive development theory, from age two until about age seven, characterized by the acquisition of language and symbolic thinking.

Preparation stage The third stage of change when the person is seriously considering taking steps toward changing their behavior and may have already taken small steps or made attempts to change.

Preponderance of evidence A standard of evaluating evidence by which there must be more evidence than not (greater than 50%) that the issue in question has been proven.

Prerelease anticipation stage An often super-optimistic time when an inmate is still incarcerated but their release date is in sight.

Preservation of reputation hypothesis An idea that among offenders, especially juvenile offenders, it may be seen as desirable to report antisocial behaviors; this idea is the reverse of social desirability bias where people over report their positive behaviors.

Primary intent of the murderer One of the decision points in the second stage of Crime Scene Analysis when the murderer's primary intent is classified as (1) criminal enterprise, (2) emotional, selfish or cause specific, or (3) fulfilling a sexual fantasy.

Priming The tendency of schema activation to be based on the recency and frequency with which that particular schema is activated.

Process evaluation A method of research that uses observation of program delivery and interviews with staff and clients to confirm that a program is being implemented as it was designed.

Production measures A test of an individual's moral development stage which uses vignettes followed by open-ended questions requiring the respondent to produce or articulate their level of morality.
Profiling inputs The first stage of Crime Scene Analysis that includes collecting comprehensive case materials, background information on the victim, forensic information and police reports.
Psychology The study of the mind and/or brain and its impact on behavior.
Psychopath A person diagnosed with psychopathy, a disorder with a specific set of symptoms including shallow affect, lack of empathy, charm, and deceit, among many others.
Psychopathic Personality Inventory (PPI) A self-report questionnaire used to diagnose psychopathy across two factors: Fearless Dominance and Self-Centered Impulsivity.
Psychopathy Checklist (PCL) Historically the most widely used diagnostic tool for psychopathy, with many derivative tools including the Psychopathy Checklist-Revised (PCL-R), Psychopathy Checklist-Screening Version (PCL-SV), and Psychopathy Checklist-Youth Version (PCL-YV).
Psychopharmacological violence Also called the intoxication model, the idea that the psychological effect(s) of a drug cause those who ingest it to behave violently.
Psychosis A group of psychiatric symptoms including hallucinations, paranoia, and delusions.
Publication bias The claim that scientific journals are less likely to publish empirical research that has "null" findings.
Punishment avoidance Part of the reconceptualization of deterrence theory by Stafford and Warr that recognizes that punishment is not certain and this uncertainty creates a learning opportunity which may actually increase the likelihood of future criminal behavior.
Punishment Something that is used to discourage an undesired behavior.
Reactance theory A theory in psychology that says people may react to being told what to do with defiance due to the resistance to a perceived threat to their behavioral freedom.
Reactive aggression/violence Aggression or violence that is a reaction to a real or perceived immediate threat.
Recidivism Committing another crime or reoffending after a previous conviction.
Recognition measures A test of an individual's moral development stage consisting of multiple-choice questions allowing participants to merely differentiate between the various levels of morality.
Reconceptualization of deterrence theory A theory by Stafford and Warr that incorporates the concept of punishment avoidance into deterrence theory.
Recovery and reunion stage The often joyful first two weeks after release from incarceration, usually spent reconnecting with loved ones and making plans for a future prosocial life.
Reentry The process of returning to society after a period of incarceration.
Rehabilitation One of the five main reasons for punishing people for disobeying the law; it has become a focal point in recent years, seeking to change a convict's future behavior to conform with the rules of society.
Reid Technique A method of interviewing and interrogating widely used by United States police investigators for decades.
Reinforcement schedules In operant conditioning, the different timing and delivery of a reinforcement.
Reinforcement Something that is used to encourage a desired behavior.
Relapse stage One of two possible final stages of Durnescu's (2018) reentry process theory characterized by a return to criminal behavior.
Relational desistance When others believe that someone will no longer commit crimes.
Relational risk factor In the I^3 model, interpersonal issues that are risk factors for violence that are unique to the specific relationship at hand.
Relative judgment Making comparisons among presented options and using process of elimination to make a selection.
Reliability A term used in research that means that a measure is consistent every time a measurement is taken/gathered.
Reproduction The third stage of social cognitive theory when the previously observed behavior is imitated.
Responsivity principle A principle of effective intervention (RNR model) that states that correctional treatment should use effective methods to bring about behavior changes.
Restoration One of the five main reasons for punishing people for disobeying the law; it strives to not only rehabilitate the offender but to repair the broken relationships between the perpetrator, the victim, and society at large.

Retention The second stage of social cognitive theory which recognizes that the observer must remember the behavior that they observed in order to imitate it.

Retribution One of the five main reasons for punishing people for disobeying the law; we punish people because they deserve it for the wrong they have done.

Retrieval The third and final stage of the memory process that entails recalling a memory from where it is stored.

Reuptake The return of neurotransmitter molecules to neurons so that they can be reused and are not causing lingering effects.

Reward deficiency syndrome The hypothesis that low levels of dopamine are associated with chronic substance use and sensation-seeking behavior.

Risk principle A principle of effective intervention (RNR model) that states that correctional treatment dosage should be based on risk for recidivism as assessed by a fourth-generation risk assessment tool.

Role playing When the person who is learning a new skill practices going through the steps of the skill in a benign situation, such as with their treatment provider.

Role schema Ideas and impressions we have about people in specific roles.

Routes In the General Aggression Model, the three pathways through which the inputs are processed to lead to the outcomes of the episode, including the present internal states of cognition, affect, and arousal.

Rule 702 of the Federal Rules of Evidence Part of many rules enacted by Congress in 1975, a standard for evaluating the admissibility of expert evidence or testimony that states that expert testimony should be admitted to trial if it accurately applies information obtained via the scientific method and will help the trier(s) of fact to better understand aspects of the case.

Sanction grids Prison punishment policies that recommend less severe repercussions for less severe behavior and reserve more punitive punishments, such as solitary confinement, for the most severe and/or prolonged negative behavior.

Schemas Mental shortcuts based on previous experience to help us process and manage the bombardment of sensory information we receive all the time.

Scientific Jury Selection A method of evaluating jurors using data and empirical knowledge usually employed by hired jury consultants.

Script Also known as an event schema, ideas and impressions we have about events that reoccur with some frequency.

Second Chance Act A federal law passed in 2007 that increased federal funding for corrections agencies looking to start, maintain or expand their prisoner reentry programs.

Second-generation risk assessment Offenders' risk for recidivism based on actuarial methods using research and statistics to provide a formula to determine individual risk score.

Secure attachment style The most balanced of the four attachment styles in attachment theory characterized by neither too much dependence on others nor no trust in others whatsoever.

Self schema Ideas and impressions we have about ourselves.

Self-care A range of techniques that have been shown to aid in relieving stress and may help law enforcement officers cope with difficult encounters on the job and avoid more severe consequences of trauma.

Semantic long-term memories Explicit long-term memories with a specific context, essentially general knowledge.

Sensation seeking A facet of the UPPS impulsivity assessment tool characterized by both a tendency to enjoy and pursue activities that are exciting and an openness to trying new experiences that may or may not be dangerous.

Sensorimotor stage The first stage of Piaget's cognitive development theory, from birth until approximately age two. Children develop a sense of themselves as separate from the world around them and their ability to affect the world.

Sensory deprivation The state of limiting or removing stimulation of one or more of the five senses, which likely has negative psychological effects.

Sequential lineup Lineup presentation method in which the photos are presented to the eyewitness one at a time, forcing the use of absolute judgment.

Serotonin deficiency hypothesis The idea that low levels of serotonin are correlated with increased aggression, particularly in men.

Serotonin A neurotransmitter used to regulate our mood, among many other functions.

Severity of punishment One of the requirements for effective deterrence theorized by early philosophers which suggests that punishment for criminal behavior must be harsh enough to be unpleasant, but so harsh that it is unjust and disproportionate.
Shadow jury A group of people to serve as a proxy for the actual jury who also observe the trial and of whom questions and opinions can be asked.
Shaping In operant conditioning, a method of teaching more complex tasks by reinforcing successive approximations of the end-goal behavior.
Shifting One of three roles of executive functions that allows us to ignore outside interference while performing a task or process.
Short-term memories Memories stored in the frontal lobe for an extremely short period of time, about 15–30 seconds.
SHU syndrome A cluster of psychiatric symptoms identified by Grassian (2006) that may be the result of solitary confinement, which is sometimes called a secure housing unit (SHU).
Signature An aspect of the crime that is superfluous to actions necessary to commit the crime, thought to be a psychological element needed to fulfill the fantasy of the crime.
Simon's coherence-based reasoning A theory of juror decision making that acknowledges the bidirectional feedback loop of human reasoning.
Simultaneous lineup Lineup presentation method in which all photos are presented to the eyewitness at once, promoting the use of relative judgment.
Situational risk factor In the I^3 model, risk factors for violence that result from the cognitive, affective, and physiological experiences unique to the specific situation at hand.
Skillstreaming The social skills training component of Aggression Replacement Training (ART).
Social cognition The ways we, as individuals, think about and respond in our social interactions.
Social cognitive theory Albert Bandura's theory of learning by observation and reinforcement that incorporates human agency via our ability to think about things.
Social contract orientation The fifth stage of Kohlberg's moral development theory with a focus on the social contract and recognizing that multiple viewpoints should be considered when making laws and that morality can and should evolve.
Social desirability bias A common methodological phenomenon which typically manifests as over reporting desirable behaviors and under reporting undesirable behaviors.
Social identity/deindividuation (SIDE) The view that when individuals in a group share a social identity, they are more likely to conform their behavior to that of their associates.
Social information processing theory A theory which states that there are six steps that happen as we choose our behavioral response in a social situation.
Social isolation The state of being kept away from other people, which likely has negative psychological effects.
Social learning theory In criminology, the theory put forward by Akers that suggests deviant behavior is learned via differential association, differential reinforcement, definitions, and imitation.
Social psychology The study of how we, as individuals, interact with and are impacted by society and other people.
Social skills The myriad skills needed to interact appropriately and positively with others.
Sociology The study of groups of people and societies as they develop and function as a whole unit.
Solitary confinement A separate area of a prison where inmates are housed in individual cells for 22 to 24 hours a day, being released only occasionally for physical exercise and/or showering. Also known as administrative segregation, restrictive housing, segregated housing unit (SHU), and protective custody, among other names.
Specialty courts or problem-solving courts Often an option to divert certain defendants from traditional court processes, these courts take a non-adversarial approach to treatment of problems that often lead individuals into trouble with the law.
Specific deterrence In line with direct operant conditioning, the idea in criminal justice that a criminal who has been punished for a crime will be less likely to commit that crime in the future.
Specific responsivity principle The part of the responsivity principle of effective intervention that states that treatment and treatment delivery should be matched to the person's learning style and that barriers to participation in treatment should be removed.
Stages of change Model of behavior change first articulated by Prochaska and DiClemente in their transtheoretical model.

Standard instructions A set of instructions given by the judge to the jury explaining the charges against the defendant, the verdict options, and reminders of the concepts of innocence until proven guilty and beyond a reasonable doubt; see also guidance instructions and pattern instructions.

State anxiety The experience of anxiety in the face of situational stressors.

Static risk factors Risk factors for recidivism that cannot be changed, such as criminal history.

Status pursuit in narcissism model (SPIN) A theory of narcissistic aggression which posits that a narcissist may use aggression preemptively to increase their status.

Stimulus discrimination In classical conditioning, the learned ability to tell the difference between similar but different stimuli.

Stimulus generalization In classical conditioning, the broadening of a conditioned response to stimuli that are similar to the conditioned stimulus.

Storage The second stage in our memory process whereby the sensory information taken in is stored in either our short-term or long-term memory.

Story classification The third and final part of Pennington and Hastie's story model which involves the comparison of the juror's constructed story against the possible verdict categories using the certainty principle of goodness-of-fit.

Story construction The first part of Pennington and Hastie's story model in which jurors construct a story of what happened using the evidence presented, their own schemas, and the certainty principles of coverage, coherence, and uniqueness.

Strain theory Merton's theory that aggression and crime originate from the frustration of goal-blockage in the attempted attainment of the American Dream.

Strange situation experiment An experiment created by Mary Ainsworth to test Bowlby's attachment theory and used to identify four unique attachment styles which are believed to be established in childhood and continue to affect our relationships in adulthood.

Strategic use of evidence The presentation of verified evidence to confront suspects with inconsistencies in their established narrative of what happened during the time of the crime.

Structured Professional Judgment Risk for recidivism is assessed using an actuarial tool that allows for professional judgment to provide a more individualized assessment.

Substance-defined model The drug-related actions that are labeled as criminal only because the law says that they were illegal (i.e., *mala prohibita*).

Successful psychopath Someone who meets the diagnostic criteria for psychopathy, but does not have a criminal conviction and may even have a high-power career.

Supervised consumption facilities Locations where drug users can consume or inject drugs they have purchased under the supervision of health care workers to minimize deaths due to overdose; a common harm-reduction strategy for addressing chronic drug use.

Swiftness of punishment One of the requirements of effective deterrence theorized by early philosophers and supported by research in behavioral psychology which suggests that punishment must quickly follow the criminal behavior to have a deterrent effect.

Syndemic Short for synergistic epidemic, recognizing the prevalence with which certain diseases or issues co-occur and also influence each other and advocating for treating them together.

Systematic review A gathering of all of the available empirical research on a specific topic to present a comprehensive summary of what all of this research has to say on a topic.

Systemic violence Also called the systemic model, the idea that the criminalization of drug use gives rise to crime and violence that stem from the fact that most drugs of abuse must be sold and purchased on the black market.

Testosterone A sex hormone produced by the gonad glands which is found in much higher concentrations in biological males, particularly after puberty.

Thinking for a Change A cognitive-behavioral treatment program created by the National Institute of Corrections.

Third degree A method of interrogation involving physical force and violence that was banned by the Supreme Court of the United States in *Brown v. Mississippi* in 1936.

Third-generation risk assessment Offenders' risk for recidivism assessed using an actuarial method with a focus on the Central Eight risk factors.

Thought-behavior link The idea that our thoughts contribute to our behavior and the crux of cognitive-behavioral treatment.

Threatened egoism model A theory of narcissistic aggression which suggests that narcissists will become aggressive towards those whom they feel do not share the same high opinion that narcissists have of themselves.

Time factors One of the decision points in the second stage of Crime Scene Analysis when the amount of time the perpetrator spent with the victim and/or at the crime scene is estimated.
Token economies A form of positive reinforcement where symbolic items are given for desired behavior which then can be exchanged for things of value to the individual.
Top-down approach Another term for FBI criminal profiling, due to its reliance on deductive reasoning.
Trait anxiety A generalized experience of anxiety across a variety of situations.
Transinstitutionalization The movement of inmates/patients from one institution to another, typically in reference to the mentally ill being moved out of jails and prisons and into psychiatric facilities.
Trauma psychology A branch of psychology specializing in the causes and symptoms of and treatment for trauma.
Trauma-informed policing A policing strategy that realizes, recognizes, and responds appropriately to citizens who have experienced acute and/or chronic trauma and resists re-traumatization.
Triarchic model of psychopathy A model of psychopathy containing three main concepts: disinhibition, boldness, and meanness. This model of psychopathy is diagnosed using the 58-question self-report Triarchic Psychopathy Measure.
Trust versus mistrust The first stage of Erikson's psychosocial development theory thought to take place primarily in infancy. Caregivers who respond promptly and consistently to an infant's needs will foster trust, while inconsistent and unreliable care will create mistrust.
Truth bias The psychological tendency for people to believe what others tell them, especially when it is perceived that the person has no motive to lie.
Tunnel vision The tendency to focus our attention on one thing to the exclusion of all others.
Ultimate issue testimony Testimony by an expert witness as to a legal conclusion, which is often prohibited as the ultimate issue is up to the judge or jury to decide.
Unconditioned response In classical conditioning, the reflexive and unconscious result of a stimulus.
Unconditioned stimulus In classical conditioning, something that reflexively and unconsciously elicits a response.
Uniform Crime Reports (UCR) A collection of crime data compiled by the Federal Bureau of Investigations from information voluntarily provided by all jurisdictions in the United States.
Uniqueness One of the certainty principles of Pennington and Hastie's story model; if more than one possible story is judged to be coherent and provide coverage of the evidence presented, then neither story is unique, and confidence in both is diminished.
Universal ethical principles The sixth and final stage of Kohlberg's moral development theory characterized by the idea that there are certain moral ideas that are universal to everyone and human laws that do not align with these ideas should be disobeyed.
Updating One of three roles of executive functions that allows us to replace old information with newly acquired information.
UPPS An assessment tool to measure four different characteristics of impulsivity developed using a study of all previously existing impulsivity assessment tools; later revised to be UPPS-P including a fifth characteristic.
Validity A term used in research that refers to whether a measure is really capturing the concept we wish to examine.
Validity scale A group of questions on a self-report questionnaire designed to detect untruthfulness.
Variable interval reinforcement A reinforcement schedule in operant condition whereby a reinforcement is delivered after a random and changing amount of time, provided the desired behavior has been completed at least once during that time.
Variable ratio reinforcement A reinforcement schedule in operant condition whereby a reinforcement is delivered after the desired behavior has been repeated a random and changing number of times.
Venire A group of eligible jurors brought to court to undergo questioning and evaluation of impartiality by the judge and attorneys on the case.
Verdict category establishment The second part of Pennington and Hastie's story model when jurors learn the details of their verdict options.
Verdict-driven jury A style of jury deliberation that relies heavily on early and frequent juror polls and discussion aimed at consensus rather than exhaustive consideration of the evidence.
Vicarious reinforcement Indirect reinforcement of a behavior by seeing the model be reinforced for the behavior and therefore expecting reinforcement for the same behavior.

Victim risk One of the decision points in the second stage of Crime Scene Analysis when the victim is classified as low, moderate, or high risk for victimization based on factors such as age, occupation, lifestyle, physical stature, resistance ability, and location.

Violence An act, usually physical, that causes immense harm to another.

Violent crime Crime that inflicts immediate, physical harm on another.

Voir dire The process of eliminating people from the jury pool (venire) through either peremptory challenges or challenges for cause by the judge and attorneys on the case to ultimately arrive at the appropriate number of jurors for the jury (usually 12).

Voluntary false confession An untrue self-incriminating statement that is offered without external pressure from the police.

Vulnerable Dark Triad A reconceptualizing of the Dark Triad which consists of vulnerable narcissism, Factor 2 psychopathy, and borderline personality disorder, suggesting the original Dark Triad includes grandiose narcissism, Factor 1 psychopathy, and Machiavellianism.

Vulnerable narcissism A theoretically distinct type of narcissism characterized by a more defensive and fragile grandiosity that may serve primarily as a mask for feelings of inadequacy.

Weapon focus A well-established psychological phenomenon whereby our attention is naturally drawn to any weapon present and therefore away from other details of the scene.

Wrap-around services Correctional services that address all of a person's needs including continued support in the community after release from prison.

Index

Note: Page numbers in **bold** and *italics* refer to tables and figures, respectively.

For Product Safety Concerns and Information please contact our EU
representative GPSR@taylorandfrancis.com
Taylor & Francis Verlag GmbH, Kaufingerstraße 24, 80331 München, Germany

www.ingramcontent.com/pod-product-compliance
Ingram Content Group UK Ltd.
Pitfield, Milton Keynes, MK11 3LW, UK
UKHW050234200926
475702UK00020B/3031
* 9 7 8 1 0 3 2 1 6 8 1 3 5 *